SO-ARM-120

Holt Reading Solutions

- Intervention
- English-Language Learners
- Special Education

HOLT, RINEHART AND WINSTON

A Harcourt Education Company

Orlando • **Austin** • New York • San Diego • London

ISBN 0-03-079043-3

4 5 6 367 09 08

CONTENTS IN BRIEF

Table of Contents

NOTE TO THE TEACHER: We realize that it will probably be impossible to cover all the material in the *Elements of Literature* student anthology with your ELL and special education students. In this book, we have provided lesson plans for only those selections that we believe *all* students at this grade level should read. (Please note that there is a lesson to accompany each selection included in *The Holt Reader.* Support provided in the *Holt Adapted Reader* is indicated in individual lesson plans.) You will find, however, that the activities, teaching strategies, and visual organizers included in these lesson plans can be applied in teaching many of the other stories, poems, and informational materials in the *Elements of Literature* student book.

Collection 1 Lesson Plans
The Anglo-Saxons: 449–1066

Collection 2 Lesson Plans
The Middle Ages: 1066–1485

Collection 3 Lesson Plans
The Renaissance: 1485–1660

Collection 4 Lesson Plans
The Restoration and the Eighteenth Century: 1660–1800

Collection 5 Lesson Plans
The Romantic Period: 1798–1832

Collection 6 Lesson Plans
The Victorian Period: 1832–1901

Collection 7 Lesson Plans
The Modern World: 1900 to the Present

Lesson Plans & Copying Masters, *continued*

III. CORE READING SKILLS AND STRATEGIES LESSONS WITH MINIREADS

Overhead transparencies for the Reading Skills and Strategies Lessons can be found in the front cover pocket of this book.

Literary Comprehension Skills

IV. Adapted Readings

Adapted Readings, *continued*

To the Teacher

Two questions that more and more secondary language arts teachers ask every day are

- How can I help my struggling readers?
- How can I integrate support for my struggling readers into my mixed-ability, literature-based classes?

Holt Reading Solutions provides the answers. This book provides tools for diagnosing and targeting reading skills deficiencies as well as lesson plans for managing the suite of reading development tools provided within the ***Elements of Literature*** program.

How to Use *Holt Reading Solutions*

To get the most out of *Holt Reading Solutions,* you will first need to identify your struggling readers. This group is broadly defined as anyone reading more than two levels below grade level. It may include English-language learners, special education students, students with learning disabilities, reluctant readers, and low-achieving students.

Diagnostic Assessment for Reading Intervention

You probably know from experience which students are reading well below grade level. The Diagnostic Assessment for Reading Intervention in this book will give you more detailed information about these students and their specific needs. Information about this test appears in the first tabbed section of this book. From the test's results, you can identify up to ten core reading comprehension skills for which each struggling reader may require remedial lessons. Lessons on each of these skills are included in *Holt Reading Solutions.*

Lesson Plans and Copying Masters

Holt Reading Solutions shows you how to provide remediation in core reading comprehension skills and how to integrate that remediation into your mixed-ability, literature-based classroom. Each lesson plan covers a selection or selection cluster in the Student Edition. Within each lesson plan, you will find the following features that target your struggling readers.

(Core Skill) This icon appears wherever there is an opportunity for addressing one of the ten core reading skills. These features may be self-contained activities, directions to use a Reading Skills and Strategies lesson from *Holt Reading Solutions,* or directions to apply a core skill to the selection at hand.

(**Mixed Ability Group**) Because research shows that struggling readers can benefit from working with more proficient readers, most lesson plans include ideas for placing students in small mixed-ability groups.

(**Especially for ELL**) Many readers struggle because they are learning English as a second language. Throughout the lesson plans are tips and activities designed especially to help English-language learners understand unfamiliar concepts and vocabulary in the literature of the Student Edition.

(**Resources**) Each lesson plan contains references to the *Elements of Literature* program's resources for struggling readers. These resources include audio CD recordings (in English and Spanish), videocassettes, *The Holt Reader,* the vocabulary worksheets mentioned below, and Adapted Readings described on the following page. In addition, suggestions for integrating these resources into specific literature lessons appear throughout each lesson plan.

Reading Skills Development These self-contained activities appear in the majority of full-length lesson plans. They generally provide further practice in the reading skill covered on the Before You Read page in the Student Edition or practice in a prerequisite skill.

Vocabulary Development Research tells us that vocabulary development is critical to the acquisition of superior word-recognition skill among older struggling readers. For this reason, many full-length lesson plans include extra support and practice for the Vocabulary Development features in the Student Edition. In addition, two copying masters, **Vocabulary and Comprehension** and **Additional Vocabulary Practice,** accompany each selection or selection cluster.

Targeted Strategies for Special Education Each lesson plan contains a separate section dedicated to special education students. Like the core lesson plans, these lesson plans provide activities and strategies for prereading, reading, and post-reading.

Reading Skills and Strategies

In this section of *Holt Reading Solutions,* you will find ten core reading comprehension skills lessons, five informational and five literary—the same skills assessed in the Diagnostic Assessment for Reading Intervention. These self-contained lessons include easy-to-read instructions for the students. With minimal teacher guidance, students can work through these lessons independently, in small groups, or as a class.

Each lesson introduces students to an easy-to-use strategy or procedure for comprehending texts. The lessons include notes for teachers and students and practice activities based on MiniReads—short below–grade-level practice reads. Each lesson comes with an application activity to assess student mastery. You can tie the application of the reading skill back into any part of the Student Edition—bringing your struggling readers in line with the rest of your class—by selecting a passage from the Suggested Selections for Reading Skills Application list on page 225.

Adapted Readings

This section of *Holt Reading Solutions* contains adapted prose selections and annotated versions of longer poetry and drama selections found in the Student Edition. The adaptations are highly condensed and written two to four grades below the textbook's grade level.

The adapted readings can be used in a number of ways. They provide excellent material for fluency practice (which requires material written at the student's reading level) and for the application portion of the Reading Skills and Strategies lessons. The prose adaptations can also be used for prereading. The lesson plans for selections that include an adapted reading advise having all students read the adaptation in prereading. This activity can be completed quickly, even by struggling readers, and it provides a schema in a reader's mind as he or she approaches the original version. (For students who struggle with the language of the original selection, the lesson plans provide numerous options—listening to the audio recording, reading the selection in small groups, and so on.)

Fluency, Decoding, and Phonics

Teachers with struggling readers know that each reader has different strengths and weaknesses. For example, some may struggle more with informational comprehension skills than with literary comprehension. Others may have difficulty with fluency and decoding.

As mentioned earlier, vocabulary is a cornerstone of reading proficiency. The vocabulary development activities and worksheets in *Holt Reading Solutions* provide ample support for vocabulary building. When you help students improve their vocabulary skills, you help them improve their ability to recognize words automatically. Improved automaticity helps them to focus on comprehension rather than on decoding.

Fluency, the ability to read automatically and with comprehension, can be improved by having students read aloud. Some lesson plans in *Holt Reading Solutions* include fluency activities, and the adapted readings can be used for fluency practice. The Vocabulary and Comprehension worksheets in *Holt Reading Solutions* serve as a quick comprehension check in conjunction with fluency activities.

If you note students having problems with pronunciation during fluency practice or other speaking activities, work with these students individually. Some struggling readers, especially English-language learners, have trouble hearing the differences between different pairs of vowel sounds or consonant sounds. Use the Phonics Chart and Decoding section in *Holt Reading Solutions* (page xxxiv) as a resource to help these students distinguish between different letter-sound correspondences.

The resources described above, combined with your professionalism and creativity, are powerful tools for reading intervention. By addressing struggling readers' specific needs yet still including them in your whole-class instruction, you can help them become confident, proficient readers. The following professional articles provide more detailed information on helping English-language learners and special education students.

Closing the Gap:

What Research Tells Us About Effective Strategies for Special Education Students and English-Language Learners

. . . [T]hose who suffer most from unsound teaching methods are the students most in need: learning disabled, impoverished, and nonnative speakers of English—the so-called at-risk students.

—Doug Carnine

Today's Classroom

Diversity defines today's classroom. Today's teacher in the mainstream classroom faces students with diverse needs. According to the National Center for Learning Disabilities' "23rd Annual Report to Congress," children classified as having learning disabilities have increased substantially, from roughly three quarters of a million in 1976 to more than 2.9 million in 2001. In their executive summary of the research, Gersten *et al.* also point to the rise in English-language learners (ELLs). Who are the students most at risk for reading failure? According to Lyon, they are "those who enter school with limited exposure to the English language."

Considering all the other demands on the classroom teacher's time and attention, meeting the needs of special education students and ELLs may sound overwhelming. What can the classroom teacher with no special training in teaching these students do? What does the research tell us about creating more effective programs for these students? What special needs must be met?

What the Research Says

We know that reading instruction is affected positively when direct instruction is combined with strategy instruction. In their synthesis of the research, Collins et al. show how "contemporary reforms in reading curricula . . . emphasize integrating metacognition, motivation, and strategies."

Why is the teaching of strategies so important? A key difference between strategic readers and special education students is that strategic readers know how to choose strategies to apply to reading, while special education students do not. These students need systematic and explicit instruction showing them how to choose strategies that fit their text, their purpose, and the occasion. Special education students benefit from strategies that help them overcome problems in

- comprehending what they read
- recognizing text patterns
- distinguishing between relevant and irrelevant information
- recalling information

Principles

Dickson, Carnine, and Kameenui's research for the National Center to Improve the Tools of Educators at the University of Oregon reveals six instructional principles for meeting the needs of special education students. They are

- big ideas
- conspicuous strategies
- mediated scaffolding
- strategic integration
- primed background knowledge
- judicious review

Big Ideas

Big ideas are "concepts and principles that facilitate the most efficient and broadest acquisition of knowledge across a range of examples in a domain." In other words, some ideas are more important than others and serve as umbrellas under which other ideas fit. By concentrating on big ideas, special education students will spend time mastering what is essential. This is particularly helpful since these students generally have more "catch-up" to do and face the "tyranny of time."

For special education students a big idea for instruction concerns the importance of text structure. Good readers know how to use the structure of the text and its special features to make sense from that text. Students with learning difficulties do not. According to Seidenberg, special education students benefit from instruction in how to do this.

Conspicuous Strategies

What is a strategy? Dickson et al. define a strategy as "an organized set of actions designed to accomplish a task." Conspicuous strategies are just that—conspicuous. In other words, they are made apparent to the student through identification and definition, modeling, guided practice, and appropriate feedback. To be effective, conspicuous strategies should be neither too narrow nor too broad and they should be generalizable. Conspicuous strategies are essential for special education students, who need "an array of strategies to enhance their understanding of the narrative and expository material they read."

Mediated Scaffolding

Dickson et al. define mediated scaffolding as "the external support provided by teacher/peers, content, tasks, and materials during initial instruction." The first method of mediated scaffolding involves the way teachers interact with students and the way peers interact. It is called teacher-peer scaffolding. When the teacher models, he or she shows how to do something and then guides students' practice. In addition, the teacher may have students, or peers, tutor one another or share work with one another. In their synthesis of the research, Elbaum et al. discuss the results of students' tutoring one another: "Researchers found clear benefits to tutoring both in cases when the students with disabilities acted as reciprocal tutors-tutees and in cases when they were only tutors." They recommend peer-mediated instruction in reading as "an effective complement to other instructional practices for students with disabilities." Gersten et al. also find the benefits of peer-assisted learning strategies promising.

The next three methods of mediated scaffolding concern content, tasks, and materials. In other words, how should teachers differentiate the content they present, the tasks they ask students to do, and the materials they give students to use in order to meet the needs of diverse students? *Content scaffolding* involves presenting easier content before more difficult content. *Task control scaffolding* involves starting with easier tasks and building toward more difficult tasks. *Material scaffolding* involves providing materials—such as key words, think sheets, and interactive graphic organizers—to guide students' thinking.

Strategic Integration

Diverse learners benefit from material that is strategically integrated, since they have difficulty making these connections on their own. In other words, they find it helpful when connections between materials are pointed out or made clear. Dickson et al. define strategic integration as "the integrating of content, skills, or concepts that (a) mutually support each other, (b) communicate generalizations, or (c) transfer to areas further and further removed from the original area of instruction." Strategic integration, then, is the "careful combination of new information with what the learner already knows to produce a more generalizable, higher order skill."

Primed Background Knowledge

The research of Weaver and Kintsch has shown the importance of activating prior knowledge. Prior knowledge consists of not only background information about topics, themes, and concepts but also knowledge about text structure, academic language, and the conventions of English. In citing the converging evidence, Lyon says, "Students who comprehend well are able to activate their relevant background knowledge when reading—they can relate what has been read to their own experiences and background." On the other hand, special education students are not skilled at this. Effective instruction for these students includes ample time spent developing background knowledge, since that addresses the students' "memory and strategy deficits."

Judicious Review

According to Dickson et al., judicious review refers to "the sequence and schedule of opportunities students receive to apply and develop facility with the conventions of well-presented text and the organizational patterns of text structures." To be effective, review should be sufficient, distributed over time, cumulative, and varied.

Good Classroom Practices

How do these principles translate into good classroom practices? Most likely, they describe things you and other good teachers have already been doing, including the following practices:

- spending more time on big ideas, or umbrella concepts
- identifying and modeling strategies to use
- using scaffold instruction, moving from heavy support to lighter support or from easier concepts, tasks, and materials to more challenging concepts, tasks, and materials
- showing connections
- activating prior knowledge and building background
- reviewing often and regularly

How Does *Elements of Literature* Address These Principles?

Principles	Access
Big ideas	Collections are organized around a well-defined set of skills that serve as a foundation for instruction. Instruction in focused skills takes place in various contexts. Interactive notes point out text structure. Graphic organizers support text structure. Comprehension check tests academic language dealing with text structure.
Conspicuous strategies	Pretaught strategies are included in each collection. Modeling uses the strategies. Transparencies for modeling are included in *The Holt Reader* Teacher's Edition. Guided practices using the strategies are included. Strategies are applied to many selections. Use of strategies is evaluated.
Mediated scaffolding Teacher-peer	Three-step instructional design in *Holt Reading Solutions*: • diagnostic assessment • appropriate presentation with instruction and immediate practice • reteaching and remediation options Program organization • scaffolded instruction within a grade and from grade to grade • reteaching and remediation focused on core skills • skill instruction in multiple contexts

How Does *Elements of Literature* Address These Principles? *(continued)*

Principles	Access
Content	• systematic organization • leveled interactive selections and lessons supporting core content instruction • selections available online • selections available on audio CDs • guided and independent strategies for selections
Task control	Lesson Plans in *Holt Reading Solutions*
Materials	Graphic organizers CDs
Primed background knowledge	Strategy Launches Before You Read notes
Judicious review	Skills practice notes Vocabulary checks Comprehension checks

Bibliography

R. Barr, M.L. Kamil, P.B. Mosenthal, and P.D. Pearson, eds. *Handbook of Reading Research,* vol. 2. White Plains, N.Y.: Longman, 1991.

Carnine, Douglas. "Introduction to the Mini-Series: Diverse Learners and Prevailing, Emerging and Research-Based Educational Approaches and Three Tools." *School Psychology Review* 23, No. 3 (1994): 341–350.

Collins, Vicki L., Shirley V. Dickson, Deborah C. Simmons, and Edward J. Kameenui. *Metacognition and Its Relation to Reading Comprehension: A Synthesis of the Research.* National Center to Improve the Tools of Educators, 1996. *<http://idea.uoregon.edu/~ncite/documents/techrep/tech23.html>.*

Dickson, Shirley V., Douglas Carnine, and Edward J. Kameenui. "Curriculum Guidelines for Diverse Learners." *National Center to Improve the Tools of Education.* Eugene, Ore.: U of Oregon, 1992.

Dickson, Shirley V., Deborah C. Simmons, and Edward J. Kameenui. *Text Organization: Curricular and Instructional Implications for Diverse Learners.* National Center to Improve the Tools of Educators, 1995. *<http://idea.uoregon.edu/~ncite/documents/techrep/tech18.html>.*

Dickson, Shirley V., Deborah C. Simmons, and Edward J. Kameenui. *Text Organizational and Its Relation to Reading Comprehension: A Synthesis of the Research.* National Center to Improve the Tools of Educators, 1995. *<http://idea.uoregon.edu/~ncite/documents/techrep/tech17.html>.*

Gersten, Russell, Scott Baker, Susan Unok Marks, and Sylvia B. Smith. "Effective Instruction for Learning Disabled or At-Risk English Language Learners: An Integrative Synthesis of the Empirical and Professional Knowledge Bases." *Research News.* National Center for Learning Disabilities, 1999. *<http://www.ld.org/research/osep_at_risk.cfm>.*

Gersten, Russell, and Scott Baker. "Reading Comprehension Instruction for Students with Learning Disabilities." *Research News.* National Center for Learning Disabilities, 1999. *<http://www.ld.org/research/ncld_reading_comp.cfm>.*

"Getting Education Back on Track." *Inquiry,* Spring 1997.

Kameenui, Edward J. "Diverse Learners and the Tyranny of Time: Don't Fix Blame; Fix the Leaky Roof." *The Reading Teacher* 46, no. 5 (1993): 376–383.

Kameenui, Edward J., and Carnine., eds. *Effective Teaching Strategies That Accommodate Diverse Learners.* Columbus, Ohio: Merrill–Prentice Hall, 1998.

Lyon, G. Reid. "The NICHD Research Program in Reading Development, Reading Disorders, and Reading Instruction." *Research News.* National Center for Learning Disabilities, 1999. *<http://www.ld.org/research/keys99_nichd.cfm>.*

Paris, S. C., B. A. Wasik, and J. C. Turner. "The Development of Strategic Readers." Barr, Kamil, Mosenthal, and Pearson. 609–640.

Pearson, P. D., and L. Fielding. "Comprehensive Instruction." Barr, Kamil, Mosenthal, and Pearson. 815–860.

Seidenberg, P. L. "Relating Text-Processing Research to Reading and Writing Instruction for Learning Disabled Students." *Learning Disabilities Focus* 5, no. 1 (1989): 4–12.

Simmons, Deborah C., and Edward J. Kameenui, eds. *What Research Tells Us About Students with Diverse Learning Needs.* Mahwah, N.J.: Lawrence Erlbaum Associates, 1998.

Swanson, Lee H. "Intervention Research for Adolescents with Learning Disabilities: A Meta-Analysis of Outcomes Related to High-Order Processing." *Research News.* National Center for Learning Disabilities, 1999. *<http://www.ld.org/research/ncld_high_order.cfm>.*

Swanson, Lee H. "Intervention Research for Students with Learning Disabilities: A Meta-Analysis of Treatment Outcomes." *Research News.* National Center for Learning Disabilities, 1999. *<http://www.ld.org/research/osep_swanson.cfm>.*

Weaver III, C. A., and W. Kintsch. "Expository Text." R. Barr, Kamil, Mosenthal, and Pearson. 230–244.

Mixed Ability Grouping

General Strategies for Grouping Students

What Is Mixed Ability Grouping?

Today's English language arts classroom includes students with varying abilities, needs, and backgrounds—and, as a result, different ways of experiencing reading. One way to address this diversity while connecting students to the excitement of literature is to create a learning environment composed of small, heterogeneous groups. **Mixed ability grouping,** also referred to as **heterogeneous grouping,** is defined in this essay as a group of two to five students of varying abilities who learn together. Such grouping allows all students access to high-level instruction and has positive effects on achievement, self-esteem, intergroup relations, and acceptance of mainstreamed students with special needs.

A major goal of mixed ability grouping is to provide a way of teaching in which students of differing abilities and backgrounds can reach their potential by learning to work together despite their individual differences. Educators who favor the small-group learning approach believe that it allows the classroom to emulate the real world, where people often function as members of a larger unit. While prizing individuality, many people recognize that a large part of life involves working in a myriad of situations toward goals that benefit the group as well as its individual members.

Within a heterogeneous-group environment, all members of a group take responsibility not only for their own learning but for that of their teammates as well. For example, following a presentation on rhythm and meter in poetry, students might gather into groups to practice distinguishing various meters (such as iambic pentameter, dactylic hexameter, and so on). Group members who quickly grasp the concepts can help fellow students mark feet and syllables in practice poems. In this way, strong students practice and strengthen their own knowledge through peer coaching while other students receive necessary individual instruction.

Why Create Mixed Ability Groups?

Small heterogeneous groups help students develop and improve communication skills needed both within and outside the classroom. By discussing literature in small groups, for example, students learn to articulate their ideas and to comprehend the logic behind others' statements and viewpoints. Encounters with different personalities and perspectives allow students to see the ambiguities and complexities inherent in any issue.

The mixed ability small-group approach to classroom organization promotes peer interaction and provides a comfortable forum for discussion. In traditional whole-class situations, only one person speaks at a time, and the period may end before everyone has had a chance to participate. Small-group discussions, on the other hand, allow students plenty of opportunity to voice their opinions and to engage in dialogue. Students who are reluctant to address the entire class will likely feel more comfortable sharing ideas in a small group of peers. Less able students have a chance to practice and pose questions they might hesitate to ask in a whole-class situation. Maximally heterogeneous classrooms encourage students to interact and achieve in ways and at levels not easily reached in other settings.

Problem solving is also enhanced by small-group work. Members of the group pool their resources, collaborating on difficult assignments and working together as peer tutors. For example, students who are having difficulty interpreting a poem or recognizing figures of speech can look to their classmates for help. When confronted with a challenging task, such as what to say in the opening paragraph of an essay about an author, students can consult one another, listing as many possible suggestions as they can within a five- or ten-minute period and reserving the evaluation of their ideas for later.

The mixed ability small-group approach provides students an ideal forum to

- read aloud to each other and help with explication/interpretation
- discuss and read literature
- study and practice literary concepts, using their combined knowledge to help each other learn
- write together and act as an audience for one another's writing
- help one another study/prepare for tests
- develop group projects (reports, book reviews, research papers, poems, and stories)
- prepare formal presentations (such as panel discussions)

How to Create Mixed Ability Groups

In creating small mixed ability groups, the teacher may want to consider the following additional factors:

- heterogeneity
- number of members
- length of time

A successful small group is heterogeneous, including a mix of high, average, and low achievers (achievement and ability are not necessarily the same thing), boys and girls, and students of any social and ethnic groups in the class. This grouping strategy promotes appreciation of and tolerance for diversity.

Another factor in creating small groups is the number of students. Many teachers have

discovered five to be an optimum number. In any case, odd numbers—three or five—may work best, as groups with even numbers of students tend to break up into pairs and stop working together as a unit.

The length of time a group works together is also important. Keeping a single group intact (that is, not changing members) is recommended, especially when students are working on long projects, sharing writing tasks, or responding to literature through the expression of personal experiences or feelings. Over time, group members tend to develop camaraderie and empathy for each other. As a result, they become increasingly comfortable sharing their thoughts.

The teacher's role in facilitating a heterogeneous small-group learning environment is to

- identify students' instructional objective
- form groups (consider the number of students in each group, how to group, length of time group works together)
- assign students to groups
- explain tasks and goals clearly
- explain criteria for success and give students a hard copy of these criteria (for example, to ensure that all students participate, everyone in group must speak once before any take a second turn)
- monitor and intervene, if necessary
- provide closure to group work, including synthesis or summary of the results of the learning. This may include soliciting student feedback about the activity.
- evaluate the group process and the final product

Specific Group Activities

The activities below may be used by mixed ability groups and can be especially helpful for struggling readers. The activities are divided into three sections: Access the Text, Reading Comprehension, and General Meaning-Making. Some activities are designed for work in pairs and may be adapted for use in a group setting.

Access the Text: Fluency Activities

- **Echo Reading** This activity can be used when it is important that all students have access to a text. Students of differing reading abilities can share in the process of reading a text. A fluent reader reads aloud while another reader reads along silently and then echoes what the first student says. Partners read a passage with one partner repeating what the first partner reads aloud.

- **Partner Reading** Partner Reading gives all students a chance to read aloud with a partner. Students read the story silently first. Then, students take turns reading the story aloud with partners, alternating readers after each paragraph. As one partner reads, the listener follows along and corrects any errors the reader makes, such as mispronunciations, omissions, and so on.

- **Popcorn Reading** This activity can be used to give every student a chance to share in the reading of a text and can be used to prepare students to explore a piece of literature in depth. Students take turns reading a text aloud. In small groups one person reads aloud while others in the group follow along. When he or she chooses, the reader says "popcorn" and the name of someone else in the group. Then, the named person reads aloud and then "pops" to another group member.

- **Break-in Reading** One variation of Popcorn Reading is Break-in Reading, in which one person reads aloud while others follow along. When another student in the group wants to read aloud, they "break in" and the other reader returns to following along with the group.

- **Words Out Loud** Words Out Loud gives students an opportunity to become familiar with vocabulary words in a text. Students are given a list of new or difficult words from the text. After the teacher presents the words, students practice reading their lists with partners or in small groups until they can read the words smoothly. Students should be able to read the words in any order without hesitating or stumbling.

Reading Comprehension: Developing an Understanding of the Text

- **Story Impressions** This prereading activity makes use of background knowledge to improve literary comprehension through prediction. The teacher selects key words about plot, setting, and character from the assigned story. The teacher lists the words connected by arrows to show the order of the key words in the story. Students read the words and make predictions about the story either as a whole-class or as a small-group activity. Using the predictions generated, small groups of three to four students write a collaborative story. Students independently read the assigned story and in their writing groups compare the predicted version with the real version.

- **Think Aloud** Think Aloud is a reading strategy that emphasizes thinking processes and improves comprehension. The teacher first models with a passage that is both new and difficult and then has pairs of students (one with good comprehension skills and one with difficulties) practice the strategy. To model, the teacher reads a passage and breaks in at points to demonstrate comprehension strategies such as predicting, summarizing, making analogies, and using fix-up strategies. For example, the teacher may read a portion of a passage to the class and then summarize aloud what he or she has just read. For pairs practice, one student reads orally and thinks aloud while the other listens and adds comments to what the reader says. Then, roles are switched. Finally, students are encouraged to do the activity independently.

- **Think-Pair-Share** This prereading activity draws on students' background knowledge about the topic or theme of a selection. Students first independently develop their own definitions of a topic word (for example, *love*). Then, in small groups of two or three, students work together to come up with a group definition before sharing it with the entire class.

General Meaning-Making: Synthesis Activities

- **Charting** This is a synthesizing activity in which the elements of a work (for example, themes, symbols, and so on) are drawn on a large piece of paper for later presentation. The activity may be done during or after reading a text. The teacher divides students into small groups when the reading of the selection is completed. Groups then create charts using lines, words, and color to make sense of the literature in a new and different way that will be shared with the class.

- **Duologue** This activity can help students to develop an understanding of the thoughts and actions of two characters. The activity consists of a conversation between two students who assume the personae of characters in a piece of literature. After reading a piece of literature, students choose a scene from the story in which an unrecorded conversation *could* have taken place between two characters. Students talk to each other in character and develop a conversation as it might have occurred if it were incorporated into the story.

- **Found Poem** This postreading activity enables students to return to a text to focus on vivid words and phrases that contribute to the meaning of the text. A Found Poem is a collection of "luminous" words or phrases that are extracted from a text. When read aloud, these words or phrases form a poem that expresses the essence of that text. The Found Poem can be created after a chunk of text has been read or after an entire text has been read. Groups of at least three students look back at the text to select approximately eight luminous words or phrases (not sentences or paragraphs) that they feel best express the essence of the text. After each group has narrowed their selection to no more than four words or phrases, the groups should take turns reading one word or phrase without interruption between groups. The class, together, will have created a Found Poem about the selection.

- **Hot Seat** This activity gives each student an opportunity to assume the persona of a character in literature. After a portion of text has been read, students form small groups of three to five students. In groups each student assumes a different role and takes a turn responding to questions (in character) posed by other group members. The questions asked may focus on character motivation and feelings about the consequences of action. Hot Seat can also be used as a whole-class activity.

- **Reciprocal Teaching** This is an activity that teaches students to focus on what they are reading by developing and answering questions and by providing summaries. This activity can be used at any point during the study of a text. The teacher should model this activity before students attempt it on their own. First, all students in a pair or small group silently read a portion of the text. One student asks his or her partner or the rest of the group questions that came to mind about the reading—questions about content, relations to other lessons or selections, and so on. The partner or group answers as many questions as possible. For the next section of the text, the roles are reversed or exchanged, with another student asking questions and the partner or group answering them. At teacher-designated stopping points, the reading stops and one or all students summarize what they understand of the text to that point.

- **Silent Dialogue** The purpose of this activity is to help students make connections between two pieces of literature or to develop an understanding of the behavior of two characters in the same text. This is a silent written activity among a small group of students who each assume the persona of a character in literature. After a piece of literature is read or after two different literary works have been read, the teacher groups students (two to three per group) and has each group member select a character. The teacher gives students a question, an issue, or a topic of discussion to begin the conversation. Then, students pass around one sheet of paper to write on as members "talk" to each other in character about the assigned question, issue, or topic. Students pass around their conversation papers until time is called. Students then read their scripts aloud to the class.

• **Storymap** This activity can give students a better understanding of the significance of the order in which the events of a story occur. Following the reading of a piece of literature, small groups retell important events of a story through illustrations. First, groups verbally retell a story in order to identify the main events. Group members then draw the events on a large piece of paper in a logical sequence. Finally, groups share their storymaps with the whole class.

Bibliography

Adams, P. E. "Teaching *Romeo and Juliet* in the Nontracked English Classroom." *Journal of Reading* 38 (1995): 424–431.

Baumann, I. F., Seifert-Kessell, N., and Jones, L. A. "Effect of Think-Aloud Instruction on Elementary Students' Comprehension Monitoring Abilities." *Journal of Reading Behavior* 24 (1992): 143–172.

Bromley, K. D. *Webbing with Literature: Creating Story Maps with Children's Books.* 2nd ed. Boston: Allyn & Bacon, 1996.

Lyman, F. T. "The Responsive Classroom Discussion: The Inclusion of All Students." In A. Anderson (Ed.), *Mainstreaming Digest,* College Park: University of Maryland Press (1981): 109–113.

McGinley, W. J., and Denner, P. R. "Story Impressions: A Prereading/Writing Activity." *Journal of Reading* 31 (1987): 248–253.

Palinscar, A. S., and Brown, A. L. "Reciprocal Teaching of Comprehension-Fostering and Comprehension-Monitoring Activities." *Cognition and Instruction* 1 (1984): 117–175.

Focus on English-Language Learners: Characteristics, Diagnosis, and Best Practices

Throughout *Elements of Literature* you will find strategies and activities designed to help English-language learners become active participants in classroom learning communities with their English-speaking peers. Based on current and proven practices for teaching content area subject matter to ELL students, these strategies and activities reflect important ideas about the learner's role and about *language* and *communication*.

More specifically, the strategies in *Holt Reading Solutions* address the needs of ELL students who are in the early advanced stage of English language acquisition. It is important to note that even though these students may demonstrate oral language proficiency, their proficiency with written language may be behind. The use of intervention strategies begins by identifying where students are having difficulty with language and why, and then guiding them toward strategies that they can use to handle various problems.

Goals for ELL Students

- To facilitate the development of academic language in order to promote concept acquisition

- To facilitate the development of vocabulary required to learn new concepts

- To facilitate the production of oral and written language to express new concepts

The ELL Student and Learning Needs

Understanding the ELL Student

ELL students probably come from cultures with different traditions and routines. If they were born abroad, ELL students must become familiar with a new environment, a new culture, a new country, a new neighborhood, and a new school. Take into account the following points while working with ELL students in your classroom:

- ELL students may be experiencing culture shock and feel overwhelmed by all of the changes in their environments.

- Many ELL students have experienced deprivation and loss. They may have left people, belongings, and surroundings that were important to their lives. Therefore, they may feel sad or angry about living in a new country.

- ELL students may feel isolated because they do not know English well and do not understand the practices and the traditions in their new environments. They need to feel accepted and encouraged in order to gain confidence and experience a rise in self-esteem.

Detecting ELL Students' Difficulties

Since concept acquisition and development are intricately related to language ability, difficulties related to language acquisition may prevent students from developing new concepts fully. It is important to recognize when ELL students experience such difficulties so that you can help them by reteaching a lesson, reinforcing a learning activity, or clarifying an idea previously presented. Below are some of the classroom behaviors that may be indicative of the difficulties related to the development of academic language.

<table>
<tr><th colspan="2">Behaviors That Indicate Problems</th></tr>
<tr><th>Behavior</th><th>Example</th></tr>
<tr><td>Lack of participation</td><td>The student may put his or her head down or refuse to answer a question.</td></tr>
<tr><td>Incorrect responses</td><td>The student continually gives incorrect responses even when questions have been simplified or additional prompts have been provided.</td></tr>
<tr><td>Mixing native language and English</td><td>The student speaks or writes in both English and his or her native language because a concept is not completely understood.</td></tr>
<tr><td>Over- or under-extension of concepts</td><td>The student fails to recognize examples of a concept (under) or includes examples that are not part of the concept (over).</td></tr>
<tr><td>Misunderstanding</td><td>The student may not be able to answer questions or follow directions because he or she does not understand what is being asked.</td></tr>
<tr><td>Difficulty in literal or inferential reading comprehension</td><td>The student may not be familiar with the words in the text or the ideas that the words represent. The student may not have prior knowledge of a concept.</td></tr>
<tr><td>Native language interference</td><td>The student may inappropriately generalize native language elements into English. For example, Spanish-speaking students may omit the verbs do, does, and did in interrogative phrases or sentences since in Spanish they are not used.</td></tr>
<tr><td>Cultural miscues</td><td>The student may not have prior knowledge or personal experiences from which to draw a correct response.</td></tr>
<tr><td>Inappropriate rhythm</td><td>The student may not be familiar with the words or punctuation within a text.</td></tr>
<tr><td>Uneasiness in using idioms and expressions</td><td>The student may translate an idiom word-for-word. Therefore, the student may be confused by the meaning.</td></tr>
</table>

General Strategies for Instructing ELL Students

By recognizing ELL students' personal situations and identifying their difficulties, you can address their learning needs better. Following are general strategies you can use to motivate ELL students and to support their learning.

- Recognize that the level of literacy achievement in the students' native languages may be obscured by a lack of facility with the English language.

- Note the ELL students may show more ability to express themselves in a social situation than in a learning situation. Social and academic English vary considerably, so classroom practices should take this into account.

- Recognize that it takes time to learn concepts in a familiar language, let alone a new one. ELL students need time to show their proficiency in English.

- Recognize that ELL students' prior knowledge bases were not developed around the cultural traditions of English. They will need help in developing strategies to activate their own prior knowledge, which is important to constructing meaning.

- Draw analogies to past experiences and provide opportunities for students to share their own experiences. This will help ELL students activate their prior knowledge.

- Help ELL students deal with culturally unfamiliar topics by doing what you do when you introduce a new topic to the entire class: Place it in a familiar context. Bring the topic to life and encourage students to draw upon their personal experiences and knowledge.

- Use role-playing, objects, pictures, and graphic organizers to create associations and support meaning. Use gestures and facial expressions to cue feelings and moods.

- Paraphrase questions. By restating questions, you can reinforce ELL students' existing knowledge and encourage the acquisition of new language.

- To determine if students understand new material, ask questions and encourage ELL students to offer explanations and summaries.

- To simplify a question, try replacing lengthy or complex sentences with shorter, declarative phrases or sentences.

- Pair ELL students with proficient native English speakers. Heterogeneous grouping allows the modeling of English—both social and academic—to occur in a natural context. Cooperative-learning situations also help all students recognize the value of cultural and ethnic diversity.

Strategies to Facilitate Language Development

The following are strategies and activities that can be used for all ELL students or for those students who require additional support in vocabulary and concept development, reading, writing, and understanding and producing oral language. When using any of these strategies, explain and model the strategies to students so that they can integrate these as part of their own learning strategies. The activities can be adapted to any unit or topic.

Vocabulary Development/Concept Development

You can facilitate the acquisition of new vocabulary and new concepts by using activities or materials that provide a context familiar to the students.

- **Use context-rich activities.** Demonstrate the use of new vocabulary in situations related to ELL students' experiences. Where appropriate, use the context provided by concepts or literature the students have already learned. The use of the classroom, the school, and the students' environment to build, develop, and exemplify new vocabulary and concepts provides context in the present, which makes the activity more concrete to the student.

- **Control the content.** When teaching new vocabulary, present words and phrases embedded in sentences or text well known to ELL students. Each sentence or portion of text should focus on only one new word or phrase. This allows the students to concentrate on the acquisition of the target language without having to be concerned with new vocabulary and new concepts at the same time.

- **Control the vocabulary.** When introducing and developing new concepts, control the complexity of the language. Learning new concepts and new vocabulary at the same time is loaded with too many unknowns, which tend to impede the acquisition of new material. Therefore, use language that does not present difficulties so that the focus is on the new concept.

Reading Comprehension

The greatest challenge in the acquisition of new academic language and new concepts is to make text comprehensible to students so that concept development can proceed logically.

- **Group text in small units.** Break long text into smaller units such as paragraphs. Well-constructed paragraphs usually have one main idea with supporting details, so they can stand alone without losing meaning. Use these units to identify the students' difficulties and teach to those areas. After working with the target paragraphs, reconstruct the whole text and restate the active-reading questions or the goal of the reading.

- **Identify main ideas.** Identify the main idea in the text as well as the supporting details. Explain to ELL students how the details support the main idea.

- **Paraphrase and rephrase text.** Simplify text by paraphrasing and rephrasing sections of text, such as sentences or short paragraphs, using language familiar to ELL students. Break down complex sentences into simple sentences. Help clarify the intention and meaning of each sentence, and reconstruct the original sentence afterward.

Listening

Multiple opportunities for listening, with different goals, enhance the development of language comprehension.

- **Promote active, focused listening.** Provide different goals for listening. For example, ask ELL students to listen for specific vocabulary related to a concept during an oral discussion. Then, have students write on a piece of paper the target words and the phrases or sentences in which the target words are embedded. Students can add to this list as you continue the discussion.

- **Use checklists.** Provide lists of words and have ELL students check the ones they hear during a discussion or an oral reading activity. This strategy will reinforce the words that are necessary in understanding a concept.

- **Use text.** Provide ELL students with a hard copy of the text to which they are listening. Have them focus on different elements of diction, such as emphasis, rhythm, and accentuation. For example, students can highlight words that they notice are emphasized during a reading.

- **Ask questions.** Provide questions to ELL students that will need to be answered after listening to a discussion, an oral reading activity, or an audiotape. This allows you to check their understanding of what they have heard.

Speaking

ELL students should be encouraged to practice their linguistic skills in academic arenas. Oral activities in which ELL students are prompted to voice their opinions or share personal experiences help them build confidence in their speaking abilities.

- **Ensure comprehension.** When ELL students have difficulties in presenting oral materials, ensure comprehension of the material by clarifying, reviewing, and discussing the concepts and the vocabulary.

- **Model and tape the presentation.** Provide ELL students with a taped model presentation of their material (you or a proficient English-speaking student can record it). Help students analyze the patterns and rhythms of the language, and encourage several listening sessions. Have students practice their oral presentations with a group of peers.

Other Resources

Specific writing, listening, and speaking strategies for ELL students appear in the Lesson Plans for Language Development section of *Workshop Resources: Writing, Listening, and Speaking.*

Student Self-Monitoring

By monitoring their own learning, ELL students are able to recognize the strategies that work best for them when they encounter difficulties. Consider the following activities to help students monitor their learning:

- Encourage ELL students to check their comprehension when reading or listening. To do this, students can summarize information or answer questions.

- Ask ELL students to identify the difficulties they encounter when learning new lessons and the strategies that work for them. Then, assist students in developing a plan that includes specific strategies that will help them achieve learning. Finally, have students evaluate their plans by discussing how their plans worked and what changes they may need to make in the future.

By providing ELL students with different activities and strategies, you can help them achieve the goals of developing academic language, acquiring vocabulary to learn new concepts, and producing oral and written language. More importantly, though, you are providing a nonthreatening environment in which ELL students become more self-confident and capable of many levels of communication.

Phonics Chart

- Encourage students to experiment with sounds from their native language as well as sounds from English. Celebrate students' languages. After all, English words derive from as many as 100 other languages.

- Focus on clearing up confusion rather than on correcting pronunciation. If a student says *ban* for *van*, just repeat the correct pronunciation, "Yes, that's a *van*."

- Avoid phonics activities with no oral component.

Consider your work in meeting diverse needs as an opportunity to stretch yourself and make yourself an ever-better teacher. Embrace the challenge.

Similarities across languages which can result in confusion with reading and spelling

Problem Contrast	Chinese	French	Greek	Italian	Japanese	Korean	Spanish	Urdu	Vietnamese
/ā/-/a/			X	X	X	X		X	
/ā/-/e/			X	X	X	X	X	X	X
/a/-/e/	X		X	X	X	X	X	X	X
/a/-/o/	X	X	X	X	X	X	X	X	X
/a/-/u/	X		X	X	X		X	X	
/ē/-/i/	X	X	X	X	X	X	X	X	X
/e/-/u/	X		X		X		X	X	
/ō/-/o/	X		X	X	X		X	X	X
/o/-/ô/	X		X		X	X	X	X	X
/o/-/u/	X		X	X	X		X		X
/u/-/o͞o/	X	X	X	X			X	X	X
/u/-/o͝o/	X		X		X		X		X
/u/-/ô/	X		X	X	X	X	X	X	
/o͞o/-/o͝o/	X	X		X		X	X	X	
/b/-/p/	X					X	X		X
/b/-/v/			X		X	X	X		
/ch/-/j/				X		X	X		X
/ch/-/sh/	X	X	X		X	X	X		X
/d/-/th/	X			X	X	X	X	X	X
/f/-/th/				X		X	X	X	X
/l/-/r/	X				X	X	X		X
/n/-/ng/	X	X	X	X	X		X	X	
/s/-/sh/			X	X	X	X	X		X
/s/-/th/	X	X	X		X	X	X	X	X
/s/-/z/	X	X	X			X	X		X
/sh/-/th/				X	X	X	X	X	X
/t/-/th/	X			X	X	X	X	X	X
/th/-/th/	X	X		X	X	X	X	X	X
/th/-/z/	X	X	X	X	X	X	X	X	X

From *The ESL Teacher's Book of Lists*, ©1993 by The Center for Applied Research in Education

Decoding: Phonics Analysis

Consonants

Initial Correspondences /b/b, /d/d, /p/p
Some ELL students, including speakers of Chinese, Samoan, and Korean, may have difficulty differentiating the initial sound of *bat* from the initial sound of *pat* and *dad*.

Initial Correspondences /f/f, /p/p, /v/v
Some ELL students, including speakers of Tagalog and Vietnamese, have difficulty differentiating the initial sound of *fat* from the initial sound of *pat* or *vat*. Students must be able to hear and produce these different sounds in order to become successful readers of English.

Initial Correspondences /v/v, /b/b
Spanish-speaking students may have difficulty differentiating the initial sound of *bat* from the initial sound of *vat*, since they are used to pronouncing /b/ when the letter *v* appears at the beginning of a word. In pronouncing English words that begin with *v*, these students often substitute /b/ for /v/; thus *vest* becomes *best*, and *very* becomes *berry*.

Initial Correspondences /j/j, /y/y, /ch/ch
The sound /j/ in *jar* is difficult for ELL students who often confuse or interchange this sound with /ch/ or /y/, causing major comprehension difficulties. In addition, Spanish has a similar sound /y/ that is often substituted for the sound /j/, resulting in confusion when students try to differentiate between the words *jam* and *yam*.

Initial Correspondences /s/c,s
The letter-sound association for *c* usually follows the same generalizations in both English and Spanish. When *c* is followed by the letter *e* or *i*, it stands for the sound /s/; when *c* is followed by the letter *a, o,* or *u*, it stands for the sound /k/. In some Spanish dialects, when the letter *c* is followed by the letter *e* or *i*, the *c* stands for the sound /th/. Therefore, some Spanish-speaking students might have difficulty with this sound.

Initial Correspondences /s/s, /z/z
The sound /z/ is difficult for many ELL students to master because often it is not found in their native language. It is especially difficult for students to differentiate this sound from the sound /s/.

Initial Correspondences /n/n,kn; /l/l
The sound /n/ at the beginning of a word seems to present no special difficulties for most ELL students. However, students whose native language is Chinese, sometimes have difficulty differentiating this sound from the sound /l/ at the beginning of *lot*.

Initial Correspondences /r/r,wr; /l/l
Some ELL students, including speakers of Chinese, Japanese, Korean, Vietnamese, and Thai, may have great difficulty differentiating /r/ as in *rip* from /l/ as in *lip* . These students often pronounce both *lip* and *rip* with the beginning sound /l/.

Initial Correspondences /kw/qu, /w/w
Some ELL students have difficulty differentiating the initial sound /kw/ as in *queen* from the initial sound /w/ as in *wet*.

Initial Correspondences /v/v, /w/w
Some ELL students, including speakers of Chinese, Arabic, German, Samoan, and Thai, have difficulty differentiating /w/ as in *wet* from /v/ as in *van* . These students need much practice producing the sound /w/ in order to avoid confusing it with the sound /v/.

Initial Correspondences /g/g; /k/k,c
Some ELL students, especially speakers of Korean, Samoan, Vietnamese, Thai, and Indonesian, have difficulty differentiating /k/ as in *cat* and *king* from /g/ as in *go*. Speakers of Vietnamese and Thai especially have difficulty with these two sounds when they appear at the end of a word.

Initial Correspondences /h/h, /j/j, /hw/wh

Students who already read in Spanish may have difficulty with these sound-symbol correspondences, because in Spanish the letter *h* is silent. Students may forget to pronounce this sound in trying to decode English words, saying for example, /ot/ for *hot* and /at/ for *hat*. Because the sound /h/ is represented by the letter *j* in Spanish, this letter may be used in spelling English words that begin with *h*. Students may write *jat* for *hat, jot* for *hot, jouse* for *house,* and so on.

In addition, some ELL students may have difficulty differentiating the beginning sound of *hat* from the beginning sound of *what.* They will need practice in differentiating these two sounds.

Initial Correspondences /fr/fr, /fl/fl

The initial /fr/*fr* does not usually present difficulty for students who speak Spanish since these sounds are commonly found in Spanish. However, /fr/*fr* does present difficulty for students who speak Chinese or other Asian languages, especially when differentiating /fr/*fr* from /fl/*fl.*

Initial Correspondences /gr/gr, /dr/dr, /br/br

Some ELL students, especially speakers of Chinese and Vietnamese, may have difficulty differentiating the initial sounds of *grass* from the initial sounds of *broom* and *dress.* Much practice is needed to help students hear and produce these sounds in English in order to avoid problems when they start to work with the written symbols that represent these sounds.

Initial Correspondences /th/th, /thr/thr, /t/t

Some ELL students, especially Spanish-speaking students, may have difficulty pronouncing words that begin with /th/ and /thr/, and differentiating these sounds from/t/. Much practice is needed to help students hear and produce these sounds in English in order to avoid problems when they start to work with the written symbols that represent these sounds.

Initial Correspondences /kr/cr, /kl/cl, /gl/gl

Some ELL students, especially speakers of Chinese or Vietnamese, may have difficulty with these clusters. These clusters do not present difficulty for Spanish-speaking students since they are commonly found in the Spanish language.

Initial Correspondences /skr/scr; /sk/sk,sc; /kr/cr

The initial consonant clusters /skr/*scr* and /sk/*sk,sc* may be difficult for ELL students of various language backgrounds. Spanish-speaking students have difficulty with the *s*-plus-consonant pronunciation. Speakers of other languages may have difficulty with the initial consonant cluster /kr/*cr.*

Initial Correspondences /st/st; /str/str; /sk/sk, sch, sc

The majority of ELL students, especially those who speak Spanish, have difficulty pronouncing these consonant clusters in the initial position. In Spanish, these clusters never appear at the beginning of a word. Thus students tend to add the /e/ sound in front of a word: *school*/skōol/ becomes / eskōol/ and *street* is pronounced /estrēt/.

Initial Correspondences /tr/tr, /thr/thr, /t/t

The consonant clusters /tr/ and /thr/ are difficult for ELL students whose native languages do not have these sounds in combination. Some students have difficulty differentiating among /tr/, /thr/, /t/, and /t/ with the vowel *i.*

Initial Correspondences /sl/sl, /pl/pl

The consonant cluster *sl* presents some difficulty for Spanish-speaking students who are not used to encountering the *s*-plus-consonant sound at the beginning of words. These students often add the /e/ sound in front of a word; for example, *sleep* is pronounced / eslēp/. The /pl/ sound does not present difficulty for speakers of Spanish because it is common in Spanish. However, speakers of Chinese and Vietnamese, among others, may find it difficult to master.

Initial Correspondences /sp/sp, /sm/sm

The majority of ELL students have difficulty pronouncing the consonant clusters *sp* and *sm* in the initial position. In Spanish, these clusters never appear at the beginning of words. Often Spanish-speaking students add /e/ before the /s/; thus *spot* is pronounced /espot/.

Initial Correspondences /sh/sh, /ch/ch

The sound /sh/ presents difficulty for many ELL students because it is not found in most languages. The sound /ch/ seems to be more common. Therefore many students do not distinguish between /sh/ and /ch/ and tend to substitute one for the other, saying *cheep* for *sheep* and *chin* for *shin*. This is particularly true of Spanish-speaking students.

Final Correspondences /p/p, /b/b

Spanish-speaking students may have difficulty hearing the final sound /p/ and may confuse this sound with the final sound /b/, since the final sound /b/ and /p/ do not often occur in Spanish.

Final Correspondences /t/t, /d/d

Some ELL students may have difficulty differentiating the final sound of *bat* from the final sound of *dad*. Much practice is needed to help students hear and produce these sounds in English to avoid problems when starting to work with the written symbols that represent these sounds.

Final Correspondences /ks/x; /s/s,ss

Final consonants can present a problem, especially for students whose native languages do not emphasize these consonants as much as English does. In Spanish, for example, there are only a few consonants that appear at the ends of words (*n,s,z,d,l,j*). Many Spanish-speaking people tend to drop the final consonant sound in conversation; for example, *reloj* becomes *relo*.

Final Correspondences /z/z,zz; /s/s,ss

The sound /z/ is difficult for many ELL students to master because often it is not found in their native languages. It is especially difficult for students to differentiate this sound from the sound /s/.

Final Correspondences /k/k,ck; /g/g

The final sound /g/ may be difficult for Spanish-speaking students since this sound never occurs at the end of Spanish words. Students may have difficulty hearing this sound and may pronounce it as the sound /k/ or omit the sound completely.

Final Correspondences /f/f, ff; /p/p

Some ELL students may have difficulty differentiating the final sound of *wife* from the final sound of *wipe*. Much practice is needed to help students hear and produce these sounds in English in order to avoid problems when they start to work with the written symbols that represent these sounds.

Final Correspondences /p/p, /t/t

Some ELL students may have difficulty differentiating the final sound of *ape* from the final sound of *ate*. Much practice is needed to help students hear and produce these sounds in English in order to avoid problems when they start to work with the written symbols that represent these sounds.

Final Correspondences /d/d, /b/b

Some ELL students may have difficulty differentiating the final sound of *lad* from the final sound of *lab*. Much practice is needed to help students hear and produce these sounds in English in order to avoid problems when they start to work with the written symbols that represent these sounds.

Final Correspondences /ld/ld, /nt/nt, /nd/nd

Some ELL students may have difficulty differentiating the final sounds of *old* from the final sounds of *lint* and *find*. Having two consonant sounds at the end of a word increases the difficulty. Much practice is needed to help students hear and produce these sounds in English in order to avoid problems when they start to work with the written symbols that represent these sounds.

Final Correspondences /ng/ng, /ngk/nk

Some ELL students may have difficulty differentiating the final sounds of *sink* from the final sounds of *sing*. Much practice is needed to help students hear and produce these sounds in English in order to avoid problems when they start to work with the written symbols that represent these sounds.

Final Correspondences /s/s,ss; /st/st

Some ELL students may have difficulty differentiating the final sound of *gas* from the final sounds of *last*. Much practice is needed to help students hear and produce these sounds in English in order to avoid problems when they start to work with the written symbols that represent these sounds.

Final Correspondences /sh/sh; /ch/ch,tch

Some ELL students may have difficulty differentiating the final sound of *mush* from the final sound of *much*. Much practice is needed to help students hear and produce these sounds in English in order to avoid problems when they start to work with the written symbols that represent these sounds.

Final Correspondences /th/th, /t/t

Some ELL students, especially speakers of Spanish, may have difficulty differentiating the final sound of *bat* from the final sound of *bath*. Much practice is needed to help students hear and produce these sounds in English in order to avoid problems when they start to work with the written symbols that represent these sounds.

Vowels

Vowel Correspondences /a/a, /e/e

Short vowel sounds are the most difficult for ELL students to master. These create problems when students try to learn and apply the concept of rhyming; ELL students have difficulty differentiating the short vowel sound in *bat* from the short vowel sound in *bet*. Much practice is needed to help students hear and produce these sounds in English in order to avoid problems when they start to work with the written symbols that represent these sounds.

Vowel Correspondences /o/o, /u/u

The vowel sound in *cot* often causes great difficulty for students who speak Spanish, Chinese, Vietnamese, Tagalog, and Thai. This sound must be practiced frequently.

Vowel Correspondences /i/i, /ē/ee, ea, e_e

Words with the short *i* vowel sound are difficult for speakers of Spanish, Chinese, Vietnamese, and Tagalog, among others. ELL students in general have difficulty pronouncing this sound as they tend to confuse it with the long *e* vowel sound. Spanish-speaking students in particular have the tendency to replace the short *i* sound with the long *e* sound.

Vowel Correspondences /u/u, /a/a, /e/e

The vowel sound in *up* is one of the most difficult for ELL students to master because it does not exist in many languages and yet is one of the most common sounds in English. ELL students often have difficulty differentiating this sound from the vowel sounds in *bat* and *bet*. Much practice is needed to help students hear and produce these sounds in English in order to avoid problems when they start to work with the written symbols that represent these sounds.

Vowel Correspondences /o/o, /ō/oa, o_e; /ô/au, aw

The vowel sound in *cot* often causes great difficulty for ELL students who speak Spanish, Chinese, Vietnamese, Tagalog, or Thai. This sound must be practiced frequently, especially to differentiate it from the vowel sound in *coat* and *caught*. In addition, when the letters *oa* come together in Spanish, they stand for two separate sounds. Therefore, many Spanish-speaking students may have difficulty understanding that the letters *oa* can stand for one sound in English.

Vowel Correspondences /ā/a_e, /e/e

It is difficult for ELL students who speak Vietnamese, Spanish, or Tagalog to differentiate between the vowel sound in *race* and the vowel sound in *pet*. Much practice is needed to help students hear and produce these sounds in English in order to avoid problems when they start to work with the written symbols that represent these sounds.

Vowel Correspondences /i/i_e, /a/a

The vowel sound in *bike* may present a problem for some ELL students who have difficulty differentiating this sound from the vowel sound in *bat*. Much practice is needed to help students hear and produce these sounds in English in order to work with the written symbols that represent these sounds.

Overview of the Assessment Program

What is the Diagnostic Assessment for Reading Intervention?

The Diagnostic Assessment for Reading Intervention is an informal, criterion-referenced assessment designed to identify a student's reading level and to diagnose the specific reading comprehension skills that need instructional attention.

The Diagnostic Assessment for Reading Intervention assesses a student's ability to read literary texts and informational texts. For ease of use, the assessment is limited to multiple-choice items.

A separate Diagnostic Assessment for Reading Intervention is available for each grade from Grade 6 through 12.

Who should take the Diagnostic Assessment for Reading Intervention?

Administer this diagnostic to students whom you have identified as reading below grade level and/or to students who score poorly on the Entry-Level Test found in *Holt Assessment: Literature, Reading, and Vocabulary.*

What types of passages are found on the Diagnostic Assessment for Reading Intervention?

Each Diagnostic Assessment for Reading Intervention consists of four reading passages—two literary passages and two informational passages.

Literary passages are primarily narrative. They may be short stories, literary essays (personal narratives), excerpts from longer works, historical fiction, or fables and folk tales.

Informational passages are subject-matter centered, wherein language is used to provide information, present new ideas, solve problems, and raise questions. They may be subject-matter texts, magazine or newspaper articles, editorials, informational essays, biographies, and consumer materials.

Because the Diagnostic Assessment for Reading Intervention is designed for students who are experiencing some difficulties reading grade-level material, the passages are written below grade level as determined by readability formulas such as the Dale-Chall and the Fry Readability Graph.

What comprehension skills does the Diagnostic Assessment for Reading Intervention measure?

The Diagnostic Assessment for Reading Intervention assesses the following ten important reading comprehension skills.

Literary Comprehension Skills

- **Make predictions:** Determine the most likely outcomes; predict ideas or events that may take place; give a rationale for predictions.

- **Understand characters:** Recognize and understand characters' traits; determine characters' motivations and feelings based on clues in the text; understand character relationships; analyze interactions between main and subordinate characters; make inferences based on characters' words, actions, and reactions to other characters.

- **Recognize theme and form interpretations:** Identify ideas and insights about life and human nature expressed in literature; form interpretations of narrative text by making inferences, generalizing, drawing conclusions, and analyzing.

- **Understand figurative language:** Recognize similes, metaphors, and personification as used in literature.

- **Compare and contrast:** Compare and contrast aspects of narrative texts such as characters, settings, plot elements (for example, conflict), and themes.

Informational Comprehension Skills

- **Understand text structure:** Recognize structural patterns such as comparison-contrast, cause-effect, chronological order, and problem-solution that are used to organize ideas in informational text; analyze and connect the essential ideas, arguments, and perspectives of the text by using knowledge of text structures.

- **Identify main idea and important details:** Determine central ideas in informational text, and identify important details that support the central ideas.

- **Make inferences:** Make informed judgments based on evidence from the text, and use personal observations and prior experience to make and confirm inferences.

- **Summarize information:** Compare original text to a summary to determine whether the summary accurately captures the ideas, includes critical details, and conveys the underlying meaning; synthesize content to demonstrate comprehension.

- **Distinguish between facts and opinions and evaluate supporting evidence:** Evaluate whether the writer presents objective facts or subjective opinions; assess the adequacy, accuracy, and appropriateness of the writer's evidence to support claims and assertions; distinguish between logical and illogical statements in a piece of text; identify biases, stereotypes, and persuasive techniques in texts.

How long does it take to administer the Diagnostic Assessment for Reading Intervention?

The Diagnostic Assessment for Reading Intervention is not a timed test. Most students should be able to complete the entire test in one class period, or twenty to forty minutes. Students should be given ample time to complete the assessment, even if more than one class period is necessary.

What materials do I need to administer the Diagnostic Assessment for Reading Intervention?

Student materials
Each student will need a test booklet and an answer sheet. Blackline masters for these can be found near the front of this tabbed section. Once the test booklets are photocopied and assembled, they can be reused because students mark their answers on the consumable answer sheet.

Teacher materials
The only materials the teacher needs to administer the Diagnostic Assessment for Reading Intervention are the Directions for Administering. These can be found later in this section.

How do I score the Diagnostic Assessment for Reading Intervention?

The Diagnostic Assessment for Reading Intervention can be scored in one of the following two ways.

Using the Annotated Answer Sheet
One method of scoring is to use the Annotated Answer Sheet. This is a facsimile of the student's Answer Sheet with the correct answer bubbles filled in. Simply place the Annotated Answer Sheet alongside a student's completed answer sheet, compare the two, and mark the items answered incorrectly.

Using the List of Correct Answers and Skills
Also included in this tabbed section is a List of Correct Answers and Skills. This list identifies the correct answer as well as the reading skill assessed by each item. To score a student's assessment, simply compare the list to a student's completed answer sheet and mark the answers that were not answered correctly.

What kind of scores will I receive from the Diagnostic Assessment for Reading Intervention?

The Diagnostic Assessment for Reading Intervention yields three scores—a Total Reading Score that can be converted to a Reading Proficiency Level, a Literary Comprehension Score, and an Informational Comprehension Score.

In addition, you can create a diagnostic profile of a student's strengths and weaknesses by noting how well the student performed on each skill. Each skill is tested with four items. If a student answers three or more of the four items correctly, he or she demonstrates proficiency in that skill. If a student answers fewer than three of the four items correctly, additional instruction is needed on that skill.

How can I summarize and report a student's performance on the Diagnostic Assessment for Reading Intervention?

Included in this tabbed section is a Performance Profile. This one-page blackline master summarizes a student's performance on the Diagnostic Assessment for Reading Intervention and provides a convenient place to record scores.

To use the Performance Profile, follow these steps:

1. Make a copy of the Performance Profile for each student taking the assessment.

2. Place a blank copy of the Performance Profile alongside a student's answer sheet that has been scored.

3. Use the item numbers on the Performance Profile to determine a student's performance for each skill. Turn to the student's answer sheet to see how the student answered these items. Mark each item that was answered incorrectly.

4. Tally the number of items answered *correctly* in the "Score" column. Record the number correct beside the number possible (for example, 3/4).

5. Sum the number of items answered correctly for Literary Comprehension, and place that number in the space provided for Total Literary Comprehension (for example, 15/20).

6. Follow the same procedure to obtain the scores for each Informational Comprehension skill, Total Informational Comprehension, and Total Reading Comprehension.

7. Use the Total Reading Comprehension score (that is, the number of items answered correctly on the entire test) to determine a student's Reading Proficiency Level. Circle the level that applies.

What do the Reading Proficiency Levels mean?

The Reading Proficiency Levels are intended to give you a general sense of a student's overall reading ability. At the middle school and high school levels, various reading tests may yield contradictory results because of the variability of the texts that students are asked to read and because of the variability in prior knowledge about and interest in specific topics. Therefore, more general Reading Proficiency Levels like those described in the following paragraphs are recommended.

Proficient Level

A student who scores at the Proficient Level should be able to read and comprehend grade-level assignments. The student may experience some difficulty depending on his or her knowledge about the topic, familiarity with the vocabulary and language of the text, and personal interest in the topic. Some assistance may be needed in those situations.

Basic Level

A student who scores at the Basic Level is reading one to two years below his or her grade placement. The student will almost surely experience difficulty reading grade-level assignments. However, when a student at the Basic Level is provided with assistance for handling such texts, he or she can often rise to the occasion and process the text in a meaningful way. Such students need an ample introduction to a text before reading it independently, shorter portions of text to process at a time, scaffolding aids such as the interactive questions in *The Holt Reader* to use while reading, and opportunities to interact and discuss a text after reading it. If the student's first language is not English, the "Especially for ELL" teaching suggestions in the Lesson Plan section of this book will be helpful.

Below Basic Level

A student who scores at the Below Basic Level is reading more than two years below his or her grade placement. The student will experience great difficulty reading and comprehending grade-level assignments. Because of their inability to process many of the assignments given to them, such students frequently become frustrated, demonstrate avoidance strategies, and stop trying. If such students are expected to respond to grade-level assignments, considerable support must be given to them. Selection previews, such as the Adapted Readings contained in this book, will help below-basic level readers. Students may listen to selections on audio CDs while following along with the original text. Students may need to be paired with a student partner who can offer assistance during the reading process. Students at the Below Basic Level could profit from basic reading instruction in an individual or small-group setting. Finally, the "Especially for ELL" teaching suggestions in the Lesson Plan section of this book provide scaffolding for non-native speakers.

What diagnostic information can I obtain from the Diagnostic Assessment for Reading Intervention?

The Performance Profile is also intended to give you some insights into a student's strengths and weaknesses in reading comprehension.

Literary Versus Informational Comprehension

One of the first aspects of student performance to consider is text type. Did the student comprehend one type of text better than another? The Performance Profile provides a Literary Comprehension score and an Informational Comprehension score. By comparing the two, you can get a sense of whether the student is experiencing more difficulty with one type of text or the other.

The scores may suggest, for example, that the student needs more assistance when reading informational passages. Perhaps key vocabulary or a simplified adaptation of the text needs to be introduced *before* the student reads independently. Identifying what the student knows about the topic before reading also allows you to fill in some knowledge gaps in order to make the reading more meaningful.

If, on the other hand, the student shows more difficulty reading literary passages, assistance can be provided for those reading assignments. Introducing characters and discussing how they are related before reading a narrative selection can be helpful. Providing a skeletal plot summary or an adaptation to guide the student before or during reading can also be beneficial. Relating the "big ideas" in a literary selection to those in familiar stories, TV programs, or movies can also aid comprehension.

Reading Skills Analysis

Each Diagnostic Assessment for Reading Intervention measures ten reading comprehension skills—five in Literary Comprehension and five in Informational Comprehension. Four items assess each skill. Using the conventional standard of 75 percent or more correct, "mastery" is defined as 3 out of 4 correct. By going down the Score column on the Performance Profile, you can identify which skills a student has mastered and which skills need further instruction.

This information can be used to plan instruction and prescribe remediation. For example, you may want to use the lessons from the Reading Skills and Strategies section of this book that address a student's specific weaknesses. Lessons and assignments in the Student Edition could also be modified or augmented to focus on the specific weaknesses the student has demonstrated. Suggestions for skills-related modifications appear in the Lesson Plan section of this book.

Keep in mind that the assessment is limited to four items for each skill. Therefore, any conclusions that are drawn about a student's specific strengths and weaknesses should be confirmed or rejected by observing that student's performance on daily work in the classroom.

Distribute Testing Materials

- Each student should have a test booklet that contains four reading passages and forty test items.
- Each student should have a blank Answer Sheet.

Directions

Read to students the following directions, or phrase them in your own words.

Today you are going to take a reading assessment. The purpose of this assessment is to determine how well you comprehend what you read. This assessment is not timed, so there is no need to rush.

The assessment contains four reading passages followed by multiple-choice questions. Read each passage. Then, read the questions that follow the passage. Use the Answer Sheet I have given you to fill in your answer choices. It is best to use a pencil. That way, if you wish to change your answer, you can erase your first choice and mark your new choice.

Some of the passages and questions may be easy to read; others may be more difficult. Try to do your best on all of the passages and questions. Since I want to see how well you read independently, I cannot help you while you are taking the assessment.

When you finish answering all of the questions, go back and check your work if there is time to do so.

Go ahead, and begin the assessment.

When all students have completed the assessment, collect the test booklets and answer sheets.

Reading Comprehension

DIRECTIONS: Read each selection. Then, read each question about the selection. Decide which is the best answer to the question. On your answer sheet, mark the space for the answer you have chosen.

SAMPLE

Location, Location, Location

Some early American settlements were in poor locations. Roanoke, for example, was on an island that proved hard to reach. Rough ocean currents and storms made the voyage difficult for ships to bring much-needed supplies. The site for a later colony, Jamestown, also had problems. Jamestown sat on a marshy, disease-ridden piece of land. Because of its location, Jamestown's settlers had to endure increased incidents of illness as well as a salty water supply. However, despite the negatives, Roanoke and Jamestown shared one important advantage: The semihidden location of both colonies aided against surprise attacks.

1. The writer organizes this passage *mostly* by—
   A listing details about early settlements from least to most important
   B telling the sequence of events involved in settling early America
   C comparing and contrasting two early American settlements
   D offering solutions for the problems early American settlers faced

   1. Ⓐ Ⓑ ● Ⓓ

2. Which words *best* signal the main structural pattern used in the passage?
   A "Roanoke, for example . . ."
   B ". . . Jamestown . . . also had problems."
   C "Because of its location . . ."
   D ". . . as well as a salty water supply."

   2. Ⓐ ● Ⓒ Ⓓ

GO ON ➡

Reading Comprehension

Myra Gallencott

A   Lynn wasn't sure how she felt about Myra Gallencott. She had grown up with the quiet, painfully private woman next door for most of her seventeen years. Actually, she was closer than next door. Lynn, her parents, and her sister, Andrea, lived in one half of a duplex at the corner of Eighth Street and Woodridge Avenue; Myra lived on the other side of the central, windowless wall that divided the duplex. Their stairwell went up right along that wall, as did Myra's.

B   As a little girl, Lynn tried to visualize exactly how the stairways were constructed; but their arrangement was never completely clear to her. It remained a kind of eleven-step mystery extending into Myra Gallencott's realm. She did know that she felt like an intruder every time she went upstairs. Sometimes the girls would forget and hurry up with heavy feet; their mother explained that this would startle and offend their dignified neighbor.

C   Myra didn't complain a great deal, but she did demand a persistent awareness of her presence. She had to be quietly respected when it came to heavy feet and uncontrolled girlish squeals and shrieks.

D   It was, Andrea insisted, very intimidating: that imperious old woman "over there," sitting in her living room with its dark wooden walls and lamps glowering behind pumpkin-colored shades, just waiting for them to intrude on her solitude.

E   Yet Myra was never prying, never intrusive. She never objected to the parties they gave on the lawn. She would smile from her window as guests arrived and then close her curtains—not with disdain, Lynn understood, but out of respect for the privacy of the "young people." In her subtle, almost regal way, Myra approved of the girls' enjoying themselves.

F   Andrea had welcomed the news that Myra Gallencott was moving into a retirement center, but Lynn felt strangely sad. She stood with Andrea, looking up at Myra's half of the house, not willing to go inside where the auctioneer held sway, his voice ratcheting on and on like some giant machine.

G   Lynn was uncomfortable as she watched people carrying the woman's possessions away. As a stranger carried the lamps with the pumpkin-hued shades down the steps, they seemed to cry out to Lynn, objecting to being taken against their will.

GO ON ➡

Reading Comprehension

H   "What will it be like without Myra beyond that wall?" she asked quietly. "Who do you suppose will move in there?"

I   "Don't know, don't care," was Andrea's flippant response. "Soon, we'll graduate from high school, and our lives will change dramatically."

J   Lynn's eyes widened in awareness. Suddenly, Myra Gallencott's departure represented an unsettling reminder of the future. Lynn wanted Myra Gallencott back. She *loved* the woman, just as she loved the memories of growing up in the place they had shared with her.

1. Myra and Lynn are similar because they both—

   A are cold and uncaring
   B welcome a challenge
   C resent Andrea
   D are faced with change

2. Which of the following *best* describes Andrea's attitude toward Myra?

   A adoring
   B resentful
   C inquisitive
   D respectful

3. Which group of words from the passage is a figure of speech?

   A "quiet, painfully private woman next door"
   B "never objected to the parties they gave"
   C "his voice . . . like some giant machine"
   D "the place they had shared with her"

4. Which of the following *best* describes a theme of the story?

   A Older persons have much to teach us.
   B Memories are always joyful.
   C Life changes can be frightening.
   D Teenagers are difficult to live with.

5. Which of the following *best* describes Lynn?

   A caring
   B studious
   C demanding
   D outgoing

6. When Andrea says that "our lives will change dramatically," she probably means that she and Lynn will—

   A buy Myra's half of the duplex
   B move out on their own
   C no longer have parties on the lawn
   D help care for Myra

GO ON →

Reading Comprehension

7. How are the stairway and Myra alike?

   A Like the stairway, Myra is old and weak.

   B Lynn is frightened of both of them.

   C The stairway is grand, as Myra is elegant.

   D They are both somewhat of a mystery to Lynn.

8. Which group of words from the passage is a figure of speech?

   A "stairwell went up right along that wall"

   B "she did demand a persistent awareness"

   C "living room with its dark . . . walls"

   D ". . . the lamps . . . seemed to cry out to Lynn . . ."

9. If Lynn were to visit Myra in the retirement center, Myra would most likely react with—

   A anger

   B boredom

   C graciousness

   D merriment

10. In the final paragraph, the author writes that "Lynn wanted Myra Gallencott back." The author uses this statement to show that Lynn—

   A wants her life to remain the same

   B would like to move in with Myra

   C does not want new neighbors

   D looks up to Myra as a role model

STOP

Reading Comprehension

Space Junk

A   For the past forty years or so, we have heard much about the accomplishments of the first people to fly in space, orbit the earth, land on the moon, and live and work on a space station. We often receive news about the latest photographs from space telescopes and probes sent to explore distant planets. However, one aspect of the human exploration of space about which we hear very little is the phenomenon of space junk. Almost every time people have launched a rocket or satellite into space, bits and pieces have fallen off or been deliberately jettisoned, and they now form a vast orbiting array of debris. This is the depressing side of space exploration.

B   Tiny particles of debris, those no larger than a marble, are estimated to number in the millions! These particles include fragments as small as the chips of paint that flake off a rocket because of extreme heat or cold. However, even these minuscule bits of matter can pose a problem because each particle is traveling at about eighteen thousand miles per hour! They can scratch and damage things such as a space shuttle's windows, which are generally replaced after each mission for this very reason.

C   Slightly larger pieces of matter, up to the size of a small grapefruit, are estimated to number about 100,000. Pieces of even larger debris are so potentially dangerous that the U.S. Space Surveillance Network monitors each and every one of them. In years to come, as more and more satellites are launched to bring people everything from television broadcasts to automobile guidance systems, the Network expects a huge increase in the number of trackable pieces. The Network trackers assign a number to each large piece of space junk, and they know its location at all times. If a piece falls to Earth, as all of them eventually will, the Network can cross it off the list. We don't need to worry much about most of these objects because they burn up from the friction of reentry into Earth's atmosphere. However, very large pieces could survive reentry and touch down somewhere on Earth.

GO ON ➡

Reading Comprehension

D   To understand the nature of the situation more clearly, remember that the earth is rotating at a high rate of speed. If an object matches or exceeds the speed of the earth's rotation, the object will stay in orbit for at least a while. Objects in low-altitude orbit, two hundred to three hundred miles aboveground, generally fall within a year or two. Every decade or so, an increase in solar activity heats and expands the upper atmosphere, thus causing objects at altitudes up to four hundred miles to plummet. However, objects five hundred miles or more above the surface will remain in orbit for centuries; and it is estimated that satellites that are more than twenty thousand miles up will not come down for millions of years.

E   The big problem is the danger of a fairly large space junk object colliding with a spacecraft or communication satellite. On one occasion, this actually happened. A French satellite had been launched in 1986, and the rocket that propelled it was discarded and became a large piece of space junk. Nine months later the rocket was observed exploding into thousands of pieces. About five hundred of those pieces were large enough to track. In July 1996, one of those pieces struck a French satellite and chopped off a section of it.

F   Although that is the only known direct hit, there have been several alarming close calls. In August 1997, a five-hundred-pound rocket that had been in orbit for more than twelve years came within two miles of a multi-million-dollar research satellite that was following the space shuttle *Discovery*. Even more frightening, in September 1997, an old U.S. military satellite came within a thousand yards of the Russian space station *Mir*, causing the two Russian cosmonauts and one U.S. astronaut aboard to prepare for an emergency evacuation.

G   One proposed solution to the problem is to develop Earth-based lasers that will obliterate the chunks of debris before they can do any harm. Already, shuttle missions are carefully planned to avoid encounters with space junk. Clearly, this is a problem that must be solved.

Reading Comprehension

11. This passage would *most* likely be found in a publication written for—

    A astronomers

    B NASA employees

    C the general public

    D designers of satellites

12. Which is the *best* detail to add to paragraph C?

    A Most meteors burn up in the upper atmosphere.

    B By 1998, the Network was tracking 9,000 larger objects.

    C Friction also occurs between two solid surfaces.

    D The outer layer of the Earth is called the *crust*.

13. According to the passage, when a piece of space junk falls back to Earth is *most* dependent upon the—

    A size of the object

    B length of time it has been in orbit

    C speed at which it was launched

    D altitude of the object's orbit

14. There is enough information in the passage to show that—

    A there will be fewer shuttle missions until space debris can be destroyed

    B the problem of space junk will grow more serious in the years to come

    C scientists on space stations will track the largest pieces of space junk

    D heating of the upper atmosphere will accelerate in the next decade

15. One way the author organizes paragraph D is by—

    A listing details about the earth from least to most important

    B telling the sequence of events involved in launching a satellite

    C comparing and contrasting objects orbiting at different altitudes

    D offering a solution for the problems associated with low-altitude orbits

16. Which words *best* signal the main structural pattern used in paragraph D?

    A "If an object matches or exceeds"

    B "will stay in orbit for at least a while"

    C "Every decade or so, an increase in solar activity"

    D "However, objects five hundred miles or more"

17. Which is the *best* summary of paragraph F?

    A Space is full of dangerous debris.

    B A U.S. satellite came close to hitting the space station *Mir*.

    C Rockets used to launch satellites into orbit become debris.

    D Several near misses involving space junk have occurred.

GO ON ➡

Reading Comprehension

18. Which is the *best* evidence that the situation described in the passage is serious?

    A It has been going on for more than forty years.

    B It affects satellite equipment and human safety.

    C One solution for the situation involves lasers.

    D The author is concerned enough to write about it.

19. Which is an *opinion* expressed in the passage?

    A "This is the depressing side of space exploration."

    B "[E]ach particle is traveling at about eighteen thousand miles per hour!"

    C "[T]rackers assign a number to each large piece of space junk . . ."

    D "Objects in low-altitude orbit . . . generally fall within a year or two."

20. Which is the *best* summary of the passage?

    A Tiny particles of debris number in the millions.

    B Large pieces of space debris are dangerous and must be dealt with.

    C When pieces of space junk fall, trackers cross them off their list.

    D Objects orbit the Earth at different altitudes.

Reading Comprehension

A Soldier's Story

Prelude

In 1812, Napoleon decided to attack Russia because Czar Alexander refused to trade with France. Instead, Russia was exporting raw materials, such as timber and grain, to Great Britain in exchange for manufactured goods. Alexander ignored Napoleon's threats to discontinue trading with Great Britain, the rival power of France. Napoleon marched toward Moscow with the intent of punishing Alexander and his country. The following fictional passage is written in the form of a journal of a high-ranking commander in Napoleon's Grand Army.

June 24, 1812

A
We are about to cross over the Nemen River, the final barrier to Russia's border. The men are confident, but Napoleon's vengeful resolve would drive us even if they were not. I have ventured to reason with our dauntless leader, to try to make him understand that now is not a favorable time to besiege Russia, but our commander is firm in his resolution to take Moscow and punish the czar.

B
As I step from the tent in the cool dew of a new June morning, the lingering frost on my breath is becoming more visible. The aroma of fading fires mixed with the brisk air has created an ominous fog that hangs over the brave soldiers lining the landscape in droves. Looking about, I can scarcely see where our forces begin or end. The Grand Army blankets the countryside, a seemingly invincible monument to Napoleon's pride. I only hope that this monument endures, as I fear the Russians are plotting a cunning maneuver. Of course, my concerns are met with haughty dismissals from our great leader, Napoleon, and we march on.

September 14, 1812

C
Alas, we have infiltrated Moscow. We met with little resistance, having encountered Czar Alexander's army only twice in our two-and-a-half-month journey. At Smolensk, we vanquished Alexander's forces and established a temporary base. We met again at Borodino, but this time the opposition was more considerable. A devastating battle ensued, yet our Grand Army, under the command of Napoleon, was decidedly victorious.

GO ON ➡

Reading Comprehension

D   However, for the majority of our march upon Moscow, the Russians have disengaged and retreated like a scattered pack of petrified prey, overmatched by the sheer potency of an opponent nearly five times its size. This strategy confounds my leader's plans. In their flight, the Russians have set fire to all that they passed during their flight. Surveying the aftermath, we have discovered that the Russians have set the torch to every conceivable structure that might have been beneficial in keeping our men fortified.

E   Here in Moscow, the story is no different. The Russians have spared nothing. We encounter only smoldering ash and the dusky shadow of what was once the jewel of Russia—its magnificent capital city. The czar has vanished, leaving a clear outline of his tactical strategy. The Russian army, unable to withstand Napoleon's aggression, baited us to enter Moscow. To spite our efforts, they then retreated, luring us after them, and proceeded to lay waste to everything along the way.

F   We thought them mad for such outlandish actions, destroying precious resources in the face of the cruel winter coming. How will anyone survive? The leaves are now falling from the trees—through the frigid air—covering the ground in a blanket of gray. The night and morning inclemency has begun to numb my extremities. The descending temperature not only chills us, but also spreads a fever through the men like icy water, soaking the Grand Army in demoralizing ailments. The callous sun is setting too soon, taking with it our fading good fortune. I only hope our eminent leader has a remedy for our greater ills. With nothing left to take here in Moscow, we persist in our desire to return home. Napoleon remains confident that we have the supplies and capabilities required to survive the arctic elements. We shall see.

December 9, 1812

G   We have finally bridged the French border, but with only a fraction of our original number. The ruthless winter has robbed us of our potency. Scores of soldiers were lost to the blizzards of the past several months. The misfortune was doubled when our supplies were pillaged by sneak attacks from the Russians.

Reading Comprehension

H   We have also suffered disloyalty within our own ranks. The noble men of the once Grand Army, provoked by famine and fright, have taken to the disreputable act of raiding our dwindling rations and then deserting their comrades. The lurid events and gross miscalculations that have unfolded over the past six months have turned a once-invincible army into a vulnerable band of wanderers. My strength has left me. My body aches, my emotions are scattered, and I can do nothing but writhe in the agonies of this fever.

21. Based on these journal entries, it seems Napoleon considered himself—

    A irresponsible

    B unbeatable

    C inadequate

    D unqualified

22. In his descriptions of Napoleon, the author reveals feelings of—

    A worship

    B admiration

    C resentment

    D self-doubt

23. In contrast to Napoleon's tactics, Czar Alexander's strategy was to—

    A bait and retreat

    B attack head-on

    C use overwhelming numbers

    D attack only at night

24. How did the soldiers of Napoleon's Grand Army change during the campaign?

    A They learned to welcome death.

    B They grew to respect their opponents.

    C They readily adjusted to harsh conditions.

    D They became increasingly disillusioned.

25. Which group of words from the passage is a figure of speech?

    A "the final barrier to Russia's border"

    B "retreated like a scattered pack of petrified prey"

    C "We thought them mad for such outlandish actions. . . ."

    D "With nothing left to take here in Moscow"

26. Which group of words from the passage is a figure of speech?

    A ". . . I can scarcely see where our forces begin or end."

    B "We encounter only smoldering ash. . . ."

    C "leaves . . . covering the ground in a blanket of gray"

    D "Scores of soldiers were lost to the blizzards. . . ."

27. An important idea expressed in the journal is that—

    A revenge is justified

    B all men are brave

    C the biggest army wins

    D nature is a powerful ally

GO ON

Reading Comprehension

28. Based on the journal, in the years following 1812, the Russians would have likely—

A devoted great resources to rebuilding Moscow

B convinced Napoleon to attack Great Britain

C built a monument to honor Napoleon's bravery

D punished Czar Alexander for his treachery

29. Which group of words provides a hint of the Grand Army's fate?

A "We are about to cross over the Nemen River. . . ."

B ". . . an ominous fog . . . hangs over the brave soldiers. . . ."

C ". . . my concerns are met with haughty dismissals. . . ."

D "Here in Moscow, the story is no different."

30. Based on the diary's last entry, it is reasonable to predict that the writer will—

A decide to join Czar Alexander's army

B rob his men and desert his command

C congratulate Napoleon for his outstanding leadership

D continue to suffer both physically and emotionally

STOP

Reading Comprehension

Water, Water, Everywhere

A   It is a well-known fact that human beings cannot survive without water. Somewhere between approximately 50 and 75 percent of a person's body weight is from water. Many critical body functions, such as digestion and tissue growth, would be impossible without water. Fortunately, humans are equipped with a kind of automatic sensor that detects the body's need for water and controls when and how much one drinks. The signal sent by this automatic sensor is called "thirst." Unfortunately, it is not always a good idea to rely on thirst alone to decide how much water to drink. Sometimes a person may not feel thirsty, yet that person may be getting less water than is needed for good health.

B   Doctors and nutritionists often recommend that people drink eight to ten glasses of water every day. Extra water that your body does not need passes through your system easily, so it is very difficult to drink too much water. Remember how glorious that tall, cold glass of lemonade tasted on a hot day? Part of that great feeling came from the taste, but another part came from satisfying your thirst. Soda, tea, coffee, and other beverages taste good, and they contain some water, but they aren't as good for you as plain old water. Even a very healthful beverage, such as orange juice, cannot take the place of water. In extreme cases, people who do not get enough water can become ill from dehydration.

C   Although normal tap water is treated (cleaned) and is almost always safe to drink in this country, some people prefer filtered or bottled water. Today, there are many different types of home filtration systems and countless brands of bottled water available. Sorting out the differences among the many options can be confusing. Surprisingly, despite advertisers' claims, your home tap water may be just as pure as some bottled waters. In order to produce truly "purified" water, a complex series of processes must be performed.

D   The first step in purifying water is to remove the largest particles of impurities, such as sand or dirt. These large particles are filtered with a simple pleated-paper sediment filter. This process removes 99.7 percent of all particles that are ten microns or larger (the human eye generally cannot see particles smaller than twenty microns). This type of filter system is the most basic and is generally performed before any other processes.

GO ON ➡

Reading Comprehension

E   The next step in the process is the removal of metallic ions. In an ion-exchange system, metallic ions carrying a strong positive electric charge displace the more weakly charged potassium ions. Then an electromagnet traps the metallic ions. In addition to "softening" the water, ion exchange removes a variety of heavy metals, such as lead, iron, mercury, and cadmium.

F   After the ion exchange, carbon filtration can be used. This is the most common system for home use, and because it is simple to use and very effective at removing the taste and smell of chlorine, it is preferred by many consumers. Some home filtering systems attach directly to your tap and are very convenient.

G   To trap extremely small particles and even waterborne organisms, five-micron and one-micron carbon block filters are used. These filters trap particles that conventional chlorination and sand-filtration techniques can miss. After this process is completed, you may wonder what impurities could possibly remain, but remember that water dissolves many substances, and these substances may contain extremely tiny particles that cannot be removed easily.

H   Finally, a two-step process gets rid of dissolved impurities. In the first step, ultraviolet disinfecting eliminates dissolved impurities and microbiological contamination. Ultraviolet light can be a powerful sterilizing agent, and used at the right wavelength, it eliminates the possibility of bacterial or viral reproduction. The second step is ozonation. Ozonation uses high-voltage electric charges to split oxygen molecules and to create a form of oxygen known as ozone. Ozone is also a powerful disinfectant. Both of these processes are highly effective and chemical-free.

I   If you are still confused, just pick your favorite type of water, whether that means tap water, filtered water, bottled water, or purified water. The important thing is to drink plenty of water each day. Your body will thank you for it.

GO ON

Reading Comprehension

31. Which of these is the *best* summary of paragraph A?

   A Drinking enough water is essential for good health.

   B Humans have an automatic sensor that detects the need for water.

   C A large percentage of a person's body weight is from water.

   D Sometimes a person may need water without feeling thirsty.

32. The information in this passage is *most* likely to be reliable if written by a—

   A chemist

   B plumber

   C ordinary consumer

   D bottled-water salesperson

33. Paragraph B is mainly about—

   A how the body knows when to drink

   B different methods of purifying water

   C drinking enough water to stay healthy

   D how tap water is different from bottled water

34. The writer *mostly* organizes paragraphs D through H by providing—

   A a sequence of steps involved in purifying water

   B a description of several kinds of home filtration systems

   C a comparison and contrast of different types of drinking water

   D an explanation of the causes of water contamination

35. Which words *best* signal the main structural pattern used in paragraphs D through H?

   A "This process removes 99.7 percent. . . ."

   B "In addition to 'softening' "

   C "After the ion exchange"

   D "This is the most common"

36. Why is an electromagnet used in the purification of water?

   A to clean rust out of water pipes

   B to remove tiny metallic particles from water

   C to give the water a negative electrical charge

   D to trap potassium ions in the water

37. Which is an *opinion* expressed in the passage?

   A Tissue growth would be impossible without water.

   B Sediment filters remove the large particles in water.

   C There are many different types of home filtration systems.

   D Soda, tea, coffee, and other beverages taste good.

38. What type of evidence does the writer *mostly* use to support the main ideas in this passage?

   A facts and statistics

   B expert opinions

   C journal entries

   D quotations

GO ON

Reading Comprehension

39. There is enough information in the passage to show that—

A chlorine is no longer used to purify water

B athletes should drink citrus juice instead of water after workouts

C consumers may be wasting their money buying bottled water

D the micron is the unit used to measure visible objects

40. Which of the following is the *best* summary of this passage?

A Beverages such as tea, coffee, and soda contain some water, but plain water is better for your body. People should also make certain that the water they drink is clean and pure.

B Water is needed to sustain life, and the body closely regulates water intake. To ensure a healthful water supply, people use a variety of processes to purify water.

C Water, which makes up much of a person's weight, is required for the body to function properly. Particles in water, such as germs and dirt, can make people sick.

D In the United States, tap water is treated to make it drinkable. In addition, many people install home filtration systems. Bottled water, which is advertised as being more healthful than tap water, is also available.

NAME _____ DATE _____

Reading Comprehension

Answer Sheet

1. Ⓐ Ⓑ Ⓒ Ⓓ   21. Ⓐ Ⓑ Ⓒ Ⓓ
2. Ⓐ Ⓑ Ⓒ Ⓓ   22. Ⓐ Ⓑ Ⓒ Ⓓ
3. Ⓐ Ⓑ Ⓒ Ⓓ   23. Ⓐ Ⓑ Ⓒ Ⓓ
4. Ⓐ Ⓑ Ⓒ Ⓓ   24. Ⓐ Ⓑ Ⓒ Ⓓ
5. Ⓐ Ⓑ Ⓒ Ⓓ   25. Ⓐ Ⓑ Ⓒ Ⓓ
6. Ⓐ Ⓑ Ⓒ Ⓓ   26. Ⓐ Ⓑ Ⓒ Ⓓ
7. Ⓐ Ⓑ Ⓒ Ⓓ   27. Ⓐ Ⓑ Ⓒ Ⓓ
8. Ⓐ Ⓑ Ⓒ Ⓓ   28. Ⓐ Ⓑ Ⓒ Ⓓ
9. Ⓐ Ⓑ Ⓒ Ⓓ   29. Ⓐ Ⓑ Ⓒ Ⓓ
10. Ⓐ Ⓑ Ⓒ Ⓓ   30. Ⓐ Ⓑ Ⓒ Ⓓ
11. Ⓐ Ⓑ Ⓒ Ⓓ   31. Ⓐ Ⓑ Ⓒ Ⓓ
12. Ⓐ Ⓑ Ⓒ Ⓓ   32. Ⓐ Ⓑ Ⓒ Ⓓ
13. Ⓐ Ⓑ Ⓒ Ⓓ   33. Ⓐ Ⓑ Ⓒ Ⓓ
14. Ⓐ Ⓑ Ⓒ Ⓓ   34. Ⓐ Ⓑ Ⓒ Ⓓ
15. Ⓐ Ⓑ Ⓒ Ⓓ   35. Ⓐ Ⓑ Ⓒ Ⓓ
16. Ⓐ Ⓑ Ⓒ Ⓓ   36. Ⓐ Ⓑ Ⓒ Ⓓ
17. Ⓐ Ⓑ Ⓒ Ⓓ   37. Ⓐ Ⓑ Ⓒ Ⓓ
18. Ⓐ Ⓑ Ⓒ Ⓓ   38. Ⓐ Ⓑ Ⓒ Ⓓ
19. Ⓐ Ⓑ Ⓒ Ⓓ   39. Ⓐ Ⓑ Ⓒ Ⓓ
20. Ⓐ Ⓑ Ⓒ Ⓓ   40. Ⓐ Ⓑ Ⓒ Ⓓ

Reading Comprehension

Annotated Answer Sheet

1.	Ⓐ	Ⓑ	Ⓒ	●
2.	Ⓐ	●	Ⓒ	Ⓓ
3.	Ⓐ	Ⓑ	●	Ⓓ
4.	Ⓐ	Ⓑ	●	Ⓓ
5.	●	Ⓑ	Ⓒ	Ⓓ
6.	Ⓐ	●	Ⓒ	Ⓓ
7.	Ⓐ	Ⓑ	Ⓒ	●
8.	Ⓐ	Ⓑ	Ⓒ	●
9.	Ⓐ	Ⓑ	●	Ⓓ
10.	●	Ⓑ	Ⓒ	Ⓓ
11.	Ⓐ	Ⓑ	●	Ⓓ
12.	Ⓐ	●	Ⓒ	Ⓓ
13.	Ⓐ	Ⓑ	Ⓒ	●
14.	Ⓐ	●	Ⓒ	Ⓓ
15.	Ⓐ	Ⓑ	●	Ⓓ
16.	Ⓐ	Ⓑ	Ⓒ	●
17.	Ⓐ	Ⓑ	Ⓒ	●
18.	Ⓐ	●	Ⓒ	Ⓓ
19.	●	Ⓑ	Ⓒ	Ⓓ
20.	Ⓐ	●	Ⓒ	Ⓓ

21.	Ⓐ	●	Ⓒ	Ⓓ
22.	Ⓐ	Ⓑ	●	Ⓓ
23.	●	Ⓑ	Ⓒ	Ⓓ
24.	Ⓐ	Ⓑ	Ⓒ	●
25.	Ⓐ	●	Ⓒ	Ⓓ
26.	Ⓐ	Ⓑ	●	Ⓓ
27.	Ⓐ	Ⓑ	Ⓒ	●
28.	●	Ⓑ	Ⓒ	Ⓓ
29.	Ⓐ	●	Ⓒ	Ⓓ
30.	Ⓐ	Ⓑ	Ⓒ	●
31.	●	Ⓑ	Ⓒ	Ⓓ
32.	●	Ⓑ	Ⓒ	Ⓓ
33.	Ⓐ	Ⓑ	●	Ⓓ
34.	●	Ⓑ	Ⓒ	Ⓓ
35.	Ⓐ	Ⓑ	●	Ⓓ
36.	Ⓐ	●	Ⓒ	Ⓓ
37.	Ⓐ	Ⓑ	Ⓒ	●
38.	●	Ⓑ	Ⓒ	Ⓓ
39.	Ⓐ	Ⓑ	●	Ⓓ
40.	Ⓐ	●	Ⓒ	Ⓓ

Diagnostic Assessment for Reading Intervention
List of Correct Answers and Skills—Grade 12

		Skill			Skill
1	D	Compare and contrast	21	B	Understand characters
2	B	Understand characters	22	C	Understand characters
3	C	Understand figurative language	23	A	Compare and contrast
4	C	Recognize theme and form interpretations	24	D	Compare and contrast
5	A	Understand characters	25	B	Understand figurative language
6	B	Make predictions	26	C	Understand figurative language
7	D	Compare and contrast	27	D	Recognize theme and form interpretations
8	D	Understand figurative language	28	A	Make predictions
9	C	Make predictions	29	B	Recognize theme and form interpretations
10	A	Recognize theme and form interpretations	30	D	Make predictions
11	C	Make inferences	31	A	Summarize information
12	B	Identify main idea and details	32	A	Make inferences
13	D	Identify main idea and details	33	C	Identify main idea and details
14	B	Make inferences	34	A	Understand text structure
15	C	Understand text structure	35	C	Understand text structure
16	D	Understand text structure	36	B	Identify main idea and details
17	D	Summarize information	37	D	Distinguish between facts and opinions and evaluate supporting evidence
18	B	Distinguish between facts and opinions and evaluate supporting evidence	38	A	Distinguish between facts and opinions and evaluate supporting evidence
19	A	Distinguish between facts and opinions and evaluate supporting evidence	39	C	Make inferences
20	B	Summarize information	40	B	Summarize information

Holt Reading Solutions
Diagnostic Assessment for Reading Intervention
Performance Profile—Grade 12

Skill	Literary Comprehension Item Numbers (Mark incorrect answers.)				Score (Number correct)
Make predictions	6	9	28	30	_____ / 4
Understand characters	2	5	21	22	_____ / 4
Recognize theme and form interpretations	4	10	27	29	_____ / 4
Understand figurative language	3	8	25	26	_____ / 4
Compare and contrast	1	7	23	24	_____ / 4
Total Literary Comprehension					_____ / 20

Skill	Literary Comprehension Item Numbers (Mark incorrect answers.)				Score (Number correct)
Understand text structure	15	16	34	35	_____ / 4
Identify main idea and details	12	13	33	36	_____ / 4
Make inferences	11	14	32	39	_____ / 4
Summarize information	17	20	31	40	_____ / 4
Distinguish between facts and opinions and evaluate supporting evidence	18	19	37	38	_____ / 4
Total Informational Comprehension					_____ / 20
Total Reading Comprehension					_____ / 40

Reading Proficiency Level (circle one)		
Proficient	**Basic**	**Below Basic**
(36–40)	(24–35)	(Fewer than 24)

Collection 1
The Anglo-Saxons: 449–1066

Prereading
Vocabulary Practice

Teach Unfamiliar Vocabulary Present the following vocabulary words before reading. Explain that each word will help students answer the Think About questions on page six of the student book.

- *unifying* (p. 8): bringing together; uniting
- *dominant* (p. 9): most influential
- *morality* (p. 11): system of ideas of right and wrong conduct
- *loyalty* (p. 13): feeling of attachment and affection

Alternative Activity

Read the Adaptation Distribute copies of the below–grade-level adapted reading of "The Anglo-Saxons: 449–1066" (available in this book and, with marginal questions, in *Holt Adapted Reader*). Have all students read the selection silently.

Reading
Alternative Teaching Strategies

Read with a Purpose As they read, guide students to answer the Think About questions that are posed on student book page six. Remind them to refer to the vocabulary words from Prereading.

Use *The Holt Reader* You may have students read the on-level, shortened version of the introduction in *The Holt Reader* and respond to the instruction in the margins.

Postreading
Listening and Speaking Opportunity

Prepare to Write Lead students in a discussion of ancient and modern-day heroes to help them prepare for the writing activity "Heroism, then and now" on student book page 17. Explain the term *larger-than-life*. Then ask open-ended questions such as those shown below to help students share and formulate their ideas on the topic. Provide vocabulary and language support as needed.

- Who are some fictional larger-than-life heroes of today?
- How do people gain fame today?
- What artistic, political, or sports achievements do you respect?
- What are some prizes for these achievements?

Literary Skill
Evaluate the philosophical, political, religious, ethical, and social influences of a historical period.

Resources

In this book:
Adapted Readings

Other Resources:
- *The Holt Reader*, p. 3
- *Holt Adapted Reader*
- Video Segments 1, 2

Especially for ELL

It is important to provide a supportive environment in which students can express their ideas without worrying about the accuracy of their language. During the writing activity, invite ELLs to discuss their thoughts with one another in order to form an opinion on the topic. Once they know *what* they want to write, they can focus on the accuracy of their language production.

Literary Skill
Evaluate the philosophical, political, religious, ethical, and social influences of a historical period.

Resources

In this book:
Adapted Readings

Other Resources:
• *The Holt Reader,* p. 3
• *Holt Adapted Reader*
• Video Segments 1, 2

Teacher Tip

Use the note-taking activity to help students identify the most important ideas about each group. Have them take notes based on the questions you ask. For example, students' notes for the Celts should include the following information: *warriors; believed spirits controlled their lives; told legends of strong women and mythical, magical stories about the spirits.*

TARGETED STRATEGIES FOR SPECIAL EDUCATION STUDENTS

Prereading
Background

Preview Historical Information Read with students Political and Social Milestones on student book pages 4–5 to get an overview of the collection introduction. Explain that they will read about these topics in more detail in the rest of the collection.

Reading
Alternative Activity

Take Notes Have students list in their notebooks the following groups that settled in England: *Celts, Romans, Danes, Anglo-Saxons, Normans.* During reading, ask guided questions to focus students on details they can add to their notes. For example:

• **Celts:** Were the Celts warriors or peace-lovers? *(warriors)* Who did the Celts believe controlled every aspect of life? *(spirits)* What kind of stories did they tell? *(legends of strong women; myths full of magic and imagination)*

• **Romans:** What did the Romans build in England? *(a network of roads and a defensive wall)* Which religion did the Romans introduce? *(Christianity)* After the Romans left, were the clans united and strong or weak and divided? *(weak and divided)*

• **Danes:** Which word indicates the character of the Danes? *(fierce)*

• **Anglo-Saxons:** Who united the Anglo-Saxon countries to fight the Danes? *(King Alfred of Wessex, or Alfred the Great)* Which religion did many people begin to practice again? *(Christianity)* Who was responsible for keeping law and order? *(the leaders of each group)* What trait was most important in Anglo-Saxon society? *(loyalty)* Why was loyalty to a leader so important? *(People had to work together to protect themselves.)* How did the scops preserve some people's memories after they died? *(They told poems about them.)*

• **Normans:** Who led the Normans to defeat the Anglo-Saxons and the Danes? *(William, duke of Normandy)* Where was he from? *(northwestern France)*

Postreading
Alternative Teaching Strategy

Check Comprehension After completing the collection introduction, have students answer the Think About questions on page 6 of the student book. Encourage them to refer to the notes they took during Reading to help them find the answer to question two.

from *Beowulf* Part One

translated by Burton Raffel

Prereading

Vocabulary Practice

Sort Imagery Words Explain that authors and poets use specific words to paint mental pictures in their writing. Write the following words on separate index cards, and display them in random order:

eat, gnaw, jaws, feasting, bolted, teeth

go, strode, rushed, journeyed, sliding

hands, snatched, ripped, clutched, claws

Tell students that these words from the poem can be sorted into three categories, based on their related meanings: *eat, go,* and *hands.* Place these cards as headings for three lists. Pantomime the meanings of unfamiliar words and invite students to place the remaining words in the appropriate lists.

Practice the Key Ideas

Discuss Imagery Tell students that *imagery* is the use of descriptive language to evoke readers' emotions. Poets use imagery to paint clear mental images of characters, settings, and events. Preview some of the imagery used in the poem to prepare students to appreciate the language. Direct their attention to examples of imagery, such as in lines 407–409, 421–426, and 560–563 of the poem.

Discuss Hero Archetypes To help students complete the Quickwrite activity on page 20 of the student book, brainstorm several modern-day fictional and real-life heroes. Discuss the terms *evil, oppression, motivation,* and *virtues.* Guide students to give examples that relate to their modern-day heroes. For more practice with hero archetypes in "The Battle with Grendel," have students fill out the chart on the Before You Read page in *The Holt Reader.*

SKILLS FOCUS

Literary Skills
- Evaluate the philosophical, political, religious, ethical, and social influences of a historical period.
- Understand the archetype of the epic hero.

Resources

In this book:
- Adapted Readings
- Vocabulary and Comprehension, p. 35
- Additional Vocabulary Practice, p. 36

Other Resources:
- *The Holt Reader,* p. 10
- *Holt Adapted Reader*
- *Audio CD Library,* Disc 1
- *Audio CD Library, Selections and Summaries in Spanish*
- *Supporting Instruction in Spanish,* p. 3

Teacher Tip

Point out that the verbs in the vocabulary list appear in the poem in the past tense. Introduce the present-tense forms as well to help students build their vocabulary and language awareness.

Reading

Alternative Teaching Strategy

Read the Adaptation Distribute copies of the annotated excerpt from "The Battle with Grendel" in the Adapted Readings section of this book (also available with marginal questions in *Holt Adapted Reader*). Have all students read the selection silently.

Check Comprehension Pause after each of the sections in this excerpt from *Beowulf* to make sure students understand the main events of the section. Encourage them to summarize these events in their own words, or provide the simple summaries below. Then have students go back to the poem and find lines that describe these events.

1. Grendel went to the hall and ate a soldier. Beowulf attacked Grendel, and Grendel tried to fight against him.

2. Beowulf's men tried to help him fight the monster. Beowulf tore off Grendel's arm. Grendel left the fight and died. Beowulf's men celebrated his victory.

3. The next day the Danes continued to celebrate Beowulf's victory. They were relieved and grateful that the horrible monster was gone.

4. Grendel's mother lived in a terrible, dangerous place at the bottom of a lake. The Danes asked Beowulf to go and kill her.

5. Beowulf went to the bottom of the lake where Grendel's mother attacked him. He tried to cut her with his sword, but it didn't hurt her, so he used his hands to fight her. She tried to stab him, but his mail protected him and he continued to fight.

6. Beowulf killed Grendel's mother with a sword from her wall. He found Grendel's body and cut off its head.

Additional Support

Track the Hero Archetype Using simplified language, remind students of the main characteristics of hero archetypes: they fight oppression and evil to solve a problem for a community; they are motivated; they possess superhuman strength or powers; they reflect the virtues that the community holds most important. Students reading the selection in *The Holt Reader* can take notes on the hero archetype and respond to the instruction in the selection's margins.

Listening and Speaking Opportunity

Especially for ELL **Listen to the Poem** Remind students that the story of Beowulf is an example of oral tradition and that people used to gather to listen to the story for entertainment. Play the audio recording of the selection in English. For pronunciation support, stop periodically to have students echo read short sections.

Postreading
Alternative Activity

(Mixed Ability Group) **Connect with Native Speakers** Help
students relate the concept of imagery to their own backgrounds.
Assign groups, combining native speakers with ELLs. First, have
them identify passages in the selection that are clear examples of
imagery. Invite students to share how they feel when they read these
passages. Then, have students use imagery to describe other
characters with which they are familiar. Record on a class chart these
examples of imagery. Invite students to discuss how these images
make them feel about each character. The chart may look something
like the following:

Hercules	Chupacabras	Don Quixote
strong, muscular man	body of a pig	thin, old man
white toga	wings like a bat	big, clumsy suit of armor
sword and shield	fangs for sucking blood	old, tired horse
sandals		knight's lance

Alternative Assessment

Discuss Archetypes To reinforce the concept of the epic hero as
exemplified by the character Beowulf, have students complete this
activity.

1. An epic hero solves a terrible problem for a community. How
   does Beowulf solve a problem? For which community? *(He kills
   Grendel for the Danes.)*

2. An epic hero has superhuman strength or powers. Work with
   a partner. Find in the poem three examples of Beowulf's great
   strength or super powers. Be ready to read those parts to the
   class and explain them in your own words. *(Answers will vary,
   but may include lines such as 441–443, 496–499, 612–614.)*

Reading Skills Development

Identify Details About Character and Setting Some students may
have difficulty understanding the characters and identifying the
setting because of the long sentences and complicated syntax in
Beowulf. Tell these students to note key words and phrases from the
story as they read and to ask the questions *what? when? where? who?
why?* and *how?* For example, asking the questions *Who is the story
about?* and *Where does the story take place?* will help students identify
important details about character and setting. For more practice
identifying details, students may complete the chart on page 18 in
The Holt Reader.

(**Teacher Tip**)
Have students take turns
acting out image-rich
sections of the poem
by referring them to
appropriate, non-violent
lines. Begin by modeling
the image of Grendel
approaching Herot
(lines 392–398).

(**Especially for ELL**)
Beowulf is an important
part of the culture
of the English language.
Encourage students
to share what they know
about famous literature
or oral traditions from
their home cultures.
Invite them to make
comparisons between
these and *Beowulf.*

(**Core Skill**)
Use the resources in the
Reading Skills and
Strategies section of this
book to help students
having difficulty
understanding character.
Use the selection from
Beowulf for the application
portion of the lesson.

Literary Skills
- Evaluate the philosophical, political, religious, ethical, and social influences of a historical period.
- Understand the archetype of the epic hero.

Resources

In this book:
- Adapted Readings
- Vocabulary and Comprehension, p. 35
- Additional Vocabulary Practice, p. 36

Other Resources:
- *The Holt Reader,* p. 10
- *Holt Adapted Reader*
- *Audio CD Library,* Disc 1
- *Audio CD Library, Selections and Summaries in Spanish*
- *Supporting Instruction in Spanish,* p. 3

Teacher Tip

Help students through the difficult language of the poem. Encourage them to stop periodically and restate what is happening. Point out that they can follow the action of the main events without worrying too much about the poetic language.

TARGETED STRATEGIES FOR SPECIAL EDUCATION STUDENTS

Prereading
Background

Talk About Archetypes Tell students that the poem they will read is about an epic hero named Beowulf. Invite them to share with the class qualities that a hero usually possesses. Record their ideas on the board. Inform students that as they read they will compare the qualities they listed with those of Beowulf.

Prepare to Read Poetry Have students skim the first page of this excerpt from *Beowulf.* Model reading the first sentence of the poem for them. Point out that each line of *Beowulf* begins with a capital letter, even if it is not the beginning of a sentence. Direct students to use punctuation to determine where each sentence ends.

Reading
Alternative Activities

Identify Heroic Qualities As the class reads the selection, ask students to identify any heroic qualities of Beowulf that they mentioned in the list they made before reading. Place a check mark next to these. Encourage students to identify other heroic qualities they read about, such as strength and bravery, and add these to the list.

Read Poetry Remind students to rely on punctuation in order to determine where sentences end in *Beowulf.* You may want to use the audio recording as a model. Invite individuals to take turns reading aloud select sentences. Reading the poem one sentence at a time will aid students' comprehension.

Postreading
Alternative Assessment

Sum It Up Point out that the poem is divided into sections. Divide the class into groups, assigning one section (or more, depending on class size) to each group. Have them reread their section and then restate the main events in a few sentences. Record each group's sentences on the board. Explain that by putting all the sentences together, they can create a summary of the poem. For example, a sentence that summarizes the first section might be: *Grendel went to the hall and ate a soldier. Beowulf attacked Grendel, and Grendel tried to fight against him.*

Vocabulary and Comprehension

from *Beowulf* Part One

A. Read each definition. Write the letter(s) of the vocabulary word(s) that best matches each one.

1. ____ ____ walked quickly

2. ____ took quickly with the hand, grabbed

3. ____ eating a lot of good food

4. ____ traveled

5. ____ tore

6. ____ ____ part of the body for eating

7. ____ moving smoothly, like slipping

8. ____ ate very quickly

9. ____ held tightly

10. ____ sharp nails of an animal

11. ____ chew

A. snatched

B. clutched

C. teeth

D. sliding

E. claws

F. strode

G. rushed

H. feasting

I. bolted

J. journeyed

K. ripped

L. gnaw

M. jaws

B. Write T or F to tell if each statement about *Beowulf* is true or false.

1. ____ Grendel is an example of an epic hero.

2. ____ Beowulf eventually defeated Grendel, but first Grendel cut off Beowulf's arm.

3. ____ Grendel and his mother lived in Herot.

4. ____ The Danes were grateful to Beowulf and considered him to be a great warrior.

5. ____ Beowulf's mail helped protect him from Grendel's mother.

6. ____ Beowulf used a magic sword to cut off Grendel's mother's head.

Additional Vocabulary Practice

from *Beowulf* Part One

A. Write each word from the Word Bank in the related web.

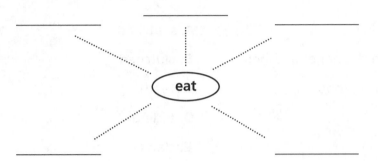

Word Bank	
claws	strode
feasting	bolted
clutched	jaws
rushed	journeyed
ripped	snatched
sliding	teeth
gnaw	

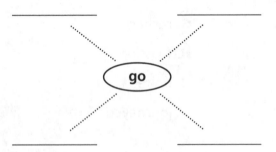 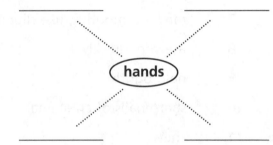

B. Write a sentence to tell how each of the following protects a soldier in battle.

1. helmet _____

_____

2. mail _____

_____

C. Write one sentence to explain one way that a sword and a dagger are alike. Write another sentence to explain how they are different.

1. _____

_____

2. _____

_____

from *Gilgamesh: A Verse Narrative*

retold by Herbert Mason

Prereading

Activate Prior Knowledge

Discuss Character Foils Remind students that a foil is a character who helps define another character by means of contrast. Explain to students that Gilgamesh, the main character of this epic poem, has a foil in his friend, Enkidu. Invite students to name foil pairs from movies, television programs, or cartoons. Help them identify contrasting characteristics in these pairs. For more practice with character foils, you may consider having students complete the chart on the Before You Read page in *The Holt Reader*.

Vocabulary Practice

Teach Unfamiliar Vocabulary Present in random order the vocabulary words shown below. Invite students to define words they know. Explain the meanings of unfamiliar words. Guide students to group the words into two general categories: words relating to strength and words relating to weakness.

- **strength:** *awesome* (line 27), *confidence* (line 38), *wisdom* (line 40), *fearless* (line 63), *unafraid* (line 102), *victorious* (line 133)
- **weakness:** *hesitations* (line 11), *cowardice* (line 40), *numb* (line 66), *paralyzed* (line 72), *despair* (line 100), *exhaustion* (line 107), *agony* (line 125), *pity* (line 173)

Ask students to identify words that describe different characters in *Beowulf*. Point out that different characters in a story may possess some of the same qualities. For example, at different times, Beowulf and the dragon are both victorious, powerful, and in agony. Tell students that at different points in *Gilgamesh*, the three main characters each demonstrate both strong and weak qualities.

Alternative Activity

Read the Adaptation Distribute copies of the annotated excerpt of the selection from *Gilgamesh* (available in this book and, with marginal questions, in *Holt Adapted Reader*). Have all students read the You Need to Know paragraph silently.

SKILLS FOCUS

Literary Skills
- Understand the use of a foil.
- Analyze the epic and the archetype of the epic hero in ancient and modern literature.
- Compare literary forms of major literary periods.

(Resources)

In this book:
- Adapted Readings
- Vocabulary and Comprehension, p. 41
- Additional Vocabulary Practice, p. 42

Other Resources:
- *The Holt Reader*, p. 19
- *Holt Adapted Reader*
- *Audio CD Library*, Disc 1
- *Audio CD Library, Selections and Summaries in Spanish*
- *Supporting Instruction in Spanish*, p. 5

(Language Tip)

Teaching vocabulary through word relationships, such as antonyms or word families, provides students with a meaningful framework for assimilating new knowledge into their working vocabularies.

Teacher Tip

Help students relate to the characters and the vocabulary words by inviting them to share times when they have displayed either strong or weak qualities. Remind them that, depending on the situation, they have probably felt and acted differently at different times.

Reading
Alternative Teaching Strategies

Use *The Holt Reader* Students reading the selection in *The Holt Reader* can take notes on character foils and respond to the instruction in the selection's margins.

Read with a Purpose As students read, encourage them to note the various times when Gilgamesh, Enkidu, and Humbaba each display the strong and weak qualities introduced in the Prereading section. Guide students through this task by prompting them to identify the vocabulary words as they encounter them in the selection. Help students to use the context surrounding each word as support for comprehension and character analysis. Connect the literary concept of a character foil to the vocabulary by encouraging students to identify instances in which Enkidu's character contrasts with Gilgamesh's.

Especially for ELL **Pantomime an Image** As the class reads this excerpt from *Gilgamesh,* call on one volunteer to read lines 162 to 167, while another pantomimes Humbaba's actions. Invite the class to name specific words in this passage that evoke an emotional reaction. For example, words like *great, huge,* and *thrashing* might evoke emotions like fear, dread, or terror. Choose a new volunteer to read the next two sentences (lines 167–173), as another student uses gestures and facial expressions to portray the image of Humbaba. Students may find that words such as *bent, slave,* and *pity* create a pitiful and sad image. Invite the class to discuss how their emotions toward the monster changed from the first section to the second.

Repeat this process with lines 176–183 and 183–192. Challenge students to decide which image of Humbaba is being described in each section. Once again, their emotional reaction to the first section might be fear evoked by his strength, and to the second, pity evoked by his weakness. Throughout this activity, use pantomime as the bridge between written language and meaning.

Use Audio Help students appreciate the sound of the poem by playing the audio recording in English. Play the selection through once while students listen and read along. Then, play specific passages and invite volunteers to mimic or echo read the audio recording. During echo reading, have students read the print as they listen to a section. Then, have them read the section aloud using the recording as a model for cadence and pronunciation.

Prepare to Write To prepare students for The Inner Quest writing activity on page 64 of the student book, stop periodically and invite them to share their ideas about what the characters might be thinking. Use guided questions to prompt students. For example, in lines 193–195, Enkidu fears Gilgamesh is weakening. Ask students what Enkidu might be thinking and why he might be afraid. As students discover similar opportunities for interior monologues, have them take notes on their ideas about what the character may be thinking.

Postreading

Alternative Assessment

Mixed Ability Group **Write a Dialogue** Assess reading comprehension and language production through this activity. Reread lines 41–50 of the selection. Model rewriting this section of the poem as dialogue, using the original language as well as paraphrasing. For example:

Gilgamesh: (shaking his finger at Enkidu and laughing) You see, my friend, you are outnumbered. (pauses) What's wrong, Enkidu?

Enkidu: I'm scared! (shakes head *no,* looks like he will cry) You have never fought Humbaba.

Divide the class into pairs, preferably mixing ELLs with native speakers. Assign each pair a section or page to reread together. Then ask them to rewrite their section as dialogue, following your model. Encourage them to be creative and to include stage directions. After each pair has practiced their completed dialogue several times, invite them to act it out for the rest of the class.

Alternative Activity

Complete the Chart For more practice comparing and contrasting Gilgamesh and Enkidu, have your students complete the postreading chart in *The Holt Reader.*

Reading Skills Development

Compare and Contrast Before students can identify one character as a foil to another character, they may need additional practice in comparing and contrasting character traits. Have pairs of students read together a selection you choose from the Comparing and Contrasting section of the list that begins on page 225 of this book. Each partner should pick a character from the story and summarize that character's qualities for the other student. After student pairs have summarized the qualities of the two characters, have them compare and contrast their attributes, compiling a list of similarities and a list of differences. Ask for volunteers to share their lists with the class.

(Especially for ELL)
Writing can be a daunting task for ELLs. Ease frustration by differentiating between the tasks of collecting and presenting content. First have students brainstorm and organize their ideas. Then they can focus on language for expression.

(Fluency Tip)
Encourage students to focus on pronunciation and fluency as they read their dialogues aloud. In writing these dialogues, students have already considered the meaning they wish to convey. In reading them, they can focus on their delivery.

(Core Skill)
Use the resources in the Reading Skills and Strategies section of this book for any student who is having difficulty comparing and contrasting. Use the excerpt from *Gilgamesh* for the application portion of the lesson.

TARGETED STRATEGIES FOR SPECIAL EDUCATION STUDENTS

Literary Skills
- Understand the use of a foil.
- Analyze the epic and the archetype of the epic hero in ancient and modern literature.
- Compare literary forms of major literary periods.

Resources

In this book:
- Adapted Readings
- Vocabulary and Comprehension, p. 41
- Additional Vocabulary Practice, p. 42

Other Resources:
- *The Holt Reader,* p. 19
- *Holt Adapted Reader*
- *Audio CD Library,* Disc 1
- *Audio CD Library, Selections and Summaries in Spanish*
- *Supporting Instruction in Spanish,* p. 5

Teacher Tip

Motivate students by making a connection between literature and popular culture. For example, teach the literary focus of the hero and his foil through examples of famous modern-day character pairs to heighten students' interest in the lesson.

Prereading

Activate Prior Knowledge

Focus on the Key Idea Review with students the Literary Focus presented on page 57 of the student book: the foil. Provide or elicit from students examples of popular heroes and their foils. For each pair, create a T-chart on the board to illustrate the contrasting qualities of the two characters. Point out that the foil does not have to be opposite from the hero in every way. A foil and the hero may both be honest, but one may be patient while the other is impatient. Explain that in the epic poem *Gilgamesh,* the hero's character is highlighted through the contrast between him and his foil Enkidu.

Reading

Alternative Activity

Complete a T-Chart Prepare students to answer Thinking Critically questions three and four on student book page 64. As they read, have students complete a T-chart similar to the ones created in Prereading. Guide them to record characteristics of Gilgamesh and Enkidu and then to compare these to emphasize Enkidu's role as a character foil. Note that these characters change throughout the poem. For example, when Enkidu is fearful, Gilgamesh encourages him. Later, when Gilgamesh is fearful, Enkidu encourages him.

Postreading

Focus on the Key Strategy

Core Skill **Compare and Contrast Epic Heroes** Provide extra support for students as they answer Comparing Literature question nine on student book page 64. Use a four-column chart like the one below to guide them in comparing and contrasting the heroes in *Beowulf* and *Gilgamesh*:

hero	evil forces	motivation	virtues
Beowulf	Grendel, dragon	Danes ask him to help.	strong, brave...
Gilgamesh	Humbaba	wants fame	strong, willful...

Vocabulary and Comprehension

from *Gilgamesh: A Verse Narrative*

A. Choose two words from the Word Bank to describe each character listed below. Then write one sentence for each word, explaining how the character demonstrates each quality in the poem.

Gilgamesh

Example:

victorious   Gilgamesh is victorious when he defeats Humbaba.

_____   _____

_____

Word Bank	
strength	weakness
victorious	hesitations
cowardice	fearless
despair	pitiful
awesome	confidence
paralyzed	

Enkidu

_____   _____

_____   _____

Humbaba

_____   _____

_____   _____

B. Answer each question below.

1. Why did Gilgamesh want to kill Humbaba?

_____

_____

2. Did the elders of Uruk like Gilgamesh's idea to kill Humbaba? How do you know?

_____

_____

3. What did Enkidu tell Gilgamesh that his dreams meant?

_____

_____

4. How did Enkidu help Gilgamesh defeat Humbaba?

_____

_____

Additional Vocabulary Practice

from *Gilgamesh: A Verse Narrative*

A. Read each pair of sentences. Decide if the two sentences have the same meaning. Write Y for yes or N for no. (Note that a vocabulary word is underlined in the first sentence of each pair).

 1. Gilgamesh told the god Shamash, "I have followed you in the way <u>decreed</u>."

 ____ Gilgamesh told the god Shamash, "I have followed your orders."

 2. Enkidu spent that night in <u>agony</u>.

 ____ Enkidu slept comfortably that night.

 3. The sea was dangerous during the <u>squall</u>.

 ____ The sea was dangerous during the storm.

 4. Gilgamesh was <u>unafraid</u> to fight the monster Humbaba.

 ____ Gilgamesh was scared to fight the monster Humbaba.

 5. Enkidu's hand became <u>numb</u> after he touched the gate.

 ____ Enkidu couldn't feel his hand after he touched the gate.

 6. At the end of the day, Enkidu and Gilgamesh were overcome with <u>exhaustion</u>.

 ____ That night, Enkidu and Gilgamesh were very, very tired.

B. Match words with definitions. Write the letter of the correct definition next to each word.

 ____ **1.** wisdom   **a.** winning a battle or contest

 ____ **2.** cowardice   **b.** amazing, wonderful

 ____ **3.** awesome   **c.** causing or deserving sympathy and sorrow

 ____ **4.** victorious   **d.** knowledge and experience

 ____ **5.** pitiful   **e.** lack of bravery

from *Book 22: The Death of Hector*

by Homer

translated by Robert Fagles

Prereading

Vocabulary Practice

Teach Unfamiliar Vocabulary Improve students' comprehension by previewing these words and their definitions:

- *mightiest* (p. 67): most powerful
- *intercept* (line 11): stop or interrupt something in progress
- *overtake* (line 16): catch up with
- *hurl* (line 23): throw forcefully.
- *venture* (line 58): dare or risk going
- *onslaught* (line 76): fierce attack
- *swear* (line 84): make a strong promise; vow
- *ransom* (line 179): payment made to release a captured person

Additional Background

Simplify the Context Prepare students to understand the selection by simplifying the background information provided on student book pages 65–66.

(**Especially for ELL**) **Prepare to Read** You may consider having Spanish-speaking English-language learners read or listen to the selection summary in Spanish in preparation for reading the selection in English.

Reteach the Key Idea

Focus on Epic Similes Remind students that a *simile* is a figure of speech that compares one thing to another using the word *like* or *as*. Provide some simple examples of common similes, such as *run like the wind* or *as strong as an ox*. Point out that Homer's epic similes also use the words *like* and *as*. Read and discuss together the simile in lines 1–3, which is mentioned in the Literary Focus on student book page 66. To provide more information on epic similes, direct students to the Before You Read page in *The Holt Reader*. Tell students that as they read, they should try to identify the selection's other epic simile. Give them the hint that the other epic simile also compares the actions of warriors to those of animals.

Literary Skills
- Understand the epic simile.
- Understand conventions of epic poetry.
- Compare epics from different literary periods.

(**Resources**)

In this book:
- Vocabulary and Comprehension, p. 47
- Additional Vocabulary Practice, p. 48

Other Resources:
- *The Holt Reader,* p. 30
- *Audio CD Library, Selections and Summaries in Spanish*
- *Supporting Instruction in Spanish,* p. 6

(**Teacher Tip**)

Provide additional background information to help students appreciate this excerpt from the *Iliad*. For example, explain that because Achilles is half-god, he has a special advantage over Hector.

Reading
Alternative Teaching Strategies

Summarize by Section Help students stay on track while reading the selection. Stop periodically and ask comprehension questions about the section students have just read. For example, stop at line 52 and ask questions like the following about the first part of the poem:

- Who is Achilles chasing? *(Hector)*
- Where are the two men running? *(around the walls of Troy)*
- Which god has helped Hector in the past? *(Apollo)* Does he help Hector now? *(no)*
- The god Zeus holds a scale that balances men's lives. Whose lives is he balancing? *(Achilles' and Hector's)*
- In line 30, who do we learn is going to die? *(Hector)*

Use *The Holt Reader* Students reading the selection in *The Holt Reader* can take notes and respond to the instruction in the selection's margins.

Read the Connection Before reading "Trojan Gold" on student book pages 77–78, you may wish to paraphrase the introduction that appears in italics. Tell students that Schliemann left his business to become an archeologist. "Trojan Gold" is about one discovery that he made during his great archeological career. As students read the selection, help them as necessary with vocabulary they find difficult.

Postreading
Alternative Activities

Especially for ELL **Revisit Similes** Ask students if they found the second epic simile mentioned in Prereading. *(lines 139–144)* Have a volunteer read aloud this simile. Discuss any vocabulary that may be difficult for English-language learners, such as "swooped," "launching," "snatch," "trembling," and "hare." Then ask questions like the following:

- Which word helped you identify this as a simile? *(like)*
- Which character is compared to an animal? *(Hector)*
- To what animal is he compared? *(an eagle)*
- What is Hector doing that an eagle does? *(swooping)*
- Is Hector really swooping down from the sky? *(No, he is attacking Achilles.)*
- What emotions are evoked by the images of a "helpless lamb" and a "trembling hare"? *(possible response: pity, fear)*

Use *The Holt Reader* Have students complete the Visualizing Imagery chart in *The Holt Reader,* either instead of or in addition to the postreading activities in the student book.

Vocabulary Development

Additional Practice

Provide Dictionary Support Prepare students to complete the Vocabulary Development activity on student book page 80. Help students become familiar with dictionary abbreviations by referring them to the page in the dictionary on which they are listed. Review some features of a typical dictionary entry as shown below.

1. **entry word** Entries are often broken into syllables.
2. **pronunciation** This appears between slashes, as in /a/.
3. **part(s) of speech** These are abbreviated and usually appear in italics. Words that function as more than one part of speech have a separate definition for each.
4. **word origin** This appears between brackets: [ ].
5. **definition(s)** These explain the meaning(s) of the word. Definitions are listed in order of most frequent usage.
6. **other forms** Some entries include other forms of the word, such as an alternative spelling.
7. **phrase and derivative lists** These list common idioms, phrases, compounds, and regularly derived forms of the word.

Grammar Link

Additional Practice

(**Especially for ELL**) **Provide Extra Support** Provide ELLs with examples of sentence fragments and run-on sentences like those below. Invite volunteers to complete the sentence fragments and revise the run-on sentences. More than one solution is often possible.

1. After she ate lunch. *(After she ate lunch, she left.)*
2. The test caught Ricardo by surprise he didn't know it would be so difficult. *(The test caught Ricardo by surprise. He didn't know it would be so difficult.)*
3. By the time I found my key and opened the door. *(By the time I found my key and opened the door, the phone had stopped ringing.)*

Reading Skills Development

(**Mixed Ability Group**) **Focus on Figurative Language** Provide additional support for students who are struggling to understand figurative language. First, have students read "The Death of Hector" with a partner. Ask students to note examples of similes, metaphors, and personification as they read. Then, go through the selection with the class, asking each student pair to point out the examples of figurative language they noted.

SKILLS FOCUS

Vocabulary Skill
Create semantic maps.

(**Geography Connection**)

Explain to students that in Homer's time and for a few hundred years afterwards, the Greeks colonized far beyond the borders of what is Greece today. Besides establishing themselves in what is now known as western Turkey, where Troy was, the Greeks also set up colonies in the eastern Mediterranean, northern Africa, Sicily, and Italy. Ask students to point out these places on a map. Invite them to share what they know about the ancient Greeks.

(**Teacher Tip**)

Have students apply what they have learned about sentence fragments and run-on sentences to their own writing. Ask them to go back and revise an earlier piece of writing, completing any sentence fragments and correctly breaking any run-on sentences that they find.

(**Core Skill**)

Use the resources in the Reading Skills and Strategies section of this book to help students having difficulty with figurative language. Use "The Death of Hector" for the application portion of the lesson.

TARGETED STRATEGIES FOR SPECIAL EDUCATION STUDENTS

Literary Skills
• Understand the epic simile.
• Understand conventions of epic poetry.
• Compare epics from different literary periods.

Resources

In this book:
• Vocabulary and Comprehension, p. 47
• Additional Vocabulary Practice, p. 48

Other Resources:
• *The Holt Reader*, p. 30
• *Audio CD Library, Selections and Summaries in Spanish*
• *Supporting Instruction in Spanish*, p. 6

Teacher Tip

Prepare students to read by paraphrasing the information provided in the Background section on student book page 66 and in the introduction to the selection on student book page 68.

Prereading
Alternative Activity

Chart Characters Explain that gods and humans both play important roles in epic poems, such as the *Iliad*. Prepare students to keep track of the selection's many characters, words and phrases used to identify them, and details which help distinguish them. On the board, complete the first column of a chart like the one shown below. As you read the selection with students, add details that will help them remember who is who. Your completed chart might resemble the following:

WHO'S WHO IN "THE DEATH OF HECTOR"		
character	god/goddess or man/woman	identifiers and details
Achilles	half god, half man	strong, fast, Greek warrior, called "Peleus' princely son"
Hector	man	strong, fast, Trojan warrior, called "breaker of horses," "gallant captain," "the fighter"
Apollo	god	"Phoebus," "son of Zeus," "Archer"
Zeus	god	father of gods
Athena	goddess	disguises herself as Hector's brother Deiphobus
Priam	man	Hector's father, King of Troy
Hecuba	woman	Hector's mother, Queen of Troy
Patroclus	man	killed earlier by Hector, had been Achilles' best friend

Reading
Alternative Teaching Strategy

Focus on Epic Similes As students read, help them understand how Homer uses epic similes at different places in the selection to evoke contrasting emotions about Hector and Achilles. For example, as they read the simile in lines 1–3, students might feel pity and fear for Hector because he is compared to a hunted fawn. Then as they read the simile in lines 139–144, they may feel contrary emotions for Hector (*possible response: awe, respect*) because he is now described as the predator.

Postreading
Speaking and Listening Opportunity

Retell the Selection After students finish reading this excerpt from the *Iliad*, challenge them to retell it using guided paraphrasing. Begin by paraphrasing the opening chase scene and then ask: *What happened next?* Help students retell the various plot events, guiding them with questions when necessary.

Vocabulary and Comprehension

from *Book 22: The Death of Hector*

A. Complete each sentence using a word from the Word Bank.

Word Bank
mightiest
venture
onslaught
swear
hurl
ransom

1. Superman is the _____ hero in the story.

2. Look out! She's going to _____ an apple at you!

3. He paid a million dollars _____ to free the hostage.

4. Because the enemy's _____ was so strong, our army lost the battle.

5. Do you _____ to tell the truth, the whole truth, and nothing but the truth?

6. Be careful! Don't _____ out in a storm.

B. Number the following sentences to indicate the order in which the events occurred, according to the excerpt from *Book 22: The Death of Hector.*

____ Achilles hurls his spear at Hector and misses.

____ Athena disguises herself as Hector's brother Deiphobus.

____ Hector hits Achilles' shield with his spear.

____ A crowd of Greeks stands over Hector's body.

____ Achilles kills Hector.

____ Achilles chases Hector around the walls of Troy.

C. Answer the questions below in complete sentences.

1. Which goddess returns Achilles' spear to him after he throws it at Hector and misses? _____

_____

2. Does Hector stop trying to kill Achilles when his spear hits Achilles shield?

_____

_____

3. What does dying Hector beg Achilles to do with his body?

_____

_____

4. Does Achilles honor Hector's dying request?

_____

_____

Additional Vocabulary Practice

from *Book 22: The Death of Hector*

A. Write each word from the Word Bank next to its definition, one letter per space. Then unscramble the shaded letters to form the name of a character from the selection.

Word Bank	
mightiest	intercept
overtake	hurl
venture	onslaught
swear	ransom

1. payment made to release a captured person
   __ __ __ __ __ __

2. catch up with __ __ __ __ __ __ __ __

3. throw forcefully __ __ __ __

4. dare or risk going __ __ __ __ __ __ __

5. most powerful __ __ __ __ __ __ __ __ __

6. make a strong promise __ __ __ __ __

7. interrupt something in progress __ __ __ __ __ __ __ __ __

8. an attack __ __ __ __ __ __ __ __ __

Hero: __ __ __ __ __ __ __ __   __ __ __ __   __ __ __ __ __ __

B. Choose three words from the Word Bank above. Use each word in a sentence.

1. _____

_____

2. _____

_____

3. _____

_____

C. Circle the letter of the answer that best completes each sentence.

1. I'm running as fast as I can, but I can't _____ Henry!
   a. hurl   **b.** overtake   **c.** swear

2. Paco hates to _____ out on cold nights like this.
   a. venture   **b.** intercept   **c.** onslaught

3. If the other team _____ the ball, we will lose the game.
   a. onslaught   **b.** intercepts   **c.** swear

4. My sister was the victim of an _____ of water balloons.
   a. venture   **b.** hurl   **c.** onslaught

Collection 2
The Middle Ages: 1066–1485

Prereading
Vocabulary Practice

(**Especially for ELL**) **Teach Unfamiliar Vocabulary** Aid English-language learners' comprehension by previewing these words and their definitions:

- *ensuing* (p. 120): taking place afterward or as a result of
- *backdrop* (p. 124): background or surrounding circumstances
- *fostered* (p. 126): promoted growth or development; encouraged
- *consciousness* (p. 127): the state or quality of being aware

Alternative Teaching Strategies

Explain Overall Text Structure Explain that the introduction is about three main topics: the Norman conquest, the features of feudalism, and the decline of feudalism. On the board, begin a chart with these topics as column headings. Then page through the selection with students, asking volunteers to predict which topic each section of the introduction will discuss.

Read the Adaptation Distribute copies of the below–grade-level adapted reading for "The Middle Ages: 1066–1485" (available in this book and, with marginal questions, in *Holt Adapted Reader*).

Reading
Alternative Activities

Focus on Key Ideas As you read the collection introduction with students, stop after each section and ask them to paraphrase main ideas and important details. Have them record each response on the chart under the appropriate topic.

Use *The Holt Reader* You may have students read the on-level, shortened version in *The Holt Reader* and respond to the instruction in its margins.

Postreading
Listening and Speaking Opportunity

Talk About It Have students refer to their completed charts as they answer the Think About questions on student book page 116.

SKILLS FOCUS

Literary Skill
Evaluate the philosophical, political, religious, ethical, and social influences of a historical period.

(**Resources**)

In this book:
Adapted Readings

Other Resources:
- *The Holt Reader*, p. 45
- *Holt Adapted Reader*
- Video Segments 1, 3

(**Teacher Tip**)

Remind students that paging through a selection before reading is a learning strategy they can use whenever they read nonfiction. Ask them to identify the best things to look for when paging through a selection, such as titles and subtitles, boxes, sidebars, and captions. Discuss how this type of prereading can prepare them to better understand a selection.

(**Core Skill**)

Use the resources in the Reading Skills and Strategies section of this book to help students having difficulty understanding text structure. Use the collection introduction for the application portion of the lesson.

TARGETED STRATEGIES FOR SPECIAL EDUCATION STUDENTS

Resources

In this book:
Adapted Readings

Other Resources:
• *The Holt Reader,* p. 45
• *Holt Adapted Reader*
• Video Segments 1, 3

Teacher Tip

Many students will have some background knowledge about the Middle Ages. As you discuss the introduction, encourage them to share any facts they already know about kings, castles, knights, and other features of the Middle Ages.

Teacher Tip

Challenge students to correct each false statement in the Postreading activity, Check Comprehension.

Prereading
Alternative Teaching Strategy

Prepare to Read Read together the Think About questions on page 116 of the student book. Highlight key words or phrases in each question, and provide a simple definition for each. Guide students in paraphrasing each question in order to better understand it. Write the paraphrases on the board for students to refer to as they read. For example, for the first question:

• Key Words: *Norman = French*
                   invasion = act of one country taking over another
                   governed = ruled or controlled

• Paraphrase: *Did the Norman invasion change England? How? Think about* who *ruled the English people and* how *they ruled.*

Reading
Alternative Teaching Strategy

Read to Find Answers As you read the introduction together with students, help them identify places in the text that might contain answers to the Think About questions. Refer to the notes you wrote on the board in Prereading. As you read each section, ask students to search for key words that look similar to those in the questions on the board. Then discuss that section to see if it provides information that answers a question. For example, after reading page 116, use a questioning strategy like the following:

• What words do you see that look like *Norman? (Normans, Normandy)*

• Is this part about the Norman Invasion or feudalism? *(the Norman Invasion)*

• Look at the first paragraph. Does it say that the Norman Invasion changed England? *(yes)* What words have a meaning similar to *changed? (radically affected)*

Postreading
Alternative Assessment

Check Comprehension Ask true/false questions like the following to check students' comprehension of the collection introduction:

1. In the feudal system, the king had power over everyone. *(T)*

2. Serfs sometimes sold the land they worked and got rich. *(F)*

3. The Black Death helped end feudalism in England. *(T)*

"The Prologue"
from *The Canterbury Tales*
by Geoffrey Chaucer, translated by Nevill Coghill

Prereading
Additional Practice

Focus on the Key Idea Reinforce the methods that writers use to portray characters, as explained in the Literary Focus on student book page 140. Provide examples such as the following to illustrate that authors can reveal their characters by telling us:

- how the character looks and dresses: *She has warm eyes and wears brightly colored clothing.*
- how the character speaks and acts: *She smiled and said she liked my idea.*
- what the character thinks and feels: *She is happy that her friend won the prize.*

Alternative Activities

Read the Adaptation Distribute copies of the annotated excerpts from "The Prologue" to *The Canterbury Tales* (available in this book and, with marginal questions, in *Holt Adapted Reader).* Have all students read the You Need to Know paragraphs silently.

Focus on Satire Students may not understand Chaucer's use of satire in characterization. Reinforce the concept using a familiar type of character, such as a teacher. Create a T-chart like the one below. Have students fill in the left side of the chart with the qualities of an ideal teacher. Complete the right column with qualities that are opposites of those on the left.

Teacher: Ideal	Teacher: Satire
energetic	lazy
smart	ignorant
loves teaching	hates teaching

Explain that Chaucer criticizes a social group by creating a character from that group whose qualities don't match what is expected, or don't match the image the group presents of itself. For more on analyzing the characters, have students read the Before You Read page in *The Holt Reader.*

SKILLS FOCUS

Literary Skills
- Understand characterization.
- Understand the characteristics of a frame story.
- Analyze imagery in characterization.

Reading Skill
Analyze style using key details.

Resources

In this book:
- Adapted Readings
- Vocabulary and Comprehension, p. 55
- Additional Vocabulary Practice, p. 56

Other Resources:
- *The Holt Reader,* p. 53
- *Holt Adapted Reader*
- *Audio CD Library,* Disc 2
- *Audio CD Library, Selections and Summaries in Spanish*
- *Supporting Instruction in Spanish,* p. 8

Especially for ELL

Teaching opposites is one way to help English-language learners build vocabulary. Present an antonym, and define a word as *the opposite of . . . .* For example, tell students that *worthy* means the opposite of *unimportant.*

By pointing out and discussing examples of satire, you will help students understand not only Chaucer's medieval world, but also the world of today. Such discussions also help students use and understand the vocabulary associated with the basic elements of society—words such as *government, social group,* and *relationship.*

Vocabulary Practice

(**Especially for ELL**) **Teach Unfamiliar Vocabulary** Help English-language learners develop their vocabularies by teaching the following words and definitions. Use each word in a sentence about a person and ask students to do the same. Point out that all the words have a positive connotation.

- *noble* (lines 50, 62): good; of very high quality; deserving respect
- *stately* (line 144): showing great dignity, importance, or royalty
- *personable* (line 204): pleasing in appearance and behavior
- *courteous* (line 254): polite; kind; having good manners
- *discreet* (line 322): careful; modest; using good judgment
- *trim* (line 375): in good physical condition; slim; neat
- *worthy* (lines 379, 455): having worth; important enough; deserving admiration
- *prudent* (line 415): careful in conduct; using good judgment or common sense
- *diligent* (line 493): persistent; careful and hardworking

Remind students that Chaucer sometimes describes a person with positive adjectives like those above, but when he shows the character's behavior, the reader gets a negative impression. Point out that such descriptions are sarcastic or ironic. For example, in line 322, Chaucer says the Lawyer is *discreet,* but the reader later finds that his discretion may come at a very high price to his clients.

Reading

Alternative Teaching Strategy

(**Mixed Ability Group**) **Focus on Character** Assign pairs of students one character for which to create a T-chart like the one made in Prereading. Have partners describe an ideal member of the character's social group on the left side of the chart. In order to help them discuss those with vocations that no longer exist, such as the Pardoner, you may need to supply some information about life in medieval society. On the right side of the chart, have students paraphrase the qualities Chaucer gives to the character. Point out that if the traits in both columns nearly match, Chaucer is idealizing that character's social group. If the two columns don't match, he is satirizing the group. Students also may read the selection in *The Holt Reader* and respond to the instruction in its margins.

Pardoner: Ideal	Pardoner: Satire
humble	shows off his golden hair
honest	lies to priests and congregations
religious	has fake religious relics

Postreading

Alternative Activities

Analyze Chaucer's England Use a chart to guide students to an understanding of the close relationships among various parts of Chaucer's medieval society. On the board, begin a chart like the one below. Choose a character such as the Cook, write *Cook* in the *character* column, and ask students to which social sphere he most obviously belongs. *(city)* In the *city* column, write the reason(s) why he is connected to that social sphere. *(He is a professional.)* Then discuss with students the reasons why he is also connected to the other two social spheres. *(Church: he tithes, or pays one tenth of his earnings to the Church; feudal system: he obeys the laws and pays taxes.)* Repeat the process with other characters. For additional practice analyzing key details of characterization in "The Prologue," have students complete the postreading activities in *The Holt Reader,* either instead of or in addition to the activities in the student book.

character	Church	feudal system	city
Cook	He tithes.	He obeys laws. He pays taxes.	He is a professional.

(Mixed Ability Group) Discuss Imagery Assign pairs of students a character from the selection. Ask them to list words that Chaucer uses to describe the character's physical appearance. Partners should be ready to share with the class what these images tell them about the character. The Yeoman (lines 103–121), for example, has bright and neat arrows at his belt, a mighty bow, a nut-brown face, a bow-string brace on his wrist, a shield and sword, and a St. Christopher medal. Students might say that all the Yeoman's weapons, in good shape and on hand, show that he is an able soldier and ready for anything. His nut-brown face shows that he spends a lot of time outside. His St. Christopher medal shows that he travels a lot.

Reading Skills Development

(Mixed Ability Group) Analyze Key Details Give students additional practice in analyzing the key details that writers use to build characterization, such as a character's words, actions, and appearance. Have pairs of students read together a selection of your choice from the "Understanding Characters" section of the list that begins on page 225 of this book. Have each pair analyze a character from the selection. Remind students to note key details about the character and then to decide what these details say about the character. After students have finished their analysis, have them share their responses with the class.

(Teacher Tip)

You might write one character on the chart and describe how that character relates to each social sphere. Then as a take-home assignment, assign each student a character to add to the chart. Have them prepare an explanation of the character's connections to the three social spheres. The next day, complete the chart with students' information.

(Core Skill)

Use the resources in the Reading Skills and Strategies section in this book for any student who is having difficulty understanding character. Use the excerpt from "The Pardoner's Tale" or "The Wife of Bath's Tale" for the application portion of the lesson.

Literary Skills
• Understand characterization.
• Understand the characteristics of a frame story.
• Analyze imagery in characterization.

Reading Skill
Analyze style using key details.

Resources

In this book:
• Adapted Readings
• Vocabulary and Comprehension, p. 55
• Additional Vocabulary Practice, p. 56

Other Resources:
• *The Holt Reader,* p. 53
• *Holt Adapted Reader*
• *Audio CD Library,* Disc 2
• *Audio CD Library, Selections and Summaries in Spanish*
• *Supporting Instruction in Spanish,* p. 8

History Connection

Chaucer mentions only a few common people, such as the Miller, who work outside the Church or the feudal system. Perhaps he chose to highlight the Church and feudal system as the two most important social spheres of the time. However, also point out to students that few common people had enough money to make pilgrimages.

TARGETED STRATEGIES FOR SPECIAL EDUCATION STUDENTS

Prereading
Alternative Teaching Strategy

Make a Chart Students can relate their personal experiences and prior knowledge to the concept of characterization. On the board, begin a chart like the one below while students reproduce it in their notebooks. The first column lists some things authors include when they depict characters. Model filling in the second column with details about a familiar character from a story or movie. Tell students that as they read, they will add new columns with details about Chaucer's main characters, beginning with the Knight.

Details	Shrek	The Knight
looks and dress	large, green, bald; wears tunic, vest	
how s/he speaks	often quiet; gruff	
what s/he thinks	thinks the princess won't love him	
reaction of others	scared at first	

Reading
Alternative Teaching Strategy

Use Audio Help students keep track of the many characters in the selection as you play the audio recording. Pause as each character is introduced so students can record the name in a new column on the chart they began above. Pause again after each characterization and ask students to record specific details Chaucer uses to describe that character. For example, for the Knight (lines 43–80), students might note the following:

• dresses plainly
• never says rude things
• noble and brave
• narrator admires him

Postreading
Alternative Activity

Play a Game Write each character's vocation on a card and place the cards in a bag. Draw a card and show it to everyone except for one student. Have the class consult their books and give the student verbal clues about the character. For example: *He won many battles. He is noble, chivalrous, and generous.* (the Knight) Once the guesser identifies the character, pick a card for the next student.

Vocabulary and Comprehension

"The Prologue"
from *The Canterbury Tales*

A. Complete each sentence about the poem with a word from the Word Bank.

> **Word Bank**
> obstinate
> agility
> frugal
> arbitrate

   1. The young Squire moved quickly and easily, with great

      _____.

   2. The men could not agree, so the Friar had to _____.

   3. The Parson could not change the _____ man's mind.

   4. The Manciple was very _____; he spent money only when necessary.

B. Choose two words from the Word Bank. Write a sentence using each one.

   1. _____

      _____

   2. _____

      _____

C. Match each character from the prologue to his or her description. Write the letter of the description next to the character.

   _____**1.** the Knight   **a.** red beard; heavy; dishonest grain seller

   _____**2.** the Nun   **b.** chivalrous and honest warrior

   _____**3.** the Monk   **c.** spoke French; sentimental; always said "By St. Loy!"

   _____**4.** the Wife of Bath   **d.** fat; loved hunting; did not like being cloistered

   _____**5.** the Miller   **e.** wore nice clothes; married many times

D. Write T or F next to each statement below to tell whether it is true or false.

   _____**1.** The Cook had an ulcer on his knee.

   _____**2.** The Oxford Cleric cared more about food and wine than philosophy.

   _____**3.** The Franklin shared his food and drinks with other people.

   _____**4.** The Wife of Bath had been to Jerusalem, Rome, and Cologne.

   _____**5.** The Reeve was a young, fat man.

Additional Vocabulary Practice

"The Prologue"
from *The Canterbury Tales*

A. Match each word on the left to its definition on the right. Write the letter of the definition next to the word.

____ **1.** arbitrate   **a.** ability to move quickly and easily

____ **2.** agility   **b.** careful in not wasting things

____ **3.** frugal   **c.** settle or decide by listening to both sides of an argument

____ **4.** obstinate   **d.** stubborn

B. Write each word from the Word Bank next to the group of words that have the *opposite* meaning.

1. _____ ugly, mean, homely

2. _____ unimportant, useless, second-rate

3. _____ vulgar, common, low-class

4. _____ rude, impolite, imprudent

5. _____ modest, humble, simple

Word Bank
discreet
noble
personable
stately
worthy

C. Use each word from the Word Bank in a sentence.

1. _____

_____

2. _____

_____

3. _____

_____

4. _____

_____

5. _____

_____

"Federigo's Falcon"
from the *Decameron* by Giovanni Boccaccio
translated by Mark Musa and Peter Bondanella

Prereading

Vocabulary Practice

Teach Unfamiliar Vocabulary Teach the following vocabulary words prior to reading "Federigo's Falcon."

- *poverty* (p. 209): the state of being poor
- *humbly* (p. 210): modestly and not proudly
- *anguish* (p. 211): agonizing physical or mental pain
- *hostile* (p. 212): unfriendly or angry
- *mourning* (p. 212): the period of time when people express grief for the dead

Alternative Activity

Read the Adaptation Distribute copies of the adapted reading of "Federigo's Falcon" (available in this book and, with marginal questions, in *Holt Adapted Reader*). Have all students read the selection silently.

Alternative Teaching Strategies

(**Especially for ELL**) **Connect to Personal Experience** Prepare English-language learners to evaluate the historical context of the *Decameron*. Ask them to focus on current social, economic, and ethical topics in a multicultural framework. For example, they might share what they know about marriage traditions from their native countries. Build language awareness by providing necessary vocabulary and restating student phrases as complete sentences. Once students have discussed cross-cultural norms, connect this prior knowledge to the *Decameron* by previewing the social, economic, and ethical realities of the Middle Ages that are discussed on page 208 of the student book.

Make a Chart Remind students that situational irony occurs when what actually happens is the opposite of what is expected. Help students grasp the concept of situational irony by contrasting the known ending of the King Midas story with an ending that a first-time reader might expect or predict. Start a story map like the one following and have students copy it. Complete the top two boxes as

SKILLS FOCUS

Literary Skill
Understand situational irony.

Reading Skills
- Evaluate historical context.
- Compare influences of different historical periods.

(**Resources**)

In this book:
- Adapted Readings
- Vocabulary and Comprehension, p. 61
- Additional Vocabulary Practice, p. 62

Other Resources:
- *The Holt Reader,* p. 69
- *Holt Adapted Reader*
- *Audio CD Library,* Disc 2
- *Audio CD Library, Selections and Summaries in Spanish*
- *Supporting Instruction in Spanish,* p. 11

(**Language Tip**)
When introducing vocabulary words, be sure to discuss and define the root from which certain words are derived. For example, *compensate* (on student book page 208) comes from the Latin verb *compendere* which means *to weigh.*

shown. Then guide students to complete the bottom two boxes by asking questions such as: *How do you think King Midas might feel? How does he expect to feel?* In the *Predictable* box, prompt students to write: *He is happy because he is very rich.* Help them understand that contrary to this expectation, he is miserable because he cannot enjoy life. Record this in the *Situational Irony* box.

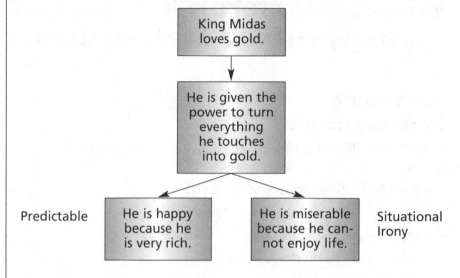

Use *The Holt Reader* For additional practice recognizing situational irony, consider having students complete the chart on the Before You Read page in *The Holt Reader*.

Reading
Alternative Teaching Strategies

Especially for ELL **Simplify Language** Many of the sentences in "Federigo's Falcon" are very long. English-language learners may become confused when reading such long sentences. Simplify the process by guiding them to divide these complex sentences into smaller chunks of meaning. For example, read aloud the second sentence on student book page 209, exaggerating the pauses indicated by punctuation to allow students time to process what you have read in each phrase. Consider having students take notes in the selection's margins in *The Holt Reader*, and paraphrase as needed for comprehension.

Complete Maps Reinforce the literary focus of situational irony as students read. On the board, start another situational irony story map like the one completed in Prereading. Use this map to help students analyze situational irony in "Federigo's Falcon."

Postreading
Additional Practice

(Core Skill) **Compare Characters** Provide support for students in writing the essay Two Medieval Women on page 213 of the student book. Review the description of the Wife of Bath from *The Canterbury Tales* (student book page 155) and her tale (student book pages 178–188). Remind students that *The Canterbury Tales* and the *Decameron* were written during the Middle Ages. Although these stories are from the same period, the Wife of Bath and Monna Giovanna are quite different.

Guide students to describe these two women, and record students' ideas on a Venn diagram. Sample responses are shown below. Help students rephrase their ideas into complete sentences as they compare these two characters.

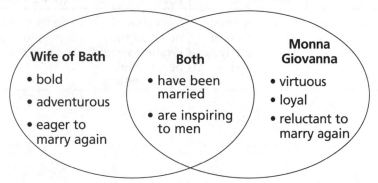

Wife of Bath
- bold
- adventurous
- eager to marry again

Both
- have been married
- are inspiring to men

Monna Giovanna
- virtuous
- loyal
- reluctant to marry again

Evaluate Historical Context For practice evaluating historical context, have students complete the postreading activities in *The Holt Reader,* either instead of or in addition to the activities found in the student book.

Reading Skills Development

(Mixed Ability Group) **Recognize Historical Detail** Students may have difficulty evaluating historical context if they are not skilled in recognizing historical detail. Using "Federigo's Falcon," have groups of students list details of character, setting, or plot that might be considered odd or uncommon today. When groups have finished, draw a chart with two columns, "Detail" and "What the Detail Suggests," on the board. As a class, fill in the "Detail" column of the chart. Then, discuss and list the class's ideas about what each detail might reveal about the work's historical context.

(Teacher Tip)
When correcting students' errors, always reinforce their successes and effort. If a student uses a vocabulary word incorrectly, praise him or her for demonstrating the meaning of the word, and subtly restate the sentence in the correct form.

(Pronunciation Tip)
Encourage students to use the pronunciation guides in parentheses that follow dictionary entries. Teach them how to read the phonetic symbols as well as the syllabic divisions and accents. Students can use these tools to pronounce unfamiliar and/or foreign words..

Literary Skill
Understand
situational irony.

Reading Skills
• Evaluate historical
context.
• Compare influences
of different
historical periods.

(**Resources**)

In this book:
• Adapted Readings
• Vocabulary and
Comprehension, p. 61
• Additional Vocabulary
Practice, p. 62

Other Resources:
• *The Holt Reader,* p. 69
• *Holt Adapted Reader*
• *Audio CD Library,* Disc 2
• *Audio CD Library,
Selections and Summaries
in Spanish*
• *Supporting Instruction
in Spanish,* p. 11

TARGETED STRATEGIES FOR SPECIAL EDUCATION STUDENTS

Prereading
Background

Connect to Personal Experience Motivate students by inviting them to connect personally with the selection. Discuss with students the historical context of the *Decameron,* specifically the social norms that dictated the relations between men and women. Then invite students to share how social norms in the United States are different today. Use a chart to organize student ideas. A partially completed chart may look something like the following:

Era	Marriage	Love	Money
Middle Ages	Women need permission of male relatives.	Men should be chivalrous. Women should be virtuous and inspiring.	Family money is passed from male to male.
Modern Day			

Reading
Alternative Activity

Refer to the Chart As they read, help students understand how the social norms of the Middle Ages affect the plot of "Federigo's Falcon." Display the chart created in Prereading. Refer to the chart as you identify examples of traditions from the Middle Ages. For example, point out that in the final paragraph, Monna Giovanna's brothers "gave her in marriage" to Federigo.

Postreading
Alternative Activity

(**Mixed Ability Group**) **Make Up a Story** Students can appreciate the concept of situational irony if they have the opportunity to apply it creatively. Help the class summarize the main events of "Federigo's Falcon." Then, using these events, guide small groups to alter some of the details to create a new story. Guide groups with prompts such as the following: *How does Federigo try to impress Monna Giovanna? What is the setting of the story? Why does Monna Giovanna go to Federigo's house?* Make sure each group maintains situational irony, but encourage students to be creative. Have volunteers retell their groups' new versions of the story.

Vocabulary and Comprehension

"Federigo's Falcon"
from the *Decameron*

A. Circle the letter of the word that best completes each sentence.

    1. The man's enemy was _____ toward him.
       a. hostile   **b.** friendly   **c.** hungry

    2. After he spent all his money, Federigo lived in _____.
       a. relief   **b.** affluence   **c.** poverty

    3. Federigo was very upset and felt _____ when Monna Giovanna asked him to prepare a meal for her.
       a. anguish   **b.** happiness   **c.** confidence

B. Complete each sentence with a definition for the underlined word.

    Example: If you make a <u>presumption</u>, you <u>take too much for granted</u>.

    1. To <u>compensate</u> someone is to _____.

    2. A <u>dire</u> situation is one that is _____.

    3. If you <u>console</u> a friend, you _____.

C. Choose one word you defined above and use it in a new sentence.

    1. _____

       _____

D. Number the sentences to show the order of events in the story.

    _____ Federigo serves Monna Giovanna the falcon for dinner.

    _____ Monna Giovanna marries Federigo.

    _____ Federigo becomes poor and moves to the countryside.

    _____ Federigo tries to win Monna Giovanna's love by participating in jousts and giving feasts.

    _____ Monna Giovanna's son gets sick and asks his mother to get him the falcon.

Additional Vocabulary Practice

"Federigo's Falcon"
from the *Decameron*

A. Write the word from the Word Bank that matches each definition. Then unscramble the letters in the shaded area to spell out a word from the story.

> **Word Bank**
> humbly   mourning
> anguish   hostile
> console

f

1. the period of time when people express grief for the dead ___ ___ ___ ___ ___ ___ ___ ___

2. modestly and not proudly ___ ___ ___ ___ ___ ___

3. to cheer up or comfort someone ___ ___ ___ ___ ___ ___ ___

4. unfriendly or angry ___ ___ ___ ___ ___ ___ ___

5. agonizing physical or mental pain ___ ___ ___ ___ ___ ___ ___

Answer: ___ ___ ___ ___ ___ ___ ___

B. Use each of the words from the Word Bank in a sentence.

1. _____

   _____

2. _____

   _____

3. _____

   _____

4. _____

   _____

5. _____

   _____

Collection 3
The Renaissance: 1485–1660

Prereading
Alternative Teaching Strategies

(**Especially for ELL**) **Set a Purpose for Reading** Have students set a purpose for reading: to answer the Think About questions on student book page 274. Read the questions and explain unfamiliar vocabulary. Record simplified versions of the questions on the board for students to refer to as they read.

Read the Adaptation Distribute copies of the below–grade-level adapted reading for "The Renaissance: 1485–1660" (available in this book and, with marginal questions, in *Holt Adapted Reader*). Have students read silently.

Reading
Alternative Teaching Strategies

Read with a Purpose As they read, remind students to refer to the questions on the board. Encourage them to focus on the headings to determine which sections are likely to answer each question. Then help students identify key words that indicate the answer to each question.

Use *The Holt Reader* You may have students read the on-level, shortened version of the introduction in *The Holt Reader* and respond to the instruction in its margins.

Postreading
Additional Practice

Prepare to Write Prepare students for the Contrasting Literary Periods writing activity on student book page 290. On the board, begin a chart with columns labeled *printing press* and *computers and the Internet*. Help students compare the impact of these inventions. First refer to "The New Technology: A Flood of Print" (student book page 279) for ideas about the printing press. Record important details on the chart under *printing press*. Then ask questions like the following to help students complete the second column of the chart:

- How have the computer and Internet changed the way people exchange information? (*The exchange is now faster and easier.*)
- What kind of information can you get from the Internet? (*information about most topics from all over the world*)
- Are computers cheaper or more costly than books? (*more costly*)

SKILLS FOCUS

Literary Skill
Evaluate the philosophical, political, religious, ethical, and social influences of a historical period.

(**Resources**)
In this book:
- Adapted Readings

Other Resources:
- *The Holt Reader,* p. 81
- *Holt Adapted Reader*
- Video Segments 1, 4, 5

(**Art Connection**)
Consider decorating the classroom with reproductions of famous works of art from the Renaissance. The works of some artists may already be familiar to students. Take this opportunity to name some famous works by these artists, such as Leonardo DaVinci's *Mona Lisa* and Michelangelo's *David*. Explain that art in all forms—not just literature—flourished during the Renaissance.

TARGETED STRATEGIES FOR SPECIAL EDUCATION STUDENTS

Prereading
Additional Activity

Prepare to Read Guide students to set a purpose for reading: to identify the main idea of each section of the collection introduction. Have students skim the section titles. Explain that these headings provide them with the topic of each section. They will read to find the main idea presented about each topic. Tell students that as they read, they will record the main idea of each section.

Reading
Additional Activity

Guide Students' Reading Help students comprehend the collection introduction by leading them to identify and record the main idea of each section. Remind students that the section titles indicate the topic and they will read to find the main idea. After reading each section, use guided questions to help students identify the main idea. For example, after reading "Rediscovering Ancient Greece and Rome" on student book page 276, ask: *What did people begin to read again during the Renaissance?* (classic Greek and Latin texts)

Postreading
Alternative Assessment

Check Comprehension Check students' comprehension of the main ideas of the collection introduction by asking questions such as the following. Encourage them to refer to their notes as they answer.

• What are some words that are used to discuss a Renaissance person? *("curiosity," "creativity," "energetic," "productive," "interested")*

• Did most Renaissance painters and writers have an optimistic or pessimistic view of humanity? *(optimistic)*

• What were the humanists' two sources of wisdom? *(the Bible and the classics)*

• What invention greatly increased the number of books available? *(the printing press)*

• What was More's *Utopia* about? *(an idealized human society)*

• Whose power did supporters of the Reformation reject? *(that of the pope and the Italian churchmen)*

• Which king broke away from the Roman Catholic church? *(Henry VIII)*

Shakespeare's Sonnets: The Mysteries of Love

Prereading

Alternative Teaching Strategies

Focus on Sonnets Help students prepare to read Shakespearean sonnets by reviewing the information presented in the Literary Focus on page 314 of the student book. Reinforce the meanings of *quatrain* and *couplet* by discussing related words, such as *quad, quadruple,* and *couple.* Also, review the meaning of iambic pentameter. Help students hear this meter by clapping it out with soft and hard claps or by saying *dah-DAH, dah-DAH, dah-DAH, dah-DAH, dah-DAH.* Read aloud lines 1–4 of Sonnet 29 as an example of a quatrain and lines 13–14 as an example of a couplet. Emphasize the rhyme scheme and iambic pentameter in this Shakespearean sonnet.

Use *The Holt Reader* You may consider having students use the Before You Read page in *The Holt Reader,* either instead of or in addition to the Before You Read page in the student book.

(Especially for ELL) Read or Listen to the Spanish Summary Spanish-speaking English-language learners may benefit from reading or listening to the sonnet summaries in Spanish in preparation for reading the sonnets in English.

Vocabulary Practice

(Especially for ELL) Teach Unfamiliar Vocabulary Many of the words in these sonnets are archaic. Focus on teaching ELLs the most globally useful words. Before reading, present the following words and definitions. Have students copy these into their notebooks.

- *Fortune* (Sonnet 29, line 1): fate or destiny
- *hymns* (Sonnet 29, line 12): sacred, religious songs
- *scorn* (Sonnet 29, line 14): reject strongly; refuse
- *grieve* (Sonnet 30, line 9): feel sad about a loss
- *alters; alteration* (Sonnet 116, line 3): changes; change made
- *sickle* (Sonnet 116, line 10): a tool for cutting grain or grass, with a curved blade and a short handle
- *coral* (Sonnet 130, line 2): underwater formations, usually red-orange or pink, made of skeletons of tiny sea creatures
- *goddess* (Sonnet 130, line 11): a female supernatural being who is worshipped

SKILLS FOCUS

Literary Skill
Understand the characteristics of Shakespearean sonnets.

(Resources)

In this book:
- Vocabulary and Comprehension, p. 69
- Additional Vocabulary Practice, p. 70

Other Resources:
- *The Holt Reader,* p. 93
- *Audio CD Library,* Disc 4
- *Audio CD Library, Selections and Summaries in Spanish*
- *Supporting Instruction in Spanish,* pp. 14–15

(Teacher Tip)

Avoid overwhelming students with new vocabulary. Focus on teaching words that are key to the comprehension of the selection and/or that will be useful outside of the classroom. You can explain other unfamiliar words as students encounter them in the reading.

Reading
Alternative Teaching Strategies

Use *The Holt Reader* Consider having students read Sonnets 29 and 116 in *The Holt Reader* so that they may make notes about the sonnets and respond to the instruction in the selections' margins.

Listen to the Audio You might have students listen to the audio recordings in English of Sonnets 18, 29, 30, 71, 73, 116, and 130 to help increase comprehension. Listening to Sonnet 130 in conjunction with the activity below, Discuss Tone, may also help students better hear the humor.

Paraphrase for Understanding Help students understand these Shakespearean sonnets by guiding them to paraphrase specific passages in the poems. Lead them to rewrite phrases in normal word order. Guide students with questions such as the following, about the first sentence in Sonnet 116:

- How can I reword "Let me not . . ." into a more familiar phrase? *(I don't want to; Don't let me)*
- What verb, or action, goes with this phrase? *(admit)* Let's add this. *(I don't want to admit)*
- What does Shakespeare not want to admit? *(impediments)* What is another word for impediments? *(obstacles)* Let's add this definition. *(I don't want to admit obstacles)*
- Shakespeare is talking about an obstacle to what? *(marriage of true minds)*
- What does the introduction to this poem say that "the marriage of true minds" is a metaphor for? *(true love)*
- Let's add this and read the whole sentence. *(I don't want to admit obstacles to true love.)*

Discuss Tone Help students appreciate the humor in Sonnet 130. Explain that Shakespeare's purpose in writing this sonnet was to ridicule the exaggerated metaphors popular in poetry at that time. As they read, guide students to find language in the poem that achieves this purpose, as modeled below.

- First have students skim the poem to identify which features Shakespeare describes. *(eyes, lips, breasts, hair, cheeks, breath, voice, walk)*
- Then ask students how they would describe attractive eyes. What could they compare them to? *(possible responses: the sky, jewels, stars, the sun)*
- Then read line 1, "My mistress' eyes are nothing like the sun."
- Ask students if they think this is a flattering comparison. *(no)*
- Point out that this description illustrates a tone that pokes fun at the exaggerated metaphors of the time.

Postreading

Alternative Activity

Use *The Holt Reader* You may have students complete the Paraphrasing chart on page 95 of *The Holt Reader*, either instead of or in addition to the postreading activities found in the student book.

Additional Practice

(Core Skill) Focus on Figures of Speech Help students appreciate the figures of speech used in Shakespeare's sonnets. Use guided questions to analyze figures of speech, like the following for Sonnet 116, line 7: "It [Love] is the star to every wandering bark."

1. Restate the figure of speech in your own words. *(possible response: Love is the guide to anyone who is lost.)*

2. How does this figure of speech make you feel about the subject (love)? *(possible responses: hopeful, secure, confident, reassured)*

Reading Skills Development

(Mixed Ability Group) Paraphrase for Comprehension Some students may be so overwhelmed by Shakespeare's vocabulary and diction that they lose the meaning of the sonnets. Give these students additional practice in paraphrasing.

First, give students these tips:

- Delete unnecessary words and phrases.
- Substitute more basic words for difficult vocabulary.
- Break complex sentences into shorter, simpler sentences.

Model using these techniques to paraphrase a line from a sonnet. For example, the first line of Sonnet 30 can be paraphrased as follows: *When I think quietly about the past, I'm sad as I remember the things I tried to get but didn't.*

Then, choose one of the sonnets in the student book. Have students work in pairs to paraphrase the sonnet. Pairs may use the Paraphrasing chart on page 95 of *The Holt Reader* to guide their work. Ask pairs to share their paraphrases with the class.

(Teacher Tip)
Capitalize on the work involved in creating visual aids such as cards, sentence strips, charts, or other graphic organizers. Keep these on display in the classroom after the lesson is over. Each time students see them, they will remember the lesson in which they were used. You may also do quick reviews of language features with these displays.

(Resources)

In this book:
• Vocabulary and
Comprehension, p. 69
• Additional Vocabulary
Practice, p. 70

Other Resources:
• *The Holt Reader,* p. 93
• *Audio CD Library,* Disc 4
• *Audio CD Library,
Selections and Summaries
in Spanish*
• *Supporting Instruction
in Spanish,* pp. 14–15

(Teacher Tip)

Play the audio recording in
English of each sonnet.
Invite students to lightly tap
their fingers to the rhythm,
emphasizing every second
syllable to practice iambic
pentameter.

TARGETED STRATEGIES FOR SPECIAL EDUCATION STUDENTS

Prereading
Alternative Activity

Practice Rhyme Explain that one of the main features of a
Shakespearean sonnet is the pattern of rhyming words at the end of
each line. Ask a volunteer for a definition of rhyme. *(common sound
at the end of words)* Have them give a few examples.

Reading
Alternative Teaching Strategy

Identify the Rhyme Scheme In advance, write Sonnet 29 on chart
paper. As students read, guide them to understand its rhyme scheme.
Write the letter *a* after line 1. Explain that in this poem, lines ending
with words that rhyme with *eyes* are labeled *a*. Ask: *Which ending
word rhymes with* eyes? (line 3: *cries*) Write the letter *a* after line 3.
Then label line 2 as *b* and challenge students to find an ending word
that rhymes with *state.* (line 4: *fate*) Continue in this way to complete
the rhyme scheme *abab cdcd efef gg.* Use Sonnet 29 as a model for
discussing the rhyme scheme of the other sonnets.

Postreading
Alternative Teaching Strategy

Discuss Tone Support students' efforts to answer Thinking
Critically questions two and three on page 315 of the student book.

• Ask students to point out words that set the desperate, hopeless
tone of lines 1–9. (*disgrace, outcast, cries, curse*)

• Help them identify the turn of the poem's tone by having them
find a word meaning *but.* (line 9: *yet*)

• Prompt students to identify words in lines 10–14 that indicate
an opposite attitude. (*sings hymns, sweet love, wealth*) Ask
students what attitude or tone these words indicate. (*hope, joy*)

Guide students to answer Thinking Critically question four on
page 319 of the student book. Remind them that the speaker
describes love as firm against impediments. Help students identify
where the turn, or change in tone, occurs by asking these questions:

• Which word means *mistake?* (line 13: *error*)

• About what does the speaker think he may be mistaken? *(the
nature of love)*

• What is the changed, or opposite, tone in the last lines?
(doubtful)

Shakespeare's Sonnets: The Mysteries of Love

A. Circle the letter of the word that best completes each sentence.

1. The old-fashioned professor showed _____ and contempt for his students' new ideas.
   a. delight   **b.** scorn   **c.** wonder   **d.** love

2. The ancient Egyptians worshipped Isis, _____ of fertility.
   a. sacrifice   **b.** aunt   **c.** goddess   **d.** architect

3. The detective _____ clues to solve the murder case.
   a. destroyed   **b.** sought   **c.** hid   **d.** scorned

4. The mayor will _____ all the townspeople for the important meeting.
   a. summon up   **b.** yell at   **c.** look down at   **d.** hide out

5. She smiled and laughed, showing her _____.
   a. shyness   **b.** scorn   **c.** doubt   **d.** delight

B. Read each line from one of Shakespeare's sonnets and the paraphrased line underneath it. Does the paraphrase express the correct meaning of the line? Write YES or NO on each line.

1. "Then can I drown an eye (unused to flow)" (Sonnet 30, line 5)

   Then I can cry (even though I am not used to crying). _____

2. ". . . black wires grow on her head" (Sonnet 130, line 4)

   She is a robot with cables on her head. _____

3. ". . . even to the edge of doom" (Sonnet 116, line 12)

   until the final judgement at the end of the world _____

4. "And look upon myself and curse my fate" (Sonnet 29, line 4)

   I am depressed about my situation. _____

5. "It is the star to every wandering bark" (Sonnet 116, line 7)

   Stars come out when dogs bark. _____

Additional Vocabulary Practice

Shakespeare's Sonnets: The Mysteries of Love

A. Write the word from the Word Bank that best matches each definition. Then unscramble the shaded letters to reveal a name. (You will not use all the words in the Word Bank.)

Word Bank	
fortune	possessed
hymns	scorn
grieve	impediments
alteration	sickle
coral	delight

1. to mourn ___ ___ ___ ▨ ___ ___

2. tool with a curved blade ___ ___ ___ ___ ▨ ___ ___

3. owned ___ ___ ___ ▨ ___ ___ ___ ___ ▨ ___ ___

4. change ▨ ___ ___ ___ ___ ___ ___ ___ ___ ___

5. natural sea formation ___ ___ ___ ___ ▨ ___

6. obstacles ___ ___ ▨ ___ ___ ___ ___ ___ ▨ ___ ___ ___

7. fate; destiny ___ ___ ___ ▨ ___ ___ ___ ___

8. religious songs ▨ ___ ___ ___ ▨

Name: ___ ___ ___ ___ ___ ___ ___ ___ ___ ___ ___

B. Choose five words from the Word Bank. Write a sentence using each one.

1. _____

_____

2. _____

_____

3. _____

_____

4. _____

_____

5. _____

_____

Elements of Literature
pages 328–335

Saint Crispin's Day Speech
by William Shakespeare

Prereading
Vocabulary Practice

Teach Unfamiliar Vocabulary Prepare students to read the Saint Crispin's Day Speech by teaching the following vocabulary words:

- *garments* (line 9): clothing
- *covet* (line 11): desire greatly (Also teach *covetous.*)
- *accursed* (line 48): being under a curse; ill-fated

Alternative Activity

Use *The Holt Reader* You may want to use the Before You Read page in *The Holt Reader,* either instead of or in addition to the Before You Read page in the student book.

Reading
Alternative Teaching Strategy

(Especially for ELL) Paraphrase for Understanding As they read, help ELLs rephrase sentences from the speech in subject-verb-complement order. Use the following steps to guide students, as modeled for "This story shall the good man teach his son" (line 39):

1. Identify the verb. *(shall teach)*
2. Identify the subject of the verb by asking who or what is performing the action. *(the good man)*
3. Identify the complement by asking whom shall the good man teach? *(his son)* What shall he teach his son? *(this story)*
4. Put it all together. *(The good man shall teach his son this story.)*

Postreading
Listening and Speaking Activity

Perform the Speech Prepare students for Performing a Speech on student book page 335. Play the audio recording of the selection as a model. Remind students that King Henry's character is brave and that their performances should reflect his courage and strength.

Alternative Activity

Use *The Holt Reader* Have students complete the Monologue and Soliloquy chart in *The Holt Reader,* either instead of or in addition to the postreading activities in the student book.

SKILLS FOCUS

Literary Skill
Understand the uses of monologue and soliloquy in drama.

(Resources)

In this book:
- Vocabulary and Comprehension, p. 73
- Additional Vocabulary Practice, p. 74

Other Resources:
- *The Holt Reader,* p. 96
- *Audio CD Library,* Disc 4
- *Audio CD Library, Selections and Summaries in Spanish*
- *Supporting Instruction in Spanish,* p. 16

(Core Skill)

Use the resources in the Reading Skills and Strategies section of this book to teach a core literary skill in which your struggling readers need remediation. Use the Saint Crispin's Day Speech for the application portion of the lesson.

Literary Skill
Understand the uses
of monologue and soliloquy
in drama.

Resources

In this book:
• Vocabulary and
Comprehension, p. 73
• Additional Vocabulary
Practice, p. 74

Other Resources:
• *The Holt Reader,* p. 96
• *Audio CD Library,* Disc 4
• *Audio CD Library,*
Selections and Summaries
in Spanish
• *Supporting Instruction*
in Spanish, p. 16

Teacher Tip

As students match
summaries with passages in
the speech, discuss how
each argument might have
appealed to the army. For
example, King Henry V
appeals to his men's egos
when he claims that their
names will be remembered
in the future.

TARGETED STRATEGIES FOR SPECIAL EDUCATION STUDENTS

Prereading

Background

Prepare to Read Before students read the Saint Crispin's Day Speech, reinforce the background information presented at the top of student book page 332. Help students understand that this speech is the king's answer to a noble's wish to have more fighting men. Have students read with a purpose: to identify persuasive language that King Henry V uses to convince his men that a small army is an advantage.

Reading

Alternative Teaching Strategy

Identify Persuasive Language As they read, help students identify the persuasive language that King Henry V employs in this speech. Record on the board in random order the brief summary sentences shown below. Pause periodically and ask students to determine which sentence paraphrases the section they just read. Students can refer to these examples later when they answer Thinking Critically question ten on student book page 335.

1. I seek honor, not wealth. (lines 5–12)

2. If you are not brave enough to join us, then depart now. (lines 18–22)

3. In the future, you will be proud of your scars, and you will enjoy telling the tale of how you fought on this day. (lines 24–34)

4. Your name will be remembered and fathers will tell their sons of your bravery. (lines 34–42)

5. If you fight with me today, you will become gentlemen. (lines 44–46)

6. Those who don't fight will regret that they missed such a heroic battle. (lines 47–50)

Postreading

Additional Practice

Read Aloud Help students bring the speech alive as they perform it. Remind them that soliloquies are supposed to sound dynamic. Invite a volunteer to read a portion of the speech, and then lead the class in critiquing the performance. Continue until everyone has had a chance to perform and receive feedback. Encourage students to incorporate this feedback into their final performances.

Vocabulary and Comprehension

Saint Crispin's Day Speech

A. Write the answer to each question on the line.

  1. Do you use *garments* to keep warm or to decorate your house?
  _____

  2. Are *wounds* a result of fighting or speaking? _____

  3. Do you *covet* something that you want to have or something that you want
  to sell? _____

  4. If you are *accursed*, do you have a positive view of the future or a negative
  one? _____

  5. Which happens first, a *scar* or a *wound*? _____

B. Circle the letter of the paraphrase that most closely matches the meaning of each
line from the speech.

  1. "But if it be a sin to covet honor / I am the most offending
  soul alive." (lines 11–12)
  a. I am an honorable man. I have not committed a sin.
  b. If it is a sin to desire honor, then I am committing that sin.

  2. "Will yearly on the vigil feast his neighbors" (line 28)
  a. His neighbors will have a feast every year.
  b. His neighbors will eat the vigil every year.

C. Circle the letter of the word or sentence that best answers each question.

  1. Reread lines 5–12. What does the king want?
  a. gold   **b.** garments   **c.** honor

  2. Reread lines 18–20. What does the king recommend to anyone who doesn't
  want to fight?
  a. That person should leave.
  b. That person should make a passport and put crowns into a purse.
  c. That person should be brave and fight anyway.

  3. Reread lines 34–42. What does the king predict will happen on Crispin's Day
  in the future?
  a. People will remember how bravely the men fought.
  b. People will eventually forget about the fight.
  c. People will talk to their brothers.

  4. Reread lines 47–50. Which word describes the way men who don't fight will
  feel on Crispin's Day?
  a. gentle   **b.** accursed   **c.** remembered

Additional Vocabulary Practice

Saint Crispin's Day Speech

A. Use the words in the Word Bank to answer the questions below.

Word Bank
accursed
garments
scars
covet
wounds

1. Which vocabulary word means *injuries*? _____

2. Which vocabulary word refers to permanent marks left after an injury? _____

3. Which vocabulary word refers to things you can wear? _____

4. Which vocabulary word describes someone who has bad luck? _____

5. Which vocabulary word means to really want something? _____

B. Write YES or NO to answer each question about the vocabulary words.

1. Can you eat garments? _____

2. If you are accursed, do you feel good? _____

3. If you covet something, do you reject it? _____

4. Can a scar be the result of a wound? _____

C. Circle the letter of the answer that best completes each sentence.

1. Covet means to _____ something a lot.
   a. fear   **b.** hate   **c.** want

2. Many soldiers received _____ in the battle.
   a. garments   **b.** covet   **c.** wounds

3. Joe felt accursed after several _____ things happened to him.
   a. bad   **b.** good   **c.** lucky

4. You will damage your garments if you _____ them.
   a. fold   **b.** save   **c.** cut

5. After a person is injured, he or she might have a permanent _____.
   a. scar   **b.** wound   **c.** hurt

"A Valediction: Forbidding Mourning" by John Donne

Prereading

Vocabulary Practice

(**Especially for ELL**) **Teach Unfamiliar Vocabulary** Help students comprehend the selection by previewing these words and their definitions:

- *virtuous* (line 1): good; full of virtue
- *refined* (line 17): very pure
- *endure* (line 22): to put up with; to suffer
- *expansion* (line 23): growth; the act of growing larger

Alternative Activity

Use *The Holt Reader* You may have students use the Before You Read page in *The Holt Reader*, either instead of or in addition to the Before You Read page in the student book.

Reading

Alternative Teaching Strategy

(**Core Skill**) **Analyze Figures of Speech** Have students work together to decipher the two extended figures of speech in the poem: the simile in the first and second stanzas and the metaphysical conceit in the final three stanzas.

- For the simile, ask: *What two things are being compared?* (lovers' good-byes and the deaths of virtuous men) *What emotion is actually named in these two stanzas?* (line 3: sad)
- For the metaphysical conceit, ask: *What two things are being compared?* (two lovers' separation and the prongs of a compass) *Which lover is the fixed foot of the compass?* (the one staying behind)

Postreading

Alternative Activity

Use *The Holt Reader* Have students complete the Recognizing Comparisons and Contrasts chart in *The Holt Reader*, either instead of or in addition to the postreading activities in the student book.

SKILLS FOCUS

Literary Skill
Understand metaphysical conceits.

(**Resources**)

In this book:
- Vocabulary and Comprehension, p. 77
- Additional Vocabulary Practice, p. 81 (includes the next selection)

Other Resources:
- *The Holt Reader*, p. 101
- *Audio CD Library*, Disc 4
- *Audio CD Library, Selections and Summaries in Spanish*
- *Supporting Instruction in Spanish*, p. 17

(**Core Skill**)

Use the resources in the Reading Skills and Strategies section of this book to help students having difficulty understanding figurative language. Use "A Valediction: Forbidding Mourning" for the application portion of the lesson.

Literary Skill
Understand metaphysical conceits.

Resources

In this book:
• Vocabulary and Comprehension, p. 77
• Additional Vocabulary Practice, p. 81 (includes the next selection)

Other Resources:
• *The Holt Reader,* p. 101
• *Audio CD Library,* Disc 4
• *Audio CD Library, Selections and Summaries in Spanish*
• *Supporting Instruction in Spanish,* p. 17

Teacher Tip

Using hands-on materials can bring meaning to a piece of literature. Manipulating a compass and relating this activity to Donne's poem will make the meaning of his metaphysical conceit more tangible and memorable for students.

TARGETED STRATEGIES FOR SPECIAL EDUCATION STUDENTS

Prereading

Additional Background

Discuss Emotions Ask students to name emotions they might feel when saying good-bye to someone they love. List these on the board. Tell them that this poem is about the sadness, loss, and hope people feel when leaving loved ones.

Reading

Alternative Teaching Strategy

Outline the Poem On a second reading of the selection, help students create an outline that paraphrases figures of speech, shows the main idea, and identifies the emotions that are evoked by each stanza. Outlines for stanzas 7–9 might look like the following:

Stanza 7

• Figure of Speech: Two lovers are like the two feet of a compass.
• Main Idea: The lover who stays behind is like the foot of the compass that sticks into the paper.
• Emotions: loyalty, love

Stanza 8

• Figure of Speech: Two lovers are like the two feet of a compass.
• Main Idea: The center foot of the compass reacts to the moving foot.
• Emotions: love, longing, loyalty

Stanza 9

• Figure of Speech: Two lovers are like the two feet of a compass.
• Main Idea: You are like the center of my compass. You provide stability to make my life perfect.
• Emotions: love, loyalty, faith

Postreading

Alternative Activity

Make a Poem Map Ask students to draw a large circle on paper and divide their circle into nine equal "pie-slices," one for each stanza of the poem. Have them create a Poem Map by writing information like that in the above outline into each section of the circle.

Vocabulary and Comprehension

"A Valediction: Forbidding Mourning"

A. Circle the letter of the correct definition for each word.

1. virtuous
   a. poisonous   **b.** full of goodness   **c.** false

2. reckon
   a. to calculate; to think about   **b.** to pick something out   **c.** to identify someone

3. refined
   a. found again   **b.** very pure   **c.** afraid

4. endure
   a. to enjoy   **b.** to wonder   **c.** to put up with; to suffer

5. expansion
   a. excitement   **b.** true love   **c.** growth; the act of growing larger

B. Choose three words from above. Write a sentence using each one.

1. _____

_____

2. _____

_____

3. _____

_____

C. Answer the questions below in complete sentences.

1. Does Donne refer to the couple's love as mainly physical or spiritual? How do you know? (Refer to lines 17–20.) _____

_____

2. How are two lovers compared to a drawing compass? _____

_____

"Meditation 17" by John Donne

SKILLS FOCUS

Literary Skill
Understand the use of tone.

(**Resources**)

In this book:
• Adapted Readings
• Vocabulary and
Comprehension, p. 80
• Additional Vocabulary
Practice, p. 81 (includes
the previous selection)

Other Resources:
• *The Holt Reader,* p. 105
• *Holt Adapted Reader*
• *Audio CD Library,* Disc 4
• *Audio CD Library,
Selections and Summaries
in Spanish*
• *Supporting Instruction
in Spanish,* p. 17

(**Core Skill**)

Use the resources in the
Reading Skills and
Strategies section of this
book to teach a core literary
skill in which your
struggling readers need
remediation. Use
"Meditation 17" for the
application portion of
the lesson.

Prereading

Vocabulary Practice

(**Especially for ELL**) **Teach Unfamiliar Vocabulary** Teach these
vocabulary words and definitions prior to reading:
• *toll* (p. 344): ring (a bell)
• *diminishes* (p. 345): makes or becomes smaller or less
• *tribulation* (p. 345): great affliction or oppression

Alternative Activity

Read the Adaptation/Use *The Holt Reader* Distribute copies of the
adapted reading of "Meditation 17" (available in this book and, with
marginal questions, in *Holt Adapted Reader*). Have students read the
selection silently. Also, consider having students use the Before You
Read page in *The Holt Reader,* either instead of or in addition to the
Before You Read page in the student book.

Reading

Alternative Teaching Strategies

Track Repetition As students listen to the audio recording in
English and read the selection, have them write down and tally
repeated words, phrases, and parallel grammatical structures. Discuss
how Donne uses repetition to emphasize his point.

Use *The Holt Reader* Consider having students read "Meditation
17" in *The Holt Reader* so that they may make notes about the
meditation and respond to the instruction in the selection's margins.

Postreading

Reteach the Key Idea

Discuss Tone Support students in answering Thinking Critically
question six on student book page 346. Guide them to find passages
that support the tones suggested in this question. For example, they
might consider the words "so ill, as that he knows not it tolls for him" to
connote a sad tone. Some students may also identify a more positive
tone in the words "affliction is a treasure."

Alternative Activity

Use *The Holt Reader* Have students complete the Understanding
Patterns of Organization chart in *The Holt Reader,* either instead of
or in addition to the postreading activities in the student book.

TARGETED STRATEGIES FOR SPECIAL EDUCATION STUDENTS

Prereading

Alternative Teaching Strategy

Understand Patterns of Organization Explain that Donne uses organizational patterns and rhythm to catch and hold the attention of the listener. To prepare students to take notes on examples of these devices as they read, create on the board a chart like the one below. Clarify the meaning of each rhetorical device with the definitions provided below. As students read, guide them in adding examples to the chart.

repetition	parallel structure	rhetorical questions
repetition of the same word, phrase, or idea	repetition of words or phrases that have the same grammatical structure or restate the same idea	questions to which no answer is expected, usually used for persuasion

Reading

Alternative Teaching Strategies

Complete the Chart Remind students to look for examples of rhetorical devices as they read to complete the chart they began in Prereading.

Focus on the Main Idea As students read, support their comprehension of the sermon by focusing on which main ideas are handled in various parts of the sermon. Each time students encounter a difficult passage, ask: *Does this support the idea that we are all connected, or does it support the idea that suffering is good?* Students will find that some passages address our interconnectedness through the Church and/or humanity, some address the benefits of suffering, and others address both.

Postreading

Alternative Assessment

Check Comprehension Ask the following questions to check students' comprehension of the selection.

1. What does Donne mean by "No man is an island"? *(possible response: Even in suffering, we are not alone in the world.)*
2. What attitude does Donne have toward God? *(He has faith in God.)* How can you tell? *(possible response: "God's hand . . . shall bind up all our scattered leaves again")*
3. Why does Donne ask a series of questions, starting with "Who casts not . . . the sun when it rises?" *(possible response: He repeats questions with* who *so the audience relates to his ideas.)*

SKILLS FOCUS

Literary Skill
Understand the use of tone.

Resources

In this book:
- Adapted Readings
- Vocabulary and Comprehension, p. 80
- Additional Vocabulary Practice, p. 81 (includes the previous selection)

Other Resources:
- *The Holt Reader,* p. 105
- *Holt Adapted Reader*
- *Audio CD Library,* Disc 4
- *Audio CD Library, Selections and Summaries in Spanish*
- *Supporting Instruction in Spanish,* p. 17

Teacher Tip

Some students may better appreciate the effect of Donne's use of repetition, parallel structure, and rhetorical questions if they hear the selection read aloud. To help students complete the Patterns of Organization Chart, play the audio recording of the selection as students read along silently.

Vocabulary and Comprehension

"Meditation 17"

A. Write on the line the letter of the word that best completes each sentence.

1. Donne feels that another person's death _____ him as a human being.
    a. diminishes   **b.** baptizes   **c.** mingled

2. Donne believes we benefit from afflictions and _____.
    a. congregation   **b.** contemplation   **c.** tribulation

3. Everyone should pay attention when the bells _____.
    a. wrought   **b.** scattered   **c.** toll

4. We should be aware of our physical and spiritual _____.
    a. fetch   **b.** state   **c.** minute

B. Choose three words you selected in part A. Use each word in a sentence.

1. _____

_____

2. _____

_____

3. _____

_____

C. Circle the letter of the correct meaning of each sentence.

1. "No man is an island."
    a. People are independent and separate from society.
    b. People are not isolated from the rest of humanity.
    c. Some men enjoy islands.

2. "When one man dies, one chapter is not torn out of the book, but translated into a better language."
    a. When someone dies, his or her books should be translated.
    b. When a person dies, he or she goes to a better place.
    c. Some languages are better than others.

3. "No man hath affliction enough that is not matured, and ripened by it."
    a. A mature man is ripe.
    b. People should never suffer.
    c. Pain and suffering can make you a better person.

Additional Vocabulary Practice

"A Valediction: Forbidding Mourning"; "Meditation 17"

A. Write a brief definition next to each word. Then write a sentence using each word.

diminishes _____

state _____

tribulation _____

toll _____

1. _____

_____

2. _____

_____

3. _____

_____

4. _____

_____

B. Circle the letter of the answer that is closest in meaning to the underlined word.

1. The <u>expansion</u> of the city destroyed the forest.
   a. shrinkage   **b.** growth   **c.** excitement   **d.** picture

2. He only bought the best and most <u>refined</u> olive oil.
   a. beautiful   **b.** thoughtful   **c.** disgusting   **d.** pure

3. If you go to the North Pole, you will have to <u>endure</u> the cold weather.
   a. run away from   **b.** enjoy   **c.** put up with   **d.** disagree with

Tilbury Speech

by Queen Elizabeth I

SKILLS FOCUS

Literary Skills
Analyze and compare political points of view on a topic.

Reading Skill
Draw inferences.

Resources

In this book:
• Adapted Readings
• Vocabulary and Comprehension, p. 86
• Additional Vocabulary Practice, p. 87

Other Resources:
• *The Holt Reader*, p. 110
• *Holt Adapted Reader*
• *Audio CD Library*, Disc 4
• *Audio CD Library, Selections and Summaries in Spanish*
• *Supporting Instruction in Spanish*, p. 19

Culture Tip

Students may better understand Queen Elizabeth's society if you help them contrast the roles of women then and now. Use a T-chart or Venn diagram to demonstrate this comparison.

Prereading

Vocabulary Practice

(**Especially for ELL**) **Teach Unfamiliar Vocabulary** ELLs may need extra practice with the following vocabulary words from the Tilbury Speech (p. 366):

• *persuaded:* convinced
• *take heed:* pay attention to
• *commit to:* decide on something; pledge
• *multitudes:* great numbers; crowds
• *treachery:* betrayal; extreme dishonesty
• *tyrants:* oppressive, brutal rulers
• *resolved:* firmly decided; very sure
• *feeble:* weak; delicate
• *foul:* very bad
• *scorn:* intense dislike; disgust and anger
• *realm:* the area and people controlled by a king or queen
• *shall:* a helping verb used to form the future tense

Alternative Activity

Read the Adaptation/Use *The Holt Reader* Distribute copies of the adapted reading of the Tilbury Speech (available in this book and, with marginal questions, in *Holt Adapted Reader*). Have students read the selection silently. Also, since the selection is included in *The Holt Reader,* you may consider having students use the Before You Read page in that book, either instead of or in addition to the Before You Read page in the student book.

Background

Prepare to Read Before you begin the selection, explain that Queen Elizabeth's goal in giving this speech was to rouse England's land forces to defend the country against Spanish invasion (student book page 366). Explain that the word *rouse* means *to wake up or provoke.* Ask: *What was Elizabeth's purpose for giving this speech? to entertain her audience? to teach them something? or to persuade them to do something or feel a certain way?* (She wanted to persuade them.) Tell students that as they read, they will think about how Elizabeth tried to persuade her audience.

Reading

Alternative Teaching Strategies

Listen to the Speech Support students' language skills by having them listen to the audio recording in English of the Tilbury Speech.

- Invite students to listen to the speech once through as they follow along silently in their books.
- As students listen a second time, address vocabulary and comprehension problems.
- Have students listen a third time with their books closed, directing them to focus on rhythm, pronunciation, and intonation. Invite them to read aloud specific lines of the speech following your model.

Use *The Holt Reader* Consider having students read the Tilbury Speech in *The Holt Reader* so that they may make notes about the speech and respond to the instruction in the selection's margins.

Paraphrase for Understanding During students' second reading of the selection, focus on paraphrasing the following passage: "I know I have the body but of a weak and feeble woman, but I have the heart and stomach of a king—and of a king of England too."

1. Ask students which words Elizabeth uses to describe a woman's body. (*weak and feeble*)
2. Ask what part of the king Elizabeth describes. (*heart and stomach*) Explain that *heart and stomach* refer to a king's spirit and bravery.
3. Point out that the second phrase begins with *but*, which implies a contrast.
4. Ask with what does Elizabeth contrast the weak body of a woman. (*the heart and stomach of a king of England*)
5. Remind them that *heart and stomach* implies spirit and bravery. Ask how they would describe a king's spirit and bravery. (*strong and powerful*)
6. Guide students in paraphrasing the passage. (*possible response: My body is weak, but my spirit is strong.*)

Next direct students to consider the rest of this sentence. "[I] think foul scorn that Parma, or Spain, or any prince of Europe should dare to invade the borders of my realm." Guide students to paraphrase how Queen Elizabeth feels about another country invading England. Review the vocabulary words *foul* and *scorn* to help them identify her beliefs on the subject. (*She feels hatred and anger toward any country that tries to attack England.*) Draw students' attention to her use of the word *dare*. Explain that this word implies a lack of fear and a belief in English superiority.

Especially for ELL

Teach words that provide clues about the relationship between phrases within a sentence. For example, take this opportunity to review other conjunctions that imply contrast, such as *even though*, *although*, or *yet*. Challenge students to use one of these conjunctions as they paraphrase the first passage in the paraphrasing activity.

Postreading

Alternative Teaching Strategies

Use *The Holt Reader* Have students complete the Drawing Inferences chart in *The Holt Reader,* either instead of or in addition to the postreading activities in the student book.

Discuss Author's Appeal Explain that a good speaker anticipates the reactions of both friendly and hostile audiences. Guide students to find examples in the Tilbury Speech in which Queen Elizabeth anticipates and addresses possible objections from her audience. Use steps such as the following:

1. Explain that a hostile audience disagrees with the speaker's idea before they hear the speech. In this example, a hostile audience might be reluctant to defend England against invasion, and Elizabeth is trying to persuade them to change their minds.

2. Paraphrase the three main objections that Elizabeth anticipates in her speech, as shown below. Ask students to locate these passages in the text.

   A. It is dangerous to arm lots of people because they may revolt. (lines 2–3)

   B. A woman cannot lead a country in battle. (lines 11–12)

   C. Those who fight should be rewarded. (lines 15–end)

3. Then present in random order the following paraphrased versions of how Elizabeth addresses each concern. Ask students to match each with the concern it addresses.

   A. I have behaved honestly, I am not a tyrant, and I trust my people to be loyal.

   B. I have the same strength of character as any king of England. I feel hatred for any country that invades us. I will lead by example and fight against them.

   C. I will lead you into battle. I will reward those who fight.

Reading Skills Development

(Core Skill)
Use the resources in the Reading Skills and Strategies section of this book to help students having difficulty making inferences. Use the Tilbury Speech for the application portion of the lesson.

(Mixed Ability Group) Make Inferences Tell students that when reading a political speech, it is particularly important to make inferences. In other words, readers must combine information in the text with what they already know in order to understand things the writer has not stated directly. Use a variation of the It Says . . . I Say . . . And So . . . strategy to help students who are struggling with this skill. First, choose a selection from Making Inferences section of the list that begins on page 225 of this book. Place students in mixed ability groups, and have each group read the selection aloud. Groups should identify key details in the text (It says). Then, group members should note what the information means to them (I Say). Finally, group members combine the information to make an inference (And So).

TARGETED STRATEGIES FOR SPECIAL EDUCATION STUDENTS

Literary Skills
Analyze and compare political points of view on a topic.

Reading Skill
Draw inferences.

Resources

In this book:
• Adapted Readings
• Vocabulary and Comprehension, p. 86
• Additional Vocabulary Practice, p. 87

Other Resources:
• *The Holt Reader,* p. 110
• *Holt Adapted Reader*
• *Audio CD Library,* Disc 4
• *Audio CD Library, Selections and Summaries in Spanish*
• *Supporting Instruction in Spanish,* p. 19

Prereading

Background

Provide Historical Context Help students place the Tilbury Speech in a historical context. Remind them that Queen Elizabeth I of England delivered the speech over four hundred years ago. At that time, England was in danger of attack from other countries in Europe. The purpose of the Queen's speech was to encourage her people to fight against England's enemies.

Reading

Alternative Activity

Create an Outline Guide students to better understand the speech by breaking it into two sections, the first ending with the words "even in the dust" on line 10. Highlight the main ideas and important details of each section on the board in the form of an outline, as shown below. Students can contribute to the creation of the outline by paraphrasing the details you point out in the text.

• Section 1 Main Idea: The Queen is united with the people.
  Detail: She doesn't fear giving weapons to the people.
  Detail: The Queen trusts the people.
  Detail: She is ready to fight and die with them.

• Section 2 Main Idea: The Queen is ready to lead the people.
  Detail: She is a woman, but she feels like a man, a king.
  Detail: She is ready to lead by example and take up arms herself.
  Detail: She promises to reward those who fight.

Postreading

Alternative Assessment

Check Comprehension Assess students' understanding of the Queen's appeal to her audience by asking questions like the following:

• Why does the Queen say she trusts her people? *(So they will join her in the fight.)*

• Why does the Queen promise to reward her people? *(Again, so they will join her in the fight.)*

• Why does the Queen mention that she is a woman, but she feels like a king? *(She anticipates that some people will fear that a woman is not strong enough to lead a country into battle.)*

Vocabulary and Comprehension

Tilbury Speech

A. Match words and definitions. Write the letter of the definition next to each word.

_____**1.** persuaded   **a.** disloyalty, trickery, betrayal

_____**2.** treachery   **b.** very weak

_____**3.** tyrants   **c.** crowds of people

_____**4.** feeble   **d.** succeeded in making someone do something

_____**5.** multitudes   **e.** cruel or unjust rulers

B. Circle the answer that has the closest meaning to each phrase or sentence from Tilbury Speech.

    1. "I have the heart and stomach of a king" means
      a. my heart belongs to the king.
      b. I am as strong and tough as a king.
      c. the king is sick and weak.

    2. "Invade the borders of my realm" means
      a. attack my kingdom.
      b. draw a line around my house.
      c. read my mind.

    3. "Take up arms" means
      a. steal some hands and elbows.
      b. throw up one's arms in the air.
      c. get ready for war.

C. Answer the following questions.

    1. Who is Queen Elizabeth addressing in her speech? How do you know?

_____

_____

    2. What promises does Queen Elizabeth make to her people?

_____

_____

Additional Vocabulary Practice

Tilbury Speech

A. Circle the letter of the definition that is closest in meaning to each underlined word or phrase.

1. She <u>resolved</u> to save money for her trip.
    a. hesitated   **b.** hurried   **c.** decided   **d.** solved

2. The rotten egg had a <u>foul</u> smell.
    a. pleasant   **b.** nice   **c.** bad   **d.** strike

3. You should <u>take heed of</u> the sign that says "No swimming allowed in this lake."
    a. eat   **b.** pay attention to   **c.** run away from   **d.** ignore

4. He felt <u>feeble</u> because he couldn't lift the heavy box.
    a. strong   **b.** smart   **c.** happy   **d.** weak

5. The speaker <u>persuaded</u> me to agree with her point of view.
    a. convinced   **b.** listened   **c.** laughed   **d.** whispered

6. The rock band attracted <u>multitudes</u> to their concerts.
    a. few animals   **b.** many people   **c.** guitars   **d.** chairs

B. Choose five of the underlined words. Write a sentence using each one.

1. _____

_____

2. _____

_____

3. _____

_____

4. _____

_____

5. _____

_____

Elements of Literature
pages 415–417

"When I consider how my light is spent" by John Milton

SKILLS FOCUS

Literary Skill
Understand the use of allusion.

Resources

In this book:
• Vocabulary and Comprehension, p. 90
• Additional Vocabulary Practice, p. 91

Other Resources:
• *The Holt Reader,* p. 113
• *Audio CD Library,* Disc 6
• *Audio CD Library, Selections and Summaries in Spanish*
• *Supporting Instruction in Spanish,* p. 24

Especially for ELL

Explain usage of the phrase *bent on.* Provide a sample sentence, such as *The team is bent on winning.*

Teacher Tip

Provide additional vocabulary support by previewing the definitions of the archaic words shown below. Present these words for students to refer to as they read. They do not need to study or memorize them.
• *ere* (line 2): before
• *therewith* (line 5): with that
• *lest* (line 6): for fear that
• *doth* (lines 7 and 9): does
• *post* (line 13): rush

Prereading
Vocabulary Practice

Especially for ELL **Preview Selection Vocabulary** Teach these words and definitions prior to reading:
• *lodged* (line 4): contained in; preserved
• *chide* (line 6): voice disapproval; find fault with someone
• *murmur* (line 9): a soft or gentle utterance; grumbling

Alternative Activity

Use *The Holt Reader* Use the Before You Read page in *The Holt Reader* in addition to the Before You Read page in the student book.

Reading
Reteach the Key Idea

Discuss Allusions As students read, guide them to understand and appreciate Milton's use of Biblical allusions in the poem.
• Point out the word "talent" (line 3) and the phrase "Lodged with me useless" (line 4). Ask students if Milton thinks he can use his talent. *(No, he thinks that the talent within him is useless.)*
• Ask students how an animal in a yoke might feel. *(restricted)* Point out that Milton talks about bearing a "mild yoke." Ask what might make Milton feel restricted. *(his blindness)*

Postreading
Fluency Practice

Use the Audio Recording Offer extra support in preparing the Listening and Speaking activity on student book page 417.
• Play the audio recording of the selection and have students mark on their copies of the poem where the speaker pauses or stops.
• Play the audio recording again to allow students to add other notes and directions for oral reading.

Alternative Activity

Use *The Holt Reader* Have students complete the Paraphrasing chart in *The Holt Reader,* either instead of or in addition to the postreading activities in the student book.

TARGETED STRATEGIES FOR SPECIAL EDUCATION STUDENTS

Literary Skill
Understand the use of allusion.

Prereading
Additional Background

Focus on Allusions To prepare students to appreciate the Biblical allusions in this poem, have them read Thinking Critically questions three and four on student book page 417 before they read the poem. Be sure that students understand each reference. Have them set a purpose for reading: to analyze the "talent" and "mild yoke" allusions in order to answer Interpretations questions three and four.

(Resources)

In this book:
- Vocabulary and Comprehension, p. 90
- Additional Vocabulary Practice, p. 91

Other Resources:
- *The Holt Reader,* p. 113
- *Audio CD Library,* Disc 6
- *Audio CD Library, Selections and Summaries in Spanish*
- *Supporting Instruction in Spanish,* p. 24

Reading
Alternative Activity

Paraphrase for Understanding Help students understand the sonnet by rewriting it in more familiar language. On the board or on chart paper, copy the original version of the poem. Then create a line-by-line paraphrase to the right. Ask volunteers for input and refer them to the definitions of archaic terms provided in the Teacher Tip on the previous page of this book. A sample paraphrase of the poem's first three lines might look like the following:

> I think about the blindness that has come to me
> before I am halfway through my life in this big, dark world,
> I think about my gift of poetry, a gift I must use . . .

Remind students that this sonnet is written in two parts. In the first part of the sonnet, Milton asks a question. In the second part, he proposes an answer to his question. As they paraphrase the sonnet, guide students to identify each part to help them answer Thinking Critically questions one and two on student book page 417.

(Teacher Tip)

To help students understand the "mild yoke" allusion, provide them with a simple definition of *yoke,* such as *a wooden frame attached to the neck of a work animal to link it to other work animals for plowing.*

Postreading
Alternative Assessment

Check Comprehension Assess students' comprehension of the poem by asking questions such as the following:

1. Why does Milton describe his world as "dark"? *(because he is blind)*

2. Does Milton still want to serve God, even though he is blind? *(yes)*

3. Reread lines 10–11. What kind of people does Milton think best serve God? *(those who accept and work with what life brings them)*

Vocabulary and Comprehension

"When I consider how my light is spent"

A. Write each word from the Word Bank next to its definition.

Word Bank
lodged
bent
chide
murmur
bidding

1. command _____

2. voice disapproval _____

3. determined to take a course of action _____

4. contained _____

5. grumbling _____

B. Circle the letter of the answer that best completes each sentence.

1. "Light" in the sonnet means _____
   a. Milton's birth.   **b.** God.   **c.** Milton's vision.

2. The "one talent" that Milton has is _____
   a. the gift of poetry.
   b. a Roman coin.
   c. a famous singer of Milton's day.

3. The best paraphrase of Milton's question in the sonnet is _____
   a. Should I get a job?
   b. How much are my poems worth?
   c. How can I continue to do God's work?

4. The sonnet says that God does not need _____
   a. a mild yoke.
   b. the work and gifts that people offer.
   c. his state.

5. According to the sonnet, those "who only stand and wait" are _____
   a. lazy.   **b.** serving God.   **c.** God's enemies.

C. Answer the questions below in complete sentences.

1. What problem does Milton face?

   _____

   _____

2. Who does Milton say answers the central question in the sonnet?

   _____

   _____

Additional Vocabulary Practice

"When I consider how my light is spent"

A. Complete each sentence with a word from the Word Bank.

> **Word Bank**
> lodged
> bidding
> bent
> chide
> murmur

1. I am _____ on learning to sing. I'm taking lessons, and I practice all the time.

2. The teacher will _____ you if you don't do your homework.

3. A _____ filled the auditorium when the principal announced the news.

4. The king has many servants to carry out his _____.

5. The cellar _____ the best wines.

B. Write YES or NO to answer each question.

1. Do you chide someone when you praise him or her? _____

2. Is a murmur a very loud noise? _____

3. If wine is lodged in the cellar, is it kept in the attic? _____

4. If you are bent on doing something, do you really want to do it? _____

5. If you do someone's bidding, do you do what he or she wants? _____

C. Write C or I to indicate whether each underlined word is used correctly or incorrectly.

1. There was a <u>murmur</u> of complaint when the teacher announced the assignment. _____

2. The workers hurry to follow the boss's orders when he tells them his <u>bidding</u>. _____

3. We <u>chide</u> the puppy for chewing on the shoe. _____

4. The student <u>bent</u> to go to college. _____

5. I found a package of crackers <u>lodged</u> under the seat of the car. _____

Elements of Literature
pages 558–578

Collection 4
The Restoration and
the Eighteenth Century: 1660–1800

Prereading

Vocabulary Practice

Teach Unfamiliar Vocabulary Present the following vocabulary words prior to reading the chapter introduction:

- *tumult* (p. 564): an uproar, commotion, or disturbance
- *reason* (p. 566): the intellectual process of drawing conclusions based on premises
- *repression* (p. 569): restraint, suppression, control
- *immorality* (p. 573): the state of not conforming to accepted standards of morality
- *wit* (p. 575): intelligence; quick understanding

Alternative Activity

Read the Adaptation Distribute copies of the below–grade-level adapted reading for "The Restoration and the Eighteenth Century: 1660–1800" (available in this book and, with marginal questions, in *Holt Adapted Reader*). Have students read silently.

Reading

Alternative Teaching Strategies

Especially for ELL Focus on Vocabulary The vocabulary words presented in Prereading all appear in the section titles of the chapter introduction. Use the above definitions to help ELLs understand the main ideas of each section.

Use *The Holt Reader* You may have students read the on-level, shortened version of the introduction in *The Holt Reader* and respond to the instruction in the margins.

Postreading

Listening and Speaking Opportunity

Talk About It Support students' efforts during the Talk About activity on student book page 578. Provide possible responses for each question. Invite students to choose the responses with which they agree and to expand on these responses as they are able.

SKILLS FOCUS

Literary Skills
Evaluate the philosophical, political, religious, ethical, and social influences of a historical period.

(Resources)

In this book:
Adapted Readings

Other Resources:
- *The Holt Reader,* p 117
- *Holt Adapted Reader*
- Video Segment 7

(Teacher Tip)
As you read, help students expand their explanations of each main idea by directing them to specific passages in the text and asking guided questions. For example, while you discuss "From Tumult to Calm," you might invite students to consider how a plague would create a period of tumult.

Literary Skills
Evaluate the philosophical, political, religious, ethical, and social influences of a historical period.

(Resources)

In this book:
Adapted Readings

Other Resources:
• *The Holt Reader,* p. 117
• *Holt Adapted Reader*
• Video Segment 7

Targeted Strategies for Special Education Students

Prereading
Background

Focus on Political and Social Milestones Spend additional time reading and discussing Political and Social Milestones on student book pages 562–563 prior to reading the main portion of the introduction. This will give students a better understanding of the historical context that serves as the background for the Restoration and the eighteenth century. Ask guided questions as students read this section. For example, after students read "The Restoration of Charles II, 1660," ask basic questions such as the following: *When did King Charles II return to the throne?* (1660) *What happened to the Church of England after King Charles II returned to the throne?* (It regained power.)

Reading
Alternative Activity

Make a Chart As students read "Life Among the Haves . . . and Life Among the Have-Nots" on student book pages 568–571, help them use a T-chart to contrast the lives of the "Haves" and the "Have-Nots." Invite students to name details about each group of people and record these on a chart on the board. Some ideas are presented below:

Haves	Have-Nots
influenced by the French	didn't have access to doctors, police, education, religion, or charity
gathered at fashionable coffeehouses	
enjoyed extravagant fashion and wigs	could be put in debtors' prisons
	lived in overcrowded tenements
spent time in London, the country, and spas	lived with waste in the streets
attended many parties	suffered crimes and deaths related to alcohol

(Teacher Tip)

When you check students' comprehension, permit them to refer to their books. Encourage them to provide specific references that support their answers. Challenge students to correct any false statements.

Postreading
Alternative Assessment

Check Comprehension Use true/false statements, like the following about "Addicted to the Theater" on student book page 572, to check students' comprehension of the chapter introduction:

1. While the Puritans held power, theaters in England thrived. *(F)*
2. King Charles II became addicted to theater while in France. *(T)*
3. When King Charles II regained the British throne, he reopened the theaters in England. *(T)*

Elements of Literature
pages 580–596

"A Modest Proposal" by Jonathan Swift

Prereading

Vocabulary Practice

Teach Unfamiliar Vocabulary Explain to students that in his proposal, Swift refers to people of the Irish lower class as if they were animals. Provide the words and definitions shown below to help students better comprehend the selection. Use each word in a sample sentence that exemplifies its meaning.

- *breeders* (p. 584): animals used to produce baby animals
- *breed* (p. 584): mate and produce young
- *dish* (p. 585): food prepared in a certain way
- *flesh* (p. 585): the meat of an animal
- *carcass* (p. 585): the body of a dead animal

Background

Discuss Irony Explain that verbal irony occurs when an author says one thing but means something very different. "A Modest Proposal" is an example of verbal irony. Tell students that Swift wrote this essay to call attention to the grave situation of Irish poverty. Explain that Swift suggested a completely outrageous solution: use babies for meat in order to reduce the number of poor people. Invite students to react to his solution, making certain they understand that Swift didn't really consider this to be an option. The proposal is ironic because he protests against the inhumane conditions in which the poor are living by suggesting something far more inhumane. For more practice understanding verbal irony, students can use the Before You Read page in *The Holt Reader.*

Prepare to Read

Set a Purpose Remind students that a speaker makes a persuasive argument to try to convince his or her audience to think or act a certain way. Explain that Swift's proposal is a coherent and persuasive argument, supported by three kinds of appeals: logical, ethical, and emotional. Break down the definition of each kind of appeal as presented on student book page 580. Have students set a purpose for reading: to identify examples of each type of appeal. On the board, create a three-column chart with the headings *logical, emotional,* and *ethical.* Have students copy this in their notebooks. They will add examples to the chart after they read.

Literary Skill
Understand verbal irony.

Reading Skills
Understand persuasive techniques (logical, emotional, and ethical appeals).

Resources

In this book:
- Adapted Readings
- Vocabulary and Comprehension, p. 99
- Additional Vocabulary Practice, p. 100

Other Resources:
- *The Holt Reader,* p. 125
- *Holt Adapted Reader*
- *Audio CD Library,* Disc 7
- *Audio CD Library, Selections and Summaries in Spanish*
- *Supporting Instruction in Spanish,* p. 25

Teacher Tip

Be sure to explain academic language so all students can participate in the lesson. For example, explain literary terms such as *persuasion, ethical, emotional,* and *logical.* Use simple examples to illustrate these techniques and concepts.

Alternative Activity

Read the Adaptation Distribute copies of the adapted reading of "A Modest Proposal" (available in this book and, with marginal questions, in *Holt Adapted Reader*). Have all students read the selection silently. .

Reading

Alternative Teaching Strategies

Analyze Structure As students read, use the following activity to help them understand how the structure of the arguments in "A Modest Proposal" contributes to the clarity of the meaning in the selection. Guide students in summarizing each of the six main arguments for using children for food, presented on student book page 587. Point out that Swift uses an organized list to present his argument. A sample summary of each argument is presented below.

1. The plan will reduce the number of Roman Catholics.
2. Poor tenants will be able to pay their landlords.
3. The nation will save money.
4. Parents won't have to spend money on their children after the first year.
5. It will benefit taverns and their customers.
6. It will encourage marriage.

Use *The Holt Reader* Students reading the selection in *The Holt Reader* can take notes and respond to the instruction in the selection's margins.

Postreading

Listening and Speaking Opportunity

Mixed Ability Group **Discuss Appeals** Direct students to reread the six advantages to this proposal that Swift identifies on student book page 587. Have them work in pairs to determine whether each argument appeals to emotions, logic, or ethics. Students may decide that certain points fall into more than one category. Pairs can use this information to complete the chart they started in Prereading. Reconvene to allow pairs to share their answers with the class. Challenge students to justify their ideas with words and phrases from the text. Provide language support as needed.

Alternative Activity

Use *The Holt Reader* For more practice recognizing Swift's persuasive techniques, students can complete the postreading activity in *The Holt Reader*.

Vocabulary Development

Alternative Teaching Strategies

(Especially for ELL) Teach New Vocabulary As students analyze the analogies in the Practice section on page 596 of the student book, they may encounter many words that they don't know. Support them by explaining any unknown words in the first word pair of each analogy. After providing definitions, guide students in determining each word's part of speech and the relationship between the two words. Remind students that they are looking for the other pair of words that has the same part of speech and relationship. For example, guide students through the first and third analogies as shown below:

- *Melancholy* means *sad* or *sorrowful*. *Melancholy* and *sad* are adjectives that mean the same thing. They are synonyms. You are looking for two adjectives that are synonyms.

- *Censure* means *condemn*. *Praise* means *show approval or admiration*. *Censure* and *praise* are verbs that have opposite meanings. They are antonyms. You are looking for two verbs that are antonyms.

Use Parts of Speech Remind students that knowing about parts of speech will help them to determine the correct answer. Point out that word endings can give clues about the part of speech of an unknown word. For example, *-y* as in *wealthy* (item 3) usually indicates an adjective. The suffixes *-less* as in *careless* and *-ous* as in *cautious* (item 3) indicate adjectives.

Reading Skills Development

Recognize Persuasive Techniques If students are having difficulty distinguishing between logical, emotional, and ethical appeals, give them these tips:

- Logical appeals include reasons and evidence, such as facts, statistics, and examples.

- Emotional appeals use words, phrases, vivid details, anecdotes, and personal experiences to arouse the reader's feelings, fears, hopes, and beliefs.

- Ethical appeals use details that convince the reader that the writer is fair and trustworthy.

Have students read in small groups the connected reading, "Top of the Food Chain," on pages 590–593 of the student book. Group members can take turns reading the story aloud. While others are reading, students should note persuasive appeals that appear in the text. After the groups have finished reading, group members should discuss the persuasive techniques they noted.

SKILLS FOCUS

Vocabulary Skill
Compare word meanings.

(Especially for ELL)

ELLs may become easily frustrated with difficult standardized testing. Throughout the year, frequently provide them with tips that demonstrate how to eliminate incorrect answers.

(Language Tip)

Encourage students to study words in pairs, either synonyms or antonyms. In this way they can learn two words without having to recall two definitions.

SKILLS FOCUS

Literary Skill
Understand verbal irony.

Reading Skills
Understand persuasive techniques (logical, emotional, and ethical appeals).

Resources

In this book:
• Adapted Readings
• Vocabulary and Comprehension, p. 99
• Additional Vocabulary Practice, p. 100

Other Resources:
• *The Holt Reader*, p. 125
• *Holt Adapted Reader*
• *Audio CD Library*, Disc 7
• *Audio CD Library, Selections and Summaries in Spanish*
• *Supporting Instruction in Spanish*, p. 25

TARGETED STRATEGIES FOR SPECIAL EDUCATION STUDENTS

Prereading
Background

Discuss Verbal Irony Write the following question and answer on the board and have students read it silently: *How was the test? Easy! I got every question right.* Then read the question aloud and answer in an ironic (sarcastic) tone. Ask the class to describe the difference in meaning between the written answer and the spoken one.

Explain that since writers can't use tone of voice to show when they are being ironic, they sometimes use several examples in order to make the irony clear. Tell students that Swift uses verbal irony throughout "A Modest Proposal" to get the reader's attention. He is not serious about the suggestion he makes in this essay. Then explain that the irony in "Top of the Food Chain" results from the speaker's attitude and ignorance. As they read each selection, help students determine the message that each author is trying to make through irony.

Reading
Alternative Teaching Strategy

Core Skill Identify the Main Ideas As students read "A Modest Proposal," pause after each paragraph to summarize its main idea. Lead them to determine whether each point appeals to readers' emotions, logic, or ethics. Guide them to identify Swift's message. (*English policies toward the Irish are wrong. A solution is needed.*)

Postreading
Alternative Assessment

Check Comprehension Assess students' comprehension of "A Modest Proposal" and "Top of the Food Chain" by asking the following questions:

• What problem does Swift address? (*the mistreatment of the Irish people by the English government*)
• Is he serious about the solution that he offers? (*no*)
• Then why does he suggest this solution? (*to get people's attention*)
• What point to do you think Boyle is trying to make in "Top of the Food Chain"? (*Answers will vary. Possible: We need to consider the consequences of our actions; it is wrong to interfere with nature and other cultures.*)

Vocabulary and Comprehension

"A Modest Proposal"

A. Complete each sentence with a word from the Word Bank.

1. The speaker _____ and then returned to the subject.

2. The teacher approved of the _____ and shortness of Sammy's essay.

3. The poor mothers beg for _____ to feed their children.

4. People should stop fighting and forget the _____ they have for one another.

5. A _____ person carefully considers what is right and wrong.

B. Summarize in your own words each of the six advantages of Swift's proposal.

1. _____

_____

2. _____

_____

3. _____

_____

4. _____

_____

5. _____

_____

6. _____

_____

Additional Vocabulary Practice

"A Modest Proposal"

A. Write the word from the Word Bank next to its one-word definition.

1. condemn _____

2. obtain _____

3. shortness _____

4. respect _____

5. overfilled _____

Word Bank
brevity
censure
deference
glutted
procure

B. Use each of the above words in a sentence.

1. _____

_____

2. _____

_____

3. _____

_____

4. _____

_____

5. _____

_____

C. Circle the letter of the answer that best completes each sentence.

1. Swift compares poor women to _____, whose only purpose is to have children.
   a. employees   **b.** breeders   **c.** lawyers

2. Swift states that young children might make a tasty _____, or meal.
   a. dish   **b.** plate   **c.** ornament

3. Swift says that there are many uses for the _____ of a baby.
   a. carcass   **b.** smile   **c.** intelligence

Heroic Couplets;
from *An Essay on Man* by Alexander Pope

Prereading
Vocabulary Practice

Teach Unfamiliar Vocabulary Prepare students to appreciate the language in Pope's work by teaching the following words and definitions prior to reading. Model using each word in a sentence.

- *merit* (couplet 5): a good point or quality
- *praise* (couplet 5): words of approval or admiration
- *commend* (couplet 5): to express approval of; to praise
- *eternal* (couplet 7): lasting forever
- *mischief* (couplet 9): behavior that causes annoyance or harm to others
- *discreet* (couplet 10): showing self-restraint in speech and behavior
- *isthmus* (from *An Essay on Man*, line 3): a narrow strip of land that lies between two bodies of water and connects two land masses
- *ignorance* (from *An Essay on Man*, line 11): the condition of being uneducated, unaware, or uninformed
- *chaos* (from *An Essay on Man*, line 13): total confusion

In addition, preview the vocabulary and references defined in the numerous side notes throughout the Pope selections. These are essential for comprehension.

Teach Academic Vocabulary Prepare students to discuss poetry by previewing academic vocabulary. Use examples from the readings to teach the following terms:

- *couplet* (p. 598): two rhymed lines with the same meter
- *antithesis* (p. 598): a contrast of ideas expressed in a grammatically balanced statement
- *heroic couplet* (p. 598): couplets of iambic pentameter, used in translations of epic poems
- *iambic pentameter* (p. 599): a line of poetry with ten syllables that are alternatively accented and unaccented
- *triplet* (p. 599): three rhyming lines of poetry
- *closed couplet* (p. 599): a couplet that expresses a complete thought in a sentence
- *epigram* (p. 602): a short poem with a clever ending

SKILLS FOCUS

Literary Skill
Understand antithesis.

Reading Skill
Identify the writer's stance.

(Resources)

In this book:
- Vocabulary and Comprehension, p. 105
- Additional Vocabulary Practice, p. 106

Other Resources:
- *The Holt Reader,* p. 141
- *Audio CD Library,* Disc 7
- *Audio CD Library, Selections and Summaries in Spanish*
- *Supporting Instruction in Spanish,* p. 26

(Especially for ELL)

Make sure to provide ELLs with academic vocabulary to help them understand and participate in classroom discussions.

Alternative Teaching Strategies

Use *The Holt Reader* Have students use the Before You Read page in *The Holt Reader*, either instead of or in addition to the Before You Read page in the student book.

Especially for ELL **Focus on Figurative Language** Discuss imagery to help ELLs appreciate Pope's use of figurative language. Read and paraphrase or simplify some examples of image-rich language, such as:

- "Hope springs eternal in the human breast" (couplet 7)
- "Placed on this isthmus of a middle state" (from *An Essay on Man*, line 3)

Invite students to share the mental images the words create for them and to discuss how these images make them feel. For example, in couplet 7, students might picture hope as an object or creature jumping from a person's chest. They might relate this to an excited or hopeful feeling.

Reading
Alternative Teaching Strategies

Listen to the Meter Help students appreciate the sound of Pope's language by playing the audio recording of each selection in English. Reinforce the meter of the heroic couplets by tapping out the rhythm as students read along. Encourage individuals to echo read (repeat each line after the audio recording) to internalize the pace and rhythm of the poetry.

Focus on Meaning Break down the language within couplets to help students analyze them. For couplet 7, you might focus first on the imagery of hope springing eternally. Then focus on the verbs and adverbs in the second line of the couplet. Remind ELLs that in the phrase "Man never is," the verb *is* expresses a state of being in the present tense. If needed, review the meaning of *never*. Then ask if the phrase "Man never is" expresses a complete idea. Help students determine that the thought is completed at the end of the line with the word *blest*. Focus next on the second part "but always to be blest." Remind students that *but* signifies contrast. In this case, *but* signifies the contrast of *never is* to *always*. Explain that in this sentence, *to be* is used to show the future tense. If needed, present other sentences with this form of the future tense, such as: *I am going to be there; she is to be married next week.*

Interpret Poetry Help students understand how each couplet provides insight into Pope's beliefs about human nature. Begin by breaking down the language in each couplet, then inviting students to share their impression of Pope's message. For example, after reading couplet 7, some students may interpret Pope's message to be that hope hinders the human race because people always look ahead and are rarely satisfied with the present. Others may think he felt that hope inspires the human race to strive for perfection. Accept all justified interpretations.

Postreading

Alternative Assessment

(**Mixed Ability Group**) **Review and Assess** Assess students' mastery of the academic language used to discuss poetry. Begin by reviewing the following words: *couplet, antithesis, heroic couplet, iambic pentameter, triplet, closed couplet, epigram.* Then divide the class into small groups. Give a definition or an example of one the above terms. Have each group decide together to which word you are referring. Provide corrections and reinforcement as needed. Continue until you have discussed each term at least twice.

Alternative Activities

Discuss Human Characteristics Prompt students to revisit their answers to Thinking Critically question four on student book page 602. Review the human characteristics that Pope thinks humans should be proud of and ashamed of. Extend the activity to allow students to share their own opinions about the characteristics of the human race. You might begin by prompting students to rephrase some of Pope's ideas. For example, they might restate the flattery and criticism in "a being darkly wise" (line 4) as *Humans are very smart, but sometimes they use their intelligence to do harmful things.* Next encourage students to express their own observations about characteristics of the human race.

Use *The Holt Reader* Have students complete the Identifying the Writer's Stance chart in *The Holt Reader,* either instead of or in addition to the postreading activities in the student book.

Reading Skills Development

Identify the Writer's Stance Identifying the writer's stance can be a challenging skill to master since writers often do not explicitly state their perspectives on the subjects they write about. Tell students that a writer's stance involves both *motivation* (why the writer wants to write about a particular topic) and *tone* (the writer's attitude toward the topic). Have students read the selection from *An Essay on Man* with a partner. While reading, students should pause occasionally to discuss the text and to make notes about the writer's tone and motivation. After students complete the reading, have them use their notes to identify the message the writer is trying to communicate.

SKILLS FOCUS

Literary Skill
Understand antithesis.

Reading Skill
Identify the writer's stance.

<hr>

(**Resources**)

In this book:
• Vocabulary and
Comprehension, p. 105
• Additional Vocabulary
Practice, p. 106

Other Resources:
• *The Holt Reader,* p. 141
• *Audio CD Library,* Disc 7
• *Audio CD Library,*
Selections and Summaries
in Spanish
• *Supporting Instruction*
in Spanish, p. 26

TARGETED STRATEGIES FOR SPECIAL EDUCATION STUDENTS

Prereading
Alternative Activity

Prepare to Read Prepare students to identify and appreciate the antitheses Alexander Pope employs in his poetry. Record on the board in random order the following words and then guide students to match each word to its contrast, as shown below:

- *first*   • *last* (couplet 3)
- *new*   • *old* (couplet 3)
- *knowledge*   • *weakness* (*An Essay on Man,* lines 5–6)
- *rise*   • *fall* (*An Essay on Man,* line 15)

Preview the referenced lines to show how contrast is used in each. Also direct students' attention to the parallel structure of lines 5–6.

Reading
Alternative Teaching Strategy

Relate to Personal Experience Help students analyze Pope's beliefs about human nature by guiding them to identify the main idea of each couplet and to relate it to their own experiences. For example:

- In couplet 6, illustrate "to err is human" by inviting students to share times when they have made mistakes. Continue by inviting students to share times when someone has made them angry or hurt their feelings.
- Illustrate "to forgive, divine" by discussing how difficult it is to forgive someone. Invite students to share how this description of forgiveness makes them feel as they relate it to their experiences. Guide them to discuss the view of human nature Pope relates in this and other examples.

Postreading
Additional Practice

Evaluate Couplet Structure Discuss how the sound of Pope's poetry educates and delights his audience. Choose an example of a couplet to rephrase as simple prose. For example, you may reword couplet 2 as: *It is risky to assume that with limited knowledge of a topic you know it all. It is only through in-depth study of a topic that you can achieve true appreciation and complete understanding.* Invite students to decide which version is more enjoyable to listen to and which more effectively communicates Pope's philosophy of human nature.

Vocabulary and Comprehension

Heroic Couplets; from *An Essay on Man*

A. Choose the word from the Word Bank that best completes each sentence.

1. The _____ connects the two
large islands in the lake.

2. Everyone will _____ you for
your effort.

Word Bank	
merit	discreet
commend	isthmus
mischief	ignorance

3. Any secret is safe with her because she is very _____.

4. He always behaves badly and makes _____.

5. She explained each _____, or good point, of her invention.

6. He hadn't studied and his _____ about the subject was obvious.

B. Next to each item, write whether it is a couplet, a triplet, an epigram, or an antithesis.

1. _____ "Here lies our sovereign lord the king,
whose word no man relies on;
he never says a foolish thing
nor ever does a wise one."

2. _____ "Know then thyself, presume not God to scan;
The proper study of mankind is man."

3. _____ "Created half to rise, and half to fall"

4. _____ "Music resembles poetry: in each
Are nameless graces which no methods teach,
And which a master hand alone can reach."

C. Next to each line of Pope's poetry, write the letter of the corresponding topic.

_____ **1.** "To err is human, to forgive, divine."

_____ **2.** "The proper study of mankind is man."

_____ **3.** "True ease in writing comes from art,
not chance"

_____ **4.** "Hope springs eternal in the
human breast"

a. self-discovery and knowledge

b. the importance of practice

c. dreams about the future

d. human imperfection
and tolerance

Additional Vocabulary Practice

Heroic Couplets; from *An Essay on Man*

A. Match each word to its description. Write the letter of the description next to the word.

_____ **1.** antithesis   **a.** short, witty poem

_____ **2.** heroic couplet   **b.** syllables alternate between stressed and unstressed

_____ **3.** iambic pentameter   **c.** contains contrasting ideas or descriptions

_____ **4.** epigram   **d.** used to translate epic poems

B. Find the word on the right that most closely describes the *opposite* of each word on the left. Write the word on the line.

1. chaos _____   ending

2. merit _____   rude

3. praise _____   wisdom

4. discreet _____   order

5. eternal _____   fault

6. ignorance _____   criticism

C. Choose four of the numbered words from Part B. Write a sentence using each one.

1. _____

_____

2. _____

_____

3. _____

_____

4. _____

_____

from *Don Quixote* by Miguel de Cervantes
translated by Samuel Putnam

Prereading
Vocabulary Practice

Teach Unfamiliar Vocabulary Teach the following words and definitions before students read the selection:
- *windmills* (p. 628): mills worked by the action of the wind on their sails (You might draw a picture to provide a clear image of a windmill.)
- *lance* (p. 629): a long weapon like a sword or spear
- *chivalry* (p. 629): the medieval knightly system with its religious, moral, and social code
- *peaceful* (p. 631): tranquil and serene; not inclined to violence

Alternative Activities

Read the Adaptation Distribute copies of the adapted reading of the selection from *Don Quixote* (available in this book and, with marginal questions, in *Holt Adapted Reader*). Have all students read the selection silently.

(**Especially for ELL**) **Use Spanish Resources** Spanish-speaking English-language learners may benefit from reading or listening to the selection summary in Spanish.

Identify Characteristics of Parody For more on identifying parody, students can use the Before You Read page in *The Holt Reader*, either instead of or in addition to the Before You Read page in the student book.

Reading
Alternative Activities

Make a Chart As students read, help them identify the characteristics of parody that Cervantes employs in *Don Quixote*. On the board, begin a chart like the one shown on the next page and invite students to copy it in their notebooks. As students read, lead them to add examples to each section of the chart. Note that these charts will help students answer question three on student book page 632. A partially completed chart may resemble the one shown on the next page.

SKILLS FOCUS

Literary Skill
Understand the characteristics of parody.

(**Resources**)

In this book:
- Adapted Readings
- Vocabulary and Comprehension, p. 111
- Additional Vocabulary Practice, p. 112

Other Resources:
- *The Holt Reader*, p. 145
- *Holt Adapted Reader*
- *Audio CD Library*, Disc 8
- *Audio CD Library, Selections and Summaries in Spanish*
- *Supporting Instruction in Spanish*, p. 27

(**Teacher Tip**)

By previewing target vocabulary as it is used in the selection, you prepare students to better comprehend what they read. When they encounter a vocabulary word in the reading, they will know the word's meaning and have a general overview of the scene in which it is used.

exaggeration	verbal irony	incongruity	humorously twisted imitation
an impression of a thing that makes it seem larger or greater than it really is Don Quixote engages in "righteous warfare" with the windmills.	saying one thing and meaning another Sancho Panza says, "I believe everything that your Grace says. . . ."	deliberately pairing things that don't belong together Don Quixote rides on an old nag with a dislocated shoulder, and Sancho rides on a donkey. These animals do not belong with the image of a brave knight and his squire.	imitation that pokes fun at something Don Quixote replaces his broken lance with a "withered bough" from a tree.

Use *The Holt Reader* Students reading the selection in *The Holt Reader* can take notes and respond to the instruction in the margins.

Additional Practice

(Core Skill) **Compare the Character and His Foil** Remind students that a foil is a character who is used as a contrast to another character. As students read, guide them in contrasting the behaviors of Don Quixote and his foil, Sancho Panza. You might record their ideas on a chart like the one below. Students can use this chart when they answer Thinking Critically questions five and six on student book page 632:

Don Quixote	Sancho Panza
thinks the windmills are lawless giants	knows the windmills are windmills
doesn't complain of pain because he is a "knight-errant"	promises to complain "over the least little thing that ails me"
doesn't eat, drink, or sleep	eats, drinks, and sleeps
is searching for adventures and battles	is peaceful and "not fond of meddling in the quarrels and feuds of others"

Postreading

(Mixed Ability Group) **Complete the Chart** You may consider having students work in groups to complete the postreading chart in *The Holt Reader*.

Alternative Assessment

Identify the Sequence of Events Before students answer the questions on student book page 632, make sure they can recall and place in correct sequence the main events in this excerpt from *Don Quixote*. On the board, present the events on the next page in random order. Ask students to place these in correct story order. Point out that the correctly sequenced list summarizes the plot of this selection. Invite students to provide details about each event.

(Teacher Tip)

To help students appreciate how Sancho Panza's character serves as a foil to Don Quixote, invite them to recall other character foils they have encountered. For example, students may recall that Gilgamesh's character is highlighted through the contrast between him and his foil Enkidu (student book pages 58–65).

1. Don Quixote and Sancho Panza see thirty or forty windmills.

2. Don Quixote claims the windmills are giants, but Sancho Panza says they are windmills.

3. Don Quixote attacks a windmill, but its whirling wing knocks him and his horse over and he loses his sword.

4. Sancho Panza eats some food and drinks something from his flask.

5. Sancho Panza goes to sleep, but Don Quixote stays awake, thinking about Dulcinea.

6. When he awakens, Sancho Panza drinks some more. Don Quixote declines any food or drink, because he claims to be nourished by his memories of Dulcinea.

7. Don Quixote and Sancho Panza arrive at Puerto Lápice. Don Quixote warns Sancho not to defend him if he gets into a fight with gentlemen.

8. Sancho Panza promises to obey Don Quixote, unless he himself is attacked, in which case he will not hesitate to defend himself.

Vocabulary Development
Alternative Activity

Especially for ELL **Provide Questions** English-language learners may have difficulty creating their own questions for the Vocabulary Development exercise on student book page 633. As an alternative activity, provide the questions yourself and ask students to answer them. You might use questions like the ones given below. Note that students' answers will vary.

• How can you show *enmity* toward someone? *(scowl at him or her; glare at him or her; say mean things about him or her)*

• What *victuals* do you think Sancho had in his bag? *(slices of cheese; pieces of bread; little cakes; morsels of meat)*

• If a police officer keeps a *vigil*, for what is he watching? *(robbers; criminals; crimes being committed)*

• Why might your muscles be *flaccid*? *(You are not in good shape; you are tired; you are old.)*

• How does someone with a friendly *disposition* behave? *(He or she smiles; he or she says hello to everyone; he or she talks to everyone.)* How does someone with a cruel *disposition* behave? *(He or she is mean to people; he or she makes fun of people; he or she scowls all the time.)*

SKILLS FOCUS

Vocabulary Skill
Demonstrate word knowledge.

Especially for ELL
Provide ELLs with language support as they write their parodies. Have students record their ideas and then read these aloud to you. Make any needed revisions in sentence structure before students commit their ideas to a final product.

Teacher Tip
Extend the Vocabulary Development activity on student book page 633 by asking additional questions using the vocabulary presented in this lesson's Prereading section. For example: *How do cowards behave?* (They cry or scream a lot; they run away; they hide.)

Core Skill
Use the resources in the Reading Skills and Strategies section of this book to teach a core literary skill in which your struggling readers need remediation. Use the selection from *Don Quixote* for the application portion of the lesson.

Literary Skill
Understand the
characteristics of parody.

(Resources)

In this book:
• Adapted Readings
• Vocabulary and
Comprehension, p. 111
• Additional Vocabulary
Practice, p. 112

Other Resources:
• *The Holt Reader,* p. 145
• *Holt Adapted Reader*
• *Audio CD Library,* Disc 8
• *Audio CD Library,*
Selections and Summaries
in Spanish
• *Supporting Instruction*
in Spanish, p. 27

(Teacher Tip)

Aid students' comprehension
by having them summarize
the main events of the story
as they read. After students
read a paragraph in the
selection, invite a volunteer
to restate what just
happened. This way,
students can check their
comprehension as they
keep track of the plot.

TARGETED STRATEGIES FOR SPECIAL EDUCATION STUDENTS

Prereading
Background

Prepare to Read Review with students the qualities of an idealized knight that are described in the Background section of student book page 626. Explain that Don Quixote tries to emulate the ideal knight by imitating these qualities. Tell students that, as they read, they will note when and how Don Quixote imitates a knight and how Cervantes uses the character's behavior to ridicule the medieval literature that created this ideal.

Reading
Alternative Teaching Strategy

Identify Examples of Satire As students read, guide them in identifying instances in which Don Quixote imitates the behaviors of an ideal knight. For example, he stays awake to keep a "wakeful vigil" (student book page 631). Help students understand how his behavior is actually a parody of the knightly chivalry that is idealized in medieval literature. *(He is keeping a vigil, but he is watching for danger that does not exist.)* Ask students to identify which technique(s) Cervantes uses in each example of parody. *(In this case, he is using incongruity and humorous imitation.)*

Postreading
Alternative Teaching Strategy

Prepare to Write Prepare students for the writing activity on student book page 633. Use prompts and questions like those listed below to help them plan their writing. Direct students to keep in mind their answers to these questions as they plan and write their parodies.

- A parody is "a mocking imitation of a writer's style or of a particular genre" (student book page 615). Ask: *Do you want to make fun of a specific writer's style or of a particular genre?*

- Parody is a form of satire. Satires "expose errors and absurdities that we no longer notice because custom and familiarity have blinded us to them" (student book page 614). Ask: *What errors and absurdities do you want to expose? What flaws can you identify in the object of your parody?*

- Parodies use exaggeration, verbal irony, incongruity, and humorous imitation. Ask: *How will you ridicule the flaws you identified above? Which techniques will you use?*

Vocabulary and Comprehension

from *Don Quixote*

A. Write the word from the Word Bank that most closely matches the meaning of each group of words.

Word Bank
disposition
enmity
flaccid
succor
victuals
vigil

1. nourishment, provisions, food _____

2. relief, aid, support _____

3. nature, inclination, personality _____

4. watch, lookout, surveillance _____

5. unfriendliness, hatred, ill will _____

6. floppy, sagging, limp _____

B. Number the following sentences to indicate the order in which the events occur in the excerpt from *Don Quixote*.

____ Don Quixote tells Sancho Panza about Machuca.

____ Don Quixote and Sancho find a group of windmills.

____ Don Quixote and Sancho arrive at Puerto Lápice.

____ Don Quixote and Sancho spend the night under a group of trees.

____ Don Quixote gives Sancho permission to eat whenever he chooses.

____ Don Quixote, riding his horse, attacks a windmill.

C. Answer the questions below in complete sentences.

1. What does Don Quixote use to replace his broken lance?

_____

2. How does he get this idea?

_____

3. What does Don Quixote tell Sancho to do if common men attack him?

_____

4. What does Don Quixote tell Sancho to do if gentlemen attack him? Why?

_____

_____

Additional Vocabulary Practice

from *Don Quixote*

A. Circle the letter of the answer that best completes each sentence.

1. The guard kept a nightlong _____ in case the enemy attacked.
   a. victual   **b.** enmity   **c.** vigil

2. She was well-liked by everyone, thanks to her sweet _____.
   a. disposals   **b.** disposition   **c.** bitterness

3. We want to _____ the victims of the earthquake.
   a. flaccid   **b.** succor   **c.** vigil

4. These pieces of bread are our only _____ for the hike up the mountain.
   a. dispositions   **b.** victuals   **c.** victories

B. Write each word from the Word Bank next to its definition, one letter per space. Then unscramble the shaded letters to form a word from the selection.

Word Bank
chivalry
cowards
lance
magician
memories
peaceful

1. a person skilled in performing magic __ __ __ __ __ __ __ __

2. code of knights __ __ __ __ __ __ __ __

3. calm and tranquil __ __ __ __ __ __ __ __

4. people who are easily frightened __ __ __ __ __ __ __

5. a long, spear-like weapon __ __ __ __ __

6. recollections, thoughts __ __ __ __ __ __ __ __

Word: __ __ __ __ __ __ __ __

C. Choose three words from the Word Bank above. Use each word in a sentence.

1. _____
   _____

2. _____
   _____

3. _____
   _____

Collection 5

The Romantic Period: 1798–1832

Prereading

Vocabulary Practice

Teach Unfamiliar Vocabulary To aid students' comprehension, introduce the following words before reading the introduction.

- *laissez faire* (p. 705): the economic theory that the government should not interfere in the free-enterprise system of the market
- *romantic* (p. 712): characterized by interest in nature, emphasis on emotion and imagination, and rebellion against social rules and conventions

Alternative Activity

Read the Adaptation Distribute copies of the below–grade-level adapted reading for "The Romantic Period: 1798–1832" (available in this book and, with marginal questions, in *Holt Adapted Reader*). Have students read silently.

Reading

Alternative Teaching Strategy

(**Mixed Ability Group**) **Guide Students' Reading** You may consider having students read in groups, using the Break-in Reading group activity on page xxv of this book. Have students read the on-level, shortened version of the introduction in *The Holt Reader* and respond to the instruction in its margins as they read.

Postreading

Alternative Assessment

Check Comprehension After students read the chapter introduction, check their comprehension. Present two paraphrased versions of the information and ask students to decide which one is accurate. For example, present the following options for the first bulleted point:

A. Romanticism copied the eighteenth-century style. The Romantics liked logic and used clever writing techniques.

B. Romanticism rejected the eighteenth-century style. The Romantics liked imagination and naturalness. *(correct)*

SKILLS FOCUS

Literary Skill
Evaluate the philosophical, political, religious, ethical, and social influences of a historical period.

(**Resources**)

In this book:
Adapted Readings

Other Resources:
- *The Holt Reader*, p. 161
- *Holt Adapted Reader*
- Video Segment 7

(**Especially for ELL**)

As they read, draw English-language learners' attention to key words in the text. For example, as they read student book page 708, point out words such as *American Revolution, England,* and *revolution in France.* These words indicate a discussion of political events in America, England, and France as addressed in the first bulleted question on student book page 706.

Literary Skill
Evaluate the philosophical, political, religious, ethical, and social influences of a historical period.

Resources

In this book:
Adapted Readings

Other Resources:
• *The Holt Reader,* p. 161
• *Holt Adapted Reader*
• Video Segment 7

Teacher Tip

Use the timeline on student book pages 702–703 to preview the events that students will read about in the introduction. Invite them to share any prior knowledge about these events. As students pool their background knowledge, they will achieve a sense of confidence resulting from their knowing something about the topic they will study.

TARGETED STRATEGIES FOR SPECIAL EDUCATION STUDENTS

Prereading
Alternative Teaching Strategy

Check Comprehension As students read Political and Social Milestones on student book pages 704–705, pause periodically to check their comprehension. For example, after reading the first two sentences in "The Industrial Revolution in England," ask: *Why did people move to the cities?* (They didn't have land; their only choice was to work in factories in cities.)

Reading
Alternative Activity

Sum Up the Main Ideas To ensure that students understand the main ideas of the introduction, help them create a brief summary of the information that appears in each section. Summaries for the first six sections might look like the following:

• The Romantic period in England was a turbulent and revolutionary time.

• The independence of the American colonies was a setback for England. England's ruling class feared the revolution in France and its radical principles would spread to England.

• French revolutionaries killed many aristocrats in the "September massacre," and many English liberals turned against France. England and France went to war against each other. Napoleon seized power in France and became a tyrant.

• England used strict measures to avoid revolutionary changes like those which had occurred in France. England defeated Napoleon.

• Individual owners took over much of the farmland in England, and many people moved to the cities to look for work in factories.

• Under the economic philosophy of laissez faire, the rich got richer, and the poor suffered even more. Children suffered the most under this system.

Postreading
Additional Activity

Discuss Individual Freedom Remind students that the Romantics embraced political changes that led to greater personal freedom. Guide students to talk about current attitudes toward political change and individual freedom. For example, say: *Today security cameras often tape people in public places.* Invite students to discuss whether this measure preserves their safety or intrudes on their privacy.

Elements of Literature
pages 735–742

"Lines Composed a Few Miles Above Tintern Abbey" by William Wordsworth

Prereading

Vocabulary Practice

(Especially for ELL) **Teach Unfamiliar Vocabulary** Provide brief definitions for the following words to help English-language learners appreciate the emotional impact this place had on the poet: *lonely* (line 25): not visited by people; *weariness* (line 27): tiredness; *raptures* (line 85): expressions of great happiness; *sublime* (line 95): supreme; *faith* (line 133): trust in something; *solitude* (line 143): the state of being alone; *grief* (line 143): great sadness; *zeal* (line 154): enthusiasm.

Reading

Alternative Teaching Strategy

Focus on Emotions Invite volunteers to take turns reading aloud small sections of the poem. Encourage students to identify each emotion with a situation in the poem.

Alternative Activities

Read the Adaptation Distribute copies of the annotated version of "Lines Composed a Few Miles Above Tintern Abbey" (available in this book and, with marginal questions, in *Holt Adapted Reader*). Have students read the selection silently.

Use The Holt Reader Have students read the selection in *The Holt Reader* and use the margins to make notes and respond to instruction.

Postreading

Listening and Speaking Opportunity

Listen to the Audio Recording Remind students that Wordsworth composed this poem aloud. He spoke the words to hear the rhythm and fluency of each line. Allow students to listen to the audio recording of the selection to help them appreciate this style of conversational blank verse. Then, to practice identifying main idea and mood, have students complete the postreading activity in *The Holt Reader*.

SKILLS FOCUS

Literary Skill
Understand blank verse.

Reading Skill
Recognize patterns of organization.

(Resources)

In this book:
- Adapted Readings
- Vocabulary and Comprehension, p. 117
- Additional Vocabulary Practice, p. 124 (includes the next two selections)

Other Resources:
- *The Holt Reader*, p. 168
- *Holt Adapted Reader*
- *Audio CD Library*, Disc 9
- *Audio CD Library, Selections and Summaries in Spanish*
- *Supporting Instruction in Spanish*, p. 30

(Language Tip)
Point out that the vocabulary words for this selection may be useful to students outside of the classroom setting. If time permits, encourage them to pool their knowledge and make a list of these and other words that refer to emotions.

Literary Skill
Understand blank verse.

Reading Skill
Recognize patterns of organization.

Resources

In this book:
• Adapted Readings
• Vocabulary and Comprehension, p. 117
• Additional Vocabulary Practice, p. 124 (includes the next two selections)

Other Resources:
• *The Holt Reader,* p. 168
• *Holt Adapted Reader*
• *Audio CD Library,* Disc 9
• *Audio CD Library, Selections and Summaries in Spanish*
• *Supporting Instruction in Spanish,* p. 30

Teacher Tip

It is often helpful for students to break up long or difficult readings into shorter sections. In this way, they can successfully achieve smaller goals. This makes the task of reading and analyzing a selection less daunting.

TARGETED STRATEGIES FOR SPECIAL EDUCATION STUDENTS

Prereading
Alternative Teaching Strategy

Discuss Style Prepare students to comment on the author's style. Explain that this poem is a meditation; the poet reflects on a place in nature that inspires him. Wordsworth composed this poem in informal, conversational blank verse. This style tends to mimic the fluency and rhythm of natural speech. Ask students to consider as they read why the poet chose this style for this particular poem.

Reading
Alternative Teaching Strategy

Set Purposes for Reading Help students comprehend the poem by setting specific purposes for reading small sections. Guide the class in reading the poem as described below.

• Have students read silently through all the reading stops to get an idea of what the poem is about.
• Have a volunteer read aloud the first reading stop and the corresponding question for lines 1–22.
• Use this question as a purpose for reading this section.
• Call on a volunteer to read this section aloud.
• Discuss the question and answer it together as a class.
• Continue in this way to help students read the rest of the poem.

You may wish to make additional comments on sections of the poem that are not explained in the reading stops. For example, the poet addresses the Wye River Valley itself in lines 55–57.

Postreading
Additional Practice

Listen to the Poem Help students answer Thinking Critically question nine on student book page 742. Play the audio recording of the selection to model how the poem should sound. Demonstrate with your hand the rhythm and rolling movement of the language. After students choose the stanza they will focus on for the question, help them by asking them questions like the following:

• What does the speaker see, hear, and smell?
• What emotions does the speaker describe?
• Is the speaker talking about the past, present, or future?

Vocabulary and Comprehension

"Lines Composed a Few Miles Above Tintern Abbey"

A. Match words and definitions. Write the letter of the definition next to the word.

_____	**1.** grief	**a.**	the state of being alone
_____	**2.** lonely	**b.**	trust in something
_____	**3.** weariness	**c.**	anxiety caused by danger
_____	**4.** pain	**d.**	expressions of great happiness
_____	**5.** raptures	**e.**	great sadness
_____	**6.** fear	**f.**	supreme
_____	**7.** solitude	**g.**	tiredness
_____	**8.** zeal	**h.**	not visited by people
_____	**9.** faith	**i.**	enthusiasm
_____	**10.** sublime	**j.**	physical hurt or great sadness

B. Choose a word from above and use it in a sentence.

1. _____

_____

C. Write T or F to tell if the following statements about the poem are true or false.

1. The speaker addresses the Wye River Valley in part of the poem._____

2. The speaker feels that five years have passed very quickly. _____

3. The speaker compares his younger self to a deer. _____

4. The stanzas in this poem are all the same length. _____

5. Wordsworth uses a formal rhyming structure to create the rhythm in this poem. _____

6. The speaker shows a love for the beauty of nature. _____

"Kubla Khan"

by Samuel Taylor Coleridge

SKILLS FOCUS

Literary Skill
Understand alliteration.

(Resources)

In this book:
• Adapted Readings
• Vocabulary and Comprehension, p. 120
• Additional Vocabulary Practice, p. 124 (includes the previous and the next selection)

Other Resources:
• *The Holt Reader,* p. 176
• *Holt Adapted Reader*
• *Audio CD Library,* Disc 9
• *Audio CD Library, Selections and Summaries in Spanish*
• *Supporting Instruction in Spanish,* p. 30

(History Connection)

Explain that the word *khan* refers to a medieval ruler of a Mongol tribe. Kubla Khan was emperor of Mongolia at its height.

(Core Skill)

Use the resources in the Reading Skills and Strategies section of this book to help students having difficulty with figurative language. Use "Kubla Khan" for the application portion of the lesson. (See lines 18–22.)

Prereading

Vocabulary Practice

Teach Unfamiliar Vocabulary Prepare students to appreciate the poem's shifts in mood by teaching the following vocabulary words prior to reading: *Xanadu* (line 1): a perfect, beautiful place; *pleasure* (line 2): happiness; *blossomed* (line 9): flowered; *delight* (line 44): happiness; *savage* (line 14): wild, fierce; *haunted* (line 15): inhabited by ghosts; *wailing* (line 16): crying; *demon* (line 16): devil or bad spirit; *turmoil* (line 17): confusion; *tumult* (line 28): disorderly commotion.

Sort Vocabulary Words Make a two-column chart on the board with the headings *light* and *dark*. Explain to students that in "Kubla Khan" the mood shifts from light (happy, good) to darker (more mysterious, dangerous, bad). Guide students to sort the vocabulary above into these two categories to prepare them to identify and discuss the mood throughout the poem.

Reading

Alternative Teaching Strategy

Read with a Purpose Guide students to use the chart they created in Prereading to help them identify the mood as it changes throughout the poem.

Alternative Activities

Read the Adaptation Distribute copies of the annotated version of "Kubla Khan" (available in this book and, with marginal questions, in *Holt Adapted Reader*). Have students read the selection silently.

Use *The Holt Reader* Have students read the selection in *The Holt Reader* and use the margins to make notes and respond to instruction.

Postreading

Alternative Activity

Explore Alliteration For more practice with alliteration, have students complete the postreading activity in *The Holt Reader,* either instead of or in addition to the activities found in the student book.

TARGETED STRATEGIES FOR SPECIAL EDUCATION STUDENTS

Prereading

Background

Provide Background Information Prepare students to appreciate the dreamlike setting and sequence of events in "Kubla Khan." Remind them that, as they learned in the chapter introduction, the Romantic poets believed that imagination is the best means of understanding the changing world around us. The Romantic era was also characterized by a turn toward nature and dream worlds that were more beautiful than the harsh, industrial cities of the time. Invite students to talk about illogical events in dreams and how dreams progress. Explain that this poem demonstrates these dreamlike qualities.

Reading

Additional Practice

Appreciate Language Read the poem aloud. Point out examples of alliteration (such as in lines 2–6, 11, 16, 17, 19, 25, 27, 33, 37, 43, 44, 45). (Many examples contain only two words with the same consonant sound.) Talk about how alliteration helps create the magical mood of the poem. *(It helps the language to flow, adding to its dreamlike quality.)* Play the audio recording of a passage and then rephrase the same passage using basic vocabulary and normal word order. Help students determine which is more enjoyable to listen to. Lead them to conclude that the alliteration, rhyme, and meter of the poem create sounds and images that give the poem an enchanted mood and dreamlike quality.

Postreading

Alternative Teaching Strategy

Analyze Imagery Invite students to reread the poem, this time focusing on the imagery that Coleridge creates. Explain that he emphasizes some of the images by using alliteration. For example, guide students to discuss the image of a "sunless sea" (line 5). Ask them to describe what picture these words create in their minds and to share how it makes them feel. Drawing on the previous discussion of alliteration, ask students to talk about the value of alliteration in emphasizing the image.

SKILLS FOCUS

Literary Skill
Understand alliteration.

Resources

In this book:
- Adapted Readings
- Vocabulary and Comprehension, p. 120
- Additional Vocabulary Practice, p. 124 (includes the previous and the next selection)

Other Resources:
- *The Holt Reader*, p. 176
- *Holt Adapted Reader*
- *Audio CD Library*, Disc 9
- *Audio CD Library, Selections and Summaries in Spanish*
- *Supporting Instruction in Spanish*, p. 30

Geography Connection

It has been suggested that Cambuluc, the great capital city of the Mongol empire, is featured in the poem "Kubla Khan." This city is now called Beijing. Invite students to find Beijing on a world map.

Vocabulary and Comprehension

"Kubla Khan"

A. Write each word from the Word Bank next to its definition.

Word Bank	
blossomed	demon
haunted	pleasure
savage	turmoil
wailing	Xanadu

1. _____ confusion

2. _____ making loud cries

3. _____ feeling of enjoyment or satisfaction

4. _____ flowered

5. _____ devil or evil spirit

6. _____ a perfect, ideal, beautiful place

7. _____ fierce, wild

8. _____ inhabited by ghosts or spirits

B. Answer the following questions in complete sentences.

1. Reread the first stanza of "Kubla Khan." In your own words, briefly describe Xanadu.

_____

_____

_____

2. What does the narrator say he once saw in a vision?

_____

_____

C. Write T or F next to each statement to tell if it is true or false.

1. _____ Xanadu is a place of pleasure and delight.

2. _____ A wall and towers surround Xanadu.

3. _____ The chasm in the earth is a place of turmoil and tumult.

4. _____ A wailing woman haunts the chasm.

5. _____ A small fountain trickles from the chasm.

"Ozymandias" by Percy Bysshe Shelley

Prereading

Vocabulary Practice

Teach Unfamiliar Vocabulary Support students' efforts to understand the poem by teaching them key vocabulary prior to reading. Use contextually-rich sentences and pantomime to clarify the following words and definitions:

- *vast* (line 2); *colossal* (line 13): huge
- *sneer* (line 5): a scornful, ironic smile
- *remains* (line 12): is left behind
- *decay* (line 12): rot; a decline in quality

Alternative Activity

Focus on Irony To provide an introduction to irony, consider having students use the Before You Read page in *The Holt Reader*, either instead of or in addition to the Before You Read page in the student book.

Reading

Additional Practice

(**Core Skill**) **Focus on Theme** As students read, help them visualize the condition of the sculpture by focusing their attention on words such as "half sunk," "shattered," "decay," and "wreck." Then shift their attention to lines 10–11 and invite them to imagine how the sculpture looked when it was first built. Guide students to identify the situational irony of the poem by asking them to imagine what Ozymandias might have felt when he first saw this grand sculpture that he had built. Then contrast these emotions with how he might feel if he saw the current condition of the sculpture.

Use *The Holt Reader* Consider having students read the selection in *The Holt Reader* and use the margins to make notes and respond to instruction.

Postreading

Additional Practice

Compare and Contrast For practice using comparison and contrast to reveal situational irony, have students complete the postreading activity in *The Holt Reader*, either instead of or in addition to the activities found in the student book.

SKILLS FOCUS

Literary Skills
Understand irony and situational irony.

(**Resources**)

In this book:
- Vocabulary and Comprehension, p. 123
- Additional Vocabulary Practice, p. 124 (includes the previous two selections)

Other Resources:
- *The Holt Reader,* p. 181
- *Audio CD Library,* Disc 10
- *Audio CD Library, Selections and Summaries in Spanish*
- *Supporting Instruction in Spanish,* p. 34

(**Language Tip**)

When you introduce vocabulary, refer to the selection to teach each word's part of speech. Then point out words that can be used differently. For example, *remains, decay,* and *wreck* can all be used as either a noun or a verb.

(**Core Skill**)

Use the resources in the Reading Skills and Strategies section of this book to help students having difficulty with theme. Use "Ozymandias" for the application portion of the lesson.

SKILLS FOCUS

Literary Skills
Understand irony and
situational irony.

(Resources)

In this book:
• Vocabulary and
Comprehension, p. 123
• Additional Vocabulary
Practice, p. 124 (includes
the previous two
selections)

Other Resources:
• *The Holt Reader,* p. 181
• *Audio CD Library,* Disc 10
• *Audio CD Library,
Selections and Summaries
in Spanish*
• *Supporting Instruction
in Spanish,* p. 34

(Teacher Tip)

Relate a new concept to a
familiar context to support
students' comprehension
and assimilation. For
example, students will
better understand
situational irony if it is
applied to a familiar
context or experience.

TARGETED STRATEGIES FOR SPECIAL EDUCATION STUDENTS

Prereading
Background

Make the Connection Guide students in considering whether humans can achieve immortality through their words and works. Discuss speeches, music, and works of art that have remained famous after their creators have died. Consider the following: Martin Luther King's "I have a dream" speech; Francis Scott Key's "The Star-Spangled Banner"; Leonardo da Vinci's *Mona Lisa.*

Reading
Additional Practice

Focus on the Sound of Language As students read, encourage them to discuss their emotional reactions to the language of the poem. Restate each idea in more conventional prose and ask students to choose the version that is more compelling. For example, the beautiful, rhythmic language that describes the wrecked sculpture (lines 12–14) might evoke feelings of pity, lament, or nostalgia. Students may feel less emotional about a prose version of this description, such as: *The wrecked sculpture is in the desert.*

Postreading
Alternative Activity

Focus on the Key Idea Help students answer Thinking Critically question two on student book page 804 by applying the concept of situational irony to various contexts. Create a three-column chart with the headings *situation, expectations,* and *reality.* Record in the first column a situation that is familiar to students, such as *going to the supermarket.* In the second column, record their expectations for going to the supermarket. *(You buy food; you see shelves of goods; you pay when you leave.)* In the third column, record an event that is clearly inappropriate or unexpected in the situation. *(They sell cars; there is no food to buy; you bring food and they give you money.)*

Then use the situation in the poem to complete the chart and analyze its situational irony. Guide students in completing column one *(a sculptor created a huge sculpture to honor a king),* column two *(the sculpture will immortalize the king),* and column three *(the sculpture deteriorates and becomes a huge wreck surrounded by sand).*

Vocabulary and Comprehension

"Ozymandias"

A. Match a word from the Word Bank to each group of related words. One word will be left over.

Word Bank	
frown	decay
wrinkled	shattered
remains	vast

1. rot, decompose, wood _____

2. colossal, immense, monumental

_____

3. stays, is left over, persists _____

4. displeasure, disapproval _____

5. pieces, broken, glass _____

B. Complete each sentence with a word from the Word Bank.

1. The _____ on the woman's face showed that she was not happy.

2. A person's skin usually becomes _____ as she or he gets older.

3. When I dropped the glass, it _____ into many pieces.

C. Answer the following questions.

1. Who does the statue represent?

_____

2. What expression does the statue have on its face?

_____

3. What three parts of the statue remain?

_____

4. What surrounds the wreck of the statue?

_____

Additional Vocabulary Practice

"Lines Composed a Few Miles Above Tintern Abbey"; "Kubla Khan"; "Ozymandias"

A. Write each word in the Word Bank under the category that is most closely related to its meaning.

Word Bank	
solitude	pain
joy	lonely
grief	delight
pleasure	wailing

alone

_____

_____

_____

happy

_____

_____

_____

sad

_____

_____

_____

B. Circle the letter of the answer that best completes each sentence.

1. The baby is _____ because she is hungry.
   a. smiling   **b.** wailing   **c.** laughing   **d.** shopping

2. With tender care, water, and sunlight, the rosebush _____.
   a. blossomed   **b.** withered   **c.** haunted   **d.** shattered

3. The children showed their happiness and _____ when their father brought them candy.
   a. anger   **b.** temper   **c.** delight   **d.** contempt

4. You can see the _____ skyscraper from miles away.
   a. colossal   **b.** savage   **c.** wrinkled   **d.** tumult

C. Write C or I to tell if the underlined word is used correctly or incorrectly in the sentence.

1. We found the <u>wreck</u> of what had once been a small ship. _____

2. When the crystal ball fell to the ground, it <u>shattered</u> into hundreds of pieces. _____

3. The <u>vast</u> germ could only be seen under a microscope. _____

4. When she heard the funny joke, she began to <u>frown</u> with laughter. _____

5. The baby had soft, smooth, <u>wrinkled</u> skin. _____

"Jade Flower Palace" by Tu Fu

Prereading

Vocabulary Practice

(**Especially for ELL**) **Teach Unfamiliar Vocabulary** Prepare students to appreciate Tu Fu's use of vivid language by teaching the following verbs: *swirls* (line 1); *moans* (line 1); *scurry* (line 2); *whistle* (line 9); *roar* (line 9); *scatters* (line 10); *crumbled* (line 12); *slips (away)* (line 19).

Alternative Activity

Focus on Mood To provide practice recognizing mood, consider having students use the Before You Read page in *The Holt Reader*, either instead of or in addition to the Before You Read page in the student book.

Reading

Additional Practice

Focus on Language Discuss with students that Tu Fu uses a minimum of words to evoke emotions and create images. As students read, highlight the target vocabulary to help them see how Tu Fu uses precise, carefully chosen verbs.

Use *The Holt Reader* Consider having students read the selection in *The Holt Reader* and use the margins to make notes and respond to instruction.

Postreading

Additional Practice

Interpret the Poem Help students answer Thinking Critically question one on student book page 818 by asking guided questions such as:

- Which words in line 3 tell you that the poet is thinking about the past? ("*long ago*") Which words tell you that Tu Fu thinks the past was grand? (line 3: "*prince*"; line 4: "*palace*"; line 13: "*gold chariots*"; line 16: "*glory*")
- What tense are "moans" (line 1), "whistle," "roar" (line 9), and "scatters" (line 10)? (*present*) Based on these lines, how does Tu Fu feel about the present? (*It is not as good as the past.*)

(**Core Skill**) **Recognize Theme** For additional practice recognizing theme, have students complete the postreading activity in *The Holt Reader*.

SKILLS FOCUS

Literary Skill
Understand mood.

(**Resources**)
In this book:
- Vocabulary and Comprehension, p. 127
- Additional Vocabulary Practice, p. 128

Other Resources:
- *The Holt Reader,* p. 184
- *Audio CD Library,* Disc 10
- *Audio CD Library, Selections and Summaries in Spanish*
- *Supporting Instruction in Spanish,* p. 34

(**Teacher Tip**)
Help students retain new vocabulary by engaging them in a concrete activity related to the new words. For example, acting out verbs is a meaningful way to reinforce these words.

SKILLS FOCUS

Literary Skill
Understand mood.

Resources

In this book:
• Vocabulary and
Comprehension, p. 127
• Additional Vocabulary
Practice, p. 128

Other Resources:
• *The Holt Reader,* p. 184
• *Audio CD Library,* Disc 10
• *Audio CD Library,
Selections and Summaries
in Spanish*
• *Supporting Instruction in
Spanish,* p. 34

TARGETED STRATEGIES FOR SPECIAL EDUCATION STUDENTS

Prereading
Background

Connect to World Literature Prepare students to appreciate the lyrical imagery that is characteristic of Chinese poetry and exemplified in "Jade Flower Palace." Refer to the explanation of lyrical imagery on student book pages 811–812, focusing specifically on the minimalist approach. Explain that in "Jade Flower Palace," Tu Fu uses simple language to evoke vivid images. Also point out that the process of change is a common focus of Chinese poetry.

Reading
Alternative Teaching Strategy

Analyze Minimalist Language Explain that the poet's choice of precise vocabulary is effective because it allows him to use fewer words than if he used less specific, vague language. Illustrate the power of minimalist language through a discussion like the following, about "The stream swirls" in line 1.

• Rephrase the sentence as: *The stream moves.* Explain that *swirls* and *moves* are both verbs, but *swirls* more accurately describes the movement of the water.

• Rephrase the sentence as: *The stream moves in a circular motion.* Explain that while both sentences mean the same thing, the original version uses one precise word—*swirls*—to create a clear image of how the stream moves.

Postreading
Additional Practice

Teacher Tip

During the activity Analyze Mood, help students identify the mood of the poem by allowing them to consider words that are not verbs, such as "broken" (line 3) and "pathos" (line 17).

Analyze Mood Support students in answering Thinking Critically question two on page 818 of the student book. Remind students that the mood of a poem refers to its atmosphere. Explain that the poet uses precise vocabulary to create vivid images in the poem. These images combine to create an overall feeling or mood. Point out examples of minimalist language that help create a mood of sadness, loneliness, or depression, such as "moans" (line 1), "crumbled" (line 12), and "slips . . . away" (line 19). Then invite students to locate other words or phrases in the poem that contribute to this mood.

Vocabulary and Comprehension

"Jade Flower Palace"

A. Write the verb from the Word Bank that relates to each of the following nouns from the poem.

Word Bank	
swirls	moans
scurry	whistle
roar	scatters
crumbled	slips (away)

1. storm _____ leaves

2. the future _____

3. stream _____

4. organ pipes _____ and _____

5. wind _____

6. painted cheeks _____

7. rats _____

B. Choose two words from the Word Bank. Write a sentence for each one.

1. _____

   _____

2. _____

   _____

C. Tell whether each of the following can be found in the palace, according to Tu Fu's poem. Write Y for yes or N for no.

1. gray rats _____

2. gold chariots _____

3. tree branches _____

4. a statue of a horse _____

5. dark rooms _____

6. stray cats _____

7. a prince _____

8. red leaves _____

Additional Vocabulary Practice

"Jade Flower Palace"

A. Write the word from the Word Bank that fits each definition, one letter to a space. Then unscramble the shaded letters to form a word related to the poem.

Word Bank	
swirls	moans
scatters	roar
slips (away)	crumbled

1. moves in circles __ __ __ __ __ __

2. moves quickly and quietly __ __ __ __ __

3. hurries away in different directions __ __ __ __ __ __ __ __

4. broke into small pieces __ __ __ __ __ __ __ __

5. makes a low, sad sound __ __ __ __ __

6. make a loud, deep noise __ __ __ __

Answer: __ __ __ __ __ __ __

B. Use each word from the Word Bank in a sentence.

1. _____

   _____

2. _____

   _____

3. _____

   _____

4. _____

   _____

5. _____

   _____

6. _____

   _____

"When I Have Fears" by John Keats

Prereading
Vocabulary Practice
Teach Unfamiliar Vocabulary Teach the following vocabulary prior to reading to aid students' comprehension of the selection.
- *gleaned* (line 2): collected together; gathered after the harvest
- *garners* (line 4): *(n)* stores or deposits

Alternative Activity
Focus on Sonnet Structure To provide additional information about sonnet structure, consider having students use the Before You Read page in *The Holt Reader,* either instead of or in addition to the Before You Read page in the student book.

Reading
Alternative Teaching Strategies
Identify Rhyme Scheme Remind students that "When I Have Fears" is a sonnet in the Shakespearean form. As they read, guide students to label and identify the rhyme scheme of the poem.

Use *The Holt Reader* Consider having students read the selection in *The Holt Reader* and use the margins to make notes and respond to instruction.

Postreading
Additional Support
Analyze the Simile Use the following steps to guide students in answering Thinking Critically question five on student book page 828:
- Question five asks about "books the speaker hopes to write." In the poem, what words relate to writing a book? *("pen," "brain," "books")*
- In harvesting, a garner holds wheat. Can your brain have a garner (store) of something? *(yes—ideas, experiences, imagination)*
- In the same part of the poem as "pen," "brain," and "books," the words "gleaned," "garners," and "full-ripened grain" appear. What do these words usually refer to? *(harvesting wheat)*

Focus on Text Structure For additional practice reading inverted syntax, have students complete the postreading activity in *The Holt Reader,* either instead of or in addition to the activities found in the student book.

SKILLS FOCUS

Literary Skill
Understand the sonnet form.

Reading Skill
Understand inverted syntax.

Resources

In this book:
- Vocabulary and Comprehension, p. 131
- Additional Vocabulary Practice, p. 135 (includes the next selection)

Other Resources:
- *The Holt Reader,* p. 188
- *Audio CD Library,* Disc 10
- *Audio CD Library, Selections and Summaries in Spanish*
- *Supporting Instruction in Spanish,* p. 35

Especially for ELL
Practice pronunciation and aural discrimination as students identify the rhyme scheme of the poem.

Core Skill
Use the resources in the Reading Skills and Strategies section of this book to help students having difficulty with figurative language. Use "When I Have Fears" for the application portion of the lesson.

TARGETED STRATEGIES FOR SPECIAL EDUCATION STUDENTS

Prereading
Alternative Teaching Strategy

Preview the Selection Prepare students to read "When I Have Fears" by reinforcing the information about sonnets presented on student book page 825. Have students set a purpose for reading: to identify the idea or problem presented in the first part of the poem, and to identify how the second part of the poem emphasizes or resolves this.

Reading
Alternative Teaching Strategies

Read with a Purpose As they read, help students fulfill the purpose for reading set during Prereading. Help them paraphrase the first line of the poem. *(possible: When I am scared that I will die)* Then focus on the use of "never" in lines 7, 10, and 11. Help students determine that the poet fears he will die too soon. He is afraid he won't have the chance to do all the things that he wants to do, and he fears he won't again have the chance to do the things he enjoys. Invite students to discuss how the author emphasizes this point at the end of the poem by stating that he will stand alone until the end.

(Core Skill) Analyze the Simile Remind students that a simile is a figure of speech that uses the word *like* or *as* to compare two things. Provide an example, such as *he is as hungry as a horse.* Then explain that in this poem, Keats uses a simile that is less obvious. Direct students to the word "like" in line 4. Help them understand how Keats uses the image of a stockpile of ripened grain to describe all the ideas in his imagination that he wants to include in a book.

Postreading
Additional Practice

Discuss Emotions Help students answer Thinking Critically question eight on student book page 828. Remind students that tone refers to the attitude with which a speaker presents a subject. Lead students to identify the tone(s) of the poem by focusing on specific passages. For example, the word "fears" in the first line denotes a fearful tone. The speaker's references to things he will never again be able to do might create for students a melancholy feeling or tone. Finally, students might think the end of the poem has a resigned tone because the speaker decides to overcome his fears alone.

Vocabulary and Comprehension

"When I Have Fears"

A. Complete each sentence with a word from the Word Bank.

> **Word Bank**
> cease
> gleaned
> garners
> ripened

1. The farmer saw that the grain had fully developed and _____.

2. So the farmer _____ the grain from the field.

3. The field was so big, he feared his work would never _____.

4. After he gleaned all the grain, he stored it in his _____.

B. Now complete each sentence about the poem with a word from the Word Bank.

1. The speaker fears his life will _____ before he has a chance to do everything that he wants to do.

2. The speaker compares _____ grain to his ideas and his imagination.

3. The speaker's mind is like the _____ that hold grain.

4. The speaker hopes to have _____ all the great ideas he holds in his mind before he dies.

C. Write T or F next to each sentence about the poem to tell if it is true or false.

1. _____ The speaker wants to write a book.

2. _____ The poem is about farming.

3. _____ The speaker does not want to die until he has experienced romantic adventures.

4. _____ The speaker's tone might be considered humorous and witty.

D. Choose a word from the Word Bank. Use it in a sentence.

1. _____

_____

Elements of Literature
pages 835–838

"Ode on a Grecian Urn" by John Keats

SKILLS FOCUS

Literary Skill
Understand metaphor.

Reading Skill
Visualize imagery.

(Resources)
In this book:
• Vocabulary and
Comprehension, p. 134
• Additional Vocabulary
Practice, p. 135 (includes
the previous selection)

Other Resources:
• *The Holt Reader,* p. 191
• *Audio CD Library,* Disc 10
• *Audio CD Library,
Selections and Summaries
in Spanish*
• *Supporting Instruction
in Spanish,* p. 36

(Core Skill)

Use the resources in the
Reading Skills and
Strategies section of this
book to help students
having difficulty with
figurative language. Use
"Ode on a Grecian Urn" for
the application portion
of the lesson.

Prereading

Vocabulary Practice

Teach Unfamiliar Vocabulary Prepare students to appreciate
Keats's use of rich language. Present the following adjectives and
their definitions prior to reading:
• *flowery* (line 4): full of detailed expressions
• *parching* (line 30): drying
• *silken* (line 34): smooth
• *desolate* (line 40): deserted, lifeless
• *trodden* (line 43): walked on

Alternative Activity

(Core Skill) Focus on Figurative Language: Metaphor To
provide additional information about metaphors, have students use
the Before You Read page in *The Holt Reader,* either instead of or in
addition to the Before You Read page in the student book.

Reading

Alternative Teaching Strategies

Discuss Imagery Point out new vocabulary in context. Replace the
adjectives with less vivid words to show how word choice affects
imagery. For example, substitute *detailed* for "flowery" (line 4) and
ask which word gives more information about the tale. *("flowery")*

Discuss Metaphors Reread the poem to focus on Keats's use of
metaphors. Revisit the explanation of "Thou still unravished bride
of quietness . . ." on student book page 835. Discuss the feelings this
comparison evokes, such as patience or innocence. Reword the line
in simple language: *You have been on the shelf for a long time.* Ask if
this statement has the same effect as the metaphor.

Use *The Holt Reader* Consider having students read the selection
in *The Holt Reader* and use the margins to make notes and respond
to instruction.

Postreading

Additional Activity

Visualize Imagery For additional practice visualizing imagery, have
students complete the postreading activity in *The Holt Reader,* either
instead of or in addition to the activities found in the student book.

TARGETED STRATEGIES FOR SPECIAL EDUCATION STUDENTS

SKILLS FOCUS

Literary Skill
Understand metaphor.

Reading Skill
Visualize imagery.

Resources

In this book:
• Vocabulary and Comprehension, p. 134
• Additional Vocabulary Practice, p. 135 (includes the previous selection)

Other Resources:
• *The Holt Reader,* p. 191
• *Audio CD Library,* Disc 10
• *Audio CD Library, Selections and Summaries in Spanish*
• *Supporting Instruction in Spanish,* p. 36

Prereading

Background

Set a Purpose for Reading Prepare students to appreciate Keats's use of metaphors and imagery. Prior to reading the poem, review the explanations of these literary devices on page 835 of the student book. Remind students that poets use such devices to provide vivid descriptions of their subject matter. Guide students to read the poem with a purpose: to identify and analyze metaphors and examples of imagery.

Reading

Alternative Teaching Strategy

Read with a Purpose Guide students in identifying and analyzing figures of speech in the poem. As they read, help them visualize specific images, such as the following: the "heifer lowing at the skies . . . her silken flanks with garlands dressed" (lines 33–34) and "forest branches and the trodden weed" (line 43). For each example, ask students why Keats might have chosen to use such rich language in his description. *(This language brings the subject matter to life by helping the reader visualize the image.)*

Remind students that imagery may appeal to senses other than vision. Direct students' attention to the following lines and ask which sense each appeals to: "Heard melodies are sweet, but those unheard/ Are sweeter" (lines 11–12: *hearing*); "A burning forehead, and a parching tongue" (line 30: *touch*). Ask students to share specific emotions each description makes them feel, such as *longing, adoration, desperation,* or *pain.*

Postreading

Additional Support

Make the Connection Support students' efforts to answer Thinking Critically question number eight on student book page 838. Discuss characteristics of Romantic poetry mentioned in the chapter introduction and in other poetry from this period that students have read. Refer students to the discussion of Romanticism on student book pages 712–713. Guide them to conclude that Keats's vivid appeals to the imagination are typical of poetry from the Romantic period.

Vocabulary and Comprehension

"Ode on a Grecian Urn"

A. Write each word from the Word Bank next to the word that has almost the same meaning.

Word Bank		
flowery	sweet	fair
bold	burning	parching
silken	desolate	trodden

1. brave _____

2. fiery _____

3. trampled _____

4. pleasant _____

5. detailed _____

6. drying _____

7. smooth _____

8. deserted _____

9. pretty _____

B. Answer the following questions.

1. Name three things in the first stanza to which the speaker compares the urn.

_____

_____

2. In the third stanza, why does the speaker say that the boughs and the melodist are so happy?

_____

_____

3. In the fourth stanza, what is the priest doing?

_____

_____

Additional Vocabulary Practice

"When I Have Fears";
"Ode on a Grecian Urn"

Circle the letter of the word that best completes each sentence.

1. The farmer picked the wheat as soon as it had _____.
   a. ceased **b.** gleaned **c.** garners **d.** ripened

2. The farmer _____ the wheat so he could store it during the winter.
   a. cease **b.** gleaned **c.** garners **d.** ripened

3. The farmer stores the wheat in _____ on his farm.
   a. cease **b.** gleaned **c.** garners **d.** ripened

4. Once the farmer begins work, he does not _____ until it is dark.
   a. cease **b.** gleaned **c.** garners **d.** ripened

5. The countries will _____ to fight, and there will be peace.
   a. roar **b.** trodden **c.** cease **d.** gleaned

6. He was constantly thirsty in the _____ heat of the desert.
   a. parching **b.** freezing **c.** bold **d.** flowery

7. The crushed flowers and leaves had obviously been _____.
   a. eaten **b.** trodden **c.** happy **d.** bold

8. The poet wrote in a _____ style. She used rich and exciting details.
   a. flowery **b.** boring **c.** burning **d.** parching

9. There were no animals or humans on the _____ island.
   a. populated **b.** desolate **c.** sweet **d.** silken

10. All the men in the kingdom loved the _____ princess.
   a. silken **b.** fair **c.** flowery **d.** desolate

11. The _____ firefighter risked his life to save the child from the burning building.
   a. bold **b.** parching **c.** hungry **d.** trodden

Collection 6
The Victorian Period: 1832–1901

Prereading

Vocabulary Practice

Teach Unfamiliar Vocabulary Teach the following words and definitions prior to reading.

- *middle class* (p. 876): class of society between the lower and upper, including professional workers and their families
- *aristocracy* (p. 877): the highest socioeconomic class in a society
- *working-class* (p. 877): of the class of people who are employed for wages, especially in manual or industrial labor

Alternative Activity

Read the Adaptation Distribute copies of the below–grade-level adapted reading for "The Victorian Period: 1832–1901" (available in this book and, with marginal questions, in *Holt Adapted Reader*). Have students read silently.

Reading

Alternative Teaching Strategy

Guide Students' Reading As an alternative to using the student book, consider having students read the on-level, shortened version of the introduction in *The Holt Reader* and use the margins to make notes and respond to instruction as they prepare to answer the Think About questions on student book page 878. As they read each section of the introduction, invite them to decide if it addresses one of these questions. Begin a three-column chart on the board, one column for each question. Each time students encounter an answer to one of these questions, record the information in the appropriate column on the chart. For example, after reading "The Idea of Progress" on student book page 880, students should add the word *progress* to the second column of the chart.

Postreading

Alternative Assessment

(**Core Skill**) **Reinforce the Main Ideas** Lead students to recap the main points of the chapter introduction. Refer them again to the questions on student book page 878 and the class chart on which they noted responses to these questions.

SKILLS FOCUS

Literary Skill
Evaluate the philosophical, political, religious, ethical, and social influences of a historical period.

(**Resources**)

In this book:
Adapted Readings

Other Resources:
- *The Holt Reader,* p. 197
- *Holt Adapted Reader*
- Video Segment 9

(**Especially for ELL**)

Use the timeline on student book pages 874–875 as a springboard for discussing world events during the 19th century. Invite English-language learners to share prior knowledge about their home countries during this period.

(**Core Skill**)

Use the resources in the Reading Skills and Strategies section of this book to help students having difficulty determining main idea. Use the collection introduction for the application portion of the lesson.

SKILLS FOCUS

Literary Skill
Evaluate the philosophical, political, religious, ethical, and social influences of a historical period.

<hr>

Resources

In this book:
Adapted Readings

Other Resources:
• The Holt Reader, p. 197
• *Holt Adapted Reader*
• Video Segment 9

<hr>

Teacher Tip

Taking notes is a skill that requires guidance and practice. As you read, stop at appropriate times and say: *This detail seems pretty important. Maybe we should record it.* Or challenge students by stopping and asking: *Does this seem important enough to write down? How can we summarize this passage?*

<hr>

Teacher Tip

Challenge students to correct each false statement in the Check Comprehension activity during Postreading.

TARGETED STRATEGIES FOR SPECIAL EDUCATION STUDENTS

Prereading
Additional Practice

Prepare to Read As students read Political and Social Milestones on student book pages 876–877, have them record specific details in their notebooks. For example, at the beginning of the first section, they might note: *The middle class wants more power in the government.* Have students record similar details for the remainder of this and the other two sections. Explain that they will read more about these details in the chapter introduction. Tell students they will add details to their notes as they read.

Reading
Alternative Teaching Strategy

Identify Paradoxes Point out these words in the chapter title: "paradox" and "progress." Explain that *progress* means *improvement.* Explain that a *paradox* is a seemingly contradictory or absurd statement that may be true. Help students identify paradoxical elements of the Victorian period as they read the introduction. For example, after reading "The Idea of Progress" and "The Hungry Forties" on student book pages 880–881, ask questions like the following: *How did Macaulay and his contemporaries feel about industrialization in England?* (They were confident that it improved society.) *Did it improve every element of society?* (No. Child labor, slum living, and pollution were all problems created by rapid industrialization.)

Postreading
Alternative Assessment

Check Comprehension Ask true/false questions like the ones below to check students' comprehension of the selection. Allow students to refer to their notes as they discuss the following:

1. England fought a major war against France during this era. *(F)*
2. The middle class agreed with Macaulay's positive view of English progress. *(T)*
3. During the 1840s, the cleanliness of the Thames River was considered a sign of progress. *(F)*
4. Attacks like Dickens's on the excesses of Victorian affluence were common in Victorian literature. *(T)*
5. Victorian literature caused people to think about the good and bad aspects of the era's progress. *(T)*

"Ulysses" by Alfred, Lord Tennyson

Prereading

Vocabulary Practice

Teach Unfamiliar Vocabulary Help students develop their vocabulary by teaching these words and their definitions:

- *hoard* (lines 5, 29): keep to oneself; store
- *margin* (line 20): the outside limit of something; the edge
- *yearning* (line 30): longing for sadly; wanting persistently

Use *The Holt Reader* You may consider having students use the Before You Read page in *The Holt Reader*, either instead of or in addition to the Before You Read page in the student book.

Reading

Alternative Teaching Strategy

(**Core Skill**) **Identify Personification** Challenge students to find the instance of personification in line 44. *("the vessel puffs her sail")* Ask what the vessel is doing. *(puffing her sails)* Ask if a boat can really puff her own sails. *(no)* Point out that a person can puff out his or her chest to show he or she is proud. Ask what this personification implies about what the ship wants or feels. *(Like Ulysses, the proud ship wants to sail again.)*

Alternative Activity

Read the Adaptation Distribute copies of the annotated version of "Ulysses" (available in this book and, with marginal questions, in *Holt Adapted Reader*). Have students read the selection silently.

Postreading

Alternative Activities

(**Mixed Ability Group**) **Discuss Theme** Guide students to discuss the theme of "Ulysses" through the following steps:

- Have pairs of students each write a sentence they think accurately states the theme of "Ulysses."
- Ask volunteers to write sentences on the board.
- Decide together which sentence most clearly states the theme of the poem.

Summarize the Poem For practice summarizing, have students complete the postreading activity in *The Holt Reader*.

Literary Skill
Understand theme.

(**Resources**)

In this book:
- Adapted Readings
- Vocabulary and Comprehension, p. 141
- Additional Vocabulary Practice, p. 145 (includes the next selection)

Other Resources:
- *The Holt Reader*, p. 206
- *Holt Adapted Reader*
- *Audio CD Library*, Disc 11
- *Audio CD Library, Selections and Summaries in Spanish*
- *Supporting Instruction in Spanish*, p. 37

(**Especially for ELL**)

If necessary, model reading aloud difficult lines for English-language learners. Then ask them to repeat, mimicking your pace, rhythm, and intonation.

(**Core Skill**)

Use the resources in the Reading Skills and Strategies section of this book to help students having difficulty recognizing theme. Use "Ulysses" for the application portion of the lesson.

SKILLS FOCUS

Literary Skill
Understand theme.

(**Resources**)

In this book:
• Adapted Readings
• Vocabulary and
Comprehension, p. 141
• Additional Vocabulary
Practice, p. 145 (includes
the next selection)

Other Resources:
• *The Holt Reader,* p. 206
• *Holt Adapted Reader*
• *Audio CD Library,* Disc 11
• *Audio CD Library,
Selections and Summaries
in Spanish*
• *Supporting Instruction
in Spanish,* p. 37

(**Mixed Ability Group**)

Depending on the number
of students in your class,
you may wish to jigsaw the
outline activity, assigning
each section of the poem
to one individual, pair, or
group of students for
analysis. Students can then
work as a whole group
to compile their
separate findings into a
completed outline.

TARGETED STRATEGIES FOR SPECIAL EDUCATION STUDENTS

Prereading

Alternative Teaching Strategy

Preview the Selection Remind students that Ulysses was an ancient Greek hero who traveled widely, fought bravely, had many adventures, and later became a king. Explain that, in this poem, Tennyson uses the hero Ulysses to say something about old age. Guide students to set a purpose for reading: to think about the poem's theme—its specific message about old age.

Reading

Alternative Activity

Outline the Poem Help students better understand "Ulysses" by having them focus on one short section of the poem at a time. On the board, provide the poem's main ideas in the form of this outline starter:

    I. Ulysses tells about his past and present. (lines 1–21)

    II. Ulysses gives an opinion about quiet old age. (lines 22–32)

    III. Ulysses introduces his son Telemachus. (lines 33–43)

    IV. Ulysses thinks about having more adventures before he dies. (lines 44–70)

Have students copy the outline starter into their notebooks. Instruct them to use a whole side of a sheet of paper, leaving plenty of space between each of the four main ideas. First read the poem once through, or play the audio recording as students follow along silently. Then have them read it again, focusing on the numbered sections in the outline. Ask them to complete the outline with details that support the main idea of each section.

Postreading

Alternative Activity

(**Core Skill**) **Determine the Theme** Write on the board the following statements about old age:

    • Old age is a time for peace and quiet, not action.

    • You can't teach an old dog new tricks.

    • Getting old doesn't mean that you can't learn and do new things.

Have students discuss which sentence best states the theme of the poem. *(Getting old doesn't mean that you can't learn and do new things.)* Invite them to identify and read aloud lines that support this statement.

Vocabulary and Comprehension

"Ulysses"

A. Choose the word from the Word Bank that best completes each sentence. Write the word on the line.

Word Bank	
hoard	margin
mild	toil
yearning	yield

1. _____ is hard, exhausting work.

2. If you are wishing for something, you are _____ for it.

3. If you give up in a struggle or fight, you _____.

4. If you keep everything to yourself, you _____ things.

5. The outside border of something is its _____.

6. If someone is _____, he or she is very gentle.

B. Choose three words from the Word Bank. Use each word in a sentence of your own.

1. _____

_____

2. _____

_____

3. _____

_____

C. Write YES or NO to tell whether each sentence below sounds like something Ulysses would say. Use what you read about his character in the poem to help you.

1. "I am happy to stay home with my young wife." _____

2. "I have been to many places and met many different people." _____

3. "I am leaving my son Telemachus in charge of the kingdom."_____

4. "I have a group of loyal sailors who have traveled with me many times." _____

5. "This journey is not dangerous." _____

6. "I plan to have lunch with Achilles tomorrow." _____

"My Last Duchess" by Robert Browning

SKILLS FOCUS

Literary Skill
Understand the characteristics of dramatic monologue.

Reading Skill
Draw inferences from textual clues.

(**Resources**)

In this book:
• Vocabulary and Comprehension, p. 144
• Additional Vocabulary Practice, p. 145 (includes the previous selection)

Other Resources:
• *The Holt Reader*, p. 211
• *Audio CD Library,* Disc 11
• *Audio CD Library, Selections and Summaries in Spanish*
• *Supporting Instruction in Spanish*, p. 38

Prereading

Vocabulary Practice

Teach Unfamiliar Vocabulary Help students understand the selection by teaching these words and their definitions:

- *countenance* (line 7): a face showing mood or emotion
- *earnest* (line 8): serious and eager
- *stoop* (line 43): submit; descend from higher to lower dignity
- *pretense* (line 50): a claim made, especially one that is not supported by fact
- *dowry* (line 51): the money, goods, or estate that a woman brings with her when she marries

Use *The Holt Reader* To teach students how to make inferences, you may consider having them use the Before You Read page in *The Holt Reader*, either instead of or in addition to the Before You Read page in the student book.

Reading

Alternative Teaching Strategy

Focus on the Speaker As students read, remind them that the Duke is trying to impress the Count's representative. Consider having students read the selection in *The Holt Reader* and use the margins to make notes or highlight specific passages in which this attempt to influence is obvious.

Postreading

Listening and Speaking Opportunity

(**Especially for ELL**) **Make Associations** Prepare English-language learners for the Listening and Speaking activity on student book page 912 by discussing interpretations of the Duke's tone. Students might think of a villain as they try to read with a sinister tone or of something sad as they try to read with a mournful tone.

Alternative Activity

Discover Details For practice using details to make inferences, have students complete the postreading activity in *The Holt Reader*, either instead of or in addition to the activities found in the student book.

TARGETED STRATEGIES FOR SPECIAL EDUCATION STUDENTS

Prereading
Reteach the Key Idea

Discuss Dramatic Monologues Revisit the Literary Focus lesson on student book page 908. Highlight the idea that in dramatic monologues, speakers reveal information about themselves, the other characters, and the situation by dropping indirect clues. Tell students that as they read, they will look for indirect clues that tell about the speaker and his last Duchess.

Reading
Alternative Activities

Use a Chart As they read, help students complete the Reading Skills activity on student book page 908. Simplify the activity by focusing on only the Duke and his last Duchess. Point out that because the Duke is relating all the information, the reader only knows his point of view. For example, the reader can infer that he thinks the Duchess is flirtatious, but she may have been only young, fun-loving, and naïve. Record students' ideas on a chart like the one shown below.

character	personality	situation	motives
Duke	jealous (lines 3–15, 24, 29–32)	looking for a new wife (lines 49–53)	wants to impress (lines 33, 54–56)
Duchess	flirtatious (lines 19–29)	enjoying the duke's wealth (lines 25, 28–29, 32–33)	young (student book page 908)

(Mixed Ability Group) Jigsaw the Reading Have students read "Scenes from a Modern Marriage" together as a class. Then have small groups work together, each group paraphrasing one paragraph. Finally, reconvene and have groups share their paraphrased sections.

Postreading
Listening and Speaking Opportunity

Prepare with Audio Prepare students for the Listening and Speaking activity on student book page 912. Have them listen to the audio recording of the selection. As they listen, ask them to imagine what facial expressions and gestures the speaker might use. For example, suggest that a sinister Duke might speak slowly, squint his eyes and frown as he reads lines 45–47. A regretful Duke might hang his head in sorrow and wipe away his tears as he reads the same lines.

SKILLS FOCUS

Literary Skill
Understand the characteristics of dramatic monologue.

Reading Skill
Draw inferences from textual clues.

(Resources)
In this book:
- Vocabulary and Comprehension, p. 144
- Additional Vocabulary Practice, p. 145 (includes the previous selection)

Other Resources:
- *The Holt Reader,* p. 211
- *Audio CD Library,* Disc 11
- *Audio CD Library, Selections and Summaries in Spanish*
- *Supporting Instruction in Spanish,* p. 38

Vocabulary and Comprehension

"My Last Duchess"

A. Match each word from the Word Bank to the related group of words. Write the word on the line.

> **Word Bank**
> countenance
> dowry
> earnest
> exceed

1. _____ serious, eager, intent

2. _____ face, expression, looks

3. _____ outrun, outdo, more

4. _____ money, marriage, wife

B. Choose three words from the Word Bank. Use each word in a sentence of your own.

1. _____

_____

2. _____

_____

3. _____

_____

C. Circle the letter of the answer that is closest in meaning to each quotation from the poem.

1. "not the first/ Are you to turn and ask thus" (lines 12–13)

a. You are the first to turn around.

b. It's your turn to ask questions.

c. You are not the first person to ask this.

2. "to make your will/ Quite clear to such an one" (lines 36–37)

a. I don't understand what you said.

b. to make someone understand what you want

c. to write a will that is easy to read

3. "and I choose/ Never to stoop" (lines 42–43)

a. I do not enjoy bending over to pick things up.

b. I don't like those steps.

c. I will never lower my standards for conduct.

Additional Vocabulary Practice

"Ulysses"; "My Last Duchess"

A. Use the Word Bank and the clues to complete the crossword puzzle below. Note that not all the words in the Word Bank are used in the puzzle.

Word Bank		
countenance	dowry	earnest
exceed	pretense	stoop
hoard	margin	mild
toil	yearning	yield

Across

3. wanting something

4. a claim made that is not supported by fact

5. to keep to oneself; to store

7. serious and eager

Down

1. face or expression

2. outside limit

3. to give in

6. marriage money

B. Choose five words from the Word Bank. Use each word in a sentence.

1. _____

    _____

2. _____

    _____

3. _____

    _____

4. _____

    _____

5. _____

    _____

Sonnet 43 by Elizabeth Barrett Browning

SKILLS FOCUS

Literary Skill
Understand the Petrarchan sonnet form.

(Resources)

In this book:
• Vocabulary and Comprehension, p. 148
• Additional Vocabulary Practice, p. 152 (includes the next selection)

Other Resources:
• *The Holt Reader,* p. 216
• *Audio CD Library,* Disc 11
• *Audio CD Library, Selections and Summaries in Spanish*
• *Supporting Instruction in Spanish,* p. 38

(Especially for ELL)

Point out to English-language learners that *thee* and *shall* are words that are not commonly used in modern-day English. Explain that *thee* means *you* and *shall* means *will.*

(Core Skill)

Use the resources in the Reading Skills and Strategies section of this book to help students having difficulty recognizing theme. Use Sonnet 43 for the application portion of the lesson.

Prereading

Vocabulary Practice

Teach Unfamiliar Vocabulary Present the following words and definitions to help students appreciate the language of Sonnet 43.

• *breadth* (line 2): distance from one side of something to the other
• *soul* (line 3): an entity thought to be the moral or spiritual part of a person
• *strive* (line 7): make a great effort
• *passion* (line 9): a very strong feeling, such as anger, love, or hatred

Alternative Teaching Strategies

(Mixed Ability Group) Prepare to Read Poetry Have students work in pairs to determine the rhyme scheme of the poem. Then, refer to the explanation of sonnet rhyme scheme on page 914 of the student book. Ask if the rhyme scheme of Sonnet 43 matches this explanation. *(yes)* Also remind students that commas and dashes indicate pauses while reading.

Focus on Paraphrasing To introduce paraphrasing, have students use the Before You Read page in *The Holt Reader,* either instead of or in addition to the Before You Read page in the student book.

Reading

Listening and Speaking Opportunity

Listen and Read Aloud Play the audio recording of Sonnet 43. Encourage students to listen a few times as they read along in *The Holt Reader,* using the margins to make notes and respond to instruction. Then, invite them to read the poem aloud along with the recording, keeping in mind the rhyme scheme and punctuation.

Postreading

Alternative Teaching Strategy

Discuss Emotional Effects Prepare students to answer Thinking Critically question four on page 915 of the student book. Guide students to use the chart in the postreading section of *The Holt Reader* as they paraphrase each idea in Sonnet 43.

TARGETED STRATEGIES FOR SPECIAL EDUCATION STUDENTS

Prereading
Background

Activate Prior Knowledge To help students complete the Quickwrite activity on page 914 in the student book, invite them to think about someone they love. Encourage them to consider family members or friends as well as romantic interests. Have them privately make notes of reasons why they love that person. Tell students that Sonnet 43 is a love poem that expresses the poet's feelings for her beloved.

Reading
Alternative Teaching Strategy

Listen to Poetry Prepare students to answer Thinking Critically question three on page 915 of the student book. Play the audio recording of the selection as students read the poem silently. Play the recording again, this time having them focus on the rhythm of the poem. Guide students to pay special attention to how the rhythm of the last three lines differs from that of the others. In addition to the change in rhythm, point out that words such as "tears" and "death" provide clues about the change in meaning at the end of the poem.

Postreading
Alternative Activity

Write a Poem Guide students to write short love poems that answer the question: How do I love you? Provide the following frame for their writing, based on Sonnet 43. To help students maintain the rhythm of a sonnet, explain that each blank space represents a syllable. Remind students that each line in their poem should contain ten syllables.

How do I love you? _____ _____ _____ _____ _____.

I love you _____ _____ _____ _____ _____ _____ _____

_____ _____ _____ _____ _____ _____ _____ _____ _____

_____ _____ _____ _____ _____ _____ _____ _____ _____.

Guide students in writing by having them:
- refer to their Prereading notes about someone they love.
- brainstorm rhyming words as a class to help them follow the rhyme scheme *abba*.
- use commas to separate ideas and clarify meaning.

Literary Skill
Understand the Petrarchan sonnet form.

Resources

In this book:
- Vocabulary and Comprehension, p. 148
- Additional Vocabulary Practice, p. 152 (includes the next selection)

Other Resources:
- *The Holt Reader*, p. 216
- *Audio CD Library*, Disc 11
- *Audio CD Library, Selections and Summaries in Spanish*
- *Supporting Instruction in Spanish*, p. 38

Teacher Tip

As students' poems may be emotional and highly personal, assure them that you will not read their writing unless they would like to share it.

Vocabulary and Comprehension

Sonnet 43

A. Write C or I next to each sentence to indicate whether the underlined word is used correctly or incorrectly.

1. I want to explore the ocean's <u>depth</u>. _____

2. The woman ate <u>breadth</u> with her soup. _____

3. That man's <u>height</u> is 6 feet. _____

4. His death made me sad and pained my <u>soul</u>. _____

5. She will <u>strive</u> the salad at lunch. _____

6. The lady plants <u>passion</u> in her garden. _____

B. Choose four words that are underlined in the previous exercise. Use each word correctly in a new sentence.

1. _____

_____

2. _____

_____

3. _____

_____

4. _____

_____

C. Write T or F to tell whether each statement below is true or false.

1. Elizabeth Barrett Browning translated all her sonnets from Portuguese. _____

2. An octave consists of eight lines. _____

3. Sonnet 43 is about the great love the speaker feels for someone. _____

4. Petrarchan sonnets are written in iambic pentameter. _____

5. The rhyme scheme for Petrarchan sonnets is *abacadababbcca*. _____

"Dover Beach" by Matthew Arnold

Prereading

Vocabulary Practice

(**Especially for ELL**) **Teach Unfamiliar Vocabulary** Help English-language learners understand the selection by previewing these words and their definitions:

- *grating* (line 9): making a scraping sound
- *cadence* (line 13): the rhythmic repetition of a sound
- *ebb* (line 17): when the tide goes down and back out to sea

Alternative Teaching Strategy

Focus on Mood To introduce mood, you may consider having students use the Before You Read page in *The Holt Reader*.

Reading

Alternative Teaching Strategies

Discuss Mood and Imagery As students read, focus on specific lines to prepare them to answer Thinking Critically questions two and three on page 924 of the student book. For example, after reading lines 1–6, ask: *Which words describe a beautiful seascape?* ("calm," "fair," "glimmering," "tranquil," "sweet")

Use *The Holt Reader* Consider having students read the selection in *The Holt Reader* and use the margins to make notes and respond to instruction.

Postreading

Alternative Teaching Strategies

(**Core Skill**) **Discuss Theme** Remind students that the poem talks about society's moving away from faith and concerning itself only with concrete reality. Reread the last stanza. Ask: *Which lines state that the world does not really provide all the pleasures that some people think it does?* (lines 30–34) *Which words describe a world without faith?* ("darkling," "confused alarms," "struggle," "flight," "ignorant," "clash")

Determine Mood For practice determining mood, have students complete the postreading activity in *The Holt Reader*.

SKILLS FOCUS

Literary Skill
Understand mood.

(**Resources**)

In this book:
- Vocabulary and Comprehension, p. 151
- Additional Vocabulary Practice, p. 152 (includes the previous selection)

Other Resources:
- *The Holt Reader*, p. 219
- *Audio CD Library*, Disc 11
- *Audio CD Library, Selections and Summaries in Spanish*
- *Supporting Instruction in Spanish*, p. 38

(**Core Skill**)

Use the resources in the Reading Skills and Strategies section of this book to help students having difficulty recognizing theme. Use "Dover Beach" for the application portion of the lesson.

Literary Skill
Understand mood.

(**Resources**)

In this book:
• Vocabulary and
Comprehension, p. 151
• Additional Vocabulary
Practice, p. 152 (includes
the previous selection)

Other Resources:
• *The Holt Reader*, p. 219
• *Audio CD Library*, Disc 11
• *Audio CD Library,
Selections and Summaries
in Spanish*
• *Supporting Instruction
in Spanish*, p. 38

TARGETED STRATEGIES FOR SPECIAL EDUCATION STUDENTS

Prereading
Alternative Teaching Strategies

Discuss the Subject Refer to the Quickwrite activity on page 921 of the student book and ask students to share their lists of people, places, or things they would depend on in times of trouble. Point out that "Dover Beach" contains a lot of imagery about the sea, but it is really about a subject that is similar to that of their lists.

Review Background Explain that "Dover Beach" is a poem that involves a person and a place that were both very important to the poet Matthew Arnold. Have students read about the background of the poem on student book page 921. Ask: *Who is the person that was important to Arnold?* (his wife) *What is the place that was important to him?* (Dover Beach) *Why was that place important?* (He and his wife spent part of their honeymoon there.)

Reading
Alternative Activity

Discuss the Poem Guide students to understand the poem by helping them identify some words and phrases that help create the images and mood of each stanza. For example:

Stanza One
- Imagery: the sea coast at Dover Beach at night—"calm," "moon," "cliffs," "glimmering," "vast," "tranquil," "line of spray," "grating roar," "draw back," "fling," "cadence"
- Mood: happiness and beauty—"fair," "glimmering," "tranquil"; mystery—"vast," "eternal note of sadness"

Stanza Two
- Imagery: Sophocles gazing at the sea long ago—"Sophocles," "Aegean," "sea"
- Mood: thoughtful—"mind," "thought"

Postreading
Alternative Teaching Strategy

Sum Up the Theme Help students sum up the poem's message about faith by asking questions such as the following:
- Does Arnold think the world is gaining or losing faith? Where does he show this? (lines 24–28: *losing*)
- What faith does he consider important to maintain? Where does he show this? (lines 29–30: *faith in loved ones*)

Vocabulary and Comprehension

"Dover Beach"

A. Use a word from the Word Bank to complete each sentence.

Word Bank	
cadence	ebb
flight	glimmering
grating	tide

1. The _____ is when the sea recedes or goes away from the shore.

2. The act of escaping or running away is _____.

3. A _____ is the rhythmic repetition of a sound.

4. The _____ is the cycle in which the sea level rises and falls.

5. When something is shining faintly, it is _____.

6. If you are making a scraping or scratching sound, you are _____.

B. Circle the letter of the answer that most closely matches the meaning of each phrase or sentence from the poem.

1. "The tide is full" means
   a. that the sea is at its highest point.
   b. that the sea is filled with water.
   c. that the sea is at its lowest point.

2. "[I]t brought/ Into his mind" means
   a. that his mind was brought out.
   b. that it erased his memory.
   c. that it reminded him.

3. "[L]et us be true/ To one another" means
   a. everything we say is a lie.
   b. we should be faithful and honest with one another.
   c. we can never truly know people.

C. Answer the questions below.

1. What historical character does Arnold talk about to link the past and the present?

   _____

   _____

2. In the third stanza, to what does Arnold compare the receding shoreline?

   _____

   _____

Additional Vocabulary Practice

Sonnet 43; "Dover Beach"

A. Write the word from the Word Bank that best fits each
definition. Write one letter in each space. Then unscramble
the letters in the shaded areas to form a phrase that is
repeated in Sonnet 43. (You will not use all of the words
in the Word Bank.)

Word Bank	
depth	breadth
height	soul
strive	passion
griefs	

1. it indicates how wide something is __ __ ▢ __ __ ▢

2. spiritual part of a person __ ▢ __ ▢

3. a strong feeling towards something __ __ __ __ ▢ __ __

4. it indicates how tall something is __ ▢ __ __ __ ▢

5. make an effort __ __ __ __ ▢ ▢

Phrase: __   __ __ __ __   __ __ __ __

B. Write C or I after each sentence to tell if the underlined word is used correctly or
incorrectly. If the word is used incorrectly, write a sentence using it correctly.

1. He <u>tide</u> the two pieces of string together.

_____

_____

2. She loved the <u>cadence</u> of Matthew Arnold's poems.

_____

_____

3. If you keep <u>glimmering</u> the french fries, you will burn them.

_____

_____

4. For breakfast, I had a fried <u>ebb</u> and some orange juice.

_____

_____

5. The guards did not know about the prisoners' <u>flight</u> from jail.

_____

_____

"The Bet" by Anton Chekhov,
translated by Constance Garnett

Prereading

Vocabulary Practice

(**Especially for ELL**) **Teach Unfamiliar Vocabulary** To provide English-language learners with extra vocabulary support, introduce the words and definitions below before they read the selection. Use contextually-rich scenarios to reinforce meanings. For example, explain the words within the context of an imaginary criminal and his potential fate.

- *capital punishment* (p. 967): punishment by being put to death
- *death penalty* (p. 967): punishment by being put to death
- *imprisonment* (*for life*) (p. 967): confinement; the state of being put in jail
- *solitary confinement* (p. 967): isolation of a prisoner in a separate cell as a punishment
- *speculation* (p. 970): the act of investing money in stocks or businesses in the hope of gain but with the possibility of loss

Alternative Activities

Read the Adaptation Distribute copies of the adapted reading of "The Bet" (available in this book and, with marginal questions, in *Holt Adapted Reader*). Have all students read the selection silently.

(**Core Skill**) **Focus on Theme** To introduce the multiple themes found in "The Bet," you may consider having students use the Before You Read page in *The Holt Reader,* either instead of or in addition to the Before You Read page in the student book.

Use Spanish Resources Spanish-speaking students can read the printed Spanish summary or listen to the recording of the story in Spanish.

SKILLS FOCUS

Literary Skill
Understand theme.

Reading Skills
- Make predictions.
- Revise predictions.

(**Resources**)

In this book:
- Adapted Readings
- Vocabulary and Comprehension, p. 157
- Additional Vocabulary Practice, p. 158

Other Resources:
- *The Holt Reader,* p. 224
- *Holt Adapted Reader*
- *Audio CD Library,* Disc 13
- *Audio CD Library, Selections and Summaries in Spanish*
- *Supporting Instruction in Spanish,* p. 42

(**Teacher Tip**)

Capital punishment is an emotional and controversial topic. As you discuss the vocabulary and subject matter of "The Bet," be sensitive to students' personal beliefs and religious orientations.

Teacher Tip

The Reading activities on this page leave room for individual opinions. Encourage students to talk about and share their interpretations without worrying about whether they are right or wrong.

Background

Connect to the Author's Biography After students read the author's biography on student book page 965, provide them with additional information about the author's style. As students complete the chart in the Focus on Character activity on the next page, they should consider how this selection is typical of Chekhov's style.

Reading

Alternative Teaching Strategies

(Core Skill) Make Predictions Using steps like the ones shown below to guide students in making predictions as they read, have students read the selection in *The Holt Reader* and use the margins to make notes and respond to instruction. Note that students' predictions may vary.

1. Ask: *What do you think is going to happen?*

2. Provide options to help students express themselves such as: *Do you think the lawyer will stay in the lodge for fifteen years and win the bet, or do you think he will leave early?*

3. Have students record their predictions in their notebooks, for example: *I think that the lawyer will leave early.*

4. Challenge students to justify their predictions with examples from the story, such as: *Fifteen years is a long time. The banker says that voluntary confinement is more difficult than compulsory confinement. If the lawyer leaves only two minutes before fifteen years have passed, the banker does not have to pay. The lawyer is depressed and lonely in the first year.*

5. After students read passages that confirm or disprove their predictions, model sentences to help them express themselves, such as: *I thought the lawyer would leave early because he was sad. Instead he left early because he renounced the money.* Instruct students to revise their predictions in their notebooks by writing what actually happened.

Especially for ELL

As you make the character chart, reinforce subject-verb agreement between the pronoun *he* and the present-tense verbs. For example, record *He _____ capital punishment is worse than imprisonment for life.* Ask students whether the verb should be *think* or *thinks*.

(Mixed Ability Group) Focus on Character As students read "The Bet," focus their attention on how Chekhov develops the two main characters: the lawyer and the banker. Create on the board a two-column chart, one column for each character. After students have finished reading, have small groups add to the chart details about each character. For example, after reading the first two paragraphs, students may note the following: *the banker hosts a party; the banker considers the death penalty more humane than life imprisonment.* After the fourth paragraph, students can add: *the lawyer considers life imprisonment preferable to capital punishment.* Continue to note important details about these characters' actions, beliefs, and feelings. Students will use this chart during Postreading to analyze the selection's theme.

Postreading

Alternative Teaching Strategies

(Core Skill) **Focus on Theme** Explain that readers can analyze characters to gain insight into how a selection represents a comment on life. Revisit the two-column character chart you created during Reading. Guide students in understanding how the changes that each character undergoes represent a view or comment on life. For example, you might ask questions like the following about the banker:

- Is the banker wealthy at the beginning of the story? *(yes)*
- What bet does the banker make? *(He bets that the lawyer can't endure solitary confinement for fifteen years.)*
- How does the banker feel at the beginning? Is he confident and happy or desperate and miserable? *(confident and happy)*
- How does the banker's financial position change by the end of the story? *(He becomes poor.)* How does he become poor? *(He gambles away all his money in the stock market.)*
- At the end, is the banker still confident and happy? *(No, he is miserable and desperate.)* Why? *(He knows he will lose the bet. If he loses and pays the lawyer, he won't have any money left.)*
- Based on the banker's experiences, how do you think Chekhov feels about gambling and money? *(possible: Gambling is dangerous; money makes people act desperately and immorally.)*

(Core Skill) **Check Predictions** To compare students' predictions with the story's events, have them complete the postreading activity in *The Holt Reader,* either instead of or in addition to the activities found in the student book.

Reading Skills Development

(Mixed Ability Group) **Make Predictions** Emphasize to students that one purpose of making predictions is to become more aware of the different twists and turns a plot might take. Choose a selection from the Making Predictions section of the list that begins on page 225 of this book. Group students of mixed ability levels, and direct each group's members to use a variation of Popcorn Reading to read aloud the selection. Instead of saying "popcorn" to pass the reading turn on to the next member, students should share a prediction about what might happen next in the story. Encourage the other group members to suggest their own imaginative predictions. The group as a whole should discuss reasons for discarding some predictions and revising and keeping others. After the groups have finished, have volunteers share their groups' reading experiences and predictions.

(Core Skill)

Use the resources in the Reading Skills and Strategies section of this book to help students having difficulty making predictions. Use "The Bet" for the application portion of the lesson.

Literary Skill
Understand theme.

Reading Skills
• Make predictions.
• Revise predictions.

(Resources)
In this book:
• Adapted Readings
• Vocabulary and
Comprehension, p. 157
• Additional Vocabulary
Practice, p. 158

Other Resources:
• *The Holt Reader*, p. 224
• *Holt Adapted Reader*
• *Audio CD Library*, Disc 13
• *Audio CD Library,
Selections and Summaries
in Spanish*
• *Supporting Instruction
in Spanish*, p. 42

(Teacher Tip)
Encourage students to
make predictions without
worrying whether they are
right or wrong. Explain that
two people can interpret
the same set of clues
differently. For example,
students might consider the
lawyer's confidence before
the bet a clue that he will
win, or they might think his
confidence will fade
and he will lose.

Targeted Strategies for Special Education Students

Prereading
Reteach the Key Idea

(Core Skill) **Discuss Theme** Before students read, reinforce the definition of theme presented on student book page 966: the overall meaning of a work of literature that usually expresses a view or comment on life. Use the example about growing up on student book page 966 to illustrate the difference between theme and subject. (In this case, the subject of the story is *growing up* while the theme is *disillusionment is part of the maturation process*.)

Then provide a simple summary of "The Bet," such as: *A banker makes a bet with a lawyer. He bets the lawyer cannot stay in solitary confinement for fifteen years. If the lawyer wins, the banker will pay him two million dollars.*

Help students name the subject of this story. (*a bet*) Have students set a purpose for reading: to determine the theme of "The Bet."

Reading
Alternative Teaching Strategy

(Core Skill) **Make Predictions** As students read, point out clues that suggest what will happen to the characters in the story. For example, from the beginning of section two on student book page 970 until the banker reads the lawyer's letter, there are numerous clues that foreshadow the banker's intent to kill the lawyer. Point out lines in this section such as "If I do pay him . . . I shall be utterly ruined" and "The one means of being saved . . . is the death of that man!" As students read this section, ask them what they think the banker will do. Once they finish reading the lawyer's letter on student book page 972, invite them to revise their predictions before they read the story's conclusion.

Postreading
Alternative Teaching Strategy

(Core Skill) **Identify the Theme** After students read, guide them in identifying the theme of the story. Note that students may name different themes. Accept all reasonable answers, provided they are justified with textual support. For example, one student might believe Chekhov's message to be: *Knowledge and wisdom are more important than a lot of money.* This student can support his or her analysis with details about the lawyer's change and development during his fifteen years of solitude.

Vocabulary and Comprehension

"The Bet"

A. Write YES or NO to answer each question based on the definition of the underlined word.

1. If you completely <u>renounce</u> chocolate, do you stop eating it? _____

2. If something is <u>compulsory</u>, do you have to do it? _____

3. If you buy clothes <u>indiscriminately</u>, do you make careful choices about them? _____

4. If you want to learn something very well, do you study it <u>zealously</u>? _____

5. If you feel <u>contempt</u> for something, do you like it? _____

6. If you have the <u>intention</u> of doing something, do you plan to do it? _____

B. Match the activities with the time periods in which the lawyer did them. Write the letter of each activity next to its corresponding time.

1. _____ first year
2. _____ second year
3. _____ fifth year
4. _____ sixth to tenth years
5. _____ eleventh to thirteenth years
6. _____ last two years

a. ate, drank wine, slept, wrote
b. read the Bible and theology books
c. played the piano, read light novels and fantastic stories
d. read about natural sciences, chemistry, and medicine
e. read only classic works of literature
f. studied languages, philosophy, and history

C. Answer the questions below in complete sentences.

1. According to the terms of confinement, what was the lawyer *not* allowed to do?

_____

_____

2. How did the lawyer ask for and receive the things he wanted?

_____

_____

3. Why did the banker decide to kill the lawyer on the last day of the bet?

_____

_____

4. Why didn't the banker kill the lawyer?

_____

_____

Additional Vocabulary Practice

"The Bet"

A. Select two terms from the Word Bank that best complete each sentence. Write the words on lines.

Word Bank	
despise	punishment
solitary confinement	speculation
contempt	imprisonment
death penalty	intention

1. When you invest in a risky business

   through _____,

   your _____ may be to quickly make money.

2. The most extreme form of _____ is the _____,

   when a person is executed.

3. If you hate or _____ someone, you might treat them

   with _____, or lack of respect.

4. _____, in which a prisoner doesn't have contact with

   other people, is a form of _____.

B. Draw a line from the vocabulary word to the best definition.

1. caprice   **a.** not serious

2. ethereal   **b.** sudden desire

3. frivolous   **c.** false

4. illusory   **d.** descendants

5. posterity   **e.** heavenly

C. Select three words from Part B. Use each word in a sentence.

1. _____

   _____

2. _____

   _____

3. _____

   _____

Collection 7
The Modern World: 1900 to the Present

Elements of Literature
pages 1016–1036

Prereading

Additional Practice

Focus on Historical Background Help students appreciate the historical context of the collection introduction by reviewing certain events in the timeline on student book pages 1018–1019. Discuss each section of the timeline to provide students with additional information about these topics.

Alternative Teaching Strategy

Read the Adaptation Distribute copies of the below–grade-level adapted reading for "The Modern World: 1900 to the Present" (available in this book and, with marginal questions, in *Holt Adapted Reader*). Have students read silently.

Reading

Alternative Teaching Strategies

Check Comprehension Check students' comprehension as they read, rather than at the end of the selection. This allows you to clarify misunderstandings and eliminate confusion while students' questions are fresh in their minds and before asking them to move on to the next section. For example, you might ask questions like the following after reading the first paragraph in "The Great War: 'A War to End All Wars'" on student book page 1025:

- Who were Britain's allies in the Great War? *(France and Russia)*
- Whom did they unite against? *(Germany and Austria-Hungary)*
- What name was later given to the Great War? *(World War I)*

Use *The Holt Reader* You may have students read the on-level, shortened version of the introduction in *The Holt Reader* and respond to the instruction in its margins.

Postreading

Listening and Speaking Opportunity

(**Especially for ELL**) **Talk About It** Support ELLs during the Talk About activity on student book page 1036 by pointing out clues in the text.

Literary Skills
Evaluate the philosophical, political, religious, ethical, and social influences of a historical period.

(**Resources**)

In this book:
- Adapted Readings

Other Resources:
- *The Holt Reader*, p. 237
- *Holt Adapted Reader*
- Video Segments 10, 11

(**Cultural Tip**)

During Prereading, invite students to share other events from modern history with which they are familiar.

(**Especially for ELL**)

ELLs may have difficulty expressing their ideas in a manner consistent with the standards of their age group. Because receptive language skills develop prior to expressive skills, use the former to elicit the latter. For example, suggest two conflicting ideas using advanced language, and ask students to determine with which idea they agree.

Literary Skills
Evaluate the philosophical, political, religious, ethical, and social influences of a historical period.

Resources

In this book:
• Adapted Readings

Other Resources:
• *The Holt Reader,* p. 237
• *Holt Adapted Reader*
• Video Segments 10, 11

Teacher Tip

Provide students with model summaries of specific sections in a reading to build their reading skills. In this way you also support comprehension by helping them determine what each section is about.

Teacher Tip

During the Postreading discussion, invite students to share examples of popular culture. Encourage a variety of opinions about shock value by being open to different views and ideas.

Targeted Strategies for Special Education Students

Prereading
Alternative Activity

Set a Purpose for Reading Prepare students to read by setting a purpose for reading. Provide summaries like the ones shown below. Tell students that as they read, they will identify the section each summary addresses. For example:

• The writings of these philosophers caused people to question the social, religious, and economic beliefs of the Victorian period. *("Darwin, Marx, and Freud: Undermining Victorian Ideas")*

• This terrible event caused many British people to doubt their government as well as certain values, such as national honor and glory. *("The Great War: 'A War to End All Wars'")*

• Writers and artists experimented with form and content to challenge traditional ideas of beauty and propriety. *("Experimentation in the Arts: Shocking in Form and Content")*

• The depression of the 1930s led to the dictatorships in Europe. These dictatorships led to World War II. *("The Rise of Dictatorships: Origins of World War II")*

Reading
Alternative Activity

Core Skill **Find Main Idea and Details** As students read each section of the introduction, have them compare the information in the passage with the summaries presented during Prereading. Help them match each section with its summary. Then invite students to name details that support the main idea of each section. For example, for "Darwin, Marx, and Freud: Undermining Victorian Ideas," students might note details such as the following:

• Darwin developed a theory of evolution based on natural selection. *(Origin of Species)*

• Marx advocated the end of private property and developed theories about social and economic injustice. *(Das Kapital)*

• Freud found motives for human behavior in the irrational and sexually driven unconscious. *(The Interpretation of Dreams)*

Postreading
Alternative Teaching Strategy

Prepare to Write Prepare students for the writing activity on student book page 1036. Lead a discussion to flesh out students' ideas on the topic before they commit them to paper. Note specific facts and opinions on the board for students to refer to as they write.

"The Hollow Men" by T. S. Eliot

Prereading

Vocabulary Practice

(**Especially for ELL**) **Teach Unfamiliar Vocabulary** To build vocabulary and help students better appreciate the selection, introduce the following words and definitions before they read. Use pantomime, drawings, and contextually rich sentences to help students understand these words. For example, you can demonstrate how to *whisper*, draw a house with a *cellar*, or describe a *violent* storm.

- *whisper* (line 6): speak very softly
- *cellar* (line 10): a basement
- *violent* (line 16): involving or using great physical force; wild; passionate; furious
- *fading* (line 28): losing strength; growing dim
- *twinkle* (line 44): a slight flash of light
- *trembling* (line 49): shaking involuntarily from fear, excitement, or weakness
- *whimper* (line 98): a low, crying sound

Alternative Teaching Strategy

Prepare to Read Provide students with a fuller appreciation of the poem. After reading the Literary Focus on student book page 1044, preview some of the allusions Eliot makes in "The Hollow Men." Discuss the information provided in the Literary Focus, the reading stops, and the footnotes. Make simple notes on the board, to which students can refer during reading. Include additional information that is not presented in the student book. For example, provide notes like those below for "Eyes I dare not meet in dreams" (line 19). Guide students to see that Dante does not meet Beatrice's eyes because he is ashamed. Suggest that the speaker may feel the same way.

- an allusion to Dante's *Purgatorio*
- Beatrice comes to Dante in his dreams.
- She tries to direct him to a more virtuous life.
- He ignores her.

Discussing these references ahead of time will increase reading fluency and comprehension without disrupting the reading process.

SKILLS FOCUS

Literary Skill
Understand allusion.

Reading Skill
Make inferences about an author's philosophical argument.

(**Resources**)

In this book:
- Vocabulary and Comprehension, p. 165
- Additional Vocabulary Practice, p. 169 (includes the next selection)

Other Resources:
- *The Holt Reader*, p. 247
- *Audio CD Library, Selections and Summaries in Spanish*
- *Supporting Instruction in Spanish*, p. 45

(**Language Tip**)

When introducing new vocabulary, teach parts of speech as well. For example, explain that in this selection, the word *whisper* is used as a verb, but *whisper* can also be used as a noun.

(**Especially for ELL**)

ELLs benefit from repeated exposure to new language. By introducing the allusions in Eliot's poem prior to reading and then reviewing them during reading, you can help students to appreciate the language in the poem.

Alternative Activities

Use *The Holt Reader* You may consider having students use the Before You Read page in *The Holt Reader*, either instead of or in addition to the Before You Read page in the student book.

Focus on Language Before reading, guide students to appreciate the comparisons Eliot makes in "The Hollow Men." Present the comparative forms and examples below:

as . . . as

- Our voices are *as* quiet *as* wind in dry grass. (Refer to lines 5–10.) (*Our voices* are compared to the sound of *wind in dry grass* because they are both quiet.)

more . . . than

- Voices are *more* distant *than* a fading star. (Refer to lines 25–28.) (*Voices* are compared to a *fading star*. A fading star is distant, but voices are *more* distant.)

Reading

Alternative Teaching Strategies

Use *The Holt Reader* Consider having students read "The Hollow Men" in *The Holt Reader* so that they may make notes about the poem and respond to the instruction in the selection's margins.

Focus on Language As students read lines 5–10 of the poem, prepare them to answer question two on page 1049 of the student book. Encourage them to use the grammar skills they learned in Prereading to analyze the simile. To begin, reorder the words in lines 5–6 and then paraphrase the entire sentence on the board as follows: *When we whisper together, our dried voices are* as *quiet and meaningless as wind in dry grass or rats' feet walking on broken glass in our dry cellar*. Then ask the following questions:

1. In the first half of the sentence, what adjectives describe *our voices*? (*dried; quiet; meaningless*)
2. In the second part of the sentence, what is described as dry? (*the grass; the cellar*)
3. What two sounds are compared to *our voices*? (*wind in dry grass; rats' feet walking on broken glass on the dry cellar floor*)
4. How are *our voices* like the sound of wind in dry grass or rats' feet on broken glass? (*They are quiet and meaningless.*)
5. Are the words "dry," "quiet," and "meaningless" used in the poem to make the reader feel excited and emotional or bored and empty? (*bored and empty*)

Postreading

Additional Practice

(Mixed Ability Group) Examine the Philosophical Approach

Help students answer question eleven on page 1049 of the student book. Begin by simplifying the language of the opening question in order to make it more accessible.

Then guide students in discovering how the quality of the poem helps create feelings of futility and anarchy. Write the following words on the board and ask small groups of students to underline those that describe the feelings Eliot creates in the poem: *importance, uselessness, hope, despair, fullness, emptiness, depression, happiness, order, disorder*. Then, write the following questions on the board to guide groups in finding evidence from the poem to support their opinions.

- Does "hollow" mean empty or full? *(empty)*
- Which word in line 7 means that something is *useless*? *("meaningless")*
- Which phrase in lines 29–36 describes a disorderly, unpredictable way of acting? *("Behaving as the wind behaves")*
- Are there any words in the third section of the poem that make you feel depressed? *(possible: "dead," "fading," "death's," "alone," "broken")*

Alternative Activity

Use *The Holt Reader* You may have students complete the Analyzing Philosophical Views chart on page 253 of *The Holt Reader*, either instead of or in addition to the postreading activities in the student book.

Reading Skills Development

Practice Inference Skills Before students attempt to analyze an author's philosophical argument, they may benefit from additional practice in making inferences. Remind students that they must combine information in the text with what they already know in order to infer things the writer has not stated directly. Making inferences is an important skill in informational reading as well as literary reading. If you would like your students to practice making inferences from informational texts, use the lesson in the Reading Skills and Strategies section of this book. Refer to the Making Inferences section of the list of selections that begins on page 225 of this book for the application portion of the lesson. Ask students to read the selection and write one inference. Then, have students list up to three supporting details for each inference.

TARGETED STRATEGIES FOR SPECIAL EDUCATION STUDENTS

Prereading

Alternative Teaching Strategy

Prepare to Read Spend additional time discussing Make the Connection on student book page 1044. This section provides valuable insight into Eliot's views on the world and humanity and will aid students' comprehension of the selection. Ask questions such as the following to make sure students understand the paragraph:

1. What is a plague? *(a deadly, contagious disease that spreads rapidly)* If humanity is plagued by something, can we say it is bothered by a dangerous problem that spreads quickly? *(yes)*

2. What problem does Eliot think plagues humanity? *(a loss of will and faith)*

3. According to the paragraph, what kind of world does Eliot's poem show? *(a world of godless despair; an empty world without religion or the promise of salvation)*

4. Do you think this poem will have a cheerful and positive tone and mood? *(No, because the poem is about the weaknesses of humanity. Words like* despair *and* empty *imply something grim.)*

Reading

Additional Practice

Focus on the Key Idea Help students appreciate the allusions made in "The Hollow Men" by following this procedure for each section:

• Before you read the section, highlight and explain the allusions made in that section.

• Read the section through once.

• Ask students to consider if and how the allusion adds to the meaning of the section.

Postreading

Alternative Teaching Strategy

Core Skill **Interpret the Poem** Help students answer question three on student book page 1049. Reread Section III together and ask students to note specific words or phrases that evoke emotions or help create a mood. You might ask questions such as the following:

• How do the words "dead" and "death's" make you feel? *(possible: sad, scared)*

• Does the image of a fading star create a hopeful mood? *(no)*

• How is the idea of "waking alone" intended to make you feel? *(possible: empty, lonely)*

Vocabulary and Comprehension

"The Hollow Men"

A. Circle the letter of the answer that best completes each sentence.

    1. If you don't want them to hear what you tell me, you should _____.
        a. shout   **b.** whisper   **c.** cellar

    2. The battery was running out, so the flashlight started _____.
        a. whimpering   **b.** fading   **c.** brightening

    3. She stored cans of food down in the _____ of the house.
        a. cellar   **b.** twinkle   **c.** grass

    4. When he saw the large bear growling, Jack began _____ with fear.
        a. whispering   **b.** fading   **c.** trembling

B. Write T or F to tell if each of the following statements about the poem is true or false.

    1. In the poem, the speaker makes references to what comes after death. _____

    2. Voices are often described as loud, powerful, and important. _____

    3. In the poem, eyes are compared to prickly pears. _____

    4. The speaker claims the world ends with a deafening bang. _____

C. Answer the questions below.

    1. List four phrases from the poem that suggest the image of a scarecrow.

    _____

    _____

    2. In the first stanza, to what are the voices compared?

    _____

    _____

    3. In lines 39–44, what three phrases refer to a graveyard?

    _____

    _____

"Blood, Sweat, and Tears"

by Winston Churchill

SKILLS FOCUS

Reading Skills
Identify and critique an author's argument.

Resources

In this book:
• Vocabulary and Comprehension, p. 168
• Additional Vocabulary Practice, p. 169 (includes the previous selection)

Other Resources:
• *The Holt Reader*, p. 254
• *Audio CD Library*, Disc 14
• *Audio CD Library, Selections and Summaries in Spanish*
• *Supporting Instruction in Spanish*, p. 47

Core Skill

Use the resources in the Reading Skills and Strategies section of this book to teach a core informational skill in which your struggling readers need remediation. Use "Blood, Sweat, and Tears" for the application portion of the lesson.

Prereading

Vocabulary Practice

(**Especially for ELL**) **Teach Unfamiliar Vocabulary** Aid students' comprehension of the selection by teaching the following vocabulary prior to reading:

• *urgency* (p. 1069): requirement of immediate attention or action
• *confidence* (p. 1069): firm trust
• *ordeal* (p. 1069): a horrific experience
• *tyranny* (p. 1069): an especially unjust or cruel absolute power

Use *The Holt Reader* You may consider having students use the Before You Read page in *The Holt Reader*, either instead of or in addition to the Before You Read page in the student book.

Reading

Alternative Activity

Focus on Persuasive Language As students read, ask them to identify words that are powerful and persuasive. For example, Churchill uses "ordeal" instead of *experience* to convince the audience that the situation is grave. Other powerful words include: "unity," "urgency," "confidence," "greatest," "crisis," "hope," "struggle," "suffering," "victory," "survival," "strength."

Postreading

Alternative Activity

Use *The Holt Reader* You may have students complete the postreading chart in *The Holt Reader*, either instead of or in addition to the postreading activities in the student book.

Additional Practice

Evaluate the Speech Make sure students can answer questions nine and ten on student book page 1070 by asking the following:

1. What was Churchill's purpose? (*possible answer: to elicit confidence in his new government; to inspire Britain to unite against the enemy*)

2. Does he appeal to emotion, ethics, and logic? (*yes to all three*)

TARGETED STRATEGIES FOR SPECIAL EDUCATION STUDENTS

Reading Skills
Identify and critique an author's argument.

Prereading

Background

Focus on Historical Context Help students appreciate Churchill's purpose in giving this speech. Ask the following questions about the Background section on student book page 1067:

- What country was Britain fighting? *(Germany)*
- Were the Germans winning the war? *(yes)*
- What was Churchill's new position? *(prime minister of Britain)*
- What did he just do? *(He just formed a coalition government.)*
- What did he have to do in this speech? *(inspire the country)*

Reading

Alternative Teaching Strategy

Focus on the Key Idea As students read the final two paragraphs of the selection, prepare them to answer question six on student book page 1070. Review each device named in the question. Help students identify these devices in the text through prompts, such as the following:

- In the first sentence of paragraph three, what does Churchill emphasize? *(the grave situation of the country)*
- Which words does he repeat in the fourth paragraph? *("wage war," "victory," "survival," "British Empire")*
- What other words does he use that might inspire his audience? *("crisis," "ordeal," "tyranny," "goal," "hope," "united strength")*
- What does Churchill say he has to offer at the end of the third paragraph? *(He has "nothing to offer but blood, toil, tears, and sweat.")*
- What is the purpose of the final line in this speech? Is it a call to action or a statement of fear? *(a call to action)*

Postreading

Additional Practice

Analyze Persuasive Techniques Prepare students to answer question eight on student book page 1070. Remind them that Germany was the enemy. Discuss how Churchill might have wanted to appear before the enemy. Point out that phrases like "I feel sure that our cause will not be suffered to fail among men" illustrate a confident, resolute, and hopeful tone. Also, Churchill uses words like "our," "united," and "all" to imply that the country is united behind him.

Resources
In this book:
- Vocabulary and Comprehension, p. 168
- Additional Vocabulary Practice, p. 169 (includes the previous selection)

Other Resources:
- *The Holt Reader,* p. 254
- *Audio CD Library,* Disc 14
- *Audio CD Library, Selections and Summaries in Spanish*
- *Supporting Instruction in Spanish,* p. 47

Vocabulary and Comprehension

"Blood, Sweat, and Tears"

A. Write C or I next to each sentence to indicate whether the underlined word is used correctly or incorrectly.

   1. We went to the movies to see a <u>grievous</u>, funny comedy. _____

   2. He demonstrated his <u>buoyancy</u> by wailing and crying hysterically. _____

   3. It is <u>lamentable</u> that you can't come with us on this trip. _____

   4. She didn't wear glasses because her <u>provision</u> was 20/20. _____

   5. The judge applied the <u>rigor</u> of the law when he decided the sentence. _____

B. Circle the letter of the answer that correctly restates the meaning of each quotation.

   1. "On Friday evening last I received His Majesty's Commission to form a new Administration."
      a. Last Friday, I went out to eat with the King at the new restaurant.
      b. Last Friday, the King officially appointed me to form a new government.
      c. Last Friday, I earned some money selling new things to the King.

   2. "I have nothing to offer but blood, toil, tears, and sweat."
      a. I wish to donate my blood and sweat to the hospital.
      b. I cannot continue to be a leader of this country.
      c. I will give and sacrifice everything I have, even my life.

   3. "I feel sure that our cause will not be suffered to fail among men."
      a. I believe our people will suffer greatly from this cause.
      b. I am confident that our people will make sure this mission succeeds.
      c. I think some people cause pain and suffering to others.

C. Answer the questions below in complete sentences.

   1. Describe the new Administration that Churchill formed.

   _____

   _____

   2. What does Churchill state is the main policy of his new government?

   _____

   _____

Additional Vocabulary Practice

"The Hollow Men";
"Blood, Sweat, and Tears"

A. Using the words from the Word Bank, write the word for each definition, one letter per space. Then write the letters in the corresponding numbered spaces to answer the question.

Word Bank
cellar
disguises
fading
trembling
twinkle
violent
whimper

1. costumes used to hide identity __ __ __ __ __ __ __ __ __
$_{6}$

2. a slight flash of light __ __ __ __ __ __ __
$_{4}$

3. shaking with fear __ __ __ __ __ __ __ __ __
$_{5}$

4. a low, crying sound __ __ __ __ __ __ __
$_{1}$

5. involving great force __ __ __ __ __ __ __
$_{2}$

6. gradually becoming weaker __ __ __ __ __ __
$_{7}$

7. room below ground level __ __ __ __ __ __
$_{3}$

Who speaks at the beginning of the poem? __ __ __ __ __ __   __ __ __
$_{1}$ $_{2}$ $_{3}$ $_{3}$ $_{2}$ $_{4}$ $_{5}$ $_{6}$ $_{7}$

B. Use each word below in a sentence.

1. confidence _____

_____

2. ordeal _____

_____

3. tyranny _____

_____

"In the Shadow of War" by Ben Okri

SKILLS FOCUS

Literary Skill
Understand the limited-third-person point of view.

Reading Skill
Make predictions.

(Resources)

In this book:
• Adapted Readings
• Vocabulary and Comprehension, p. 174
• Additional Vocabulary Practice, p. 180 (includes the next selection)

Other Resources:
• *The Holt Reader,* p. 260
• *Holt Adapted Reader*
• *Audio CD Library,* Disc 15
• *Audio CD Library, Selections and Summaries in Spanish*
• *Supporting Instruction in Spanish,* p. 48

(Especially for ELL)

Take this opportunity to reinforce the different pronunciations of -ed in past-tense verbs:
• /ed/ as in *strutted, threaded, glided, hesitated, surrounded*
• /d/ as in *stumbled, disappeared*
• /t/ as in *tripped, thrashed* Demonstrate proper pronunciation and invite ELLs to repeat after you.

Prereading

Vocabulary Practice

(Especially for ELL) **Teach Unfamiliar Vocabulary** Teach the following verbs and their definitions prior to reading "In the Shadow of War."

• *disappeared* (p. 1095): stopped being visible; vanished
• *strutted* (p. 1095): walked with a self-important, confident manner
• *glided* (p. 1095): moved in a smooth, continuous manner
• *stumbled* p. 1096): proceeded unsteadily or clumsily
• *hesitated* (p. 1096): paused
• *surrounded* (p. 1097): encircled; encompassed
• *tripped* (p. 1097): stumbled or slipped after catching or entangling one's feet
• *thrashed* (p. 1097): moved or flung the limbs about violently or in panic

Background

Focus on the Historical Context Help students appreciate the historical context of war-torn Nigeria before they read the selection. As they read the Background section on page 1094 of the student book, pause after each sentence to check students' comprehension of what they have read. For example, after reading the first sentence, you might ask: *What war is going on as this story takes place?* (the Nigerian Civil War) Paraphrase each sentence whose structure may be confusing for ELLs. For example, you might paraphrase the second sentence as follows: *First Nigeria gained independence from Great Britain. Then the Nigerian people tried to create a stable government.*

Alternative Activity

Read the Adaptation/Use *The Holt Reader* Distribute copies of the adaptation of "In the Shadow of War" (available in this book and, with marginal questions, in *Holt Adapted Reader*). Have students read silently. Also since the selection is included in *The Holt Reader,* you may consider having students use the Before You Read page in that book, either instead of or in addition to the Before You Read page in the student book.

Reading

Alternative Teaching Strategies

Use *The Holt Reader* Consider having students read "In the Shadow of War" in *The Holt Reader* so that they may make notes about the story and respond to the instruction in the selection's margins.

(Especially for ELL) Listen to the Story Students may increase their comprehension of the story by listening to the audio recording in English. Spanish-speaking English-language learners may also benefit from listening to or reading the selection summary in Spanish.

(Core Skill) Make Predictions As students read, prepare them to answer question three on page 1100 of the student book. Help them make predictions based on Omovo's feelings, as modeled below. Have students record their ideas in their notebooks to refer to later.

Use the following steps to help students identify Omovo's feelings towards the soldiers and predict later events.

- After reading the first paragraph, ask students if the image of the soldiers drinking "amidst the flies" is a flattering one. *(no)*

- As students read page 1096, point out that the soldier sprays spit on Omovo's face, his face is "crowded with veins," and he makes fun of Omovo's lips. Ask if these soldiers seem like good people that Omovo trusts, or bad people he might mistrust. *(bad people he might mistrust)*

- Then help students predict. Ask: *What do you think these soldiers will do?* (possible: They will do something scary or bad.)

Use the following steps to help students identify Omovo's feelings toward the woman and predict later events.

- After reading the third paragraph on page 1095, remind students that the woman is described as a strange woman who disappears into the forest. Ask if this description makes her seem like a normal person from the town. *(no)*

- Focus on the last paragraph on the same page. Point out that the woman glides. The children say that she has no shadow and that her feet never touch the ground. She does not react when the children throw things at her. Ask if she seems like an everyday person. *(No, she seems like a ghost or a witch.)*

- Then help students predict. Ask: *What do you think will happen to this woman?* (possible: Something mysterious or out of the ordinary will happen to her.)

(Especially for ELL) As you read passages from the story that are particularly descriptive, invite more advanced ELLs to describe these scenes in their own words. Have them reread the passage to themselves, imagining the scene they are reading about. Then ask them to cover the text and try to describe the scene as they imagined it.

Postreading

Alternative Teaching Strategy

Interpret the Story Help students answer question six on student book page 1100. Direct them to reread the last complete paragraph on page 1096 ("He passed unfinished estates . . ."). Guide students in visualizing the scene as Omovo sees it by focusing on words such as "unfinished," "flaking," "collapsing," "empty," "crumbled," "deserted," and "skeleton". Ask:

- Does this riverbank seem like a pleasant place to visit, or is it a sad and scary place? *(It's a sad and scary place.)*
- Why is it sad and scary? *(possible: There are no people; there is a dead animal; it is empty and abandoned.)*
- Why are these buildings abandoned? Why are there no people? *(Answers will vary, but lead students to consider the war's impact. It seems as if something happened to scare all the people away and destroy what was there.)*
- How would you feel if you were walking in the woods and suddenly saw this scene? How do you think Omovo feels when he sees the riverbank? *(possible: scared, confused, sad)*
- What do you think Okri is trying to tell the reader about how war affects children? *(It scares and confuses them.)*

Alternative Activity

Use *The Holt Reader* You may have students complete the Making Predictions chart in *The Holt Reader,* either instead of or in addition to the postreading activities in the student book.

Reading Skills Development

(**Mixed Ability Group**) **Practice Making Predictions** Remind students that in order to make predictions about a character in a story, a reader must recognize the effects of various story elements on a character—for example, character motivations, words, actions, decisions, accidents, and coincidences. Also, point out to students that story developments might require that they revise their predictions as they read. Have mixed ability groups of two or three students look for these elements while reading together a selection chosen from the Making Predictions section of the list that begins on page 225 of this book. Groups should discuss the possible consequences of these elements. (Have groups use the Think Aloud activity found on page xxv of this book as they discuss and revise their predictions.) After groups have finished the selection, discuss with them their experiences. Did the predictions students make come true? Why or why not?

(**Core Skill**)
Use the resources in the Reading Skills and Strategies section of this book to help students having difficulty making predictions. Use "In the Shadow of War" for the application portion of the lesson.

TARGETED STRATEGIES FOR SPECIAL EDUCATION STUDENTS

Prereading

Background

Make the Connection Guide students in completing the Quickwrite activity on student book page 1093 by expanding on the questions. For example, ask:

- How can you protect children from learning about harsh realities? (*possible: Don't let them watch, listen to, or read the news; don't let them go outside.*)

- Why is it good to forbid children from watching the news? Is it good to keep children inside all the time? Why would it be bad for children never to read a newspaper? (*Answers will vary.*)

Reading

Alternative Activity

Core Skill **Make Predictions** As students read, guide them in predicting what will happen to the characters by creating on the board a chart like the one shown below. As students predict an event, record it on the class chart. After students read a section that either confirms or disproves their prediction, invite them to revise the chart. Note that students' ideas may vary from the following predictions:

Prediction	Revision
Omovo will see the strange woman.	He sees her go into the woods.
The soldiers will do something evil.	It is unclear. The soldiers seem to attack the strange woman, but they also carry the boy home from the woods.

Postreading

Alternative Teaching Strategy

Analyze Author's Style Prepare students to answer question eight on student book page 1100 by asking questions like the ones below about "The End and the Beginning." (You might ask similar questions about "In the Shadow of War.")

- Is the language in this poem complex or simple? (*simple*)

- Has the speaker experienced a war? (*Yes, there are references to specific details associated with war in stanzas 2, 3, 4, 5, 6.*)

- Does the speaker focus on the war or its aftermath? (*aftermath*)

- How does the speaker describe a town after a war? (stanzas 1–3: *It is a mess*; stanzas 4, 6: *it needs to be rebuilt*; stanzas 7–10: *some people remember why the war happened and some do not.*)

Literary Skill
Understand the limited-third-person point of view.

Reading Skill
Make predictions.

Resources

In this book:
- Adapted Readings
- Vocabulary and Comprehension, p. 174
- Additional Vocabulary Practice, p. 180 (includes the next selection)

Other Resources:
- *The Holt Reader*, p. 260
- *Holt Adapted Reader*
- *Audio CD Library*, Disc 15
- *Audio CD Library, Selections and Summaries in Spanish*
- *Supporting Instruction in Spanish*, p. 48

Teacher Tip

Remind students that this story is told from the point of view of a young boy. His lack of experience and understanding of the world are reflected in his perception of the images and events around him.

Vocabulary and Comprehension

"In the Shadow of War"

A. Match each word from the Word Bank to the group of related words.

Word Bank
dementedly
oppressive
ostentatious
stupefying
succumbed

1. dulling, numbing, sedating, _____

2. surrendered, yielded, submitted, _____

3. unbearable, harsh, suffocating, _____

4. crazily, madly, wildly, _____

5. showy, vain, pretentious, _____

B. Number the following sentences to show the sequence of events in the story.

_____ Omovo follows the soldiers when they follow the woman with the black veil.

_____ A soldier offers Omovo money to tell him about the mysterious woman.

_____ Omovo tries to explain to his father what happened to him.

_____ Omovo hears a shot.

_____ Three soldiers arrive at Omovo's village.

_____ The woman with the black veil goes into a cave.

C. Answer the questions below in complete sentences.

1. What does Omovo's father tell him about eclipses?

_____

_____

2. What happens after the woman with the black veil reaches the cave?

_____

_____

"Shakespeare's Sister" by Virginia Woolf

Prereading

Vocabulary Practice

Teach Unfamiliar Vocabulary Prepare students to read the selection by teaching the following idiomatic expressions and their definitions. Use each expression in a sample sentence that clearly demonstrates its meaning.

- *let alone* (p. 1107): not to mention; much less
- *the apple of* [*someone's*] *eye* (p. 1107): a person who is treasured
- *on the sly* (p. 1107): secretly; in a way intended to escape notice
- *with child* (p. 1107): pregnant
- *more or less* (p. 1107): about; approximately
- *at any rate* (p. 1110): whatever the case may be

Additional Background

Read "Votes for Women!" Have students read "Votes for Women!" on pages 1111–1112 of the student book before they begin "Shakespeare's Sister." Guide their reading to help them understand the issue of women's suffrage at the time that Woolf was writing. Explain key vocabulary, such as "suffrage," "campaigned," and "rallies." Then help students summarize the main idea of each paragraph. Depending on the level of your students, you might provide main idea statements such as those shown below, but in random order. Have them decide to which paragraph each main idea statement best corresponds.

- **Paragraph 1:** Some women compared their struggle for the right to vote to Joan of Arc's fight for liberty.
- **Paragraph 2:** Woolf supported the suffragist movement in various pacifist ways.
- **Paragraph 3:** People had been fighting for universal suffrage since the middle of the 19th century.
- **Paragraph 4:** Suffragists continued their struggle through rallies, marches, plays, protests, and hunger strikes.
- **Paragraph 5:** Public opinion started to change, and most people felt that women should have the right to vote.

SKILLS FOCUS

Literary Skill
Understand the characteristics of the essay.

Reading Skill
Identify an author's beliefs.

(Resources)

In this book:
- Adapted Readings
- Vocabulary and Comprehension, p. 179
- Additional Vocabulary Practice, p. 180 (includes the previous selection)

Other Resources:
- *The Holt Reader,* p. 269
- *Holt Adapted Reader*
- *Audio CD Library,* Disc 15
- *Audio CD Library, Selections and Summaries in Spanish*
- *Supporting Instruction in Spanish,* p. 49

(Teacher Tip)

Periodically remind students to use learning strategies—such as those they used to help them remember target vocabulary words—in their daily learning. Point out that they can apply these strategies to any topic they study or want to remember.

Alternative Activity

Read the Adaptation/ Use *The Holt Reader* Distribute copies of the adapted reading of "Shakespeare's Sister" (available in this book and, with marginal questions, in *Holt Adapted Reader*). Have students read the essay silently. Encourage students to write notes, questions, predictions, reactions, and comments on the worksheets as they read. Also, since the selection is included in *The Holt Reader,* you may consider having students use the Before You Read page in that book, either instead of or in addition to the Before You Read page in the student book.

Reading

Alternative Teaching Strategies

Use *The Holt Reader* Consider having students read "Shakespeare's Sister" in *The Holt Reader* so that they may make notes about the essay and respond to the instruction in the selection's margins.

Mixed Ability Group **Identify the Author's Beliefs** As small groups of students read the selection aloud, guide them to practice the reading skill presented on page 1105 of the student book: "Identifying the Author's Beliefs." Prompt them to identify some of Woolf's beliefs by asking questions such as those shown below. Write the following questions on the board, and have groups record their responses in a list in their notebooks.

- In the first paragraph, draw students' attention to the word "odd" and ask: *Does Woolf think it would have been likely for a woman in Shakespeare's time to have written plays like those of Shakespeare?* (No, she thinks it would have been strange.)

- In the third paragraph, focus on the words "must have existed" and ask: *What does Woolf think about women who possessed genius?* (She thinks there must have been some women who possessed genius in Shakespeare's time.)

- In the fourth paragraph, note the words "feared" and "mocked." Ask: *How does Woolf believe people would have treated a woman who had a gift or talent?* (They would have feared her and made fun of her.)

- In the fourth paragraph, emphasize the word "unsigned" and ask: *How does Woolf think a female author would have signed her name to her work?* (She thinks that a female author wouldn't have signed her work at all.)

- In the seventh paragraph, direct students' attention to the phrase "infinitely more formidable" and ask: *Does Woolf think that men or women face more difficulties in writing?* (women)

- In the seventh paragraph, point out the words "hostility" and "guffaw." Ask: *According to Woolf, what would have been the world's reaction to a woman's writing?* (hostility and laughter)

Postreading

Alternative Teaching Strategies

Use *The Holt Reader* You may have students complete the Identifying the Author's Beliefs chart in *The Holt Reader,* either instead of or in addition to the postreading activities in the student book.

Discuss Tone Support students' efforts to answer Thinking Critically question four on page 1113 of the student book. To help them identify the conversational tone of the essay, point out phrases such as the following:

- "Let me imagine" (page 1106) in which Woolf addresses the reader
- "This may be true or it may be false—who can say?" (page 1108) in which Woolf poses a rhetorical question
- "At any rate" (page 1110), an idiomatic expression which is more commonly used in spoken language than in written language

Vocabulary Development

Alternative Teaching Strategy

(Especially for ELL) Focus on the Key Idea Many of the words in this activity will be unfamiliar to English-language learners. Provide students with example sentences that clearly demonstrate the meaning of each word. Ask them to infer from these sentences the meanings of unknown words, as well as the difference between the words in each word pair. Use the following prompts:

1. In many modern relationships, men and women are mutually *helpful*—that is, they cooperate. During Shakespeare's time, many men expected women to be *servile* and to do whatever they were told.

2. The governor's staff *suppressed* the unflattering story, and it never reached the press. The police *restrained* the people, so they could not get very close to the building.

3. A four-leaf clover is a *propitious* sign, but a black cat is a *foreboding* one.

4. You might pass an English exam with *prodigious* difficulty after studying English for only one year. If you never studied English, then it would be an *overwhelming* task to pass the exam.

5. George Washington, Dr. Martin Luther King, Jr., and Mother Teresa are *famous.* Adolf Hitler, Joseph Stalin, and Al Capone are *notorious.*

6. Reading one paragraph is an *approachable* assignment, but reading an entire novel might be a *formidable* one.

7. After hearing a funny joke, a child might let out a *laugh*, while a big man might let out a *guffaw.*

SKILLS FOCUS

Vocabulary Skill
Clarify word meanings.

(Teacher Tip)

In the Vocabulary Development activity, have students explain how each example helps them understand the meaning of the word. This requires them to demonstrate a higher level of comprehension. In item five, for example, you might ask students which word, *notorious* or *famous*, has a negative connotation. Then ask how the people named in the example make this clear.

(Core Skill)

Use the resources in the Reading Skills and Strategies section of this book to teach a core informational skill in which your struggling readers need remediation. Use "Shakespeare's Sister" for the application portion of the lesson.

(**Resources**)

In this book:
• Adapted Readings
• Vocabulary and Comprehension, p. 179
• Additional Vocabulary Practice, p. 180 (includes the previous selection)

Other Resources:
• *The Holt Reader,* p. 269
• *Holt Adapted Reader*
• *Audio CD Library,* Disc 15
• *Audio CD Library, Selections and Summaries in Spanish*
• *Supporting Instruction in Spanish,* p. 49

TARGETED STRATEGIES FOR SPECIAL EDUCATION STUDENTS

Prereading
Background

Read About the Era Before beginning "Shakespeare's Sister," have students read "Votes for Women!" on student book pages 1111–1112. Ask questions such as the following after each paragraph to ensure that students comprehend the article:

• In the first paragraph, what did the women want? *(the right to vote)* What did they compare their struggle to? *(They compared their fight for suffrage to Joan of Arc's fight for liberty.)*

• According to the second paragraph, what movement did Woolf support? *(the movement to give women the right to vote)* How did she help? *(She helped in various, pacifist ways.)*

Reading
Alternative Teaching Strategy

Identify the Author's Beliefs Help students identify some of Woolf's beliefs as they read. Ask questions about statements that suggest these beliefs. For example, after the third paragraph ask:

• Does Woolf think there was some genius among women? *(yes)*

• Does she think that women used this genius to write? *(no)* Why not? *(It would have been very strange for a woman of that time to be a writer. She would have been looked upon with hostility and fear.)*

• What does she think happened to the women who did possess genius? *(They never wrote anything; they went crazy; they wrote, but didn't sign their work; they used their genius to invent songs for their children.)*

Postreading
Additional Support

Discuss the Literary Focus Help students analyze "Shakespeare's Sister" as an informal essay. Refer them to the Literary Focus on student book page 1105 to identify characteristics of this subgenre. Lead students to find examples of these in the text, such as:

• highly subjective: "[I]t would have been impossible...." (p. 1106) (Woolf states that there is no way that she is wrong about her idea.)

• dominated by the author's own feelings, beliefs, and biases: "[S]he found herself with child...." (p. 1107) (Woolf states her opinion as to what would have happened to a female genius at that time.)

• humorous and casual in tone: "Let me imagine...." (p. 1106) (Since Woolf doesn't have facts, she'll make up a story.)

Vocabulary and Comprehension

"Shakespeare's Sister"

A. Write each word from the Word Bank next to the word that is closest in meaning.

> **Word Bank**
> formidable   guffaw
> notorious   prodigious
> propitious   servile
> suppressed

    1. disreputable _____

    2. prevented _____

    3. enormous _____

    4. laughter _____

    5. submissive _____

    6. challenging _____

    7. favorable _____

B. Circle the letter of the expression that best completes each sentence.

    1. A woman in Shakespeare's time had no chance of learning grammar, _____ reading the great classics of literature.
      a. on the sly   **b.** let alone   **c.** at any rate

    2. Shakespeare's sister would have written _____.
      a. out in the open   **b.** let alone   **c.** on the sly

    3. Virginia Woolf describes, _____, the life of a woman with Shakespeare's genius.
      a. more or less   **b.** the apple of his eye   **c.** let alone

    4. A woman in Shakespeare's time would have found herself married and _____ at a young age.
      a. with the apple of someone's eye   **b.** with child   **c.** more or less

C. Write T or F next to each statement to indicate whether it is true or false.

    1. Women and men had the same access to education in the 17th century. _____

    2. Women generally did not work as actors in Shakespeare's time. _____

    3. George Eliot, George Sand, and Currer Bell were pen names used by women. _____

    4. Virginia Woolf states that writing a work of genius is easy for men. _____

    5. Woolf believes that society accepts women's writings more readily than men's. _____

Additional Vocabulary Practice

"In the Shadow of War"; "Shakespeare's Sister"

A. Choose the word from the Word Bank that best completes each sentence. Write the word on the line.

> **Word Bank**
> dementedly
> oppressive
> ostentatious
> stupefying
> succumbed

   1. The movie was so boring, it was _____.

   2. The queen always wore expensive jewelry and clothes, which made her seem _____.

   3. He ran around _____, shouting loudly at everyone he saw.

   4. Wendy abandoned her diet and _____ to the temptation of eating chocolate.

   5. The _____ dictator did not allow people to hold elections.

B. Answer each question with YES or NO, based on the meaning of the underlined word.

   1. If an object <u>disappeared</u>, would you be able to see it? _____

   2. If a person <u>hesitated</u> to do something, would he or she do it quickly? _____

   3. Is an island <u>surrounded</u> by water? _____

   4. Mia <u>thrashed</u> about. Did she stand still? _____

   5. Juan <u>tripped</u> over a small rock. Did he stumble? _____

C. Use each word below in a sentence.

   1. formidable _____

   _____

   2. suppressed _____

   _____

   3. propitious _____

   _____

"Shooting an Elephant" by George Orwell

Prereading

Vocabulary Practice

(**Especially for ELL**) **Teach Unfamiliar Vocabulary** Teach the following words and definitions prior to reading.

- *baited* (p. 1117): harassed or annoyed
- *hideous* (p. 1117): frightful, repulsive, or revolting
- *sneering* (p. 1117): smiling in a mocking or taunting way
- *guilt* (p. 1118): feeling of shame for committing an offense or sin
- *agony* (p. 1119): extreme mental or physical suffering
- *corpses* (p. 1119): dead bodies
- *paralyzed* (p. 1122): made powerless and unable to move

Additional Background

Focus on the Historical Context Prepare students to appreciate how the historical period influenced Orwell. Review with students the points listed below. During this discussion, ask students to consider why Orwell might have felt like an outsider in Burma, as well as why the Burmese people might have felt resentment toward the British.

- Colonialism refers to the rule of one nation over a group of people in a geographically distant land—usually to maintain control of that land's resources (p. 1114).
- Between the 1600s and the 1800s, Great Britain colonized many areas of the world. Great Britain took control of millions of people, their land, and their resources through colonization (p. 1114).
- British people went to live in the colonies and to govern over the people there (p. 1116).
- The British people who lived in the colonies were outsiders and a minority (p. 1116).
- The colonial subjects were resentful of the British (p. 1116).

Alternative Activity

Use *The Holt Reader* You may consider having students use the Before You Read page in *The Holt Reader*, either instead of or in addition to the Before You Read page in the student book.

SKILLS FOCUS

Literary Skills
- Analyze points of view on a topic.
- Understand irony.

Reading Skill
Identify an author's purpose.

(**Resources**)

In this book:
- Vocabulary and Comprehension, p. 185
- Additional Vocabulary Practice, p. 191 (includes the next selection)

Other Resources:
- *The Holt Reader*, p. 280
- *Audio CD Library*, Disc 16
- *Audio CD Library, Selections and Summaries in Spanish*
- *Supporting Instruction in Spanish*, p. 49

(**Multicultural Tip**)

Invite students to share their prior knowledge about colonialism. For example, some students might come from countries that were also colonized by the British, such as China or India. Some might come from other colonizing countries, such as France or Spain.

Reading
Alternative Teaching Strategies

Use *The Holt Reader* Consider having students read "Shooting an Elephant" in *The Holt Reader* so that they may make notes about the essay and respond to the instruction in the selection's margins.

Focus on Irony As they read, prepare students to answer Thinking Critically question six on page 1123 of the student book. Remind them of the definition of irony given on student book page 1116: a discrepancy between expectations and reality or between appearances and reality. As students read, discuss the following points in the essay that highlight Orwell's use of irony.

- Before students read the first two paragraphs of the selection, prepare them to appreciate the irony by asking questions such as: *Who controlled Burma at the time of the essay?* (the British) *Orwell was British. Did his countrymen have more political power than the Burmese people?* (yes) *Who was oppressed in colonial Burma?* (the Burmese people)

- After students read the first two paragraphs, use the following questions to guide them in understanding the irony of Orwell's situation: *How does Orwell feel?* (oppressed by his guilt) *Does he feel like he has power over the Burmese population?* (No, they always make fun of him and make his job difficult.)

- Before students read paragraph five (page 1119 in the student book), ask them to imagine how the elephant will look and act. Predictions will vary, but lead students to consider clues in the text that imply the elephant is wild and violent. For example, it goes "must" and ravages a bazaar, destroys a hut, kills a cow, turns over a van (page 1118), and kills a man (page 1119).

- After students read paragraph six (student book pages 1119–1120), ask the following: *What is the elephant doing?* (eating) *What word does Orwell use to describe how the elephant eats?* ("peacefully") *Is the elephant as dangerous as you expected?* (probably not)

- After students read "I should have about as much chance as a toad under a steamroller" on student book page 1121, ask them how they would feel if they were Orwell confronting the elephant. Suggest words such as *frightened* and *anxious* to help them express themselves.

- After students finish reading paragraph nine, ask: *Is Orwell in danger?* (Yes, the elephant might trample and kill him.) *Is Orwell afraid the elephant will hurt him?* (no) *Is he afraid of something else?* (Yes, he is afraid of the crowd that is watching him. He fears they will laugh at him if he misses and the elephant attacks him.)

Postreading

Alternative Activity

Use *The Holt Reader* You may have students complete the Identifying the Author's Purpose chart in *The Holt Reader,* either instead of or in addition to the postreading activities in the student book.

Alternative Assessment

Check Comprehension Use the following activity to help students compare main ideas across texts. On the board, write: *How does Orwell feel about the issue of British colonialism?* Lead students through the following steps to help them answer this question, using elements of the text to defend and clarify their interpretations.

1. Direct students to reread the following quotation: "And it was at this moment . . . that I first grasped the hollowness, the futility of the white man's dominion in the East" (student book page 1120). Explain any unfamiliar vocabulary, such as "grasped" (in this case meaning *understood*), "hollowness" (the state of being without significance or meaning), "futility" (uselessness), and "dominion" (rule or control).

2. Direct students to reread the following quotation: "And my whole life, every white man's life in the East, was one long struggle not to be laughed at" (student book page 1120). Explain the word "struggle" (a determined effort under difficulties) and clarify the meaning of the negative infinitive "not to be."

3. Ask students to consider the above quotations and the rest of the essay to determine which of the following statements Orwell might make:
   - British colonialism is insignificant and useless. *(yes)*
   - The Burmese people are very friendly to me. *(no)*
   - I feel guilty about my role in British colonialism. *(yes)*
   - I feel like an enemy within another culture. *(yes)*
   - I am proud of the job I do. *(no)*

Reading Skills Development

(Mixed Ability Group) Identify the Main Idea Students may have difficulty identifying an author's purpose if they are not able to identify the main idea of a selection. Choose a selection from the Determining Main Idea section of the list that begins on page 225 of this book. Have small groups of students read the selection and practice identifying the main idea. As groups read the selection aloud (see Popcorn or Break-in Reading on page xxv of this book), have them make lists of key words and phrases from the selection. After groups finish reading, members should review their notes and look for common themes that will point to the main idea of the selection. Then, have groups share their themes with the class.

(Core Skill)
Use the resources in the Reading Skills and Strategies section of this book to help students having difficulty determining main idea. Use "Shooting an Elephant" for the application portion of the lesson.

TARGETED STRATEGIES FOR SPECIAL EDUCATION STUDENTS

Prereading
Alternative Teaching Strategy

Focus on Background Prepare students to evaluate how the influences of the period shaped Orwell's experiences in Burma. As they read the Points of View section on page 1116 of the student book, ask questions to check their comprehension. For example, after reading the first two sentences, ask: *How did the British people who went to the colonies feel?* (like outsiders) *How did the colonists feel about the British holding power?* (resentful)

Reading
Alternative Activity

Focus on the Key Skill As students read, help them analyze Orwell's purpose for writing this essay: "to reveal his own personal dilemma and to reveal the cultural dilemma presented by colonialism itself" (student book page 1116). Highlight passages in the essay that develop this twofold purpose. For example, after students read the second paragraph, ask guided questions such as:

• How does Orwell feel about imperialism? *(It is wrong.)* Which clues in the first two paragraphs show this? *(possible: "imperialism was an evil thing"; "I was . . . all against . . . the British"; " the dirty work of Empire"; "my hatred of the empire")*

• How does Orwell feel about the Burmese people? *(He dislikes them.)* Which clues in the first two paragraphs show this? *(possible: "hideous"; "wretched"; "evil-spirited little beasts"; "the greatest joy . . . to drive a bayonet into a Buddhist priest's guts")*

Then help students identify the dilemma developed in these paragraphs: "I was stuck between my hatred of the empire . . . and my rage against the evil-spirited little beasts. . . ."

Postreading
Additional Practice

Interpret the Irony Use questions to guide students in answering the first part of question six on student book page 1123:

• Generally, who has freedom—tyrants or the people they oppress? *(tyrants)*

• In this essay, who are the tyrants? *(the British)*

• As an agent of the British tyrants, does the reader expect Orwell to be free? *(yes)*

• Is he truly free? *(No, he is not free to follow his conscience; the hatred of the Burmese people and his fear of their ridicule control him.)*

Vocabulary and Comprehension

"Shooting an Elephant"

A. Choose the word from the Word Bank that best completes each sentence. Write the word on the line.

Word Bank
labyrinth
pretext
squalid
supplant

1. To _____ something is to replace it.

2. An excuse is a _____.

3. A _____ is another name for a maze.

4. Something that is _____ is very dirty or unclean.

B. Circle the letter of the answer that best completes each sentence.

1. As a British police officer, Orwell endured the constant _____ of the Burmese people.
   a. praise   **b.** love   **c.** insults

2. The treatment of prisoners by the British police filled Orwell with a sense of _____.
   a. indifference   **b.** guilt   **c.** happiness

3. The man who had been killed by the elephant had an expression of _____ on his face.
   a. agony   **b.** peacefulness   **c.** anger

4. Orwell's first shot _____ the elephant, but didn't knock it down.
   a. paralyzed   **b.** shocked   **c.** missed

C. Write YES or NO to answer each of the questions below.

1. Was Orwell the head of the fire department in Lower Burma? _____

2. Did Orwell approve of the British rule over Burma? _____

3. Did a tiger ravage the town's bazaar? _____

4. Did an elephant kill an Indian man? _____

5. Did Orwell want to shoot the elephant? _____

6. Did Orwell capture the elephant and take him to the zoo? _____

"No Witchcraft for Sale" by Doris Lessing

SKILLS FOCUS

Literary Skill
Understand theme.

Reading Skill
Identify historical context.

(Resources)

In this book:
• Vocabulary and Comprehension, p. 190
• Additional Vocabulary Practice, p. 191 (includes the previous selection)

Other Resources:
• *The Holt Reader*, p. 292
• *Audio CD Library, Selections and Summaries in Spanish*
• *Supporting Instruction in Spanish*, p. 50

(Teacher Tip)

For selections that are rich in new vocabulary, a good strategy is to provide a context to which students can associate words. Though they may not learn the exact definition for every word, teaching words in context provides an idea of their meanings and aids in retention.

Prereading

Vocabulary Practice

Teach Unfamiliar Vocabulary Help students develop their vocabulary by previewing these words and definitions:

• *impulse* (p. 1127): a sudden, spontaneous feeling
• *bush* (p. 1127): a large, unsettled, natural area in Africa
• *sulk* (p. 1129): to act with moody silence
• *distorted* (p. 1129): twisted out of natural or normal appearance
• *inflamed* (p. 1130): swollen, reddened, and hot from disease
• *exasperation* (p. 1130): anger from being irritated or annoyed
• *grudgingly* (p. 1131): unwillingly; reluctantly
• *sullen* (p. 1131): gloomily silent and full of resentment
• *mischievously* (p. 1132): playfully, in a naughty or teasing way

(Especially for ELL) **Reinforce Target Vocabulary** The vocabulary in this selection may be difficult for some English-language learners. While teaching the above words and the target words on page 1126 of the student book, provide sample sentences to clarify each word's meaning. Whenever possible, use simple sentences from within the context of the selection so students get a head start on understanding what they will read. For example:

• It was *inevitable* that Teddy would encounter animals. He grew up in rural Africa, and animals were everywhere; they were impossible to avoid.
• Gideon acted *perversely* when the doctor came to ask him questions. He wouldn't cooperate at all.

Alternative Activities

Use *The Holt Reader* You may consider having students use the Before You Read page in *The Holt Reader*, either instead of or in addition to the Before You Read page in the student book.

(Especially for ELL) **Use Spanish Resources** Spanish-speaking English-language learners may benefit from reading or listening to the selection summary in Spanish in preparation for reading the selection in English.

Reading

Alternative Teaching Strategies

(Core Skill) **Review Theme** Review with students the information about theme presented on page 1126 of the student book. Remind them that a theme is the central idea, or insight, embodied in a work of literature. Theme can also be explained as the development of a one-word subject, such as *colonialism*, into a statement or two about that subject, such as *Colonialism is unjust.*

(Mixed Ability Group) **Create a Chart** On the board, begin a T-chart with the headings *cooperative* and *uncooperative*. As students read the selection, have them work in pairs to identify passages that characterize the relationship between the Farquars and Gideon as either cooperative or uncooperative. Have students record these under the appropriate headings of their charts. Their charts might resemble the following:

cooperative	uncooperative
The servants rejoice in Teddy's birth.	Teddy scares the black boy.
Gideon and Teddy feel affection for each other.	Gideon can't completely forgive Teddy.
The Farquars and Gideon are fond of each other.	Gideon won't share his medical secret.
The Farquars and the servants share religious values.	Gideon leads the Farquars and the doctor on a long and unnecessary search.
Gideon saves Teddy's eyes.	The doctor knows Gideon won't share his secret.
Both sides joke about the medicine incident.	

Identify Author's Attitude As students read and complete the above chart, pause periodically to ask what feelings about colonialism Lessing is expressing. Consider positive feelings, such as love and faith, as well as negative feelings, such as frustration and resentment. For example, when Teddy scares the black boy on student book page 1129, Lessing may be expressing her anger toward the disrespect that many whites displayed toward blacks.

Use *The Holt Reader* Students reading the selection in *The Holt Reader* can take notes and respond to instruction in the selection's margins.

Postreading

Focus on the Key Idea

(Core Skill) **State the Theme** After students read "No Witchcraft for Sale," guide them in a discussion of the comment about colonialism Lessing makes in this selection. Remind them that by stating such a comment, they are stating the theme of the story. If students have trouble formulating a statement of theme, offer them alternatives and ask them to choose the best one. For example:

A. When one culture imposes itself on another, true cooperation between the two is rare. (*yes*)

B. No one has ever been happy under colonial rule. (*no*)

C. Colonists are always fair to the people they colonize. They always treat them with great respect. (*no*)

Analyze Historical Context Help students answer Literary Criticism question ten on student book page 1133.

- Review the information about the story's historical context as discussed during Prereading.

- Guide students in understanding the question by simplifying the language and explaining any unfamiliar vocabulary.

- Ask them to identify passages from the story in which either the Farquars or Gideon are responsible for suffering. For example, Gideon is responsible for suffering on page 1132 when he leads the white people on a long and unnecessary journey through the bush.

- Ask: *How does this example support our statement of theme?* (See theme statement *A* in the previous activity.) This example supports the theme because Gideon's cooperation is limited to curing Teddy's eyes. Later, his lack of cooperation with the doctor and the Farquars causes them to suffer.

Use *The Holt Reader* You may also consider having students complete the postreading activity in *The Holt Reader*, either instead of or in addition to the activity in the student book.

Reading Skills Development

Apply Knowledge of Historical Context For additional practice, have students read the connected reading "I Believe in a British Empire" found in the student book. Ask them to apply what they have learned about the historical context of British colonialism to the speech. For example, ask students: *What can you infer about Chamberlain's view of British colonialism from the speech? Do you think Doris Lessing would agree with this view?*

TARGETED STRATEGIES FOR SPECIAL EDUCATION STUDENTS

SKILLS FOCUS

Literary Skill
Understand theme.

Reading Skill
Identify historical context.

(**Resources**)

In this book:
• Vocabulary and Comprehension, p. 190
• Additional Vocabulary Practice, p. 191 (includes the previous selection)

Other Resources:
• *The Holt Reader,* p. 292
• *Audio CD Library, Selections and Summaries in Spanish*
• *Supporting Instruction in Spanish,* p. 50

Prereading
Alternative Teaching Strategy

Discuss Setting Explain that "No Witchcraft for Sale" is a story about a white family living in the British colony of Southern Rhodesia (modern-day Zimbabwe). Invite volunteers to locate Africa and Zimbabwe on a map.

Reading
Alternative Activity

Summarize Story Events As students read the selection, pause periodically and ask them to summarize the main story events. Record these on the board. Their summaries for the beginning of the story might resemble the following:

1. Teddy is born.
2. Teddy and Gideon feel great affection for each other.
3. Teddy frightens the little black boy.
4. Gideon is angry with Teddy.
5. The snake spits in Teddy's eyes.
6. Gideon goes into the woods to find a medicinal root.
7. Gideon saves Teddy's eyes with the root.

Postreading
Reteach the Key Idea

Discuss the Political Point of View Discuss the summaries created during Reading to guide students in determining Doris Lessing's opinion about British colonialism. Remind students that this opinion can be considered the story's theme. Help students express Lessing's opinion. *(While there are good and bad aspects of colonialism, true cooperation between blacks and whites is difficult due to the unjust nature of the colonial system.)* If students have difficulty determining this idea on their own, ask questions like the following to guide them:

• Does Lessing show only the bad things about colonialism? *(No. For example, she describes the servants' affection for Teddy.)*

• Is colonialism just and fair? *(no)*

• Does Gideon ever cooperate with the Farquars? *(Yes. For example, he cures Teddy's eyes.)* Does he always cooperate with them? *(No. For example, he won't share the secret medicine with the white doctor.)*

(**History Connection**)

Remind students that most of Africa was targeted for colonialism by European countries including France (e.g. Senegal, Cameroon, Ivory Coast), Portugal (Equatorial Guinea), and Belgium (Central African Republic, Democratic Republic of the Congo). Have students find these countries on a map. Ask them to share what they know about each country's colonial periods and struggles for independence.

Vocabulary and Comprehension

"No Witchcraft for Sale"

A. Write each word from the Word Bank next to the word that has the closest meaning.

Word Bank
annulled
efficacy
inevitable
perfunctory
perversely
reverently

1. disagreeably _____

2. indifferent _____

3. cancelled _____

4. respectfully _____

5. effectiveness _____

6. unavoidable _____

B. Circle the letter of the character who would most likely say each sentence, based on the story "No Witchcraft for Sale."

1. I know the secret healing powers of the plants and roots of the bush.
   a. the doctor   **b.** Mr. Farquar   **c.** Gideon

2. I gave Gideon a raise in his wages because he saved Teddy's eyes.
   a. Mrs. Farquar   **b.** Teddy   **c.** Gideon

3. Look at me riding my scooter!
   a. Gideon   **b.** the cattle boy   **c.** Teddy

4. I don't believe the stories about plants that cure people!
   a. Mrs. Farquar   **b.** the cattle boy   **c.** the doctor

C. Answer the questions below in complete sentences.

1. How does Gideon save Teddy's eyes?

_____

_____

2. What happens when Gideon finally agrees to show the doctor the healing root?

_____

_____

Additional Vocabulary Practice　　　**Elements of Literature**
pages 1116–1133

"Shooting an Elephant"; "No Witchcraft for Sale"

A. Choose the word from the Word Bank that best completes each sentence. Write the word on the line.

Word Bank
despotic
hideous
sneering
unnerving
vague

1. I have only a _____ idea of how computers work. I don't know all the details.

2. The boxer kept _____ at his opponent throughout the fight.

3. Singing in front of a crowd was _____ for the young singer.

4. The _____ king made the poor peasants pay very high taxes.

5. He wore a _____ mask that frightened anyone who saw it.

B. Use each word below in a sentence.

1. annulled _____

_____

2. inevitable _____

_____

3. efficacy _____

_____

C. Write C or I next to each sentence to tell whether the underlined word is used correctly or incorrectly.

1. He did not want to work as a waiter, but he did it <u>grudgingly</u>. _____

2. We <u>achieved</u> all our goals in a very short time. _____

3. The man bought a <u>sulk</u> tie to match his expensive suit. _____

4. He drove his <u>exasperation</u> from his house to the park. _____

5. The girl's knee felt <u>tender</u> after she hit it against the wall. _____

6. The <u>sullen</u> boy laughed and played joyfully. _____

"The Second Coming" by William Butler Yeats

SKILLS FOCUS

Literary Skill
Understand theme.

Resources

In this book:
• Vocabulary and Comprehension, p. 194
• Additional Vocabulary Practice, p. 200 (includes the next selection)

Other Resources:
• *The Holt Reader,* p. 305
• *Audio CD Library,* Disc 17
• *Audio CD Library, Selections and Summaries in Spanish*
• *Supporting Instruction in Spanish,* p. 52

Cultural Tip

Invite students who have an understanding of Christian beliefs to share their knowledge of the prophecy of the Second Coming with the rest of the class.

Core Skill

Use the resources in the Reading Skills and Strategies section of this book to help students having difficulty recognizing theme. Use "The Second Coming" for the application portion of the lesson.

Prereading

Vocabulary Practice

Teach Unfamiliar Vocabulary Help improve students' comprehension by teaching these words and their definitions:

- *anarchy* (line 4): absence of order; absence of government
- *intensity* (line 8): an extreme degree of strength, force, or energy
- *gaze* (line 15): a fixed, intent look
- *reel* (line 17): turn or move round and round
- *vexed* (line 20): troubled, distressed, or agitated

Alternative Activity

Use *The Holt Reader* You may consider having students use the Before You Read page in *The Holt Reader,* either instead of or in addition to the Before You Read page in the student book.

Reading

Alternative Teaching Strategy

Especially for ELL **Use Audio** Help ELLs appreciate the poem's theme and irony by having them listen to the audio recording in English of "The Second Coming" as they read along in their books.

Postreading

Alternative Activities

Discuss Irony Help students analyze Yeats's use of situational irony through the following steps:

- Reread the Background section on student book page 1163 and ask: *What do the Christians expect after the Second Coming?* (an era of peace and justice)
- Guide students to compare this idea with the scene Yeats describes. Ask: *Does Yeats describe an era of peace and justice or one of violence and oppression?* (an era of violence and oppression) *What are some words that create his description of this era?* (possible: line 3: "fall apart"; line 4: "anarchy"; line 5: "blood-dimmed"; line 6: "drowned"; line 13: "troubles"; line 15: "pitiless")

Use *The Holt Reader* You may consider having students complete the Visualizing chart in *The Holt Reader,* either instead of or in addition to the postreading activities found in the student book.

TARGETED STRATEGIES FOR SPECIAL EDUCATION STUDENTS

Literary Skill
Understand theme.

Prereading
Alternative Teaching Strategy

Set a Purpose for Reading Review with students the Christian expectations for the Second Coming, as explained on student book page 1163. Write on the board the key words *an era of peace and justice.* Then remind students that irony is a discrepancy between what is expected and what actually happens. Have students set a purpose for reading: to identify the irony of the Second Coming that Yeats describes.

Reading
Alternative Teaching Strategy

Discuss Images As you read the poem with students, pause periodically and ask them to describe in their own words the images the language calls to mind. For example:

- After reading lines 1–2, say: "*Gyre*" *means part of a spiral or circle. What do you imagine when you read these lines?* (possible: a falcon flying in a circle; a man shouting to it)
- Read line 5 and explain that "tide" refers to the change in sea level and that "loosed" means *let loose.* Then ask: *What do you see when you read this line?* (possible: a flood of bloody water)

Postreading
Alternative Teaching Strategies

Discuss Irony Prepare students to answer Thinking Critically question five on student book page 1165. Refer to the Christian expectations for the Second Coming, as noted on the board during Prereading: *an era of peace and justice.* Ask: *What words does Yeats use to describe the Second Coming?* (possible: "pitiless as the sun"; "darkness"; "vexed to nightmare"; "rough beast") *Do these words support the expectation of peace and justice?* (no)

Relate the Poem to the Era Remind students that this poem was written after the first World War. Ask what emotions war generally evokes. *(possible: fear, hopelessness, and loss of faith)* Invite students to discuss how the poem evokes similar feelings in the reader. *(possible: through the use of words such as "anarchy" and "blood-dimmed tide"; through the image of a "rough beast")*

Resources

In this book:
- Vocabulary and Comprehension, p. 194
- Additional Vocabulary Practice, p. 200 (includes the next selection)

Other Resources:
- *The Holt Reader,* p. 305
- *Audio CD Library,* Disc 17
- *Audio CD Library, Selections and Summaries in Spanish*
- *Supporting Instruction in Spanish,* p. 52

Teacher Tip

Students may be tempted to give up trying to understand the poem after reading the first few lines. Encourage them to appreciate the poem by slowly and consistently guiding them through the language and meaning.

Vocabulary and Comprehension

"The Second Coming"

A. Write each word from the Word Bank next to the word or definition that is closest in meaning.

Word Bank
anarchy
conviction
intensity
gaze
reel
vexed

1. _____ stare

2. _____ bothered

3. _____ disorder

4. _____ go round and round

5. _____ strong belief

6. _____ extreme force

B. Write T or F to tell whether each statement below is true or false, according to the poem.

1. The falcon comes back when the falconer calls it. _____

2. The world is full of chaos and disorder. _____

3. The speaker thinks that a revelation will happen soon. _____

4. The speaker sees an image of a beautiful bird from Spiritus Mundi. _____

5. The speaker wants to visit Bethlehem. _____

C. Circle the letter of the answer that is closest in meaning to each phrase from the poem.

1. "Things fall apart" (line 3) means:
   a. things slip and tumble.
   b. things go far away.
   c. things collapse or break down.

2. "Hardly are those words out" (line 11) means:
   a. the words are harsh and mean.
   b. the words have just been spoken.
   c. the words will never come back.

3. "[I]ts hour come round at last" (line 21) means:
   a. time goes by quickly.
   b. its time has arrived.
   c. clocks that tell time are round.

"Araby" by James Joyce

Prereading

Vocabulary Practice

Teach Unfamiliar Vocabulary Help improve students' comprehension by teaching these words and their definitions:

- *musty* (p. 1175): smelling of dampness and decay
- *diverged* (p. 1175): moved in different directions from a common point
- *throng* (p. 1177): a large number of assembled persons; crowd
- *follies* (p. 1177): foolish acts or ideas
- *clenching* (p. 1178): grasping or closing tightly, as in a fist or teeth
- *turnstile* (p. 1179): a post with turning arms at the top, allowing people on foot to go through an entrance or exit only one at a time
- *murmured* (p. 1179): said in a low tone
- *derided* (p. 1179): laughed at; ridiculed

Alternative Teaching Strategies

Predict Mood Tell students that "Araby" has a very distinct mood, which they will notice as soon as they begin to read. Ask if any of the vocabulary words on student book page 1174 or those listed above suggest what the mood of the story might be. *(possible: Somber, monotonous, and* musty *all suggest a dark, quiet mood.)*

Use *The Holt Reader* You may consider having students use the Before You Read page in *The Holt Reader,* either instead of or in addition to the Before You Read page in the student book.

Reading

Alternative Activities

(**Especially for ELL**) **Read the Literary Focus First** English-language learners will benefit from reading the Literary Focus about irony on student book pages 1183–1184 before they read "Araby." Provide students with vocabulary support as they read the material. Discuss the various kinds of irony, helping students come up with additional examples of each. Remind them that the irony in "Araby" comes from the discrepancy between the narrator's romantic view and the reality of the situation.

SKILLS FOCUS

Literary Skill
Understand epiphany.

Reading Skill
Compare and contrast aspects of a story.

(**Resources**)

In this book:
- Vocabulary and Comprehension, p. 199
- Additional Vocabulary Practice, p. 200 (includes the previous selection)

Other Resources:
- *The Holt Reader,* p. 309
- *Audio CD Library,* Disc 17
- *Audio CD Library, Selections and Summaries in Spanish*
- *Supporting Instruction in Spanish,* p. 53

(**Especially for ELL**)

When you introduce vocabulary words, be sure to discuss and define the root from which certain words are derived. In this way, English-language learners can rapidly increase their vocabulary by learning related words. For example, point out that *derided, deriding, derides,* and *derision* are all related in meaning.

Core Skill **Check Predictions About Mood** Guide students in identifying language that sets the mood of the story to help them answer Reading Check question two on student book page 1182. After students read the first page of "Araby," revisit any predictions they made in Prereading about the mood of the story, and ask them to verify their predictions. Guide them to understand that the story's mood is dark and gloomy. Ask volunteers to point out words or phrases on the first page that help create this mood. *(possible: "Air, musty from having been long enclosed, hung in all the rooms"; "short days of winter"; "dusk fell"; "somber"; "feeble lanterns"; "silent street"; "dark dripping gardens"; "dark odorous stables")*

Mixed Ability Group **Complete a Chart** Have students work in pairs to complete the comparison-contrast chart assigned on student book page 1174. As students read, have one partner record details for the *Imagination* side of the chart, while the other records details for the *Reality* side. After partners read the story once, allow them time to discuss their notes. If they both recorded a story event, they can reread the part in which it occurs to see if there are any clues in the text that clearly show whether the event is imagined or real.

Identify the Main Idea After students have read "Araby" at least once, have them read silently "The Influence of James Joyce" on student book pages 1180–1181. Ask them to note down any unfamiliar vocabulary or difficult structures and address their questions about these after they read.

Then have students discuss the main idea and supporting details of the selection. Ask questions such as the following:

- What is the main idea of this reading? *(One great impact that Joyce had on literature was his development of a kind of writing called stream of consciousness.)*

- What details support this main idea? *(possible: Virginia Woolf adopted a similar style. This method has become so popular that its use is no longer considered unusual.)*

Use *The Holt Reader* Students reading the selection in *The Holt Reader* can take notes and respond to the instruction in the selection's margins.

Postreading

Alternative Teaching Strategies

Discuss Epiphany Guide students in answering Reading Check question four on student book page 1182. Have them re-read the seventh paragraph on page 1177. Ask them to describe the narrator's feelings and thoughts. *(He is enchanted and living in a dream world; he has an idealized image of love and of Araby.)*

Then have students compare the narrator's state of mind on page 1177 with the epiphany he has on the last page. *(On the last page, he is disenchanted by the normalcy of Araby; he is angry with himself for having been so vain.)* Ask them to retell the events that led up to this great disappointment for the narrator. *(possible: his great anticipation before the bazaar; his uncle making him wait so long; his arriving late for the bazaar; his watching the vendors count their money; his overhearing the common gossip of the vendors)* Note that students' responses will also help them answer Reading Check question three on student book page 1182.

Compare and Contrast Students can also complete the Comparing and Contrasting chart on page 318 in *The Holt Reader,* either instead of or in addition to the postreading activities found in the student book.

Additional Activity

Prepare to Write Prepare students to write short stories by reviewing various past-tense forms of regular verbs. Focus specifically on the first-person conjugations of these so students can employ the first-person point of view in their stories. You might use a chart like the following:

tense	form	use	example
past	I + regular verb + -ed	to describe an action that occurred in the past	I *walked* to school yesterday.
past perfect	I + *had* + past participle	to describe an action that began and ended in the past, before another action	I *had brushed* my teeth before I walked to school.

Vocabulary Development
Additional Practice

Mixed Ability Group **Create and Discuss Word Charts** Allow students to work in pairs or groups to create word charts for the Vocabulary Development activity on student book page 1183. Then reconvene so that groups can compare their work. They can discuss any differences they find in one another's charts and give suggestions for correction. During the comparison process, have students record their findings on the board in the form of a class chart for each word.

SKILLS FOCUS

Vocabulary Skill
Create semantic charts.

Teacher Tip

Encourage students to use new vocabulary throughout the day. Students benefit from seeing and using new words as often as possible.

Grammar Tip

Provide students with a list of irregular past-tense verbs, such as *ate, saw,* and *was.* Encourage them to check a dictionary for other irregular verbs as they write their stories.

Core Skill

Use the resources in the Reading Skills and Strategies section of this book to help students who are having difficulty with comparing and contrasting. Use "Araby" for the application portion of the lesson.

Literary Skill
Understand epiphany.

Reading Skill
Compare and contrast aspects of a story.

Resources

In this book:
• Vocabulary and Comprehension, p. 199
• Additional Vocabulary Practice, p. 200 (includes the previous selection)

Other Resources:
• *The Holt Reader,* p. 309
• *Audio CD Library,* Disc 17
• *Audio CD Library, Selections and Summaries in Spanish*
• *Supporting Instruction in Spanish,* p. 53

History Connection

Remind students that during the Middle Ages, England made many military expeditions to North Africa and what is now known as the Middle East. These were the Crusades. Nowadays, the word *crusade* is also used to describe a vigorous movement for a cause. Considering this background information, the narrator in the selection might be perceived as making his own crusade to the bazaar named "Araby," which he thinks will be as exotic as far-away Arabia.

Geography Connection

Remind students that James Joyce lived in Dublin, the capital of Ireland. Ask volunteers to point out Ireland and Dublin on a map.

TARGETED STRATEGIES FOR SPECIAL EDUCATION STUDENTS

Prereading
Alternative Teaching Strategy

Prepare to Read Explain to students that "Araby" has a strong element of irony. Much of this irony has to do with the situation of the narrator. He imagines things to be one way, but he finds out at the end of the story that those things are different from how he had imagined them.

Reading
Alternative Activity

Note Details As you read through "Araby" with students, help them point out details that show imagination versus reality. Record these on a chart like the one shown on student book page 1174. Help students determine whether story events are real or imagined. For example, after reading the narrator's words "I bore my chalice safely through a throng of foes" (student book page 1177), ask questions like the following:

• Is the boy really carrying a chalice through a crowd? *(no)*
• Which nearby word or phrase helps you see that the narrator is imagining this? *("I imagined")*
• Why does he imagine this? *(possible: He is obsessed with a romantic fantasy. He cures the boredom of shopping with his aunt by imagining his life is a romantic tale.)*

Later in the same paragraph, at "My eyes were often full of tears," ask:

• Are the boy's eyes really full of tears? *(yes)*
• Why does he often cry? *(He is upset and frustrated because he is in love with Mangan's sister.)*

Postreading
Alternative Assessment

Check Comprehension Ask basic questions like the following to check students' comprehension of the selection:

1. What kind of mood do words from the story, such as "somber," "odorous," "shadow," "musty," and "darkness" help create? *(a dark and gloomy mood)*
2. Why does the narrator arrive so late at the Araby bazaar? *(He has to wait for his uncle to come home.)*
3. What does the narrator buy at the bazaar? *(nothing)*

Vocabulary and Comprehension

"Araby"

A. Answer each question below with YES or NO, based on the meaning of the under-lined word.

1. Is a nervous person <u>imperturbable</u>? _____

2. Is a funeral usually sad and <u>somber</u>? _____

3. During a storm, does the rain <u>impinge</u> upon the earth? _____

4. Could you <u>annihilate</u> a wall by painting it green? _____

5. Is a <u>monotonous</u> person charming and interesting? _____

6. Would a quiet, shy person be <u>garrulous</u>? _____

7. If you <u>improvised</u> a dinner, would you prepare it three days in advance? _____

8. Can the smell of garlic <u>pervade</u> an apartment? _____

B. Number the sentences to show the order in which the events of the story occur.

_____ The narrator leaves the bazaar without buying anything.

_____ The narrator asks his aunt for permission to go to the bazaar on Saturday.

_____ The narrator follows Mangan's sister every morning.

_____ The narrator takes the train to the bazaar.

_____ The narrator waits for his uncle to arrive home on Saturday night.

_____ The narrator tells Mangan's sister he will bring her something from the bazaar.

C. Answer the questions below in complete sentences.

1. What does the narrator do every morning when he sees Mangan's sister leave her house? _____

_____

2. Why can't Mangan's sister go to the bazaar?

_____

_____

3. How much money does the narrator get from his uncle? How does he spend it?

_____

_____

Additional Vocabulary Practice   **Elements of Literature**
pages 1163–1165; 1174–1184

"The Second Coming"; "Araby"

A. Circle the letter of the answer that most closely matches the meaning of each underlined word.

1. Most people left in the middle of the politician's <u>monotonous</u> speech.
   a. loud   **b.** interesting   **c.** dull

2. The <u>garrulous</u> old man spoke with everyone he saw on the street.
   a. talkative   **b.** shy   **c.** angry

3. The submarine used torpedoes to <u>annihilate</u> the enemy ship.
   a. inflate   **b.** surrender   **c.** destroy

4. The teacher's excitement <u>pervades</u> her classroom.
   a. spreads through   **b.** washes under   **c.** passes over

5. The dark clouds and rain gave the winter day a <u>somber</u> mood.
   a. cheerful   **b.** gloomy   **c.** uneven

B. Choose the word from the Word Bank that best completes each sentence. Write the word on the line.

1. The road split into two paths that _____ .

2. The old castle dungeon was dark, dirty, and _____ .

3. Only one person at a time can pass through the _____ at the entrance.

4. A _____ had gathered in the park to hear the senator speak.

5. She barely heard when the boy _____ in a quiet voice.

6. The cruel boy constantly _____ and made fun of his younger sister.

> **Word Bank**
> derided
> diverged
> murmured
> musty
> throng
> turnstile

C. Use each word below in a sentence.

1. conviction _____

   _____

2. intensity_____

   _____

"Musée des Beaux Arts" by W. H. Auden

Prereading

Vocabulary Practice

(**Especially for ELL**) **Teach Unfamiliar Vocabulary** Aid students' comprehension of the poem by previewing these words and their definitions:

- *reverently* (line 5): in a way that shows great respect
- *pond* (line 8): a body of water that is smaller than a lake
- *martyrdom* (line 10): the act of dying for one's beliefs
- *leisurely* (line 15): unhurried; in a relaxed way
- *forsaken* (line 16): abandoned; ignored; forgotten by everyone

Alternative Activity

Use *The Holt Reader* You may consider having students use the Before You Read page in *The Holt Reader*, either instead of or in addition to the Before You Read page in the student book.

Reading

Alternative Teaching Strategy

(**Core Skill**) **Identify Theme** Help students identify the theme of the selection.

- Clarify the language in the first four lines of the poem: "they" (lines 1–2) refers to the Old Masters (such as Bruegel); "it" (line 3) refers to suffering; "just" and "dully" (line 4) imply indifference.
- Point out the contrast between the image of a frantic Icarus plunging into the sea and the images of indifferent people engaged in everyday activities, such as plowing or eating dinner.
- As students read the rest of the poem, have them keep in mind this theme: the world keeps turning, seemingly indifferent to the suffering of individuals.

Postreading

Alternative Teaching Strategies

Analyze Contrasts in Diction Help students answer Thinking Critically question four on student book page 1266. First review the Literary Focus on student book page 1264. Then ask: *What kind of expression is "anyhow in a corner"?* (colloquial) *What kind of expression is "dreadful martyrdom"?* (eloquent)

Complete the Chart For more practice identifying theme, students can complete the chart on page 323 of *The Holt Reader*.

SKILLS FOCUS

Literary Skill
Understand diction.

(**Resources**)

In this book:
- Vocabulary and Comprehension, p. 203
- Additional Vocabulary Practice, p. 204

Other Resources:
- *The Holt Reader*, p. 320
- *Audio CD Library*, Disc 19
- *Audio CD Library, Selections and Summaries in Spanish*
- *Supporting Instruction in Spanish*, p. 58

(**Art Connection**)

Explain to students that Pieter Bruegel (known as Pieter Bruegel the Elder) lived from 1525?–1569. Bruegel finished this painting in about 1558. This scene from ancient Greek mythology depicts Bruegel's view of his own world.

(**Core Skill**)

Use the resources in the Reading Skills and Strategies section of this book to help students having difficulty recognizing theme. Use "Musée des Beaux Arts" for the application portion of the lesson.

SKILLS FOCUS

Literary Skill
Understand diction.

(**Resources**)

In this book:
• Vocabulary and Comprehension, p. 203
• Additional Vocabulary Practice, p. 204

Other Resources:
• *The Holt Reader,* p. 320
• *Audio CD Library,* Disc 19
• *Audio CD Library, Selections and Summaries in Spanish*
• *Supporting Instruction in Spanish,* p. 58

(**Geography Connection**)

Remind students that the title of the poem is in French because Auden is writing about a painting that he saw in a museum in Brussels, where French is spoken. On a world map, help students find Belgium and other countries where French is spoken, such as France, Switzerland, Canada, Cameroon, Senegal, and Ivory Coast.

TARGETED STRATEGIES FOR SPECIAL EDUCATION STUDENTS

Prereading

Background

Explain the Allusion Read aloud the background material above the poem on student book page 1265. You may wish to augment the brief synopsis of the Daedalus myth in the first paragraph by reading a more detailed version that you find in the library or on the Internet. Remind students that such myths have been told and retold for thousands of years and represent different aspects of human behavior. Icarus' fall from the sky can be said to represent the imprudence and overzealous behavior of youth. Point out that in the myth, the boy's fall is a central event and a great tragedy. Contrast this with Bruegel's interpretation of the event in his painting *The Fall of Icarus.*

Reading

Alternative Activity

Refer to the Painting As you read the second stanza of the poem with students, display Bruegel's painting on student book 1264. For each direct reference to the painting in lines 15–21 of the poem, ask students to point to the people and things mentioned. Ask:

- Who is the main figure in the painting? (*The man plowing the field.*)
- Where is Icarus? Does he seem important in this scene? Why or why not? (*Icarus is off in a corner of the painting and does not seem important. He is very small, and we can't even see all of him.*)
- Do you think the peasant cares about Icarus? (*No, the peasant doesn't even notice Icarus.*)

Explain that Auden writes about the painting and uses other images to bring out a theme in his poem: the world keeps turning, seemingly indifferent to the sufferings of individuals.

Postreading

Alternative Teaching Strategy

Use Paintings to Reinforce the Theme Pieter Bruegel (The Elder) has other interesting paintings that bring out a theme similar to the one in "Musée des Beaux Arts." Examples include: *The Way to Calvary* and *Children's Games.* You may wish to obtain reproductions of these paintings from a library art book or from the Internet. Display them and talk about them with students, relating them to Auden's theme of indifference to suffering.

Vocabulary and Comprehension

"Musée des Beaux Arts"

A. Write YES or NO to answer each question. Use the underlined word as a clue.

    1. If you speak <u>reverently</u>, do you speak with great respect? _____

    2. Is a <u>pond</u> a wide river? _____

    3. If a house is <u>forsaken</u>, is it empty and abandoned? _____

    4. If you are in a great hurry, do you walk <u>leisurely</u>? _____

    5. Does <u>martyrdom</u> have to do with suffering because of one's beliefs? _____

B. Write T or F to tell whether each statement about the poem is true or false.

    _____ **1.** The poem mentions a famous piece of music.

    _____ **2.** One person can suffer while another is eating.

    _____ **3.** Old people wait for the miraculous birth while some children skate on a pond.

    _____ **4.** The poem tells how everyone rushes to save Icarus.

    _____ **5.** A ship sails by the drowning Icarus.

    _____ **6.** The plowman thinks Icarus' fall is exciting.

C. Answer the questions below about the poem.

    1. What do the dogs and a horse do while dreadful martyrdom runs its course?

    _____

    _____

    2. In line 18, what do the words "white legs disappearing into the green" describe?

    _____

    _____

"Musée des Beaux Arts"

A. Write the letter of the definition that best matches each word.

_____ **1.** forsaken   **a.** with great respect

_____ **2.** reverently   **b.** small body of water

_____ **3.** pond   **c.** ignored and abandoned

_____ **4.** leisurely   **d.** suffering for one's beliefs

_____ **5.** martyrdom   **e.** in a relaxed way

B. Choose two words from the left column of Part A. Use each in a sentence.

    1. _____

       _____

    2. _____

       _____

C. Circle the letter of the word that best completes each sentence.

    1. I was not in a hurry, so I walked down the road at a _____ pace.
       a. leisurely
       b. martyrdom
       c. reverently

    2. The woman looked _____ upon the statue of her idol.
       a. pond
       b. reverently
       c. angrily

    3. The little boy enjoys catching frogs in the _____.
       a. forsaken
       b. cafeteria
       c. pond

    4. The _____ house was left to rot.
       a. reverently
       b. forsaken
       c. loved

Elements of Literature
pages 1271–1273

"Fern Hill" by Dylan Thomas

Prereading
Vocabulary Practice

(**Especially for ELL**) **Teach Unfamiliar Vocabulary** Aid students' comprehension by previewing these words and their definitions before students read the poem:

- *wanderer* (line 28): a person who moves about without a particular purpose or place to go
- *dew* (line 29): beads of water that form on surfaces overnight
- *maiden* (line 30): a young, unmarried woman
- *loft* (line 47): room or space under the roof of a building

Alternative Activity

Use *The Holt Reader* You may consider having students use the Before You Read page in *The Holt Reader*, either instead of or in addition to the Before You Read page in the student book.

Reading
Alternative Teaching Strategies

Reteach the Key Idea As they read, prepare students to answer question six on student book page 1273. Play the audio recording of "Fern Hill" while students read along in their books. Discuss how Thomas uses alliteration and onomatopoeia to create a musical sound. Point out examples like the following: "green and golden" (lines 15, 44); "wanderer white" (line 28); "whinnying" (line 35).

Discuss Personification Help students identify instances of personification in "Fern Hill." For example, as you read line 41, ask: *What is the verb?* ("raced") *Who or what "raced"?* ("my wishes") *Can wishes race?* (No, people race. It is an example of personification.) Students can also read the poem in *The Holt Reader* and respond to the instruction about personification in the selection's margins.

Postreading
Alternative Activity

Draw Inferences For practice drawing inferences, have students complete the chart on page 328 in *The Holt Reader*, either instead of or in addition to the postreading activities in the student book.

SKILLS FOCUS

Literary Skill
Understand the characteristics of lyric poetry.

(**Resources**)

In this book:
- Vocabulary and Comprehension, p. 207
- Additional Vocabulary Practice, p. 208

Other Resources:
- *The Holt Reader*, p. 324
- *Audio CD Library*, Disc 19
- *Audio CD Library, Selections and Summaries in Spanish*
- *Supporting Instruction in Spanish*, p. 59

Literary Skill
Understand the characteristics of lyric poetry.

(**Resources**)

In this book:
• Vocabulary and Comprehension, p. 207
• Additional Vocabulary Practice, p. 208

Other Resources:
• *The Holt Reader,* p. 324
• *Audio CD Library,* Disc 19
• *Audio CD Library, Selections and Summaries in Spanish*
• *Supporting Instruction in Spanish,* p. 59

(**Teacher Tip**)

As an alternate activity, invite individual students to try to memorize a stanza from the poem. Allow them time to practice and prepare, then conduct a class poetry recital.

TARGETED STRATEGIES FOR SPECIAL EDUCATION STUDENTS

Prereading
Reteach the Key Idea

Set a Purpose for Reading Remind students that "Fern Hill" is a lyric poem; it focuses on expressing thoughts and feelings rather than on telling a story. Explain that one focus of the poem is the feeling of happiness that Thomas felt as a boy on a farm. Have students set a purpose for reading: to identify words and images that evoke this feeling of childhood happiness.

Reading
Alternative Teaching Strategies

Read with a Purpose Read the poem with students, reminding them to identify words and passages that clearly evoke feelings of childhood happiness. Students may identify words and phrases like the following: "young and easy" (line 1), "happy" (line 2), "green and carefree" (line 10), and "it was lovely" (line 19).

Focus on Form Encourage students to use punctuation and line spaces between stanzas as guides to understanding the poem. Model by reading aloud. Raise your voice and pause after commas; lower it and pause after periods. You might also play the audio recording of the selection as a model.

Postreading
Alternative Activity

(**Core Skill**) **Focus on Theme** Explain that the impressions of happiness in the poem constitute only part of its message; the poem also has a darker side that may be more difficult to grasp. Remind students that they read about one of Thomas's persistent themes—the lurking presence of death in life (student book page 1271). Help students focus on this darker theme by highlighting the words "shadow," "sleep," "dying," and "chains" from stanza six. Ask: *Do these words have to do with childhood happiness?* (no) *What do they have to do with?* (possible: dying, getting old, unhappiness) Ask students to search stanzas five and six for other words or phrases that develop this darker side of the poem's theme. *(possible examples:* line 45: *"out of grace";* line 46: *"[n]othing I cared";* line 48: *"moon that is always rising")*

Vocabulary and Comprehension

"Fern Hill"

A. Write each word from the Word Bank next to its definition.

Word Bank	
bearing	
wanderer	
dew	
maiden	
loft	

1. _____ water that forms at night

2. _____ room under the roof

3. _____ young, unmarried woman

4. _____ person who moves around

5. _____ carrying

B. Choose two of the words from the Word Bank above. Use each word in a sentence.

1. _____

_____

2. _____

_____

C. Read each line below from "Fern Hill." Circle the letter of the answer that is closest in meaning to the line of the poem.

1. "And green and golden I was huntsman and herdsman" (line 15)

   a. I hunted for gold out where the cows stood.

   b. The huntsman and herdsmen were green and gold.

   c. I pretended to be a hunter and a cattleman when I was young and bright.

2. ". . . the horses / Flashing into the dark" (lines 26–27)

   a. the horses being photographed in the dark

   b. the horses running off into the dark

   c. the horses lying in the grass

3. ". . . the sun born over and over," (line 39)

   a. The sun was like new every morning.

   b. The sun went down in the evening.

   c. The sun was behind the clouds.

Additional Vocabulary Practice

"Fern Hill"

A. Write YES or NO to tell whether or not each pair of sentences means the same thing. Use the underlined words as clues.

1. _____ The work horse was used to <u>bearing</u> the load of his wagon.
The work horse usually worked without a wagon.

2. _____ The man was a bit of a <u>wanderer</u>.
The man stayed in his hometown and never went anywhere new.

3. _____ Every morning there is <u>dew</u> on the grass.
Every morning the grass is wet.

4. _____ The <u>maiden</u> walks along the path.
The mother walks along the path.

5. _____ We keep extra blankets in a <u>loft</u> in the bedroom.
We keep extra blankets in a storage area above the bedroom.

B. Choose two underlined words from Part A. Use each in a sentence.

1. _____

_____

2. _____

_____

C. Circle the letter of the answer that best completes each sentence.

1. The man proved his strength by _____ the piano on his back.
a. playing **b.** bearing **c.** sorting

2. I never climb up to the _____ because it is a dark and scary room.
a. chimney **b.** loft **c.** basement

3. The _____ had been to over a hundred different countries.
a. wanderer **b.** spellbound **c.** carefree

4. It was dawn, and the grass was covered with _____.
a. owls **b.** dew **c.** praise

5. The knight fought many battles in honor of the young _____.
a. castle **b.** maiden **c.** daisies

"Games at Twilight" by Anita Desai

Prereading

Vocabulary Practice

Teach Unfamiliar Vocabulary To help students better comprehend the selection and appreciate Desai's use of imagery, preview the following words and definitions before reading.

- *stifled* (p. 1290): held back; suppressed; suffocated
- *choke* (p. 1290): suffocate; fail to breathe
- *veranda* (p. 1290): an open porch around the outside of a house
- *glared* (p. 1291): shined intensely and blindingly
- *brass* (p. 1291): a yellow metal made from copper and zinc
- *burrow* (p. 1292): dig a tunnel or hole in the ground
- *squashed* (p. 1293): crushed or flattened
- *howling* (p. 1294): a loud, sad noise like a cry of pain

Alternative Activity

Introduce Imagery and Details For practice analyzing imagery and details, students can use the Before You Read page in *The Holt Reader*, either instead of or in addition to the Before You Read page in the student book.

Reading

Reteach the Key Ideas

Analyze Imagery and Details Remind students of the purpose for reading in Reading Skills on student book page 1289: to jot down words and phrases that help the reader imagine the scene and share the characters' feelings and experiences. Help students appreciate Desai's use of details to create imagery as shown below:

- As they read, invite students to point out words that are key to describing each scene, including the vocabulary words above.
- Reinforce the power of details in imagery by stopping after you read examples of sensory-rich text (such as paragraph one on page 1290, and paragraph one on page 1291). Call on volunteers to describe the scene in their own words.
- Ask students to which sense each description appeals.
- Invite students to discuss how each description makes them feel.

SKILLS FOCUS

Literary Skill
Understand imagery.

Reading Skill
Analyze details.

Resources

In this book:
- Vocabulary and Comprehension, p. 213
- Additional Vocabulary Practice, p. 214

Other Resources:
- *The Holt Reader,* p. 329
- *Audio CD Library,* Disc 20
- *Audio CD Library, Selections and Summaries in Spanish*
- *Supporting Instruction in Spanish,* p. 60

Teacher Tip

To enhance students' appreciation of the vivid descriptions in this selection, invite volunteers to act out the vocabulary words that are verbs. In addition, show pictures of a veranda, brass, and fur.

Especially for ELL

Explain the English name of the game hide-and-seek: it is a game in which people hide while one person, who is *It,* looks for—or seeks—all of them.

Use *The Holt Reader* Students reading the selection in *The Holt Reader* can take notes and respond to the instruction in the selection's margins.

Postreading
Alternative Teaching Strategies

Core Skill **Discuss Theme** Guide students to discuss the theme of "Games at Twilight" and answer Thinking Critically question seven on student book page 1296. Divide the question into two parts for discussion.

First, focus on the part that asks: "What truth or insight about human life does it [the story] reveal?" Invite students to reread the Quickwrite notes they took during Prereading and to share with the class some of the lessons they learned through play when they were children. Guide them to consider which of these lessons could be a theme of this story. (*Possible themes might include the following: You need to use strategies to win—focus on your strengths and downplay your weaknesses. It is natural to either fight or run when faced with danger. Life is not always fair.*)

Then continue with the second part of the question, which asks students to consider the layers of meaning in the word *game* and to think about how the story's title reinforces its theme. Provide students with several meanings of the word *game*, and invite them to identify how each meaning relates to the story. For example:

- an activity providing entertainment or amusement (*The children play games such as hide-and-seek for fun.*)
- a competitive activity or sport in which players contend with one another according to a set of rules (*They play for fun, but also everyone wants to win. On student book page 1293, Ravi thinks of winning as "thrilling beyond imagination."*)
- wild animals, birds, or fish that are hunted for food or sport (*The hiding children are Raghu's "game." He hunts them, or tries to find them.*)
- an object of attack, ridicule, or pursuit (*The other children finished the game of hide-and-seek much earlier. They don't care who won. They think Ravi is foolish to care about it. "Don't be a fool," Raghu says on student book page 1294.*)

Complete the Chart For more practice analyzing details, students can complete the postreading chart on page 340 of *The Holt Reader,* either instead of or in addition to the postreading activities in the student book.

Vocabulary Development
Alternative Teaching Strategy

Vocabulary Skill
Use synonyms.

Practice Synonyms Provide students with extra help in completing the Vocabulary Development activity on student book page 1296. First have them review the definitions of the vocabulary words given on student book page 1289. Two strategies are listed below, followed by examples of how to apply them to each word:

- Help students understand the meaning of a word in context by identifying other words in the sentence that provide clues about its meaning.

- Help students substitute a synonym for a vocabulary word by suggesting possible alternatives from which to choose.

  1. *maniacal:* Focus on the words *burst, wild,* and *yells.* Ask: *Are maniacal yells calm or crazy?* (crazy)

  2. *stridently:* Focus on the words *white, glared,* and *sun.* Ask: *Does* stridently *mean* brightly *or* darkly? (brightly)

  3. *superciliously:* Focus on the words *idiot* and *kicking.* Ask: *Does Raghu act scornfully or happily?* (scornfully)

  4. *temerity:* Focus on the words *chuckled* and *astonishment.* Ask: *Does Ravi laugh because he is surprised by his boldness or because he is surprised by his cowardice?* (boldness)

  5. *intoxicating:* Focus on the words *lavishly* and *sweet.* Ask: *Is an intoxicating smell wonderful or horrible?* (wonderful)

  6. *dogged:* Focus on the words *determination, winner,* and *champion.* Ask: *Is dogged determination easygoing or stubborn?* (stubborn)

  7. *lugubrious:* Focus on the word *trooped.* Ask: *Does* lugubrious *mean* joking *or* serious? (serious)

  8. *ignominy:* Focus on the words *forgotten* and *face.* Ask: *Does* ignominy *mean* pride *or* shame? (shame)

(**Especially for ELL**)

Invite students from different cultures to tell about games they played as children in their home countries.

Reading Skills Development

(**Mixed Ability Group**) **Think Aloud** Hearing a story read aloud and being able to respond with their thoughts can help students who are having difficulty forming interpretations based on details. Pair students of differing comprehension levels, and have them take turns reading "Games at Twilight" aloud and identifying details. Pairs should also share their thoughts about the details by asking themselves: *How does this detail contribute to mood?* or *What is the significance of this detail?* You may want to read aloud the first two or three paragraphs for students, modeling the kinds of thoughts and questions you might have about details when reading the selection. Then, share your interpretation of the first two or three paragraphs with students.

Literary Skill
Understand imagery.

Reading Skill
Analyze details.

Resources

In this book:
• Vocabulary and Comprehension, p. 213
• Additional Vocabulary Practice, p. 214

Other Resources:
• *The Holt Reader,* p. 329
• *Audio CD Library,* Disc 20
• *Audio CD Library, Selections and Summaries in Spanish*
• *Supporting Instruction in Spanish,* p. 60

Teacher Tip

Encourage students to use charts to organize their ideas. Having them complete boxes of a chart one at a time helps them break down a task into smaller, more manageable chunks.

TARGETED STRATEGIES FOR SPECIAL EDUCATION STUDENTS

Prereading
Prepare to Read

Begin a Chart Help students prepare to read with the purpose of identifying and discussing imagery throughout the selection. Have them begin in their notebooks a four-column chart with the following headings: *page number/ paragraph, key words, sense, feelings.* Tell students that they will complete the chart as they read.

Reading
Alternative Teaching Strategy

Read with a Purpose As students read, guide them in completing the chart they began in Prereading. Point out examples of imagery from the text. Note that students' completed charts will help them answer Thinking Critically questions two and three on student book page 1296. The following partially completed chart provides two examples:

page number/ paragraph	key words	sense	feelings
page 1291, paragraph 11	clapping, chanted, melancholy unison	hearing	sadness, harmony, togetherness
page 1291, paragraph 12	flashing, scrambling, leaping; stood empty, bare	sight	hurry and panic; loss, loneliness

Postreading
Alternative Assessment

Check Comprehension Assess students' comprehension by asking questions such as the following:

1. At the beginning of the story, why are the children closed up in the house? *(because it is too hot to go outside)*

2. What game do the children decide to play together? *(hide-and-seek)*

3. First Ravi hides by sitting on a flowerpot behind the garage. Where does he hide after that? *(inside a shed next to the garage)*

4. Does Ravi win the game? *(possible: He wins according to the rules of the game, but in life, he feels like he loses.)*

5. What lesson does Ravi learn in this story? This lesson can be called the theme of the story. *(possible: Life is not always fair; winning doesn't matter if those around you don't play along.)*

Vocabulary and Comprehension

"Games at Twilight"

A. Match each word from the Word Bank with the word below that has the closest meaning. Write the word next to its synonym.

Word Bank	
dogged	ignominy
intoxicating	lugubrious
maniacal	stridently
superciliously	temerity

1. insane _____

2. harshly _____

3. scornfully _____

4. recklessness _____

5. stimulating _____

6. persistent _____

7. mournful _____

8. dishonor _____

B. Match each character to his or her description on the right. Write the letter of the description next to the character's name.

1. Mother _____   **a.** This character is the first one caught in the game of hide-and-seek.

2. Manu _____   **b.** This character is *It* in the game of hide-and-seek.

3. Mira _____   **c.** This character hides in the shed for a long, long time.

4. Raghu _____   **d.** This character tells the children to play on the veranda.

5. Ravi _____   **e.** This character organizes everyone into a circle to decide who will be *It*.

C. Circle the letter of the answer that most closely matches each underlined phrase from the story.

1. Manu was afraid he would be caught so he was <u>near to tears</u>.
   a. barely ripping up   **b.** almost crying   **c.** close to his eyes

2. Ravi <u>stood frozen</u> when he heard Ragu outside the shed.
   a. looked like ice   **b.** shook from the cold   **c.** did not move

3. Ravi sat on the edge of the tub and decided to <u>hold out</u> a bit longer.
   a. grasp   **b.** run   **c.** wait

Additional Vocabulary Practice

"Games at Twilight"

A. Circle the letter of the word that best completes each sentence.

1. The _____ and determined detective finally caught the thief.
   a. weak   **b.** dogged   **c.** catnip

2. The cruel instructor always _____ criticized his students.
   a. lovingly   **b.** temerity   **c.** stridently

3. The funeral of the senator was a _____ event.
   a. superciliously   **b.** maximized   **c.** lugubrious

4. The stuntwoman showed great _____ by walking on the tightrope without a safety net.
   a. temerity   **b.** caution   **c.** ignominy

5. The older boys teased the young child and laughed at him _____.
   a. superciliously   **b.** seriously   **c.** respectfully

B. Write YES or NO to answer each question based on the meaning of the underlined word.

1. Do you use <u>choke</u> to write on a blackboard? _____

2. Could you make a balloon <u>burst</u> by poking it with a pin? _____

3. Is a <u>veranda</u> usually located under a house? _____

4. Is a gold medal made of <u>brass</u>? _____

5. Do cows and horses <u>burrow</u> to make their homes? _____

6. If a piano fell on a watermelon, would the fruit be <u>squashed</u>? _____

7. Do roses have <u>fur</u>? _____

C. Choose three of the underlined words from above. Use each in a sentence.

1. _____

_____

2. _____

_____

3. _____

_____

Answer Key

Collection 1
The Anglo-Saxons:
449–1066

Vocabulary and Comprehension

from **Beowulf** Part One
p. 35

A. 1. F, G   4. J   7. D   10. E
   2. A   5. K   8. I   11. L
   3. H   6. C, M   9. B

B. 1. F   3. F   5. T
   2. F   4. T   6. T

from **Gilgamesh: A Verse Narrative**
p. 41

A. Sentences will vary.

B. 1. Gilgamesh wanted to prove that he was
      more powerful than Humbaba. He wanted
      to end Humbaba's power over them.
   2. Yes, the elders approved of Gilgamesh's
      idea. They gave him their blessing.
   3. Enkidu told Gilgamesh that both his dreams
      meant he would be victorious over
      Humbaba.
   4. Enkidu attacked Humbaba from low on the
      ground, causing Humbaba to fall down.

from **Book 22: The Death of Hector**
p. 47

A. 1. mightiest   4. onslaught
   2. hurl   5. swear
   3. ransom   6. venture

B. 3, 2, 4, 6, 5, 1

C. 1. Athena returns Achilles' spear to him.
   2. No, Hector doesn't give up. He attacks
      Achilles with his sword.
   3. Hector begs Achilles to give his dead body to
      his family, so they can bury him with honor.
   4. No, Achilles doesn't honor Hector's request.

Additional Vocabulary Practice

from **Beowulf** Part One
p. 36

A. For web *eat:* gnaw, jaws, feasting, bolted, teeth
   For web *go:* strode, rushed, journeyed, sliding
   For web *hands:* snatched, ripped, clutched,
   claws

B. 1. A helmet protects a person's head.
   2. Mail protects a person's body.

C. 1. Answers will vary, but students may point
      out that a sword and a dagger are both
      sharp, knife-like weapons.
   2. Answers will vary, but students may point
      out that a sword is bigger and has a longer
      blade than a dagger.

from **Gilgamesh: A Verse Narrative**
p. 42

A. 1. Y   3. Y   5. Y
   2. N   4. N   6. Y

B. 1. d   3. b   5. c
   2. e   4. a

from **Book 22: The Death of Hector**
p. 48

A. 1. ransom   5. mightiest
   2. overtake   6. swear
   3. hurl   7. intercept
   4. venture   8. onslaught

   Hero: Achilles the Greek

B. Sentences will vary.

C. 1. b   2. a   3. b   4. c

Collection 2
The Middle Ages:
1066–1485

Vocabulary and Comprehension

The Prologue from **The Canterbury Tales**
p. 55

A. 1. agility   4. frugal
   2. arbitrate
   3. obstinate

B. Sentences will vary.

C. 1. b   3. d   5. a
   2. c   4. e

D. 1. T   3. T   5. F
     2. F   4. T

Federigo's Falcon from the **Decameron**
p. 61

A. 1. a   2. c   3. a

B. 1. To compensate someone is to repay him
       or her.
    2. A dire situation is one that is extreme.
    3. If you console a friend, you comfort him
       or her.

C. Answers will vary.

D. 4, 5, 2, 1, 3

Additional Vocabulary Practice

The Prologue from **The Canterbury Tales**
p. 56

A. 1. c   3. b
     2. a   4. d

B. 1. personable   4. discreet
    2. worthy   5. stately
    3. noble

C. Sentences will vary.

Federigo's Falcon from the **Decameron**
p. 62

A. 1. mourning   4. hostile
    2. humbly   5. anguish
    3. console
    The letters in the shaded area spell *falcon.*

B. Sentences will vary.

Collection 3
The Renaissance:
1485–1660

Vocabulary and Comprehension

Shakespeare's Sonnets: The Mysteries of Love
p. 69

A. 1. b   3. b   5. d
     2. c   4. a

B. 1. yes   3. yes   5. no
    2. no   4. yes

Saint Crispin's Day Speech
p. 73

A. 1. to keep warm
    2. fighting
    3. something you want to have
    4. a negative view of the future
    5. a wound

B. 1. b   2. a

C. 1. c   2. a   3. a   4. b

A Valediction: Forbidding Mourning
p. 77

A. 1. b   3. b   5. c
     2. a   4. c

B. Sentences will vary.

C. 1. Donne considers their love more spiritual
      than physical. He says their love is "so much
      refined" that the lovers are "interassured of
      the mind." They do not care so much about
      physical features such as eyes, lips, and hands.
    2. The two lovers each represent a foot of the
      compass: one moves in a circle around the
      other. They are always somehow connected
      and can never be entirely independent or
      separated from each other.

Meditation 17
p. 80

A. 1. a   2. c   3. c   4. b

B. Sentences will vary.

C. 1. b   2. b   3. c

Tilbury Speech
p. 86

A. 1. d   3. e   5. c
     2. a   4. b

B. 1. b   2. a   3. c

C. 1. The queen is addressing her army. We know
      this because she says she is "resolved in the
      midst and heat of the battle to live or die
      amongst you" and "I myself will be your
      general." She also speaks of rewarding the
      listeners for their "virtues in the field."
    2. Queen Elizabeth promises that she will lead
      her army into battle; she will fight, and she
      promises to reward those who fight.

When I consider how my light is spent
p. 90

A. 1. bidding   4. lodged
    2. chide   5. murmur
    3. bent

B. 1. c   3. c   5. b
    2. a   4. b

C. 1. He is blind.
    2. Patience answers the question.

Additional Vocabulary Practice

Shakespeare's Sonnets: The Mysteries of Love
p. 70

A. 1. grieve   5. coral
    2. sickle   6. impediments
    3. possessed   7. fortune
    4. alteration   8. hymns
    The unscrambled letters spell "Shakespeare."

B. Sentences will vary.

Saint Crispin's Day Speech
p. 74

A. 1. wounds   4. accursed
    2. scars   5. covet
    3. garments

B. 1. NO   2. NO   3. NO   4. YES

C. 1. c   2. c   3. a   4. c   5. a

**A Valediction: Forbidding Mourning;
Meditation 17**
p. 81

A. Definitions and sentences will vary.

B. 1. b   2. d   3. c

Tilbury Speech
p. 87

A. 1. c   3. b   5. a
    2. c   4. d   6. b

B. Sentences will vary.

When I consider how my light is spent
p. 91

A. 1. bent   4. bidding
    2. chide   5. lodged
    3. murmur

B. 1. NO   2. NO   3. NO   4. YES   5. YES

C. 1. C   2. C   3. C   4. I   5. C

Collection 4
The Restoration and the Eighteenth Century: 1660–1800

Vocabulary and Comprehension

A Modest Proposal
p. 99

A. 1. digressed   4. animosities
    2. brevity   5. scrupulous
    3. sustenance

B. 1. It will reduce the number of Roman Catholics.
    2. Poor tenants will be able to pay their landlords.
    3. The nation will save money.
    4. Parents won't have to spend money on their children after the first year.
    5. It will benefit taverns and their customers.
    6. It will encourage marriage.

Heroic Couplets; from An Essay on Man
p. 105

A. 1. isthmus   4. mischief
    2. commend   5. merit
    3. discreet   6. ignorance

B. 1. epigram   3. antithesis
    2. couplet   4. triplet

C. 1. d   2. a   3. b   4. c

from Don Quixote
p. 111

A. 1. victuals   4. vigil
    2. succor   5. enmity
    3. disposition   6. flaccid

B. 3, 1, 6, 5, 4, 2

C. 1. Don Quixote uses a withered bough from one of the trees he and Sancho sleep under.
    2. Don Quixote is inspired by a Spanish knight called Diego Pérez de Vargas who tore a branch off an oak tree and used it as a weapon.
    3. Don Quixote tells Sancho Panza to help him if he is attacked by common or lowly men.
    4. Don Quixote tells Sancho not to help if he is fighting a gentleman. The code of chivalry prohibits Sancho from aiding Don Quixote, because Sancho is not a knight.

Additional Vocabulary Practice

A Modest Proposal
p. 100

A. 1. censure
2. procure
3. brevity
4. deference
5. glutted

B. Sentences will vary.

C. 1. b
2. a
3. a

Heroic Couplets; from An Essay on Man
p. 106

A. 1. c   2. d   3. b   4. a

B. 1. order
2. fault
3. criticism
4. rude
5. ending
6. wisdom

C. Sentences will vary.

from Don Quixote
p. 112

A. 1. c   2. b   3. b   4. b

B. 1. magician
2. chivalry
3. peaceful
4. cowards
5. lance
6. memories

Word: windmills

C. Sentences will vary.

Collection 5
The Romantic Period:
1798–1832

Vocabulary and Comprehension

Lines Composed
a Few Miles Above Tintern Abbey
p. 117

A. 1. e   3. g   5. d   7. a   9. b
2. h   4. j   6. c   8. i   10. f

B. Sentences will vary.

C. 1. T   2. F   3. T   4. F   5. F   6. T

Kubla Khan
p. 120

A. 1. turmoil
2. wailing
3. pleasure
4. blossomed
5. demon
6. Xanadu
7. savage
8. haunted

B. 1. Xanadu has a pleasure-dome with a river running through caves, surrounded by a long stretch of fertile ground with walls and towers. There are green forests and gardens where incense-bearing trees grow.
2. He once saw a vision of an Abyssinian (Ethiopian) woman playing on a dulcimer a song about Mount Abora.

C. 1. T   2. T   3. T   4. T   5. F

Ozymandias
p. 123

A. 1. decay
2. vast
3. remains
4. frown
5. shattered

B. 1. frown   2. wrinkled   3. shattered

C. 1. The statue represents a king named Ozymandias.
2. The statue has a frown or sneer on its face.
3. The two legs, the face, and the pedestal with the inscription remain.
4. Sand and desert surround the wreck of the statue.

Jade Flower Palace
p. 127

A. 1. scatter
2. slips (away)
3. swirls
4. whistle, roar
5. moans
6. crumbled
7. scurry

B. Sentences will vary.

C. 1. Y   3. N   5. Y   7. N
2. N   4. Y   6. N   8. Y

When I Have Fears
p. 131

A. 1. ripened
2. gleaned
3. cease
4. garners

B. 1. cease
2. ripened
3. garners
4. gleaned

C. 1. T   2. F   3. T   4. F

D. Sentences will vary.

Ode on a Grecian Urn
p. 134

A.
1. bold
2. burning
3. trodden
4. sweet
5. flowery
6. parching
7. silken
8. desolate
9. fair

B.
1. The speaker compares the urn to a bride, a foster child, and a historian.
2. All the depictions on the urn are frozen in time. The boughs are happy because they will always live in the spring, never losing their leaves. The melodist, or flute player, will always play a joyous tune, never tiring or running out of breath.
3. The priest is taking a cow to an altar to be sacrificed.

Additional Vocabulary Practice

Lines Composed a Few Miles Above Tintern Abbey; Kubla Khan; Ozymandias
p. 124

A. **alone:** solitude, lonely
happy: joy, delight, pleasures
sad: grief, pain, wailing

B. 1. b   2. a   3. c   4. a

C. 1. C   2. C   3. I   4. I   5. I

Jade Flower Palace
p. 128

A.
1. swirls
2. slips
3. scatters
4. crumbled
5. moans
6. roar

The letters form the word "palace"

B. Sentences will vary.

When I Have Fears; Ode on a Grecian Urn
p. 135

1. d   3. c   5. c   7. b   9. b   11. a
2. b   4. a   6. a   8. a   10. b

Collection 6
The Victorian Period: 1832–1901

Vocabulary and Comprehension

Ulysses
p. 141

A.
1. toil
2. yearning
3. yield
4. hoard
5. margin
6. mild

B. Sentences will vary.

C.
1. NO   3. YES   5. NO
2. YES   4. YES   6. NO

My Last Duchess
p. 144

A.
1. earnest
2. countenance
3. exceed
4. dowry

B. Sentences will vary.

C. 1. c   2. b   3. c

Sonnet 43
p. 148

A.
1. C   3. C   5. I
2. I   4. C   6. I

B. Sentences will vary.

C.
1. F   3. T   5. F
2. T   4. T

Dover Beach
p. 151

A.
1. ebb
2. flight
3. cadence
4. tide
5. glimmering
6. grating

B. 1. a   2. c   3. b

C.
1. Arnold talks about Sophocles, a writer of ancient Greek tragedies.
2. Arnold compares the receding shoreline to the world's dying faith.

The Bet
p. 157

A. 1. YES   3. NO   5. NO
   2. YES   4. YES   6. YES

B. 1. c   3. a   5. b
   2. e   4. f   6. d

C. 1. The lawyer was not allowed to leave the
      lodge, to see people, to hear people's voices,
      or to receive letters and newspapers.
   2. He had to write an order and receive the
      things through a window.
   3. The banker decided to kill the lawyer
      because he had lost a lot of money and he
      didn't want to pay the lawyer two million
      dollars.
   4. The banker did not kill the lawyer because
      he found a letter from the lawyer. The letter
      stated the lawyer's plan to leave five
      minutes early so that he wouldn't win the
      bet and the two million dollars.

Additional Vocabulary Practice

Ulysses; My Last Duchess
p. 145
A.

Across	Down
3. yearning	1. countenance
4. pretense	2. margin
5. hoard	3. yield
7. earnest	6. dowry

B. Sentences will vary.

Sonnet 43; Dover Beach
p. 152

A. 1. breadth   4. height
   2. soul   5. strive
   3. passion

   Phrase: I love thee

B. 1. I   Sentences will vary.
   2. C
   3. I   Sentences will vary.
   4. I   Sentences will vary.
   5. C

The Bet
p. 158

A. 1. speculation, intention
   2. punishment, death penalty
   3. despise, contempt
   4. solitary confinement, imprisonment

B. 1. *caprice* and *sudden desire*
   2. *ethereal* and *heavenly*
   3. *frivolous* and *not serious*
   4. *illusory* and *false*
   5. *posterity* and *descendants*

C. Sentences will vary.

Collection 7
The Modern World:
1900 to the Present

Vocabulary and Comprehension

The Hollow Men
p. 165

A. 1. b   2. b   3. a   4. c

B. 1. T   2. F   3. F   4. F

C. 1. possible: "hollow men"; "stuffed men";
      "headpiece filled with straw"; "rat's coat";
      "crowskin"; "crossed staves in a field"
   2. The voices are compared to wind in dry
      grass and rats' feet over broken glass.
   3. "dead land"; "stone images"; "dead man's
      hand"

Blood, Sweat, and Tears
p. 168

A. 1. I   3. C   5. C
   2. I   4. I

B. 1. b   2. c   3. b

C. 1. Churchill formed a War Cabinet consisting
      of five members, from both his ruling party
      and the Opposition. Three leaders of
      Churchill's party were appointed to serve
      either in the War Cabinet or in high
      executive office. The three Fighting Services
      were filled.
   2. Churchill states that the policy of his
      government is to wage war against the
      most monstrous tyranny the world has ever
      known, and to fight that war with all the
      might and strength possible by land, air,
      and sea.

220   Lesson Plans

In the Shadow of War
p. 174

A.
1. stupefying
2. succumbed
3. oppressive
4. dementedly
5. ostentatious

B. 3, 2, 6, 5, 1, 4

C.
1. Omovo's father tells him that an eclipse is when the world goes dark and strange things happen. He also tells Omovo that eclipses hate children and eat them.
2. When the woman reaches the cave, she is greeted by a group of people who lead her into the cave. She goes into the cave with a basket but leaves the cave without it. Then she is led by starving children and women halfway up a hill.

Shakespeare's Sister
p. 179

A.
1. notorious
2. suppressed
3. prodigious
4. guffaw
5. servile
6. formidable
7. propitious

B. 1. b   2. c   3. a   4. b

C. 1. F   2. T   3. T   4. F   5. F

Shooting an Elephant
p. 185

A.
1. supplant
2. pretext
3. labyrinth
4. squalid

B. 1. c   2. b   3. a   4. a

C.
1. NO   3. NO   5. NO
2. NO   4. YES   6. NO

No Witchcraft for Sale
p. 190

A.
1. perversely
2. perfunctory
3. annulled
4. reverently
5. efficacy
6. inevitable

B. 1. c   2. a   3. c   4. c

C.
1. Gideon chews the root of a special plant and spits into Teddy's eyes.
2. Gideon leads the Farquars and the doctor on a long walk to show them where the healing root is located. Gideon pretends to look for the root. Then he gives the doctor some blue flowers, which may or may not be the healing plant.

The Second Coming
p. 194

A.
1. gaze
2. vexed
3. anarchy
4. reel
5. conviction
6. intensity

B. 1. F   2. T   3. T   4. F   5. F

C. 1. c   2. b   3. b

Araby
p. 199

A.
1. NO   3. YES   5. NO   7. NO
2. YES   4. NO   6. NO   8. YES

B. 6, 3, 1, 5, 4, 2

C.
1. The narrator grabs his books and follows Mangan's sister after she leaves her house. When they near the point where they will separate, the narrator hurries and passes her.
2. Mangan's sister says she cannot go to the bazaar because she must attend a retreat in her convent.
3. The narrator's uncle gives him a florin. He spends it on the train fare and the entrance fee to the bazaar. He does not buy anything at the bazaar.

Musée des Beaux Arts
p. 203

A.
1. YES   3. YES   5. YES
2. NO   4. NO

B.
1. F   3. T   5. T
2. T   4. F   6. F

C.
1. The dogs go on with their lives; the horse scratches itself against a tree.
2. The words describe the legs of Icarus, who is disappearing into the green water of the sea.

Fern Hill
p. 207

A.
1. dew
2. loft
3. maiden
4. wanderer
5. bearing

B. Sentences will vary.

C. 1. c   2. b   3. a

Games at Twilight
p. 213

A. 1. maniacal   5. intoxicating
   2. stridently   6. dogged
   3. superciliously   7. lugubrious
   4. temerity   8. ignominy

B. 1. d   3. e   5. c
   2. a   4. b

C. 1. b   2. c   3. c

Additional Vocabulary Practice

The Hollow Men; Blood, Sweat, and Tears
p. 169

A. 1. disguises   5. violent
   2. twinkle   6. fading
   3. trembling   7. cellar
   4. whimper

Who speaks at the beginning of the poem?
hollow men

B. Sentences will vary.

In the Shadow of War; Shakespeare's Sister
p. 180

A. 1. stupefying   4. succumbed
   2. ostentatious   5. oppressive
   3. dementedly

B. 1. NO   2. NO   3. YES   4. NO   5. YES

C. Sentences will vary.

Shooting an Elephant; No Witchcraft for Sale
p. 191

A. 1. vague   4. despotic
   2. sneering   5. hideous
   3. unnerving

B. Sentences will vary.

C. 1. C   3. I   5. C
   2. C   4. I   6. I

The Second Coming; Araby
p. 200

A. 1. c   2. a   3. c   4. a   5. b

B. 1. diverged   4. throng
   2. musty   5. murmured
   3. turnstile   6. derided

C. Sentences will vary.

Musée des Beaux Arts
p. 204

A. 1. c   3. b   5. d
   2. a   4. e

B. Sentences will vary.

C. 1. a   2. b   3. c   4. b

Fern Hill
p. 208

A. 1. NO   3. YES   5. YES
   2. NO   4. NO

B. Sentences will vary.

C. 1. b   2. b   3. a   4. b   5. b

Games at Twilight
p. 214

A. 1. b   2. c   3. c   4. a   5. a

B. 1. NO   3. NO   5. NO   7. NO
   2. YES   4. NO   6. YES

C. Sentences will vary.

Table of Contents

Overhead transparencies for the Reading Skills and Strategies Lessons can be found in the front cover pocket of this book.

Suggested *Elements of Literature* Selections for Reading Skills Application

Each of the ten Reading Skills and Strategies lessons in this section includes an application activity. The following list provides suggestions for selections from the *Elements of Literature* Student Edition (or from the Adapted Readings section of this book) appropriate for the application of a given skill. All page references given refer to the *Elements of Literature* Student Edition unless otherwise noted.

Informational Comprehension Skills

Identifying Text Structure

Recognize structural patterns such as comparison-contrast, cause-effect, chronological order, description, and problem-solution that are used to organize ideas in informational text; analyze and connect the essential ideas, arguments, and perspectives of the text by using knowledge of text structures.

Each selection below, in full or in part, is representative of the text structure indicated.

Coll. 1 Life in 999: A Grim Struggle (p. 40) — *description*
Trojan Gold *from* Gods, Graves, and Scholars (p. 77) — *chronological order*

Coll. 2 Money, Gunpowder, and the Middle Class: The End of an Era (p. 126) — *cause-effect*

Coll. 3 Give Us This Day Our Daily Bread (p. 305) — *comparison-contrast*

Coll. 4 . . . and Life Among the Have-Nots (p. 570) — *cause-effect*
from The Education of Women (p. 647) — *problem-solution*

Coll. 5 *from* In Patagonia (p. 788) — *chronological order*
An Irresistible Bad Boy: The Byronic Hero (p. 799) — *comparison-contrast*

Coll. 6 Death and Other Grave Matters (p. 928) — *description*

Coll. 7 Votes for Women! (p. 1111) — *chronological order*

Determining Main Idea

Determine central ideas in informational text, and identify important details that support the central ideas.

Any short informational selection may be used to apply the skill. Below are suggested readings from each collection.

Coll. 1 The Fury of the Northmen (p. 49)

Coll. 2 "A Terrible Worm in an Iron Cocoon" (p. 120)

Coll. 3 Tilbury Speech (p. 366)

Coll. 4 *from* The Burning of Rome *from* The Annals (p. 694)

Coll. 5 The Lure of the Gothic (p. 714)

Coll. 6 An Age in Need of Heroines: Reform in Victorian Britain (p. 882)

Coll. 7 Blood, Sweat, and Tears (p. 1068)

Making Inferences

Make informed judgments based on evidence from the text, and use personal observations and prior experience to make and confirm inferences.

Any short informational selection, excluding process or "how-to" passages, may be used to apply the skill. Below are suggested readings from each collection.

Coll. 1 Women in Anglo-Saxon Culture (p. 12)

Coll. 2 Panchatantra (p. 193)

Coll. 3 The Glass of Fashion (p. 291)

Coll. 4 Top of the Food Chain (p. 590)

Coll. 5 Shelley and the Ode (p. 809)

Coll. 6 The Pre-Raphaelite Brotherhood: Challenging Artistic Authority (p. 884)

Coll. 7 "I Believe in a British Empire" (p. 1135)

Summarizing

Compare original text to a summary to determine whether the summary accurately captures the ideas, includes critical details, and conveys the underlying meaning; synthesize content to demonstrate comprehension.

Any short informational selection may be used to apply the skill. Below are suggested readings from each collection.

Coll. 1 Epics: Stories on a Grand Scale (p. 54)

Coll. 2 Places of Pilgrimage (p. 150)

Coll. 3 Of Studies (p. 361)

Coll. 4 Life Among the Haves . . . (p. 568)

Coll. 5 "Blake Is a Real Name . . ." (p. 722)

Coll. 6 The Rise of Realism (p. 946)

Coll. 7 The Influence of James Joyce (p. 1180)

Distinguishing Fact from Opinion

Evaluate whether the author presents objective facts or subjective opinions; assess the adequacy, accuracy, and appropriateness of the author's evidence to support claims and assertions; distinguish between logical and illogical statements in a text; identify biases, stereotypes, and persuasive techniques in texts.

Coll. 1 The Anglo-Saxons 499–1066 (p. 6)

Coll. 2 The Canterbury Tales: Snapshot of an Age (p. 137)

Coll. 3 *from* Female Orations (p. 368)

Coll. 4 *from* The Education of Women (p. 647)

Coll. 5 Coleridge Describes His Addiction (p. 787)

Coll. 6 Scenes from a Modern Marriage (p. 911)

Coll. 7 *from* Towards a True Refuge (p. 1325)

Literary Comprehension Skills

Making Predictions

Determine the most likely outcomes; predict ideas or events that may take place; give a rationale for predictions.

Any short literary selection may be used to apply the skill. Below are suggested readings from each collection.

Coll. 1 *from* Grendel (p. 39)

Coll. 2 *from* The Third Voyage of Sindbad the Sailor (p. 201)

Coll. 3 To His Coy Mistress (p. 303)

Coll. 4 Top of the Food Chain (p. 590)

Coll. 5 The Tyger (p. 721)

Coll. 6 Ulysses (p. 904)

Coll. 7 In the Shadow of War (p. 1095)

Understanding Characters

Recognize and understand characters' traits; determine characters' motivation and feelings based on clues in the text; understand characters' relationships; analyze interactions between main and subordinate characters; make inferences based on characters' words, actions, and reactions to other characters.

Any short literary selection featuring a character or characters may be used to apply the skill. Below are suggested readings from each collection.

Coll. 1 *from* Grendel (p. 39)
from The Seafarer (p. 87)

Coll. 2 Get Up and Bar the Door (p. 132)
Right-Mind and Wrong-Mind (p. 195)

Coll. 3 To His Coy Mistress (p. 303)
from The Pilgrim's Progress (p. 420)

Coll. 4 *from* Don Quixote (p. 627)
from The Diary of Samuel Pepys (p. 695)

Coll. 5 The Chimney Sweeper *from* Songs of Innocence (p. 726)
Kubla Khan (p. 759)

Coll. 6 My Last Duchess (p. 909)
The Bet* (*Holt Reading Solutions*)

Coll. 7 The Book of Sand (p. 1227)
The Doll's House* (*Holt Reading Solutions*)

*Adapted Reading

Recognizing Theme

Identify ideas and insights about life and human nature expressed in literature; form interpretations of narrative text by making inferences, generalizing, drawing conclusions, and analyzing.

Any short literary selection may be used to apply the skill. Below are suggested readings from each collection.

Coll. 1 The Monster's Mother (p. 36)
Coll. 2 *from* The Third Voyage of Sindbad the Sailor (p. 201)
Coll. 3 Zen Parables (p. 389)
Coll. 4 Top of the Food Chain (p. 590)

Coll. 5 A Poison Tree (p. 731)
Coll. 6 Dover Beach (p. 922)
Coll. 7 Telephone Conversation (p. 1157)

Understanding Figurative Language

Recognize similes, metaphors, and personification as used in literature.

Many poems may be used to apply the skill. Below are suggested selections from each collection. Note that some selections contain no more than two obvious figures of speech.

Coll. 1 *from* Grendel (p. 39)
        from The Seafarer (p. 87)
Coll. 2 *from* The Wife of Bath's Tale, lines 7–21 (p. 178)
Coll. 3 Sonnet 130 (p. 320)
        from the Tao Te Ching (p. 392)
Coll. 4 *from* Heroic Couplets (p. 599)
        To the Ladies (p. 646)

Coll. 5 Composed Upon Westminster Bridge (p. 744)
        When I Have Fears (p. 827)
Coll. 6 Dover Beach (p. 922)
        To an Athlete Dying Young (p. 927)
Coll. 7 The Hollow Men (p. 1046)
        Half a Day (p. 1242)

Comparing and Contrasting

Compare and contrast aspects of literary texts such as characters, settings, plot elements (for example, conflict), and themes.

Coll. 1 *from* The Seafarer (p. 87) / Break, Break, Break (p. 106) — *image, theme*

Coll. 2 Right-Mind and Wrong-Mind *from* the Panchatantra (p. 195) — *characters*

Coll. 3 The Passionate Shepherd to His Love (p. 295) / The Nymph's Reply to the Shepherd (p. 297) — *speaker*

Sonnet 130 (p. 320) / Sonnet 23 (p. 321) — *mood, writer's attitude*

Coll. 4 A Modest Proposal* (*Holt Reading Solutions*) / Top of the Food Chain (p. 590) — *theme or main idea*

from The Burning of Rome (p. 694) / *from* The Diary of Samuel Pepys (p. 695) — *setting, point of view*

*Adapted Reading

Coll. 5 The Chimney Sweeper *from* Songs of Innocence (p. 726) / The Chimney Sweeper *from* Songs of Experience (p. 727) — *point of view, details*

Ozymandias (p. 803) / Ode on a Grecian Urn (p. 836) — *theme*

Coll. 6 The Bet* (*Holt Reading Solutions*) — *characters*

Coll. 7 Dulce et Decorum Est (p. 1040) / The Rear-Guard (p. 1041) — *setting, details*

Shakespeare's Sister* (*Holt Reading Solutions*) / A Closer Look: Political Influences (p. 1111) — *point of view, tone*

Marriage Is a Private Affair (p. 1149) / Telephone Conversation (p. 1157) — *theme, mood*

(CORE SKILL) Identifying Text Structure   Teacher Notes

At a Glance

- Recognizing text structures helps students see the relationship between ideas, determine what is important, and improve comprehension and retention.

- The following encourages students to examine a text and identify its structure.

Direct Instruction

Write these titles on the board: *Reptiles and Amphibians, The History of Art, Conserving Water,* and *The Beauty of Orchids.* Point out that titles can provide clues about how the text will be structured, or organized. Then, after distributing copies of the Student Notes page, help students match the titles to the text structures listed.

Guided Practice

Distribute copies of the MiniRead, and guide students through Exercise A, using Transparency 1 and the steps below.

1. Read the title aloud, and ask students what they think the passage will be about based on the title. Then, ask students to predict, based on their experience with similar texts, how the passage might be organized.

2. As students read the first paragraph, help them underline key words or phrases that show how ideas are related. If necessary, help students revise their predictions.

3. Ask the questions on the Student Notes page to help identify text structure.

4. Repeat Steps 2 and 3 for the remaining paragraphs.

5. Have students formulate a statement that identifies the text structure and how it was used in the passage.

   If paragraphs have different text structures, help students identify the overall text structure.

Independent Practice

Have students work alone or in groups to complete Exercise B of the MiniRead.

Assessment

After choosing a selection (see suggestions, p. 225), hand out the Application activity. Once the activity is completed, have students explain how they identified the text structure.

Identifying Text Structure

At a Glance

- The way a writer organizes ideas is called **text structure.** Five common text structures are **cause-effect, chronological order, comparison-contrast, description,** and **problem-solution.**
- The strategy below will help you identify text structure.

Step-by-Step Strategy

1. Read the title, and write down what you think the passage will be about. Then, based on similar texts, predict how the ideas might be organized.

2. Read the first paragraph. Underline key words or phrases that show how the ideas are related. Then, check the prediction you made in Step 1.

3. Ask yourself the following questions to determine the text structure.

   - Does the author show how one thing leads to another? (Cause-effect)

   - Does the author list events or ideas in a time sequence? (Chronological order)

   - Does the author discuss similarities and differences? (Comparison-contrast)

   - Does the author describe a person, place, thing, or idea? (Description)

   - Does the author define a problem and offer a solution? (Problem-solution)

4. Repeat Steps 2 and 3 as you continue reading the selection.

5. Then, identify the overall text structure of the passage and how it was used.

Example

Summer Mornings	The title makes me think that the passage will describe what happens during a summer morning.
Fishing with my granddad was a summer pastime. He would wake me up <u>early</u>, and we would dig for worms. <u>Then</u>, I would follow him down the trails to the creek, where we fished <u>until</u> the <u>afternoon</u> sun glared down on us.	The author uses chronological order to describe morning fishing trips with his granddad.

TIP Look for key words and phrases to help you determine the text structure.

- Cause-Effect: *as a result of, because, consequently, effects of, process, steps*
- Chronological Order: *after, before, during, later, second, then, today, when*
- Comparison-Contrast: *although, different from, likewise, on the other hand*
- Description: *above, across, between, characteristic, for example, most important*
- Problem-Solution: *accordingly, if . . . then, in response to, option, proposal*

Identifying Text Structure

MiniRead

DIRECTIONS: Use the following MiniRead to complete Exercise A on page 234.

MiniRead A

How Languages Are Lost

A   Languages are often referred to as "living" or "dead." Living languages are those that are spoken by a group of people. Dead languages are those that are no longer spoken. For example, ancient Greek and Latin are considered dead languages because no one speaks them outside of the classroom. Many living languages, however, are just barely alive. Around the world, many speakers of rare and ancient languages now choose to communicate in more widely spoken languages. Many linguists fear that the modern world's emphasis on global communication and international markets will cause many languages to die.

B   In a region of South America known as the Peruvian Amazon, many languages have already become extinct. About a hundred and fifty languages were once spoken by the isolated jungle communities. These languages flourished in isolation. However, as outsiders came into the jungles of the Amazon, Peruvian tribes, languages, and cultures began to change. When Spanish speakers moved to the region, they established schools in which only Spanish was spoken. As the Spanish speakers grew politically and culturally powerful, Spanish became the dominant language in the region. As a result, speakers of regional tribal languages began to learn and speak Spanish.

C   At the end of the twentieth century, only fifty-seven tribal languages still existed. Twenty-five of the existing Peruvian tribal languages are in danger of being lost because they are not spoken by younger generations. The only speakers of these languages are a handful of elderly people, and they are likely to be the last native speakers of these languages. The younger generations prefer to speak Spanish and have not learned the language of their elders. Furthermore, scholars have not fully documented these endangered languages. As elderly speakers die, they take the last memories of their languages and cultures with them.

Identifying Text Structure

DIRECTIONS: Use the following MiniRead to complete Exercise B on page 234.

MiniRead B

Adjusting to a New Life

A   From the late 1700s through the middle of the twentieth century, India was part of the British Empire. Many British citizens—from government officials and merchants to religious missionaries and soldiers—left England with their families and moved to India. In their new South Asian home, they found a way of life completely different from the one they had known.

B   The first and perhaps most noticeable difference was the weather. England has a cool, damp climate with few extremes in temperature. India, in contrast, has three seasons: a cold season, a hot season, and a rainy season. Some parts of India don't even get a cool season; from mid-April until September the temperature is, simply, hot. The British were not used to living in such a hot climate.

C   Furthermore, the British ideas of dressing "respectably" were often in sharp contrast to the realities of the weather in India. Native Indians tended to wear lightweight, loose clothing in white or bright colors. Men wore *dhotis*—cloths draped around the legs to form loose trousers. Women wore *saris*—long lengths of cloth draped around the entire body to form a dress. Young Indian children would often play outdoors wearing as few clothes as possible. The British, on the other hand, often clung to their ideas of "suitable dressing"—no matter how hot the weather was. In the heat of the day, little girls were made to wear starched cotton hats and frilly, starched dresses with petticoats underneath. Also, everyone was expected to dress up for dinner. One Englishman who lived alone in the jungle insisted on dressing for dinner every evening in a dinner jacket and black tie.

D   Many of the British in India also held to their preferences in housing and furnishing. They wanted their homes in India to look like their houses in England. In India most British lived in country bungalows—one-story houses with low roofs. Indian bungalows were usually sparsely furnished, with comfortable cushions and cots and a few pieces of bamboo furniture. In contrast, the British filled their new homes with furniture, heavy fabrics, bookcases brimming with the latest books from England, and decorative knickknacks.

Identifying Text Structure

MiniRead Practice

Exercise A Use "How Languages Are Lost" to complete the following.

1. Based on the title and your prior reading, write down what you think the passage will be about and how you think the passage will be organized.

   A. The passage will be about _____

   _____

   B. The passage will organize ideas by _____

   _____

2. Write down any key words or phrases that show how the ideas are related.

   _____

   _____

3. Identify the text structure and how it is used in the passage.

   _____

   _____

   _____

Exercise B Use "Adjusting to a New Life" to complete the following.

1. Based on the title and your prior reading, write down what you think the passage will be about and how you think the passage will be organized.

   A. The passage will be about _____

   _____

   B. The passage will organize ideas by _____

   _____

2. Write down any key words or phrases that show how the ideas are related.

   _____

3. Identify the text structure and how it is used in the passage.

   _____

   _____

   _____

Identifying Text Structure

DIRECTIONS: First, look over the types of text structure and their definitions. Then, focus on the title of the selection and write down what you think the passage will be about and how the ideas will be organized. Next, read the selection, and write down the key words and phrases that show how ideas are related. Finally, identify the text structure and how it is used in the passage. Before starting, be sure to review your notes on text structure.

Text Structures

Cause-Effect—The author shows how one event or idea leads to or causes another.
Chronological Order—The author lists events or ideas in a time sequence.
Comparison-Contrast—The author discusses similarities and differences.
Description—The author describes a person, place, thing, or idea.
Problem-Solution—The author defines a problem and offers a solution.

Title: _____

The title suggests that . . .

* the passage will be about

_____

_____

* the passage will organize ideas by

_____

_____

Key words and phrases that show how ideas are related:

_____

_____

Text structure and its use:

_____

_____

(CORE SKILL) Determining Main Idea   Teacher Notes

At a Glance

- Readers struggling with the concept of main idea (especially implied main idea) often need help seeing how details, taken together, signal main idea.

- The following lesson provides a simple, three-step strategy designed to help students practice identifying main idea—whether stated or implied.

Direct Instruction

After passing out the Student Notes page, review the strategy, especially focusing on the importance of inferring main idea from a group of details.

Guided Practice

Distribute copies of the MiniRead. In guiding students through Exercise A, use the steps below and Transparency 2.

1. Read paragraph A aloud. Then, help students identify the topic of the paragraph. As a prompt, ask a question like "What is this paragraph mostly about?" To keep students from focusing on the details of the paragraph, limit descriptions of the topic to short phrases.

2. Guide students in identifying the important details that tell about the topic. For simplicity, you may want to focus on identifying one detail per sentence. Encourage the use of short phrases to describe the details.

3. Finally, ask students to identify the writer's main idea about the topic. Prompt students by asking a question like "Based on the details, what seems to be the writer's most important point about the topic?" Even if the paragraph has a stated main idea, have students rephrase the sentence as an aid to reading comprehension. Note that interpretations may vary slightly; the standard for a good statement of main idea is supportability.

Repeat the basic process for paragraphs B through D, or until you feel students are ready to use the strategy independently for the rest of the MiniRead.

Independent Practice

Have students work alone or in groups to complete Exercise B of the MiniRead.

Assessment

After choosing a selection (see suggestions, p. 225), hand out copies of the Application activity. Once the activity is completed, ask students to explain how they applied the strategy.

Determining Main Idea

At a Glance

- The **main idea** of a paragraph is the writer's most important point.
- The following three-step strategy will help you practice identifying main ideas.

Step-by-Step Strategy

1. Identify the **topic**.
   Here's how: After reading the paragraph, ask yourself, "What is this paragraph mostly about?" Write down your answer, using as few words as possible.

2. Next, identify the **important details** that tell about the topic.
   Here's how: Review the paragraph. For each sentence, write a short phrase to describe what the writer is saying about the topic.

3. Finally, determine the **main idea** about the topic.
   Here's how: Review the important details. Then, ask yourself, "What seems to be the writer's most important point about the topic?" Write down the most important point (main idea). Note that a sentence in the paragraph may already state the most important point. If so, rewrite that sentence in your own words.

Example

In 1930, Mohandas Gandhi thought of a unique way to protest British control in India. Salt, an essential part of the human diet, was regulated by the British, and British laws made it illegal for the Indian people to make their own salt. Instead, they had to buy salt that was heavily taxed. Gandhi decided to defy this law. On March 12, 1930, Gandhi and a small group marched 241 miles to the sea. This nonviolent protest encouraged people all over India to defy the salt law, which became an important first step in the movement for Indian independence.

Topic: Mohandas Gandhi's peaceful protest

Important Details: salt was controlled by British, making salt was illegal, Gandhi marched to the sea, people were encouraged to defy the salt law

Main Idea: Gandhi's peaceful and unusual protest was an important step toward Indian independence.

TIP The writer's main idea isn't always clear. In such cases, you'll need to make an educated guess. First, think about the details you've read. Then, answer this question: "If the writer could say only one thing about this paragraph, what would it be?"

Determining Main Idea

DIRECTIONS: Use the following MiniRead with the exercises on page 240.

Speaking the Words

A In the year 384, a young teacher named Augustine went to visit the bishop of Milan. When Augustine arrived, he found the bishop doing something that seemed very strange: reading silently to himself. "When he read," Augustine wrote later, "his eyes scanned the page and his heart sought out the meaning, but . . . his tongue was still . . . he never read aloud."

B Augustine's amazement might be hard for us to understand today, when almost everybody reads silently. Yet, in Augustine's time, the opposite was true: Most people read aloud. Letters on a page were just symbols representing the human voice. People spoke their words aloud as they wrote them, and they expected their readers to complete the process by using their own voices to turn the written words back into speech. When Augustine found the bishop sitting alone with an open book, he expected to hear him reading aloud to himself.

C Even after most people began reading silently in private, books were still often read aloud in groups. In Italy a century and a half after Augustine, St. Benedict wrote a list of rules that is still used to organize life in Catholic monasteries today. The Rule of St. Benedict covered all the essential daily activities of the monks, which included (in addition to eating, sleeping, and praying) reading aloud. Benedict even ordered the monks to hand all the food around the table so that nobody would have to interrupt the reader by asking for something to be passed.

D The books the monks heard at meals were always religious texts. They read these texts as a group for the same reason they prayed as a group: because they practiced their religion as a community, not as individuals. The "read alouds" were not for personal entertainment. In fact, the monks had to be quiet during the reading so that they would not comment privately on what they heard.

E Eventually, of course, silent reading was no longer the strange custom Augustine had stumbled upon; it became the normal way for an individual to read a book. Still, there were times and situations that called for the old practice of reading out loud. Workers in a nineteenth-century Cuban cigar factory, for example, returned to the old style of out-loud readings for a very practical reason.

NAME _____ DATE _____

Determining Main Idea *continued*

In 1865, a poet named Saturnino Martínez decided to publish a newspaper for factory workers. The newspaper contained poems and stories along with political articles exposing the factory owners' mistreatment of cigar workers. However, the majority of the workers were illiterate. How would they read his newspaper?

F   With the help of a local high school principal, Martínez convinced the cigar workers in one factory to have public readings. One of the workers was chosen as the official reader. The other workers chipped in and paid him to read aloud to them while they sat at tables rolling tobacco leaves into cigars. Soon, other factories followed their example.

G   These public readings became very popular. Unlike Benedict's monks, who listened to whatever their abbot thought they should hear, the cigar workers decided for themselves what they wanted to hear. They eventually chose all kinds of books—poetry, novels, histories, political tracts—in addition to Martínez's newspaper. Cigar-making was boring, repetitive work, and the readings made the time go more quickly.

H   Today, many people think of reading aloud as something for adults to do with children who are too young to read to themselves, but in fact, anyone can enjoy hearing a book read aloud. Whether sharing a "read aloud" with a friend or small group, or playing a taped reading, you can enjoy listening to books any time: when you're driving, while you're working, or just when your eyes want a break from words on a page.

Determining Main Idea

MiniRead Practice

Exercise A Use "Speaking the Words" to complete the following.

 1. Paragraph A

 A. topic _____

 B. important details _____

 _____

 C. main idea _____

 _____

 2. Paragraph B

 A. topic _____

 B. important details _____

 _____

 C. main idea _____

 _____

Exercise B Use "Speaking the Words" to complete the following.

 1. Paragraph E

 A. topic _____

 B. important details _____

 _____

 C. main idea _____

 _____

 2. Paragraph G

 A. topic _____

 B. important details _____

 _____

 C. main idea _____

 _____

Determining Main Idea

Application

DIRECTIONS: Read the selection. For two paragraphs, apply the strategy for determining main ideas. Show your work in the graphic organizers below.

Topic	
Important Details	
Main Idea	

Topic	
Important Details	
Main Idea	

(CORE SKILL) Making Inferences — Teacher Notes

At a Glance

- Making inferences, including drawing conclusions and forming generalizations, can help readers better understand and remember the ideas in a text.

- The **Inside + Outside** strategy can help readers make inferences by exploring their own questions about a text.

Direct Instruction

Begin by showing students a poster or transparency of a painting. Have students work to develop and then to answer *5W-How?* questions about the painting. Note that in answering the questions, students should use details from the painting and from their own experience. Next, pass out the Student Notes page and formally introduce the skill and strategy.

Guided Practice

Distribute copies of the MiniRead, and guide students through Exercise A, using Transparency 3 and the steps below.

1. Have students read paragraphs A–E, jotting down *5W-How?* questions as they read. Help them focus on ideas that seem most important or unusual. When they are finished, ask students to share some of their questions with the class.

2. Choose one question requiring an inference (for example, "What was a queen's life like in the 1500s?"). Have students suggest details inside the text and outside the text (from their own experiences) that will help answer the question.

3. Lead students to use the details they suggested in Step 2 to make an inference that answers the question. In particular, have them make clear connections between the ideas they find in the text and those that come from their own knowledge.

4. Choose another question requiring an inference, and repeat Steps 2 and 3.

Independent Practice

Have students work alone or in groups to complete Exercise B of the MiniRead.

Assessment

After choosing a selection (see suggestions, p. 225), hand out the Application activity. Once the activity is completed, have students explain how they used the strategy.

NAME _____ DATE _____

Making Inferences

At a Glance

- An **inference** is an educated guess. A reader makes an inference based on details *inside the text* and *outside the text* (that is, from personal experience).
- Using the **Inside + Outside** strategy will help you to make inferences that will add to your understanding of an author's ideas.

Step-by-Step Strategy

1. As you read a text, jot down a few questions about events or ideas that seem important or unusual. Leave several blank lines below each question.

2. Make two columns below each question labeled "Inside the Text" and "Outside the Text." In the first column, write details you find in the text that may help you answer your question. In the second column, make notes about related ideas from your own knowledge or experience.

3. Use all the details you noted below a question to develop an answer for it.

4. Repeat Steps 2 and 3 for any remaining questions.

Example

Question: Why doesn't the United States have a king or queen?

Inside the Text

- The Declaration of Independence lists things the king of England did that the founders thought were wrong.
- It also says that "all men are created equal" and that the powers of government should come "from the consent of the governed."

Outside the Text

- People always say that anyone can become president. It doesn't matter who your parents are or how much money you have.
- We elect our leaders and write them letters to tell them how we feel about important issues.

Answer: The founders did not want the U.S. to be ruled by a king or queen. They had seen how bad a king could be. Also, it is more fair to everyone when the people can choose and influence a leader.

TIPS

- Focus on ideas or events that stand out in some way. Such ideas might be discussed in depth or might seem out of place at first.
- Ask broad questions, not questions that can be answered in a word or two.
- To note relevant details, watch for clues that tie a detail to your question. For example, if your question is about the cause of an event, look for cause-effect clue words such as "as a result." You might also look for details that describe the situation before that event took place.

Making Inferences

DIRECTIONS: Use the following MiniRead with the exercises on page 246.

Which Queen Was That, Anyway?

A   The popular image of King Henry VIII is of a fat, bearded man chomping on roasted chickens as fast as he can throw the bones away. This image may be an exaggeration, but it's true that Henry VIII had a big appetite. He also had a strong desire to have a son who would be the next king of England, and for that Henry needed a wife. As it turned out, Henry had six wives.

B   Back in the 1500s, a wife was almost completely under her husband's control, and this was especially true of the queen of England. The king and queen were not expected to love each other. Sometimes their first meeting took place on their wedding day. The main purpose of a queen was to give birth to a prince, a future king. Another important purpose of a queen was to help the king politically by belonging to a powerful family. For example, Henry's first wife, Catherine of Aragon, was the daughter of important Spanish nobles. His marriage to Catherine helped Henry make an alliance with Spain against France.

C   Catherine of Aragon was an intelligent, able woman who helped to defend England against a Scottish invasion. She was very popular with the people, and Henry was quite taken with her. Still, when she gave birth to two sons who died in infancy and bore only a daughter who survived, Henry decided to marry one of Catherine's attendants. That attendant was the attractive and charming Anne Boleyn, with whom he had fallen in love. He asked the pope in Rome to annul his marriage to Catherine. An annulment would declare the marriage null and void, as if it had never happened. The pope refused. A long struggle between Henry and the pope began.

D   Ultimately, Henry broke away from the Catholic Church and set up the Church of England as the religion of his country. This enabled the archbishop of Canterbury, who was the leader of the Church of England, to grant Henry a divorce from Catherine and marry him to Anne. This is why England is no longer a primarily Catholic country: because Henry VIII wanted a male heir and thought Anne Boleyn would give him one.

E   Instead, Anne bore Henry a daughter, Elizabeth, who would one day become Queen Elizabeth I, one of the greatest monarchs England has ever had. Henry

Making Inferences *continued*

couldn't predict the future—he still thought he needed a son to be the next monarch. Unfortunately for Anne, she learned that she couldn't have any more children. Henry was devastated and frustrated by this turn of events. He not only fell out of love with Anne but also falsely charged her with crimes and had her beheaded. On the day after Anne's execution, Henry became engaged to Jane Seymour, with whom he had fallen in love.

F   Jane bore a son named Edward, but she died soon after giving birth. Henry had lost his beloved queen but had finally gained a male heir to the English throne. When Edward was nine years old, he would become King Edward VI. Little could Henry know that this long-awaited son would die of tuberculosis at age sixteen, after only seven years on the throne.

G   With Jane gone, Henry needed a new queen. He also needed to forge an alliance with Germany. He sent one of his top ministers to Germany to set up a politically beneficial marriage. The result was Henry's marriage to Anne of Cleves, who was the sister of a powerful German duke. However, when Henry saw Anne and spoke to her, he didn't like her. He divorced her almost immediately. She may have been the luckiest of Henry's six wives: After the divorce, Anne lived a full, comfortable life in England and was respected by all.

H   Henry's fifth queen was Catherine Howard. She was only about fifteen when the forty-nine-year-old Henry took a liking to her and married her. She is probably the least known of Henry's wives. Henry charged her with crimes and had her beheaded only a year and a half after their wedding.

I   Henry's sixth wife was also named Catherine—Catherine Parr. She was thirty-one and had been widowed twice before. Friendly, religious, intelligent, and good-looking, Catherine Parr was a positive influence on Henry. He treated her well, though they had no children together. In 1547, Henry died. Catherine Parr outlived him, but only by one year. During that year she married Thomas Seymour, the brother of Jane, Henry's third wife. Catherine died after giving birth to Thomas's child.

J   Although Henry VIII divorced two wives and beheaded two others, he did something else that was highly unusual and sensational for a monarch in the 1500s: Of the six times Henry married, four of those marriages seem to have been the result of deep affection or actual love.

Making Inferences

Exercise A Use "Which Queen Was That, Anyway?" to complete the following.

1. Write two *5W-How?* questions about important ideas in paragraphs A–E.

   _____

   _____

2. Choose the question that might have a more interesting answer or more details in the text. Jot down details from the passage (Inside the Text) and from your own knowledge or experiences (Outside the Text) that may help you answer the question.

Inside the Text	**Outside the Text**
_____	_____
_____	_____
_____	_____

3. Answer the question based on your notes in both columns above.

   _____

Exercise B Use "Which Queen Was That, Anyway?" to complete the following.

1. Here are two *5W-How?* questions about important ideas in paragraphs F–J.

   What was Henry VIII's attitude toward marriage?

   Why did Henry VIII marry so many times?

2. Choose the question that might have a more interesting answer or more details in the text. Jot down details from the passage (Inside the Text) and from your own knowledge or experiences (Outside the Text) that may help you answer the question.

Inside the Text	**Outside the Text**
_____	_____
_____	_____
_____	_____

3. Answer the question based on your notes in both columns above.

   _____

Making Inferences

Application

DIRECTIONS: As you read an informational selection, jot down *5W-How?* questions on the lines below as questions occur to you. Then, mark the question that you think is most interesting or most supported by details in the text. Use the space provided to list ideas that might help you answer that question. Connect the "Inside the Text" and "Outside the Text" details in order to write an answer to your chosen question.

My questions about the text:

_____

_____

_____

_____

_____

_____

Details to use in answering my chosen question:

Inside the Text	**Outside the Text**
_____	_____
_____	_____
_____	_____
_____	_____
_____	_____

My answer (connecting "Inside" and "Outside" details):

_____

_____

CORE SKILL **Summarizing**

Teacher Notes

At a Glance

- The **GIST** summary strategy (**G**enerating **I**nteractions between **S**chemata and **T**ext; Cunningham, 1982) is a simple, holistic approach appropriate for all readers.

- Students using the strategy learn to summarize increasingly larger chunks of text by building on summaries of smaller chunks.

Direct Instruction

After passing out copies of the Student Notes page, guide students through the explanation of the skill. Then, review the steps of the **GIST** summary strategy, focusing on the example following the strategy.

Guided Practice

Distribute copies of the MiniRead. In guiding students through Exercise A, use the steps below and Transparency 4.

1. Break the reading into sections. (The MiniRead is already broken into sections.)

2. Read aloud the first section, guiding students to identify—by underlining or circling—important words and ideas. (Additionally, you may want to have students cross out nonessential or repetitive ideas.) Record selected words and ideas in the Section Notes column of Transparency 4.

3. Focusing on the Section Notes column, have students suggest short summary sentences. The summary does not have to be a single sentence, but it should be twenty-five words or fewer. Students should use their own words as much as possible. Record a selected response.

4. Repeat the above process for the second section. This time, however, have students create a twenty-five-word summary that is a combination of the first and second sections. You may want to note that the combination summary doesn't need to contain equal amounts of information from both sections.

5. For longer selections, you would continue repeating the basic steps, with the ultimate goal of creating a single summary of the entire selection.

Independent Practice

Have students work alone or in groups to complete Exercise B of the MiniRead.

Assessment

After choosing a selection (see suggestions, p. 225), hand out copies of the Application activity. In reviewing students' completed work, pay particular attention to the final GIST statement.

Summarizing

At a Glance

- A **summary** is a short restatement of the most important ideas in a text.
- Using the **GIST** summary strategy will help you summarize long selections.

Step-by-Step Strategy

1. Divide the selection into sections.

2. Read the first section, noting important words and ideas.

3. Write a brief summary that includes only the most important ideas from the first section. Use your own words as much as possible—but try to use no more than twenty-five words in all.

4. Read the second section. Then, write another summary. This time, however, include in your summary important ideas from *both* sections.

5. Repeat Step 4 as needed. You'll be done when you have a single summary for the whole selection. Remember—try to use no more than twenty-five words!

Example

What is coincidence? Is it just random chance—"the luck of the draw"? An unlikely collision of circumstances? Although mathematicians can use statistics to predict chance, some coincidences are too unusual to be explained. Mathematicians have this to say about it: What *can* happen *will* happen, however unlikely it might seem.

Let's say you're at a party and you meet someone for the first time. What are the chances that both of you have the same birthday? If there are twenty-three people at a party, the odds are fifty-fifty. With fifty people, there is almost a 100 percent chance of at least two people having the same birthday. These "coincidences," statisticians say, are actually more likely than most people might think.

Summary of Section 1:
Coincidence is hard to understand. Statistics can predict chance, but some coincidences can't be explained. Some say coincidences just happen.

Summary of Sections 1 and 2:
Although mysterious, coincidences happen more often than people think. The odds of two strangers sharing a birthday are quite good.

TIPS

- Underline only those ideas that seem most important.
- Cross out details that simply repeat information.
- Replace big word groups with two or three words that stand for the whole group.

Summarizing

DIRECTIONS: Use the following MiniRead with Exercise A on page 252.

MiniRead A

Making Monsters

A   Tom Savini is a special-effects artist who has created many gruesome monsters for horror movies. Born in Pittsburgh in 1946, Savini began reading about and experimenting with monster makeup as a teenager. When he was fourteen, he got a job as Dracula in a traveling show. Later, he served in Vietnam as an army photographer. Sometimes he put fake scars and beards on his soldier friends for fun.

B   Although the special effects in some movies look fake, Savini's special effects are credible. Savini makes monsters using makeup and fake body parts. The fake body parts are made of modeling clay or latex, a type of plastic. Rubber, glue, paint, plaster casts, and false hair are just some of the other materials with which a designer can fabricate a monster. Special-effects artists like Tom Savini who create monsters with makeup are really sculptors and painters. They use a variety of artists' materials to create just the right scary look that a director wants a certain monster to have.

Summarizing

DIRECTIONS: Use the following MiniRead with Exercise B on page 252.

MiniRead B

Computer Monsters

A Since the 1990s, special-effects artists have begun to use computers to design monsters. Graphic artists can design a monster on-screen. These monsters are then put digitally into the movie frame. Creating monsters on a computer takes less time and a lot less space than traditional ways of creating monsters. Many of the dinosaur effects in *Jurassic Park* were designed digitally on computers.

B Many designers are also using computers to help them think up scarier monsters before building them out of the usual materials, such as latex and modeling clay. In other words, the computer screen is a kind of sketch pad. Twenty years ago, an artist would have drawn monsters with pen and paper. Now, an artist can make better drawings at the keyboard.

 People in the monster-making business are wondering which method to use: the old, makeup-and-latex way or computer graphics. Perhaps the best method will be some combination of the old and the new. No matter which method is used, though, it seems that movie monsters are getting creepier than ever.

Summarizing

Exercise A

1. Read section A of "Making Monsters." Then, create a GIST statement that summarizes section A. Use no more than twenty-five words.

_____

_____

_____

_____

2. Read section B of "Making Monsters." Then, create a GIST statement that summarizes section A *and* section B. Use no more than twenty-five words.

_____

_____

_____

_____

Exercise B

1. Read section A of "Computer Monsters." Then, create a GIST statement that summarizes section A. Use no more than twenty-five words.

_____

_____

_____

_____

2. Read section B of "Computer Monsters." Then, create a GIST statement that summarizes section A *and* section B. Use no more than twenty-five words.

_____

_____

_____

_____

Distinguishing Fact from Opinion   Student Notes

At a Glance

- A **fact** is a statement that can be proved true, while an **opinion** cannot be proved.
- Using the **Source or Signal?** strategy will help you to distinguish facts from opinions. It will also help you evaluate the strength of an author's evidence.

Step-by-Step Strategy

1. Read the selection, and underline statements that seem open to debate.

2. To figure out if a statement is a fact, ask, "Can this statement be proved true?" If you think it can, identify the type of **source** that might provide the proof.

3. If you think the statement is an opinion and cannot be proved, look for **opinion signal words.** Opinion words like those below often signal beliefs, feelings, or judgments that cannot be proved or measured.

   - love/hate
   - fascinating/boring
   - brilliant/foolish
   - in my opinion
   - best/worst
   - everyone knows that

   Think about how any signal words relate to the statement and about how believable the evidence is. Then, decide if the overall statement is an opinion.

4. Using Steps 2 and 3, continue identifying underlined statements as facts or opinions. Finally, consider whether the text seems to contain mostly facts or mostly opinions. A text with too many opinions might not be reliable.

Example

Statement: Earthworms improve soil quality, which in turn helps plants grow.	**Source:** gardening book, encyclopedia **Opinion Signal:** none FACT
Statement: No sight is more delightful to a gardener than that of a busy earthworm.	**Source:** unclear; maybe a survey of gardeners **Opinion Signal:** "delightful" OPINION

TIPS These additional tips will help you distinguish facts from opinions.

- Notice whether the author presents ideas that support only one point of view. Also, think about how believable the author is. The author's job title or the organization the author works with can be clues about the author.
- Focus on a few key statements from a passage, not every sentence. Analyze only sentences that make or support claims important to the writer's point.
- Beware of **false facts**—statements that can be proved untrue. "Ants built the Taj Mahal" is a false fact, *not* an opinion. An author may include false facts to mislead readers.

Distinguishing Fact from Opinion

MiniRead

DIRECTIONS: Use the following MiniRead with the exercises on page 258.

What's Bugging Us

A   Insects of the world, unite! For too long we have let ourselves be crushed beneath the heel of our human oppressors. (I do mean crushed beneath the heel. Have you ever heard the expression "squashed like a bug"? Where do you think it comes from?)

B   Yet, though we are small, we are many. The number of insects you can find in a few acres of cow pasture is hundreds of times the entire human population of the planet. Think about it: For every pound of people, there are *three hundred* pounds of bugs. So, what are we waiting for? It's time for us to start throwing our weight around!

C   Humans have no respect for the age and greatness of insect civilization. North Carolina may think the Wright brothers were "first in flight," but insects learned to fly long before any other living creature had wings. Humans celebrate in song and story the kingdoms and castles they had "once upon a time," but honeybee queens ruled vast societies of worker bees before there was even such a thing as a human kingdom. What's more, let's face it: Insects were the first farmers. Leafcutter ants were mixing decaying materials and leaves together to make compost for growing food (a fungus that looks like tiny heads of cauliflower) thousands of years before humans got around to inventing the wheel, let alone the plow.

D   It's time humans started giving credit where credit is due. Why won't they admit that the contributions of insects have led directly to some of the greatest achievements of human civilization? For instance, where would the arts and crafts of Asia be without the silkworm or the lac insect? Thousands of silkworms give up their lives to provide a few spools of silk thread, and it takes nearly a thousand lac insects to produce a single *ounce* of shellac varnish. Do they get credit for it? Try this: The next time you spot a beautiful Japanese kimono or a shiny antique lacquered box in a museum, be sure to read the little printed label that identifies the creator of the piece. The odds are that the insects who made it all possible don't even get an honorable mention.

Distinguishing Fact from Opinion *continued*

E   Humans say that Thomas Edison was the first person to turn night into day with the invention of electric lighting, but who was lighting up the darkness before that? You're right: We were. From the fireflies, which poor Japanese students once kept in lanterns so they could read by their light, to the bees whose beeswax made candles to illuminate the dark cabins of early American settlers, insects have done as much as Edison did to light up the night—and they did it for thousands of years.

F   Insects have even earned an honorable place in the history of science. A handful of overrated human scientists are worshipped as heroes for discovering the laws of heredity. Yet weren't the *real* heroes the millions of fruit flies who devoted their lives, generation after generation, to these genetic studies? I leave you to guess whether there is a single statue of a fruit fly in any public square anywhere on earth.

G   Still, our contributions to human culture are just the icing on the cake (or, as a scarab beetle might put it, "the bacteria on the elephant dung"). The plain fact is that if it weren't for us insects, humans would be roaming around the countryside scavenging for nuts and berries. We insects make human agriculture possible. Without insects to loosen and fertilize the soil, pollinate plants, and eat harmful weeds, there wouldn't be any vegetable gardens, fields of cotton, or apple orchards. In fact, it might not be going too far to say that humans owe their very existence to us. Yet, what thanks do we get? Instead of graciously giving us our fair share of the crops we help to produce, the farmers call us names and plot ways to kill us through chemical warfare. Homicide (the murder of humans) is a crime, but pesticide (the murder of bugs) is paid for by the government. Have they no conscience?

H   The truth is, we are the rightful inhabitants of the earth. Humans may think we exist just to bug them, but we were here before they came along, and we will still be here long after they have disappeared. Warble fly and weevil, answer the call. Firebrat, fur beetle, and froghopper, rally to the cause. Hail to the insect! Bugs rule!

Distinguishing Fact from Opinion   MiniRead Practice

Exercise A Use "What's Bugging Us" to complete the following.

1. Write one significant statement from paragraphs A–D. To decide whether the statement is a fact or an opinion, fill in the following blanks (write "none" if necessary).

   A. Statement: _____

   B. Source that might prove the statement true: _____

   C. Opinion signals or loaded language: _____

   D. Other clues about the strength of evidence: _____

   _____

2. Complete the following sentences.

   A. The statement is (a fact, an opinion) because _____

   _____

   B. The overall evidence (is, is not) strong because _____

   _____

Exercise B Use "What's Bugging Us" to complete the following.

1. Below is a significant statement from paragraph G. To decide whether the statement is a fact or an opinion, fill in the following blanks (write "none" if necessary).

   A. Statement: _"The plain fact is that if it weren't for us insects, humans would be roaming_

   around the countryside scavenging for nuts and berries."

   B. Source that might prove the statement true: _____

   C. Opinion signals or loaded language: _____

   D. Other clues about the strength of evidence: _____

   _____

2. Complete the following sentences.

   A. The statement is (a fact, an opinion) because _____

   _____

   B. The overall evidence (is, is not) strong because _____

   _____

Distinguishing Fact from Opinion   Application

DIRECTIONS: Choose a statement in your reading that seems significant or debatable. Use the steps illustrated in the flowchart below to help you determine whether the statement is a fact or an opinion.

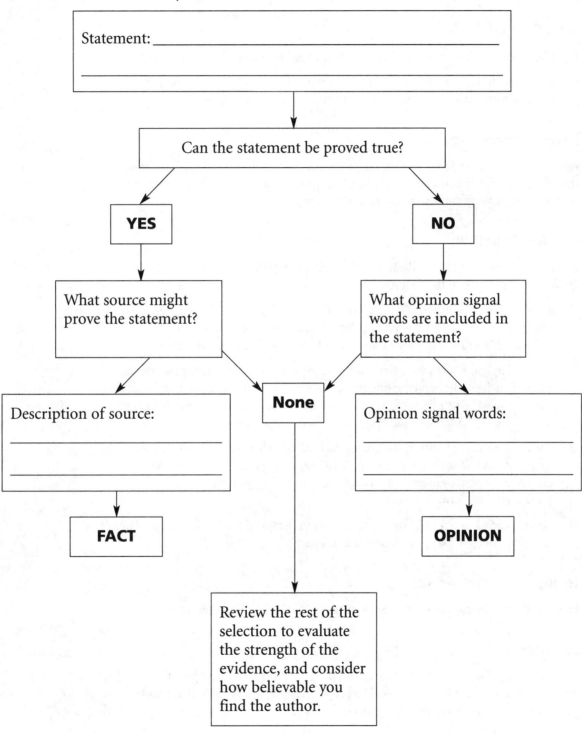

Statement: _____

_____

Can the statement be proved true?

YES

NO

What source might prove the statement?

What opinion signal words are included in the statement?

Description of source:

_____

_____

None

Opinion signal words:

_____

_____

FACT

OPINION

Review the rest of the selection to evaluate the strength of the evidence, and consider how believable you find the author.

(CORE SKILL) Making Predictions   Teacher Notes

At a Glance

- The **A-P-V** (Ask-Predict-Verify) strategy promotes purposeful, active reading.

- Readers will pause to ask questions and predict answers based on textual details and prior knowledge. Students then continue reading to verify predictions.

Direct Instruction

Pass out copies of the Student Notes page. When introducing the skill, emphasize the role of textual details and the reader's background knowledge. Then, review the A-P-V strategy steps and the accompanying example.

Guided Practice

Distribute copies of the MiniRead. Then, using the steps below and Transparency 6, guide students through the first part of the exercise.

1. Read paragraph A aloud. Then, ask questions to elicit predictions. Questions can be specific or general ("What might happen next?" or "What will character X do now?"). For simplicity, record one question on Transparency 6.

2. Ask students to make predictions about the question. Then, prompt students to support each prediction by citing the text and by using background knowledge (for example, "This might turn out to be a ghost story because the title of the story is 'Dark Shadows'"). Record one prediction on Transparency 6.

3. Continue reading, pausing after paragraph B. Ask whether students can verify the prediction. If so, record a model response, which can be broadened to include newly encountered details. Before continuing, guide students to ask questions of their own. Record one question.

4. Repeat Steps 2 and 3 until you feel students understand the basic process. Then, have students complete the Independent Practice.

Independent Practice

Have students work alone or in groups to complete the MiniRead exercise.

Assessment

After choosing a selection (see suggestions, p. 225), hand out the Application activity. Once the activity is completed, review each student's A-P-V chart and provide positive reinforcement for good questions.

Making Predictions

At a Glance

- Active readers think ahead to predict what might happen next.
- The **A-P-V** (Ask-Predict-Verify) strategy will help you make good predictions.

Step-by-Step Strategy

1. Read until you reach a good stopping place, such as at the end of an event or at a break in the action. Then, **ask** a question or two about what might happen next. Write down your questions.

2. For each question, **predict** an answer. To support each prediction, use a "because" statement ("I think . . . because . . ."). Write down your predictions.

3. Continue reading until you reach another good stopping place. If you have read enough information, **verify** your prediction and write down an explanation. Then, ask another question or two about what might happen next.

4. Repeat Steps 2 and 3 as needed. At the end of the reading, review your work. Make sure you have verified every prediction. If a prediction turns out to be wrong or is not addressed in the reading, write down an explanation.

Example

At first, all Ted and Martin could see was a small mound of black fur. The boys stood back and watched for several minutes, but the furry mound didn't move. Ted whistled loudly. There was no response. Suddenly, the animal began to move slightly. Its right paw moved up toward its face as if it were trying to wipe something off its mouth. . . .	**Ask:** What will happen next? **Predict:** I bet the animal will turn out to be dead because Ted whistled loudly and the animal didn't move. **Verify:** It's not dead, but it seems injured.

TIPS

- Good questions usually involve events or characters. "What might happen next?" "Where is this story going?" "How will this story end?" "What will this character do?" "How will this character solve the problem?"
- Good predictions are supported by details in the reading and from your own experience. "There might be a robbery next because that suspicious man has been watching the bank all day. Also, this is a detective story, so there has to be a crime."

Making Predictions

DIRECTIONS: Use the following MiniRead with the exercise on page 264.

Dark Shadows

A   One day Seth, Grimes's fellow student at Cambridge University in England, noticed that Grimes looked exhausted. Grimes should have slept deeply. His rooms were among the nicest on campus. They also were quiet because they overlooked an old graveyard. Concerned, Seth asked his friend what was wrong.

B   At first Grimes didn't want to say what was wrong, but he finally admitted that mysterious scratching on his windows had kept him awake. There were no nearby bushes or trees that could have scraped the glass. Also, the windows were covered with bars to prevent tardy students from climbing in after hours (the main entrance of the dormitory was locked late each night). Grimes said he thought someone might be playing a joke on him. Each time he jumped out of bed to examine the window, the sound stopped. When he got back under the covers, the noise began again.

C   However, another student who was listening to Grimes's story insisted the scratcher was a vampire, and that the graveyard was its home. Grimes laughed, claiming that he didn't believe in vampires. The noises stopped for about a week, and Seth forgot his friend's strange tale.

D   Seth therefore was shocked when he heard Grimes had been raced to the school medical ward one night. Grimes had been found collapsed, hysterically muttering about vampires. University officials investigated. They found badly scraped paint around the outside of one of Grimes's windows. However, the soil under the window didn't have any footprints. Students gossiped endlessly about the incident. Soon the school was divided into two camps: those who believed in the vampire, and those who didn't. Seth decided to visit Grimes and hear the real story.

E   Grimes told his friend that he had fallen asleep at about 11:00 P.M., but soon after, the scratching had awakened him. He was annoyed that the practical joker was back. Grimes turned on the light, but the sound continued. He went into his sitting room, and the scratching became noisier and quicker. Staring into the darkness outside, Grimes saw a hooded figure hammering its fingers on the windowpanes.

Making Predictions *continued*

F   Furious, Grimes yelled at the being. He threatened to fetch the porter—a university employee who lived in the dormitory—for help. In response, the figure beat its fist on the glass. Grimes was so angry that he opened the window's catch. The figure lunged against the windowpane, which slammed into Grimes's forehead, and then suddenly shoved its arm into the room. A horrified Grimes felt fingernails dig into his wrist. As he struggled to pull them out, he saw that the fingers had no flesh; they looked like eagle's long talons, or claws. The figure's hood fell off during the fight, and Grimes looked into its flaming eyes and gaping fangs. Terrified, he tried even harder to free himself. Grimes realized escape was impossible. After screaming in anguish and fainting, he woke in the medical ward.

G   Grimes showed Seth his wrist, which had several deep scars that could have been made by fingernails. He swore that the creature had not been a practical joker wearing a mask. Grimes left school for a semester and insisted on different rooms when he returned. A mathematician moved into his former rooms; he heard the scratching, too, but said it didn't bother him—he had thick shutters put across the windows. Seth claimed that although Grimes's physical scars faded after a year, the emotional scars remained forever.

        This vampire story was told by a real person—Ronald Seth, a British author—who claims it is true. (Peter Grimes, also an actual person, became a classics scholar.)

Making Predictions

Exercise

As you read "Dark Shadows," pause after each paragraph to apply the **A-P-V** prediction strategy. Be sure to support each prediction with a "because" statement. Write all of your work in a chart like the one below.

Ask	Predict	Verify

Making Predictions

DIRECTIONS: Read the story you or your teacher chose. Pause at least three times to apply the **A-P-V** strategy for making predictions. Be sure to follow the steps shown on the Student Notes page. Show your work in a chart like the one below.

Title of story: _____

Ask	Predict	Verify

CORE SKILL Understanding Characters   Teacher Notes

At a Glance

- Understanding characters enriches the literary experience, helping readers make connections to the text and its themes.
- Creating a **character web** helps students discover many facets of a character.

Direct Instruction

Ask students to name well-known characters—from movies, television shows, or literature. Choose one character that all students are familiar with, and have them discuss the traits of that character. Then, hand out copies of the Student Notes page. Discuss the skill and the strategy, focusing on the example provided.

Guided Practice

Distribute copies of MiniRead A, and guide students through Exercise A using Transparency 7 and the steps below.

1. Read the selection aloud, and have students choose a character to analyze. Guide them to choose a character about whom the author provides many details. Write the chosen character's name on Transparency 7.

2. Ask students how they learn about a character. Then, have them list the types of clues authors usually provide (speech, appearance, actions, others' reactions, thoughts/feelings).

3. Have students give details about the character, and ask them to link the details to the corresponding types of clues. Add student responses to the web.

4. Ask students to sum up the ideas in the character web in a sentence or two. What kind of person is the character?

Independent Practice

Have students choose a character from MiniRead B and complete Exercise B.

Assessment

After choosing a selection (see suggestions, p. 225), hand out the Application activity. Once the activity is completed, discuss responses with each student.

NAME _____ DATE _____

Understanding Characters

At a Glance

- Understanding characters will help you get more from the literature you read.
- A **character web** helps you think about difference aspects of a character.

Step-by-Step Strategy

1. Read the selection. Choose the character about whom the author gives the most information or the character who interests you most. Begin a character web by writing the character's name in a circle.

2. To your web, add the ways you learn about the character. For example, some authors provide clues about a character—what a character thinks or how other characters react to him or her. Identify the types of clues included in the selection (for example, "Actions" or "Others' Reactions"). Then, write each type of clue in its own circle and connect it to the character circle.

3. Review the selection you read, looking for details about the character. Add these details to your web. Make a new circle for each detail and connect it to the appropriate type of clue.

4. Use the details in your character web to sum up what kind of person the character is. Think in particular about *why* the character behaves as he or she does.

Example

Here is part of a character web and a summary statement for the character of Gulliver.

What the character is like: Gulliver learns from his struggles against the Lilliputians that he is more likely to get what he wants by treating them kindly.

TIP To develop your summary statement, try to form an idea about the character based on the details you have listed. For example, the writer of the summary statement above draws the conclusion that Gulliver changes his behavior when he sees that doing so will help him get what he wants.

Understanding Characters

DIRECTIONS: Use the following MiniRead with Exercise A on page 270.

MiniRead A

Strangers in Nowhere

A   Children's lives are often transformed while they are asleep, as decisions or events take place. The causes may not be understood for years, but the effects are immediately visible. Such a change occurred the summer when I was ten.

B   Out in the flatlands, our long, languid summers passed without our ever seeing a person we did not know. What we did not know about someone firsthand, someone else regularly reported. That was how life was.

C   You can imagine, then, how perplexed my brother and I were when we found a group of strangers sitting at the breakfast table one morning. They were a mother, two sons, and a baby from a faraway place we could not pronounce. My parents had seen them on the highway, standing forlornly beside the smoking skeleton of a car. At my mother's insistence, the family moved into our home.

D   They stayed with us for only two weeks, yet there was talk all over the county. My mother, usually sensitive to gossip, paid no heed. Despite the language barrier, she spoke to them in English, served her regular menu of meat and potatoes, and knew not to relax her instinctive attention to the activities of young boys.

E   My brother and I befriended the brothers, who knew nothing of rural life. They were jumpy around animals but were not bothered when the local grocer trailed them through the cluttered aisles. They laughed at our old dog, tried to teach us a ball game played only with feet, and flirted with our sister. We communicated mostly through gestures, although the boys learned enough English to hint at adventures they had had in a crowded city half a world away.

F   After the family moved on, people asked questions for months. I had no answers for them. I sometimes wondered why my mother had opened our home to strangers, and years later, I found a clue. After my mother's death, I found a note written in a language she did not know. Attached to it was a note in her own handwriting. It said, "If a child anywhere is in trouble, then my child is—or will be." My mother, ultimately then, had taken in the family for us. I know this simple idea, so typical of my mother, made a difference in many lives.

Understanding Characters

DIRECTIONS: Use the following MiniRead with Exercise B on page 270.

MiniRead B

Aunt Lou

A   Leaning back laughing, James comes sweeping around the end display where the store-brand cereal and syrup are on sale. A willowy girl has just taken his arm, and he is delighted. She likes him, he knows, but he isn't sure how much, so when she makes her joke about shopping like old married people, James laughs carefully.

B   As his head tilts down, white teeth still parted, an image from the far end of the aisle strikes him. It is Aunt Lou, Aunt Lou with her battered old clothes and her stiff hair pushed up any way her hand left it; Aunt Lou, who doted on him as a baby and dotes still; Aunt Lou, who thinks James looks like her dead husband. James sees her at the end of the aisle studying sugar and remembers the made-from-scratch cakes presented every birthday and the "for-a-fine-boy" birthday cards given long after he was too old for them. In an instant James knows his problem. How can he explain to this willowy girl his rough Aunt Lou, her voice louder than those of her four loud dogs, her hobbling walk, her fierce flat eyes, and her nosy questions?

C   He pivots like a dancer, takes the girl out of sight. She pulls back, wanting to visit cereal boxes she liked as a kid. James teases her about growing up on sweet junk, all the while fighting down panic. Aunt Lou might be gone now, or she might be coming this way. It dawns on him, then, that it may already be too late; his hesitation might have betrayed him. She might have recognized his retreating back, could be shuffling hurriedly this instant to thwart whatever strategy he may devise.

D   He hustles the girl toward the soft drinks, grateful for space to consider and scout. The girl is not close now. She is incurious—he seems not to have given himself away—but she is not warm, and the moment is gone. They get the soda and James steers to an express lane, where they wait while a twelve-item violator tries the clerk's patience and tortures James, who alternately slouches and periscopes store traffic. As long as he can, James avoids what he knows about himself, hopes his aunt didn't see him, prays that she won't, wishes somehow that she had, and that she would somehow understand or at least forgive a fine boy.

Understanding Characters

MiniRead Practice

Exercise A Use "Strangers in Nowhere" to complete the following.

1. Choose a character to analyze. Below, identify the character and two types of clues the author provides (one is listed for you). Then, add details from the selection. Draw your own circles as needed. If you need more space, create the web on your own paper.

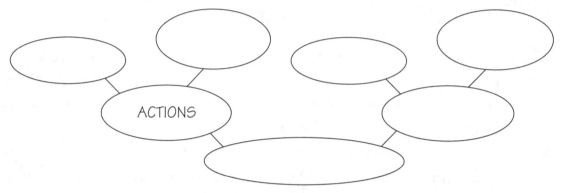

2. Write a statement that sums up what the character is like. _____

_____

Exercise B Use "Aunt Lou" to complete the following.

1. Choose a character to analyze. Below, identify the character and at least three types of clues the author provides. Draw your own circles for details. If you need more space, create the web on your own paper.

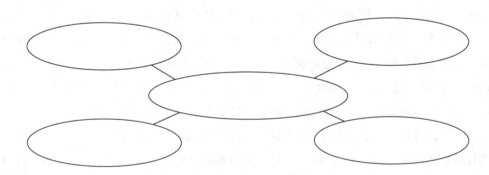

2. Write a statement that sums up what the character is like. _____

_____

Understanding Characters

Application

DIRECTIONS: Read the selection you or your teacher chose. Choose a character about whom the author provides many details or a character that interests you. Use the character web below to record the character's name and at least three types of clues the author provides. List details about the character in new circles, and connect them to the appropriate type of clue. Then, summarize what the character is like based on the details.

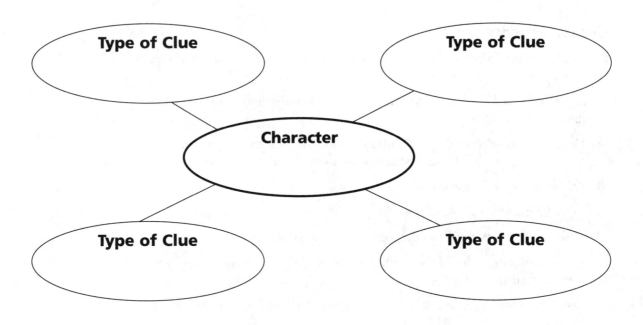

What the character is like: _____

_____

CORE SKILL **Recognizing Theme**   Teacher Notes

At a Glance

- Recognizing theme requires students to make inferences about the author's meaning and to connect the text with their life experiences.

- The **Most Important Word** strategy will help students identify theme by focusing on an important word and how it relates to narrative elements.

Direct Instruction

Write a few universal themes on the board. Then, have students list stories, movies, poems, or other works that express these themes. Next, pass out the Student Notes. Review the skill and discuss the steps of the strategy.

Guided Practice

Distribute copies of MiniRead A. In guiding students through Exercise A, use the steps below and Transparency 8.

1. As students read the selection, have them note any repeating words, images, or ideas.

2. Have students select one word that they think is the most important and write it in the space provided. Caution students not to choose a character's name.

3. Ask students how the word relates to . . .

- the characters—What are the characters like? How do they change?

- the conflict—What causes the conflict? Who is involved in the struggle?

- the resolution—How is the conflict resolved? What do the characters learn from their struggles?

4. Instruct students to write a statement of theme based on the most important word and how it relates to the story.

Independent Practice

Have students work alone or in groups to complete Exercise B of the MiniRead.

Assessment

After choosing a selection (see suggestions, p. 225), hand out the Application activity. Once the activity is completed, have students explain how they used the Most Important Word strategy to identify theme.

NAME _____ DATE _____

Recognizing Theme

At a Glance

- **Theme** is the general idea or insight about life that a story reveals. The theme usually is not stated directly. You must develop your own idea about the theme based on the story and the characters' actions.
- The **Most Important Word** strategy will help you identify the theme of a story.

Step-by-Step Strategy

1. Read the passage. Note any repeating words, images, or ideas.

2. Think about the story and how it ends. Then, select one word that you think is the most important and write it down. *(Do not choose a character's name.)*

3. Next, think about why the word is important. Write down how the word relates to

   - the characters—What are the characters like? How do they change?

   - the conflict—What causes the conflict? Who is involved in the struggle?

   - the resolution—How is the conflict resolved? What do the characters learn from their struggles?

4. Review your ideas about the word, and write a statement of theme. Remember that themes should always be written as complete sentences.

Example

Most Important Word:	Imagination
Characters:	Walter Mitty has a wild imagination and often daydreams. Walter Mitty's wife doesn't seem very imaginative and gives Walter Mitty a hard time.
Conflict:	Walter Mitty must use his imagination to keep his life from being too boring.
Resolution:	Walter Mitty continues to daydream and use his imagination to relieve his boredom.
Theme:	The power of imagination can make life more interesting.

TIPS Along with the strategy, here are some tips that will help you to identify the theme.

- After you read the selection, look at the title to see if it provides any clues about the theme of the story.
- Don't worry if the theme you identified is different from someone else's. Selections usually have more than one theme.

Recognizing Theme

MiniRead

DIRECTIONS: Use the following MiniRead with Exercise A on page 276.

MiniRead A

Distant Dreams

A   Once there was a man who had everything he needed to be happy. Handsome, with a beautiful wife, he worked for many years at a good job and made a good salary. He and his wife lived in a pretty little house with a flower garden out back bordered by a trim, green lawn. They had two lovely children, a boy and a girl. Nevertheless, the man was not content. Polite, yet distant, his eyes were often fixed on some faraway horizon, searching, restlessly searching. His patient wife and his loving children were puzzled by this. The man was with them, but his thoughts were not. Instead of joining them in family activities, the man would sit on the porch, lost in his thoughts. If they tried to engage him, he would speak to them softly and kindly, but his attention would soon drift away. Gradually, they stopped trying to draw him out and went on with their lives.

B   One day there was a change. The man realized that his search was needless. The horizon held nothing of value. Happiness dwelt not in the restless winds, which blew toward the horizon, but here, in this house, with his family. However, the years had passed, and the laughter of his wife and children as they chased fireflies or played some pretend game in the garden had faded, like the last leaves of autumn that float to the ground, there to lie as a reminder of what once was. He tried to get involved with his family and their activities, but it was too late. The children had grown up and moved away. His beloved wife, sad to see her children leave, gradually lost her vibrancy and passed away as gently as she had lived her life with a man whose eyes had been seduced by a distant horizon. The man was left alone with his distant thoughts, but now his eyes were fixed on the past.

Recognizing Theme

DIRECTIONS: Use the following MiniRead with Exercise B on page 276.

MiniRead B

Louder Than Words

A   Dad has never been good at discussing his feelings. He grew up around men who showed their affection by bringing home the monthly paycheck and supporting the interests of their children. Dad has always worked long hours, yet he made sure to attend every single game when I pitched for my high school team. I could always find him leaning forward with his intent, penetrating gaze. He did not jump up and down or shout like other parents. If we won, he said, "Good job, Son." If we lost, he said we would do better next time. Other than that, we never talked about my game. I never knew how he felt about my baseball career—or about me. When I won a baseball scholarship to a university several states away, he had simply responded with his usual "Good job, Son."

B   It wasn't until I came home for a visit between semesters that I discovered how he really felt. When I was looking for writing paper in his desk drawer, I found an overstuffed folder, brimming with newspaper clippings and photos. The photos were of me playing baseball over the years—a toddler swinging a bat that was bigger than me, a boy wearing a Little League uniform, a teenager smiling triumphantly and riding high on the shoulders of my teammates when we won the championship. Most of the newspaper clippings were old and yellowed. They were from the local paper and my high school's paper. Other clippings were new, though. They were from my university's paper. Dad must have subscribed so that he could keep up with my progress. My eyes began to sting as I leafed through the photos and clippings. They told me what he has never managed to say: He loves me and is really proud of me.

Recognizing Theme

MiniRead Practice

Exercise A

1. Write down what you believe is the most important word in "Distant Dreams."

   Most Important Word: _____

2. Describe how the word relates to the following elements.

   A. Characters: _____

   _____

   B. Conflict: _____

   _____

   C. Resolution: _____

   _____

3. Based on how the word relates to the story, write a statement of theme.

   Theme: _____

   _____

Exercise B

1. Write down what you believe is the most important word in "Louder Than Words."

   Most Important Word: _____

2. Describe how the word relates to the following elements.

   A. Characters: _____

   _____

   B. Conflict: _____

   _____

   C. Resolution: _____

   _____

3. Based on how the word relates to the story, write a statement of theme.

   Theme: _____

   _____

Recognizing Theme

DIRECTIONS: Read the selection you or your teacher chose. As you do, note any repeating words, images, or ideas. Write down the word you think is the most important. Next, write down how that word relates to the story's characters, conflict, and resolution. Then, think about how the word relates to the story and write a statement of theme.

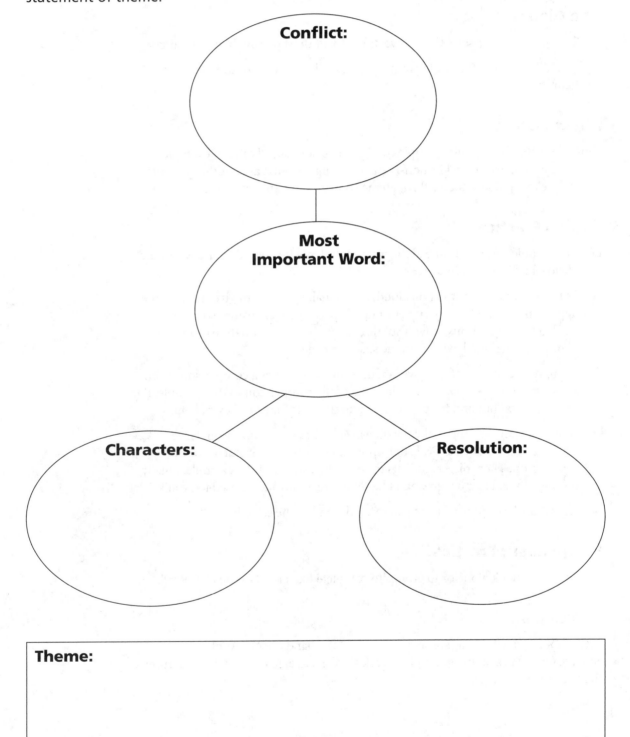

Conflict:

Most Important Word:

Characters:

Resolution:

Theme:

(CORE SKILL) Understanding Figurative Language

Teacher Notes

At a Glance

- Struggling readers sometimes have difficulty understanding figurative language.

- The following strategy will help struggling readers recognize and interpret figurative language.

Direct Instruction

Show students a few simple examples of figurative language. For each example, discuss the comparison and its non-literal meanings. Then, pass out the Student Notes page and guide students through the strategy steps and example.

Guided Practice

Distribute copies of the MiniRead. In guiding students through Exercise A, use the steps below and Transparency 9.

1. Begin by reading the selection aloud, occasionally pausing to give students the opportunity to identify examples of figurative language. Prompt students as needed (with questions or with subtle changes in your intonation). Once an example is identified, write it in the space provided.

2. Remind students that figurative language always involves a comparison. Then, ask students to identify the two elements of the comparison in the example. For implied metaphor and for personification, students may need extra help.

3. Guide students to explain the possible meaning of the comparison. Have students brainstorm a short list of similarities for the two elements of the comparison. Then, direct students to study the context of the example. Finally, prompt students with a question like "How are X and Y supposed to be alike?"

4. Repeat the basic process until you reach the end of the selection.

Independent Practice

Have students work alone or in groups to complete Exercise B of the MiniRead.

Assessment

After choosing a selection (see suggestions, p. 225), hand out the Application activity. Once the activity is completed, ask students to explain how they interpreted the figurative language.

Understanding Figurative Language — Student Notes

At a Glance

- **Figurative language** is non-literal language. For example, in the sentence "Hearing thunder, the tree shook in fear," the tree is not literally a person. The tree is simply being compared to a person. The comparison creates a colorful image by suggesting that the tree has feelings, *like* a person.
- Figurative language is common in poetry. However, it is also common in stories, informational texts, and everyday conversation.
- The following strategy will help you recognize and interpret figurative language.

Step-by-Step Strategy

1. Pause anytime you read language that is non-literal.

2. Identify the two things being compared.

3. Figure out how the two things compared are supposed to be similar, or alike. In other words, determine what the writer is suggesting in making the comparison.

Example

Fame is a bee by Emily Dickinson Fame is a bee. It has song— It has a sting— Ah, too, it has a wing.	*Fame is not really a bee. The poet is making a comparison. She is saying that fame is like a bee—that it can be pleasing like a song and hurtful like a sting, and that it can make you feel as light as if you're flying.*

TIPS

- Close your eyes and try to picture the meaning of the words. If the picture is extraordinary, you have probably found an example of figurative language.
- Look for signal words. The words *like, as, than,* and *resembles* sometimes signal similes, which are a kind of figurative language.
- Study the context of the figurative language. The words or sentences around the figurative language may provide clues about its meaning.

Understanding Figurative Language   MiniRead

DIRECTIONS: Use the following MiniRead with exercises A and B on page 282.

I Wandered Lonely as a Cloud
by William Wordsworth

A   I wandered lonely as a cloud
That floats on high o'er vales and hills,
When all at once I saw a crowd,
A host, of golden daffodils,
Beside the lake, beneath the trees,
Fluttering and dancing in the breeze.

B   Continuous as the stars that shine
And twinkle on the Milky Way,
They stretched in never-ending line
Along the margin of a bay;
Ten thousand saw I at a glance,
Tossing their heads in sprightly dance.

C   The waves beside them danced, but they
Outdid the sparkling waves in glee;
A poet could not but be gay,
In such a jocund company;
I gazed—and gazed—but little thought
What wealth the show to me had brought:

Understanding Figurative Language *continued*

D   For oft, when on my couch I lie
In vacant or in pensive mood,
They flash upon that inward eye
Which is the bliss of solitude;
And then my heart with pleasure fills,
And dances with the daffodils.

Understanding Figurative Language   MiniRead Practice

Exercise A Read the Wordsworth poem to complete the following.

1. Write down one example of figurative language from stanza A. _____

    _____

    A. What two things are being compared? _____

    B. How are the two things similar? What does the comparison mean? _____

    _____

    _____

2. Write down one example of figurative language from stanza B. _____

    _____

    A. What two things are being compared? _____

    B. How are the two things similar? What does the comparison mean? _____

    _____

    _____

Exercise B Read the Wordsworth poem again. Then, complete the following.

1. Write down one example of figurative language from stanza C. _____

    _____

    A. What two things are being compared? _____

    B. How are the two things similar? What does the comparison mean? _____

    _____

    _____

2. Write down one example of figurative language from stanza D. _____

    _____

    A. What two things are being compared? _____

    B. How are the two things similar? What does the comparison mean? _____

    _____

    _____

Understanding Figurative Language   Application

DIRECTIONS: Read the selection. Find two examples of figurative language, and complete a chart for each example.

Figurative Language

Example	
Two Things Compared	
Similarities	
Meaning	

Example	
Two Things Compared	
Similarities	
Meaning	

(CORE SKILL) **Comparing and Contrasting**   Teacher Notes

At a Glance

- Comparing and contrasting characters, events, or ideas from two literary works or within a single work can help students better understand literature.

- Creating a **Venn diagram** can help readers make clear and insightful connections between and within works of literature.

Direct Instruction

Ask students to name two well-known movies or television shows. Have them briefly discuss how the main characters, settings, plot events, and themes of each are alike and different. Then, point out that they can make the same kinds of comparisons about literature. Hand out copies of the Student Notes page. Discuss the skill and the strategy, focusing on the example.

Guided Practice

Distribute copies of MiniRead A, and guide students through Exercise A using Transparency 10 and the steps below.

1. Read the selection aloud, and have students identify details about the two main characters. Lead students to draw some conclusions about each character's personality.

2. Ask students to provide the label for each circle of the Venn diagram ("Elly" and "Madison"). Then, ask students to place the "similar" details in the center of the Venn diagram and the "different" details in the separate part of the appropriate circle.

3. Have students identify the types of details included in the diagram. If the two separate portions of the diagram do not contain the same kinds of details, have students look for more details. Add any new details to the diagram.

4. Have students summarize, in one or two sentences, the most important similarities and differences.

Independent Practice

Have students complete Exercise B, using MiniReads A and B.

Assessment

After choosing one or two selections (see suggestions, p. 225), hand out the Application activity. Once work is completed, discuss responses with each student.

NAME _____ DATE _____

Comparing and Contrasting

At a Glance

- Comparing and contrasting can help you better understand what you read.
- Using a **Venn diagram** will make it easier to find similarities and differences.

Step-by-Step Strategy

1. Read the selection. Identify two characters, two settings, two events, or two themes to compare and contrast. Then, re-read, noting characteristics or details about each of the characters, settings, events, or themes.

2. Label the two circles of a Venn diagram with the two things being compared and contrasted. Then, put the details you noted in Step 1 in the circles as follows: Details that apply to both things go in the center, where the circles overlap. Details that apply to one thing but not the other go in the separate part of the appropriate circle.

3. Review your diagram to make sure you included the same types of details for both things. For example, if you are comparing and contrasting two settings and have details about what people do in one setting but not the other, re-read the selection and add details about what people do in the other setting.

4. Use the information in your diagram to state a sentence or two summarizing the most important similarities or differences between the two things.

Example

The Venn diagram below compares and contrasts the mythological characters Eris and Loki.

Eris   **both**   **Loki**

- Greek goddess
- her mischief started Trojan War
- discord, strife

- caused problems
- got revenge for not being invited to a big celebration

- Norse god
- his deception caused death of god Balder
- trickster, evil

Summary: Although they come from different cultures' mythology, both Eris and Loki cause trouble and death through their trickery and mischief.

TIP You will need to draw conclusions based on details in the text and on your own knowledge in order to make a thorough, thoughtful comparison. Draw conclusions both to gather details for your diagram and to develop your summary statement.

Comparing and Contrasting

DIRECTIONS: Use the following MiniRead with the exercises on page 288.

MiniRead A

The Truth

A   The two girls sat in the principal's office not looking at each other, the principal, or their teacher. One girl had cheated on a test; the other knew it but wasn't going to be a snitch. The principal claimed she could figure out who did it just by watching the girls—"Guilt always shows," she said. Elly tugged on a strand of her long hair and began twisting it around her finger. She seemed bored. Madison bit a fingernail and chewed on her lips. She looked as if she was about to cry. Neither girl looked the principal in the eyes. Elly looked angry, while Madison looked scared. Madison finally said, "So what are you going to do to us?"

B   The principal leaned back in her chair. "Clearly, you two ladies don't think alike, so I'm surprised you answered an essay question the same way—word for word." Their teacher, putting on his best "tough guy" act, grunted, "Uh huh." The principal waited a beat and then leaned forward. "Elly, please explain one effect of the Industrial Revolution."

C   Elly turned red and glanced around the dimly lit office, taking in the flimsy paneling and water-stained perforated ceiling tiles. Finally, she locked eyes with the principal for a second and then looked away.

D   After what seemed like an eternal silence, the principal turned to the other girl, whose face had relaxed. "Madison, please wait outside." The girl stepped cautiously past the teacher, who gave her a slight smile.

E   The principal gave Elly a resigned look. "I appreciate your covering for a fellow student, but you need to be more careful." The astonished teacher's eyes darted back and forth between principal and student, who shared a knowing gaze. I'll let Madison know you didn't rat on her."

F   Elly nodded and gathered her things. Her teacher looked at her as if he were seeing her for the first time. "Mr. Cox, the Industrial Revolution led to the growth of the middle class, more leisure time, and better food supplies, but it also caused toxic pollution and horrible working conditions."

Comparing and Contrasting

DIRECTIONS: Use the following MiniRead with Exercise B on page 288.

MiniRead B

An Unlikely Path

A   The sun began its descent to the horizon as I walked, mulling over what my college major should be. With my mind in a daze, I didn't see the shaggy mutt following me until his tail playfully swatted my leg. He had bushy eyebrows that seemed to rise in anticipation when I bent down to pet his head.

B   "Go home, Shaggy," I told him. He didn't listen, and kept following me until I crossed the street. Interested in a bag of food scraps lying next to a wastebasket, he paused at the curb to investigate. He withdrew his wiry snout from the bag, his teeth clenching a bounty of discarded bread and cheese. Eager to show off his loot, he looked up and noticed that I had crossed the street. He bounded onto the pavement to catch up with his newfound friend.

C   "No, stop!" I shouted when I saw the oncoming car. The screeching sound of the tires and the hard smack of the bumper hitting the dog's side caused every pore on my body to open and flush with adrenaline and shock.

D   If only I had kept walking or he hadn't seen me, I thought frantically as I kneeled over the dog to see if he was still breathing. As he lay there, I brushed his matted hair away from his eyes and cradled his head in my hands. He was still breathing and tried to stand up, but his two back legs were useless.

E   "I'm so sorry. I didn't see your dog. He just bounded out before I could stop," said the driver.

F   Ten minutes later, the dog and I were in the examination room of an animal clinic. Shaggy had no internal injuries, just a cut on his head and two broken legs.

G   Because of his injuries, Shaggy would need constant care. I agreed to pay for his stay at the vet's—by working three afternoons a week—and adopt him as my pet.

H   During those afternoons at the clinic, my interest centered on the animals. As each day went by, I enjoyed work more and more. Out of the blue, I had discovered my college major: pre-veterinary medicine.

I   It seems strange that a stray dog led me to my career. Sometimes accidents can lead us to a path we may not otherwise have considered.

Comparing and Contrasting

MiniRead Practice

Exercise A

1. Complete the Venn diagram below for the characters from "The Truth."

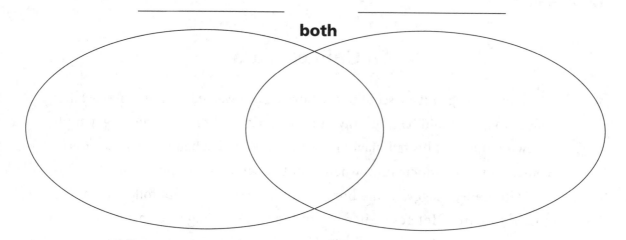

_____   _____

both

2. Write a sentence or two summarizing the characters' similarities and differences.

_____

_____

Exercise B

1. Complete the Venn diagram below for two characters, events, or themes from "The Truth" and "An Unlikely Path."

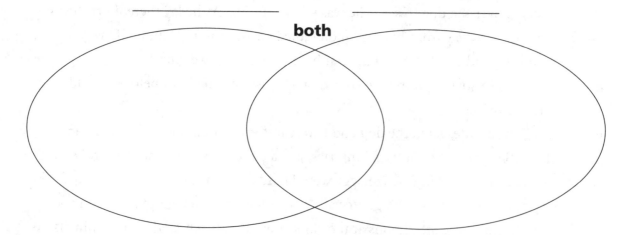

_____   _____

both

2. Write a sentence or two summarizing the similarities and differences in your diagram.

_____

_____

Comparing and Contrasting

DIRECTIONS: As you read, choose two characters, settings, events, or themes to compare and contrast. Gather details about each of the subjects, and label the two separate parts of the circles in the diagram below. List details that fit one or both subjects in the appropriate parts of the diagram. After making sure you have listed the same types of details for both subjects, write a sentence or two summarizing the most important similarities and differences.

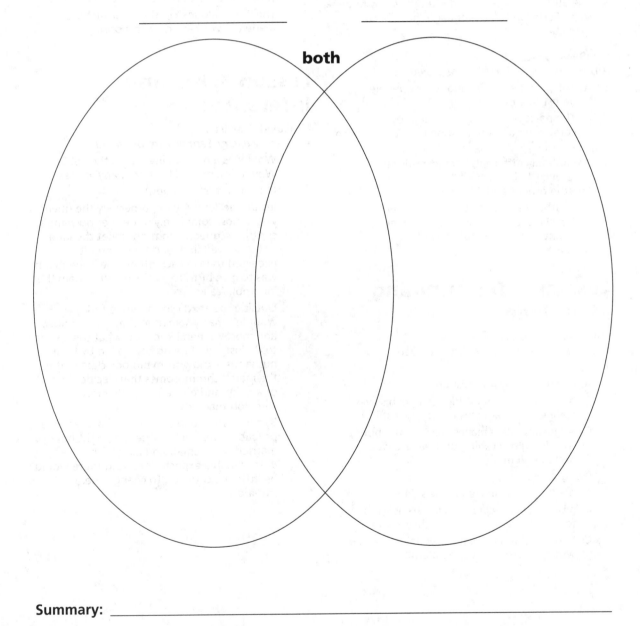

_____   _____

both

Summary: _____

_____

Answer Key

Lesson 1: Identifying Text Structure

MiniRead Exercise A
Answers will vary. Samples are provided.

1. **A.** The passage will be about the way languages are lost.
   B. The passage will organize ideas by cause and effect to show how languages die.
2. "cause," "However," "change," "As a result," "because"
3. The author uses cause and effect to show how some Peruvian tribal languages have become extinct.

MiniRead Exercise B
Answers will vary. Samples are provided.

1. **A.** The passage will be about how people adjust to a new life.
   B. The passage will organize ideas by comparing and contrasting the new life with the old life.
2. "completely different," "most noticeable difference," "in contrast," "in sharp contrast," "on the other hand," "In contrast"
3. The author uses contrast to show how the Indian climate, dress, and housing were different from the British way of life.

Lesson 2: Determining Main Idea

MiniRead Exercise A
Answers will vary. Samples are provided.

1. Paragraph A
   A. Augustine's visit to bishop
   B. bishop doing something strange; his eyes scanned the page; his tongue was still
   C. Augustine was amazed because the bishop was doing something unusual: He was reading silently.
2. Paragraph B
   A. reading aloud in Augustine's time
   B. most people read aloud; letters as symbols for voices; people spoke as they wrote
   C. In Augustine's time, most people expected written words to be read aloud.

MiniRead Exercise B
Answers will vary. Samples are provided.

1. Paragraph E
   A. reading aloud in later times
   B. silent reading became normal way for reading a book; Cuban cigar factory returned to out-loud readings; majority of workers were illiterate
   C. Although reading silently had become the normal way to read in the nineteenth century, some situations called for reading out loud.
2. Paragraph G
   A. the popularity of the public readings
   B. workers could choose what was read; they chose all kinds of books; work was boring
   C. The "read-alouds" in the cigar factories made the workers' days less boring.

Lesson 3: Making Inferences

MiniRead Exercise A
Answers will vary. Samples are provided.

1. What was a queen's life like in the 1500s? Why did Henry VIII have so many wives?
2. (based on first question)
   Inside the Text: A wife, especially the queen, was almost completely under her husband's control. A queen might not meet the king until the wedding, and they weren't expected to love each other. The queen's job was to give birth to a prince and to help the king politically.

   Outside the Text: Most women today wouldn't marry someone they didn't know, and most women I know do what they want to do instead of being controlled by their husbands. I know from biology class that it's the male's chromosomes that decide the sex of a baby, and girls are slightly more common than boys.
3. By today's standards, the life of a queen was probably stressful because she might be married to a demanding king with unreasonable expectations, and there would be little she could do to change the situation.

MiniRead Exercise B
Answers will vary. Samples are provided.

1. What was Henry VIII's attitude toward marriage? Why did Henry VIII marry so many times?

2. (based on first question)

   Inside the Text: He changed England's religion just so he could marry the woman he chose. He had six wives; he divorced two wives and had two others beheaded on false charges. He married several times for love instead of for political gain, even though most kings were not expected to love their queens.

   Outside the Text: No other ruler since Henry VIII so drastically changed England's religion. Divorce became common only in the twentieth century. Love is the most important thing in most marriages today. A ruler should obey the law.

3. Henry VIII considered it so important to be married to someone he loved—but only until he fell out of love—that he made a lasting change to England's religion, had two divorces centuries before divorce became common, and misused his country's law.

Lesson 4: Summarizing

MiniRead Exercise A
Answers will vary. Samples are provided.

1. Tom Savini is a special-effects artist who makes monsters for movies. He has been interested in monster makeup most of his life.

2. Tom Savini, a special-effects artist, uses a variety of materials to make his monsters look realistic.

MiniRead Exercise B
Answers will vary. Samples are provided.

1. Computers are used to create digital monsters, which are then added to movies. Using computers takes less time and space than traditional ways.

2. Artists use computers to sketch out ideas before creating monsters. Using computers is very efficient and helps make monsters scarier.

Lesson 5: Distinguishing Fact from Opinion

MiniRead Exercise A
Answers will vary. Samples are provided.

1. A. "For every pound of people, there are *three hundred* pounds of bugs."
   B. a book on insects or nature
   C. none
   D. major support in this section is almost all facts

2. A. The statement is (a fact) because it can be proved true.
   B. The overall evidence (is) strong because it is mostly facts, even though the writer also gets emotional and tries to make readers sympathize with insects.

MiniRead Exercise B
Answers are based on the sample statement provided.

1. A. "The plain fact is that if it weren't for us insects, humans would be roaming around the countryside scavenging for nuts and berries."
   B. none; there's no way to know what would happen without insects
   C. "plain fact," "us insects," "roaming around," "scavenging"
   D. lots of questions and loaded language; just a few facts in this section

2. A. The statement is (an opinion) because it would be impossible to prove true or false.
   B. The overall evidence (is not) strong because, even though some facts are included, the writer sounds too emotional and includes too many opinions.

Lesson 6: Making Predictions

MiniRead Exercise
Answers will vary. Samples, which are grouped by paragraph, are provided.

In Paragraph A

Question 1: What kind of story will this be?

Prediction 1: This might turn out to be a scary ghost story because the title of the story is "Dark Shadows" and because Grimes's room overlooks a graveyard.

In Paragraph B

Question 2: What is making the scratching noise?

Prediction 2: I think the noise might be from a ghost scratching on the window because most of the natural causes (tree limbs, etc.) were ruled out as explanations.

In Paragraph C

Question 3: What will happen next?

Prediction 3: I bet the scratching will start up again because it seems too early in the story for it to stop.

In Paragraph D

Verification 3: Grimes was taken to the medical ward, but I'm not sure that he heard any more scratching.

Verification 1 and 2: This is a scary story, although it's about vampires, not ghosts.

Question 4: Will this turn out to be a hoax?

Prediction 4: I think it might be a hoax because there seems to be too much evidence (scraped paint and no footprints) pointing toward a vampire. The writer probably wants to make it seem real so that the ending will be more of a surprise.

In Paragraph E

Verification 3 (continued): The scratching did start up again.

Question 5: What will Grimes do next?

Prediction 5: Because he still believes it's a practical joke, I think Grimes will chase the hooded figure to find out who it is.

In Paragraph F

Verification 4: Grimes doesn't believe it's a joke now. If it's a person playing a trick, the person has a convincing costume.

Verification 5: Grimes didn't chase the hooded figure. The figure grabbed Grimes and dug its fingernails into Grimes's wrist.

Question 6: What will happen next?

Prediction 6: Because of his terrifying experience, Grimes may move away, leaving the mystery unsolved. Lots of scary stories end with a question mark.

In Paragraph G

Verification 6 and 4 (continued): He did leave, but he came back to live in a different room. Grimes, who is a real person, told this story and said that the creature was not a practical joker wearing a mask.

Lesson 7 Understanding Characters

MiniRead Exercise A
Sample answer is based on analysis of the narrator's mother.

1. **actions:** insists that the stranded family move in; ignores gossip; maintains household routines **thoughts:** she believes that helping others helps her family **others' reactions:** the neighbors gossip about her; her sons are puzzled; the stranded family is grateful

2. Though the author's mother seems to be an ordinary, rural homemaker, she endures difficulties to help strangers, putting the welfare of children above her own reputation.

MiniRead Exercise B
Sample answer is based on analysis of Aunt Lou.

1. **appearance:** old clothes; messy hair; rough and loud demeanor; hobbling walk; fierce eyes **thoughts/feelings:** loves James; sees his resemblance to her late husband; asks nosy questions **actions:** every year makes a birthday cake from scratch for James and gives him a juvenile birthday card; keeps four loud dogs **others' reactions:** James hopes that she won't see him and that she will see him and forgive him

2. Aunt Lou may not seem socially acceptable, but she clearly loves James.

Lesson 8: Recognizing Theme

MiniRead Exercise A
Answers will vary. Samples are provided.

1. Contentment

2. A. The man is not content with his life and seems to be searching for something more.

   The wife and children don't understand why their father is not content. They try to involve him in their lives but are unsuccessful.

   B. The man's discontent does not allow him to establish a good relationship with his family. When he later tries to get involved with them, he is unsuccessful.

   C. The children move away, his wife dies, and the man is left alone with his thoughts and discontent.

3. If people spend their lives searching for something more rather than appreciating what they have, they will never find contentment.

MiniRead Exercise B
Answers will vary. Samples are provided.
1. Communication
2. A. The son plays baseball. He appreciates his father's support but wishes that his father would communicate his feelings.
   The father is not good at discussing his feelings. He shows affection by supporting the interests of his son.
   B. The father and son don't communicate as much as the son would like. The son wants to know how his father feels about him and his baseball achievements.
   C. The son realizes that his father loves him and is proud of him even though his father has never told him so.
3. A person's actions can communicate how he or she feels.

Lesson 9: Understanding Figurative Language

MiniRead Exercise A
Answers will vary. Samples are provided.
1. "I wandered lonely as a cloud / That floats o'er vales and hills"
   A. The poet compares himself to a cloud.
   B. Like a single cloud in the sky, the poet is alone and lonely.
2. "Ten thousand saw I at a glance, / Tossing their heads in sprightly dance."
   A. The poet compares flowers moving in the breeze to dancers moving their heads as they dance.
   B. The breeze moves the daffodils with the energy of a happy dance.

MiniRead Exercise B
Answers will vary. Samples are provided.
1. "The waves beside them danced, but they / Outdid the sparkling waves in glee"
   A. The poet compares both waves and flowers to happy dancers.
   B. The movement of the waves and the flowers reminds the poet of happy dancers and makes him happy.

2. "And then my heart with pleasure fills, / And dances with the daffodils."
   A. The poet compares his heart when he is happy to the flowers he saw moving in the breeze.
   B. The poet is saying that a beautiful scene in nature can reflect and reinforce his own happiness.

Lesson 10: Comparing and Contrasting

MiniRead Exercise A
1. **Elly:** acts bored; does not answer question at first
   both: don't want to tell what happened; in an uncomfortable position
   Madison: acts nervous, then relieved; did cheat
2. Though neither student wants to tell the truth, Elly's honesty is paradoxically revealed by her uncooperative attitude and Madison's reaction to it.

MiniRead Exercise B
Answers will vary. Sample response is based on comparison of themes.
1. **"The Truth":** Elly is revealed to be an honest and knowledgeable person
   both: Elly and the narrator did not choose situation they find themselves in; characters try to protect someone who makes a bad decision
   "An Unlikely Path": narrator discovers what he wants to do
2. The themes of the two stories both have to do with uncovering a truth as a result of being put in a difficult position.

The Anglo-Saxons: 499–1066
Based on the Student Edition text by David Adams Leeming

The Spirit of the Celts

In the fourth century B.C. Greek travelers visited what is now Great Britain. There they met up with tall, blond warriors who called themselves Celts. Among these Celts were a group called the Britons. The Britons gave the land one of its current names— Britain.

The Celts believed that spirit-gods were everywhere: in rivers, trees, and stones. These gods were moody and all-powerful. Rituals and sacrifices were performed by priests called Druids to keep the gods pleased. It's even possible that the Druids used Stonehenge for some of their rituals.

The Celtic Heroes and Heroines: A Magical World

Celtic myths and legends have had a lasting effect on English and Irish writers. In the 1400s, Sir Thomas Malory blended Celtic and European legends to produce *Le Morte d'Arthur*, the tale of King Arthur and his noble knights. In the early twentieth century, William Butler Yeats used Celtic myths in his poems to remind the Irish people of their past.

The Anglo-Saxon stories that came later in British history are full of strong men. Strong women, however, dominate Celtic stories. Celtic myths are full of violence, passionate love, and adventure; they take us to lands of magic and enchantment.

The Romans: The Great Administrators

Beginning in 55 B.C., the Celts were conquered by Roman invaders. The Romans had already taken over much of the known world. Their armies and their organization kept Britain safe from further invasion for hundreds of years. They built a network of roads and

Notes

a seventy-three-mile defensive wall. During Roman rule, Christianity took hold and the old Celtic religion began to fade.

Roman rule, however, did not last. Early in the fifth century A.D. the Roman Empire came under attack on several fronts. Rome was forced to withdraw from Britain, leaving it weak, unprotected, and once again open to invasion.

The Anglo-Saxons Sweep Ashore

In the middle of the fifth century, two main groups invaded Britain: the Angles and Saxons from Germany, and the Jutes from Denmark. Because of them, the Anglo-Saxon language became the most important language, and the land received yet another name—England—from the Angles. Nevertheless, the newcomers did not have an easy time of it. The Celts put up a fierce struggle before withdrawing to Wales in the west. There, traces of the Celtic culture and language can still be found.

Unifying Forces: Alfred the Great and Christianity

For a long time, Anglo-Saxon England was divided into many small kingdoms. But in the late ninth century, a fierce group of Vikings known as the Danes came storming across the North Sea. A great ruler named Alfred brought the Anglo-Saxons together to defend themselves. Nevertheless, the Danes took over parts of northern England.

King Alfred the Great played an important role in uniting the Anglo-Saxons. Another uniting force was the spread of Christianity. As Anglo-Saxon kings converted to that religion, so did their people. Under King Alfred, their strong leader, and the uniting force of their strong faith, the Anglo-Saxons fought hard to protect themselves from the Danes. The kings who came after Alfred carried on his battle against them. In 1066, though, the Anglo-Saxons and the Danes were both defeated by Norman invaders from France. Their leader was William, Duke of Normandy.

Anglo-Saxon Life: The Warm Hall, the Cold World

The Anglo-Saxons were not uncivilized barbarians, though they are often represented that way. On the other hand, they did not have much luxury, learning, or art in their lives. Warfare was their focus. They needed great leaders to provide law and order, and they achieved fame or success through loyalty to their leaders. True loyalty, especially in war, was rewarded with gifts from the leader. It was also rewarded by fame. Beowulf, for example, earns both glory and wealth by defending King Hrothgar against the monster Grendel.

This pattern of loyalty came from a need to protect the group from a wilderness full of enemies. Especially in winter, the Anglo-Saxon world was cold, dark, and threatening. To protect themselves, the Anglo-Saxons lived close together. A group of small wooden homes usually surrounded a warm, fire-lit meeting hall. This arrangement helped the people in the community feel safe. It also meant that leaders and followers knew each other well. Such closeness meant that everyone could take part when decisions had to be made.

The Anglo-Saxon Religion: Gods for Warriors

When Christianity came to England, it blended with the old Anglo-Saxon religion. This religion had come with the Anglo-Saxons from Germany, and had much in common with what we think of as Norse mythology. For example, the Norse gods Odin and Thor appear in the Anglo-Saxon culture as Woden and Thunor. Woden (from which our Wednesday, or "Woden's Day," comes) was the god of death, poetry, and magic. He played an important part in a culture that produced great poetry and battled daily against death. Thunor (who gave us a name for our Thursday) was the god of thunder and lightning. His sign was the hammer and possibly the twisted cross we call the swastika. This sign is found on many Anglo-Saxon graves.

In general, the Anglo-Saxon religion was practical and useful. It focused not on ideas that were hard to understand, but on the down-to-earth values of bravery, loyalty, and friendship.

The Bards: Singing of Gods and Heroes

The Anglo-Saxon meeting hall offered shelter and a place to hold meetings. During the long, dark evening hours, it was also used for entertainment. Storytellers called bards sang about gods and heroes. Bards were as important as warriors. Strumming a harp, they sang stories from a rich supply of heroic tales. *Beowulf* tells us that even King Hrothgar would take up the harp and sing wonderful stories of heroism and battle, weeping when his stories touched on old age.

Hope in Immortal Verse

Anglo-Saxon literature has many works that remember heroic events of the past. For non-Christians, who lived a hard life with no promise of life after death, being remembered in poetry was a defense against death. Perhaps this is why bards were so honored by the Anglo-Saxons.

A Light in Ireland

In the fifth century, the remote island of Ireland was not threatened by Germanic invaders. In 432, though, Ireland was converted to Christianity by Patrick, a Briton who had adopted the Roman way of life. When he was a teenager, Celtic slave traders took Patrick to Ireland. Six years later, he escaped. After becoming a Christian bishop, he returned to Ireland, and in a few short years had converted the whole island to Christianity. Irish monks opened monasteries that became havens of learning. While the rest of Europe sank into constant warfare, confusion, and ignorance, Ireland enjoyed a Golden Age.

The Christian Monasteries: The Ink Froze

(Notes)

Like the song of the bard—the poet and singer—Christianity also offered hope in the dark Anglo-Saxon world. As the bard preserved the memory of heroes, so the monasteries preserved the great Latin and Greek myths and stories. They also preserved other popular works such as *Beowulf.*

Some of the monks who lived in monasteries were scribes. They spent most of the day in a writing room, copying out texts by hand. The writing room was actually no more than a covered walkway; in winter, the ink would sometimes freeze.

The Rise of the English Language

Until King Alfred's reign, Latin was the language of scholars and learning in England. But Alfred decided to have a history of England written in the Anglo-Saxon language. This work, the *Anglo-Saxon Chronicle,* helped to establish English as a language of learning and culture. The Old English stories copied by the monks began to be seen and understood as great works of literature.

from Beowulf

Part One, translated by Burton Raffel

(Notes)

from The Battle with Grendel

You Need to Know The monster Grendel comes up from his swamp at night, thirsting after human blood. Reaching Herot, the home of the Danish king and his warriors, he rips the door from its hinges and enters the hall, which is filled with sleeping warriors. Grendel grabs the first soldier he sees and gobbles him down. Then the monster's claw reaches out for another warrior—but this warrior is Beowulf, and he is ready.

1

Out from the marsh, from the foot of misty
Hills and bogs, bearing God's hatred,
Grendel came, hoping to kill
Anyone he could trap on this trip to high Herot.
He moved quickly through the cloudy night,
Up from his swampland, sliding silently
Toward that gold-shining hall. He had visited Hrothgar's
Home before, knew the way—
But never, before nor after that night,
10   Found Herot defended so firmly, his reception
So harsh. He journeyed, forever joyless,
Straight to the door, then snapped it open,
Tore its iron fasteners with a touch,
And rushed angrily over the threshold.
He strode quickly across the inlaid
Floor, snarling and fierce: His eyes
Gleamed in the darkness, burned with a gruesome
Light. Then he stopped, seeing the hall

From *Beowulf,* translated by Burton Raffel. Copyright © 1963 and renewed © 1991 by Burton Raffel. Reproduced by permission of **Dutton Signet, a division of Penguin Putnam Inc.**

Crowded with sleeping warriors, stuffed

20   With rows of young soldiers resting together.

And his heart laughed, he relished the sight,

Intended to tear the life from those bodies

By morning; the monster's mind was hot

With the thought of food and the feasting his belly

Would soon know. But fate, that night, intended

Grendel to gnaw the broken bones

Of his last human supper. Human

Eyes were watching his evil steps,

Waiting to see his swift hard claws.

30   Grendel snatched at the first Geat

He came to, ripped him apart, cut

His body to bits with powerful jaws,

Drank the blood from his veins, and bolted

Him down, hands and feet; death

And Grendel's great teeth came together,

Snapping life shut. Then he stepped to another

Still body, clutched at Beowulf with his claws,

Grasped at a strong-hearted wakeful sleeper

—And was instantly seized himself, claws

40   Bent back as Beowulf leaned up on one arm.

In Other Words Beowulf has Grendel firmly in his powerful grasp, and the monster is terrified. He expected an easy meal. Now, all he wants to do is run home and hide. But Beowulf has sworn to kill Grendel with his bare hands, and he will not let the monster go. Their struggle shakes the strong walls of Herot. The soldiers cower. Then a horrible scream rips through the night. It is Grendel.

That shepherd of evil, guardian of crime,

Knew at once that nowhere on earth

Had he met a man whose hands were harder;

His mind was flooded with fear—but nothing

Could take his talons and himself from that tight

Hard grip. Grendel's one thought was to run

(Notes)

From Beowulf, flee back to his marsh and hide there:

This was a different Herot than the hall he had emptied.

But Higlac's follower remembered his final

50 Boast and, standing erect, stopped

The monster's flight, fastened those claws

In his fists till they cracked, clutched Grendel

Closer. The infamous killer fought

For his freedom, wanting no flesh but retreat,

Desiring nothing but escape; his claws

Had been caught, he was trapped. That trip to Herot

Was a miserable journey for the writhing monster!

　　　The high hall rang, its roof boards swayed,

And Danes shook with terror. Down

60 The aisles the battle swept, angry

And wild. Herot trembled, wonderfully

Built to withstand the blows, the struggling

Great bodies beating at its beautiful walls;

Shaped and fastened with iron, inside

And out, artfully worked, the building

Stood firm. Its benches rattled, fell

To the floor, gold-covered boards grating

As Grendel and Beowulf battled across them.

Hrothgar's wise men had fashioned Herot

70 To stand forever; only fire,

They had planned, could shatter what such skill had put

Together, swallow in hot flames such splendor

Of ivory and iron and wood. Suddenly

The sounds changed, the Danes started

In new terror, cowering in their beds as the terrible

Screams of the Almighty's enemy sang

In the darkness, the horrible shrieks of pain

And defeat, the tears torn out of Grendel's

Taut throat, hell's captive caught in the arms

80 Of him who of all the men on earth

Was the strongest.

In Other Words Beowulf's men rush to his aid. But Grendel is protected by a magic spell, and their swords cannot hurt him. Fortunately, their help is not needed. Grendel, trying to twist out of Beowulf's grip, feels his arm being ripped off. Mortally wounded, Grendel flees back to his swamp. Beowulf has rescued the Danes from the monster that tormented them. The victorious hero hangs the arm of Grendel from the rafters of the great hall.

2

That mighty protector of men
Meant to hold the monster till its life
Leaped out, knowing the fiend was no use
To anyone in Denmark. All of Beowulf's
Band had jumped from their beds, ancestral
Swords raised and ready, determined
To protect their prince if they could. Their courage
Was great but all wasted: They could hack at Grendel
From every side, trying to open
90 A path for his evil soul, but their points
Could not hurt him, the sharpest and hardest iron
Could not scratch at his skin, for that sin-stained demon
Had bewitched all men's weapons, laid spells
That blunted every mortal man's blade.
And yet his time had come, his days
Were over, his death near; down
To hell he would go, swept groaning and helpless
To the waiting hands of still worse fiends.
Now he discovered—once the afflictor
100 Of men, tormentor of their days—what it meant
To feud with Almighty God: Grendel
Saw that his strength was deserting him, his claws
Bound fast, Higlac's brave follower tearing at
His hands. The monster's hatred rose higher,
But his power had gone. He twisted in pain,
And the bleeding sinews deep in his shoulder

Notes

Snapped, muscle and bone split

And broke. The battle was over, Beowulf

Had been granted new glory: Grendel escaped,

110 But wounded as he was could flee to his den,

His miserable hole at the bottom of the marsh,

Only to die, to wait for the end

Of all his days. And after that bloody

Combat the Danes laughed with delight.

He who had come to them from across the sea,

Bold and strong-minded, had driven affliction

Off, purged Herot clean. He was happy,

Now, with that night's fierce work; the Danes

Had been served as he'd boasted he'd serve them; Beowulf,

120 A prince of the Geats, had killed Grendel,

Ended the grief, the sorrow, the suffering

Forced on Hrothgar's helpless people

By a bloodthirsty fiend. No Dane doubted

The victory, for the proof, hanging high

From the rafters where Beowulf had hung it, was the monster's

Arm, claw and shoulder and all.

In Other Words The next morning, crowds of people begin to arrive from far away, eager to see the place where Grendel was defeated. They follow his bloody footprints to the lake where he went down to his death. Beowulf is a hero, and there is great rejoicing.

3

And then, in the morning, crowds surrounded

Herot, warriors coming to that hall

From faraway lands, princes and leaders

130 Of men hurrying to behold the monster's

Great staggering tracks. They gaped with no sense

Of sorrow, felt no regret for his suffering,

Went tracing his bloody footprints, his beaten

And lonely flight, to the edge of the lake

Where he'd dragged his corpselike way, doomed

And already weary of his vanishing life.

The water was bloody, steaming and boiling

In horrible pounding waves, heat

Sucked from his magic veins; but the swirling

140 Surf had covered his death, hidden

Deep in murky darkness his miserable

End, as hell opened to receive him.

       Then old and young rejoiced, turned back

From that happy pilgrimage, mounted their hard-hooved

Horses, high-spirited stallions, and rode them

Slowly toward Herot again, retelling

Beowulf's bravery as they jogged along.

And over and over they swore that nowhere

On earth or under the spreading sky

150 Or between the seas, neither south nor north,

Was there a warrior worthier to rule over men.

(But no one meant Beowulf's praise to belittle

Hrothgar, their kind and gracious king!) . . .

Notes

from Gilgamesh, A Verse Narrative

retold by Herbert Mason

(Notes)

The Head of Humbaba

You Need to Know The following is an excerpt from the selection in the Student Edition (lines 154–208). Gilgamesh goes to cut down a cedar tree. The monster Humbaba hears the sound of the ax and rushes toward Gilgamesh and Enkidu. When the two men see the deformed monster, slave to the gods, they almost feel pity and do not attack immediately. Humbaba attacks first and nearly kills Enkidu. Frozen with horror, Gilgamesh looks on as Humbaba aims a final blow. Just in time, Enkidu drags himself out of the way, and Humbaba falls. Gilgamesh snaps out of his daze and raises his ax to kill the monster. Humbaba pleads for his life, offering to serve Gilgamesh instead of the gods. Gilgamesh pauses, as if tempted, but Enkidu cries out not to trust Humbaba. Gilgamesh raises his ax again and chops off the monster's head.

At dawn Gilgamesh raised his ax

And struck at the great cedar.

When Humbaba heard the sound of falling trees,

He hurried down the path that they had seen

But only he had traveled. Gilgamesh felt weak

At the sound of Humbaba's footsteps and called to Shamash[1]

160   Saying, I have followed you in the way decreed;

Why am I abandoned now? Suddenly the winds

Sprang up. They saw the great head of Humbaba

Like a water buffalo's bellowing down the path,

His huge and clumsy legs, his flailing[2] arms

Thrashing at phantoms in his precious trees.

His single stroke could cut a cedar down

1. **Shamash** (SHAH mahsh): the sun god who has been guiding the hero.

2. **flailing:** swinging.

And leave no mark on him. His shoulders,

Like a porter's[3] under building stones,

Were permanently bent by what he bore;

170   He was the slave who did the work for gods

But whom the gods would never notice.

Monstrous in his contortion, he aroused

The two almost to pity.

But pity was the thing that might have killed.

It made them pause just long enough to show

How pitiless he was to them. Gilgamesh in horror saw

Him strike the back of Enkidu and beat him to the ground

Until he thought his friend was crushed to death.

He stood still watching as the monster leaned to make

180   His final strike against his friend, unable

To move to help him, and then Enkidu slid

Along the ground like a ram making its final lunge

On wounded knees. Humbaba fell and seemed

To crack the ground itself in two, and Gilgamesh,

As if this fall had snapped him from his daze,

Returned to life

And stood over Humbaba with his ax

Raised high above his head watching the monster plead

In strangled sobs and desperate appeals

190   The way the sea contorts under a violent squall.[4]

I'll serve you as I served the gods, Humbaba said;

I'll build you houses from their sacred trees.

Enkidu feared his friend was weakening

And called out: Gilgamesh! Don't trust him!

As if there were some hunger in himself

That Gilgamesh was feeling

That turned him momentarily to yearn

For someone who would serve, he paused;

3. **porter's:** A porter is a person who carries things.

4. **squall:** sudden, brief storm.

(Notes)

And then he raised his ax up higher
200   And swung it in a perfect arc
Into Humbaba's neck. He reached out
To touch the wounded shoulder of his friend,

And late that night he reached again
To see if he was yet asleep, but there was only
Quiet breathing. The stars against the midnight sky
Were sparkling like mica[5] in a riverbed.
In the slight breeze
The head of Humbaba was swinging from a tree.

5. **mica** (MY kuh): colored, translucent mineral.

The Middle Ages: 1066–1485
Based on the Student Edition text by David Adams Leeming

In October 1066, a daylong battle was fought near the channel of water that divides England from France. In that battle, Duke William of Normandy, France, defeated Harold, the last of the Anglo-Saxon kings. So began what is known as the Norman Conquest.

Notes

William the Conqueror and the Norman Influence

William wanted to rule the Anglo-Saxons, not wipe them out. Today, as a result, England's language and culture have both Norman and Anglo-Saxon elements. The Normans brought administrative abiltiy to the more democratic and artistic Anglo-Saxons. One of William's greatest accomplishments was an inventory of all property in England and a tax system based on what people owned.

The Normans Changed England

William and many of the Norman kings who followed him kept their titles as Norman dukes. In addition, William gave the property of defeated Anglo-Saxons to his own Norman followers. These men brought two things to England: the French language and the European social system—feudalism. These changes made England part of mainstream Europe.

Feudalism: From the Top Down

Feudalism was like a pyramid of power. The king sat at the top of the pyramid. He appointed barons—noblemen—to serve him as his **vassals**—dependent tenants. The barons gave the king money, military support, or both. The barons, in turn, chose vassals of their own—and so on down the pyramid. At the bottom were

(Notes)

serfs—laborers who were like slaves since they were not free to leave the nobleman or his land.

The feudal system did not always work. Sometimes a vassal would switch his loyalty to a more powerful lord, and battles would follow. Indeed, we cannot think of the Middle Ages without thinking of knights in armor.

Knights in Shining Armor

Males above the level of serf were expected to serve as warriors; they began training for the knighthood at an early age. Once knighted, a youth became a man with the title "sir."

Knights had to behave according to a strict code known as chivalry. This code was based on loyalty, bravery, and courtly behavior. Breaking one of the code's rules would weaken the knight's position—and the whole of knighthood itself.

Women in Medieval Society: No Voice, No Choice

Women had no political rights under feudalism. A woman had to depend entirely on a man, whether husband, father, or brother. For peasant women, life was a tiring round of childbearing and labor. Women of higher rank spent their time having children and managing their households. If the men were away at war, such women might also govern the estate—but only until the men came home.

Chivalry and Courtly Love: Ideal but Unreal

The code of **chivalry** ruled how a knight must behave toward his lord and toward his enemy. It also dictated how he must behave toward women. **Courtly love**—the practice of adoring a worthy lady—was thought to make the knight braver and better. Ideally, this love was not sexual. A knight's ideal woman must always remain pure and out of reach. The resulting tension gave poets and storytellers plenty of drama to work with. When Sir Lancelot had an affair with Queen Guinevere, for example, Camelot crumbled because they violated the rules of courtly love.

(Notes)

The Rise of Romance

Under chivalry, women became idealized objects—perfect in every way. A woman was not valued for her abilities and talents, but rather for land she could bring to a marriage. The code and practice of chivalry brought about a new form of literature—the romance.

The New City Classes: Out from Under the Overlords

Society in the Middle Ages centered on the feudal castle. But as England's population grew, so did its towns and cities. The people of the cities were free, tied neither to the land and its owner nor to knighthood and chivalry. The new merchant class had its own money and its own tastes in the arts. Therefore, much art from this time reflects the lives and interests of the middle class.

The Great Happenings

Against the backdrop of feudalism, several major events changed the course of English history and literature.

• **The Crusades: Bloodbath over the Holy Land**
In Chaucer's *The Canterbury Tales,* we meet a knight who has fought in "heathen" places. His adventures in the 1300s were really an extension of the **Crusades** (1095–1270). In this series of "holy wars," European Christians tried to conquer the Muslims of the Middle East. Although the Crusades were a military failure, they brought together people from Europe and the Middle East. Contact with eastern mathematics, astronomy, and art enriched European culture—and made possible the lively world of Chaucer.

Notes

- **The Martyrdom of Thomas à Becket: Murder in the Cathedral**

When Chaucer's pilgrims set out for Canterbury, their goal was the shrine of Saint Thomas à Becket (c. 1118–1170). Becket, a Norman, had risen to power under King Henry II (reigned 1154–1189). At that time, all Christians belonged to the Catholic Church. Even King Henry was a vassal—or servant—of the pope, the powerful head of the Church. However, Henry hoped to take on some of the power of the pope. To help do this, he made his friend Becket the archbishop of Canterbury, the most powerful church leader in England. The plan backfired, though, as Becket was independent-minded and often took the pope's side. Seeing how Becket enraged Henry, four of the king's loyal knights murdered Becket in the archbishop's own cathedral. Becket became a martyr—someone who died for his beliefs—and Henry's power against the pope was weakened.

The power of the Church had both good and bad effects. Priests and other clergy often misused their powers. Chaucer's Monk, for example, lives a life of luxury, and his Friar chases women. But the Church also brought together all the nations and peoples of Europe. The Church continued to be the center of learning, as well, and Latin remained the language of educated Europeans.

- **The Magna Carta: Power to (Some of) the People**

In 1215, a group of English barons forced King John to sign the **Magna Carta,** or "Great Charter." This document emphasized the rights of common people and later became the basis for much of English law. At the time, though, the barons did not care about commoners. They wanted to use the Magna Carta to curb the power of the king—which it did.

- **The Hundred Years' War (1337–1453):**
  The Arrow Is Mightier Than the Armor

This war, fought in Europe, was based on claims to the French throne by two English kings, Edward III and Henry V. England lost the war, but gained a new society in the process. Most English armies in France were made up of small landowners, or **yeomen.** Dressed in green, these landowner-warriors shot long arrows over castle walls. Chivalry and knighthood faded into the past, and a new, democratic England was born.

- **The Black Death**

The **Black Death,** or bubonic plague, struck England in 1348–1349. Spread by fleas carried on rats, this easily spread disease killed off one third of England's population. It also created a labor shortage and gave the lower classes more power than ever before. One long-term effect was the serfs' freedom— and with that came the end of feudalism.

from The Prologue to The Canterbury Tales

by Geoffrey Chaucer, translated by Nevill Coghill

(**Notes**)

The Knight

You Need to Know The first pilgrim is the Knight, who has had a long and famous military career. He has taken part in battles all over Europe and Africa and been victorious in all of them. The Knight is described as truthful, honorable, generous, well mannered, noble, and wise. He does not brag or boast about his achievements. Although he has fine horses—a mark of his wealth—he does not show off in fancy clothes. Instead, he wears a simple long coat, still stained from being worn under his armor. He has just come back from the war, and is eager to give thanks to God. (This excerpt can also be found starting on line 43 of the Student Edition.)

> There was a *Knight*, a most distinguished man,
> Who from the day on which he first began
> To ride abroad had followed chivalry,
> Truth, honor, generousness, and courtesy.
> He had done nobly in his sovereign's war
> And ridden into battle, no man more,
> As well in Christian as in heathen places,
> 50 And ever honored for his noble graces.
> When we took Alexandria,[1] he was there.
> He often sat at table in the chair
> Of honor, above all nations, when in Prussia.
> In Lithuania he had ridden, and Russia,
> No Christian man so often, of his rank.
> When, in Granada, Algeciras sank
> Under assault, he had been there, and in

1. **Alexandria:** city in Egypt captured by the Crusaders in 1365. In the next few lines, Chaucer is indicating the knight's distinguished and extensive career.

From "The Prologue" from *The Canterbury Tales* by Geoffrey Chaucer, translated by Nevill Coghill (Penguin Classics 1951, Fourth Revised Edition 1977). Copyright 1951 by Nevill Coghill; copyright renewed © 1958, 1960, 1975, 1977 by the Estate of Nevill Coghill. Reproduced by permission of **Penguin Books Ltd.**

North Africa, raiding Benamarin;

In Anatolia he had been as well

60 And fought when Ayas and Attalia fell,

For all along the Mediterranean coast

He had embarked with many a noble host.

In fifteen mortal battles he had been

And jousted for our faith at Tramissene

Thrice in the lists, and always killed his man.

This same distinguished knight had led the van

Once with the Bey of Balat, doing work

For him against another heathen Turk;

He was of sovereign value in all eyes.

70 And though so much distinguished, he was wise

And in his bearing modest as a maid.

He never yet a boorish thing had said

In all his life to any, come what might;

He was a true, a perfect gentle-knight.[2]

Speaking of his equipment, he possessed

Fine horses, but he was not gaily dressed.

He wore a fustian[3] tunic stained and dark

With smudges where his armor had left mark;

Just home from service, he had joined our ranks

80 To do his pilgrimage and render thanks.

The Nun

You Need to Know The Prioress is very different from the Knight. Although she is a nun—a sister in a religious order—she wants to appear polite, dainty, and well mannered. In fact, she loves to show off. When she takes part in a religious service, she is thinking not of God but of her own singing. She speaks French, but not very well; she is greatly concerned with table manners. She shows off her love for animals and spoils her little pet dogs. The Prioress is

2. **gentle-knight:** In Chaucer's day, *gentle* meant "well bred and considerate."

3. **fustian** (FUHS chuhn): coarse cloth made of linen and cotton.

Notes

large, has a small mouth and a wide forehead, and wears a rather showy set of coral prayer beads.

There also was a *Nun,* a Prioress,
Her way of smiling very simple and coy.
Her greatest oath was only "By St. Loy!"[4]
And she was known as Madam Eglantyne. [5]
And well she sang a service, with a fine
Intoning through her nose, as was most seemly,
And she spoke daintily in French, extremely,
After the school of Stratford-atte-Bowe[6]

130 French in the Paris style she did not know.
At meat her manners were well taught withal;
No morsel from her lips did she let fall,
Nor dipped her fingers in the sauce too deep;
But she could carry a morsel up and keep
The smallest drop from falling on her breast.
For courtliness she had a special zest,
And she would wipe her upper lip so clean
That not a trace of grease was to be seen
Upon the cup when she had drunk; to eat,

140 She reached a hand sedately for the meat.
She certainly was very entertaining,
Pleasant and friendly in her ways, and straining
To counterfeit a courtly kind of grace,
A stately bearing fitting to her place,
And to seem dignified in all her dealings.
As for her sympathies and tender feelings,
She was so charitably solicitous
She used to weep if she but saw a mouse
Caught in a trap, if it were dead or bleeding.

4. **St. Loy:** Saint Eligius, known for his perfect manners.

5. **Eglantyne:** a kind of a rose and also the name of several romantic heroines. The Prioress herself is a romantic.

6. **Stratford-atte-Bowe:** Benedictine convent near London where inferior French was spoken.

NAME _____ DATE _____

150 And she had little dogs she would be feeding
With roasted flesh, or milk, or fine white bread.
And bitterly she wept if one were dead
Or someone took a stick and made it smart;
She was all sentiment and tender heart.
Her veil was gathered in a seemly way,
Her nose was elegant, her eyes glass-gray;
Her mouth was very small, but soft and red,
Her forehead, certainly, was fair of spread,
Almost a span[7] across the brows, I own;

160 She was indeed by no means undergrown.
Her cloak, I noticed, had a graceful charm.
She wore a coral trinket on her arm,
A set of beads, the gaudies tricked in green,[8]
Whence hung a golden brooch of brightest sheen
On which there first was graven a crowned A,
And lower, *Amor vincit omnia.*[9]

The Monk

You Need to Know Next comes the Monk. Like the Prioress, he is rather worldly for a religious person. He does not shut himself away in his monastery to study and work; he considers such a life strict and old-fashioned. Instead, he loves to ride out hunting—not at all traditional for a monk! He spends a lot of money on his hobby, and has many fine horses and hunting dogs. The Monk adorns himself with fur and gold, and he enjoys such extravagant dishes as whole roasted swan. He is fat and bald, with a shiny face.

A *Monk* there was, one of the finest sort

170 Who rode the country; hunting was his sport.
A manly man, to be an Abbott able;
Many a dainty horse he had in stable.

7. **span:** nine inches.

8. **a set of beads . . . green:** Beads are a rosary, or prayer beads and a crucifix on a string or chain. Every eleventh bead is a gaud, a large bead indicating when the Lord's Prayer is to be said.

9. ***Amor vincit omnia*** (AY mawr VIHN ciht OM nee ah): Latin for "Love conquers all."

Notes

Notes

His bridle, when he rode, a man might hear

Jingling in a whistling wind as clear,

Aye, and as loud as does the chapel bell

Where my lord Monk was Prior of the cell.

The Rule of good St. Benet or St. Maur[10]

As old and strict he tended to ignore;

He let go by the things of yesterday

180 And took the modern world's more spacious way.

He did not rate that text at a plucked hen

Which says that hunters are not holy men

And that a monk uncloistered is a mere

Fish out of water, flapping on the pier,

That is to say a monk out of his cloister.

That was a text he held not worth an oyster;

And I agreed and said his views were sound;

Was he to study till his head went round

Poring over books in cloisters? Must he toil

190 As Austin[11] bade and till the very soil?

Was he to leave the world upon the shelf?

Let Austin have his labor to himself.

      This Monk was therefore a good man to horse;

Greyhounds he had, as swift as birds, to course.[12]

Hunting a hare or riding at a fence

Was all his fun, he spared for no expense.

I saw his sleeves were garnished at the hand

With fine gray fur, the finest in the land,

And on his hood, to fasten it at his chin

200 He had a wrought-gold, cunningly fashioned pin;

Into a lover's knot it seemed to pass.

His head was bald and shone like looking-glass;

---

10. **St. Benet** [Benedict] **or St. Maur** [Maurice]: Saint Benedict (c. 480–c. 547) was an Italian monk who founded numerous monasteries and wrote a famous code of regulations for monastic life. Saint Maurice was a follower of Benedict.

11. **Austin:** Saint Augustine (354–430), bishop of Hippo in North Africa. He criticized lazy monks and suggested they do some hard manual labor.

12. **course:** to cause to chase game.

So did his face, as if it had been greased.

He was a fat and personable priest;

His prominent eyeballs never seemed to settle.

They glittered like the flames beneath a kettle;

Supple his boots, his horse in fine condition.

He was a prelate fit for exhibition,

He was not pale like a tormented soul.

210 He liked a fat swan best, and roasted whole.

His palfrey[13] was as brown as is a berry.

The Oxford Cleric

You Need to Know The Oxford Cleric is a thin, quiet, serious-looking man; his coat is almost worn out; even his horse is underfed. He has no profession, and he spends all his time studying. If his friends give him money, he spends it on another book instead of food or clothes, and repays them by praying for them.

An *Oxford Cleric*, still a student though,

One who had taken logic long ago,

Was there; his horse was thinner than a rake,

And he was not too fat, I undertake,

But had a hollow look, a sober stare;

300 The thread upon his overcoat was bare.

He had found no preferment in the church

And he was too unworldly to make search

For secular employment. By his bed

He preferred having twenty books in red

And black, of Aristotle's[14] philosophy,

Than costly clothes, fiddle, or psaltery.[15]

Though a philosopher, as I have told,

Notes

---

13. **palfrey:** horse.

14. **Aristotle's** (AR ih STOT uhlz): Aristotle (384–322 B.C.) was a Greek philosopher.

15. **psaltery** (SAWL tuhr ee): a stringed instrument that is plucked.

Notes

He had not found the stone for making gold.[16]

Whatever money from his friends he took

310 He spent on learning or another book

And prayed for them most earnestly, returning

Thanks to them thus for paying for his learning.

His only care was study, and indeed

He never spoke a word more than was need,

Formal at that, respectful in the extreme,

Short, to the point, and lofty in his theme.

A tone of moral virtue filled his speech

And gladly would he learn, and gladly teach.

The Doctor

You Need to Know The Doctor appears to know a great deal about medieval medicine. He has studied medical writings from ancient times until the Middle Ages. He treats patients using astronomy and ideas about the four "humors." In Chaucer's eyes, the Doctor is more interested in making money by prescribing treatments his patients do not need than in actually helping his patients.

A *Doctor* too emerged as we proceeded;

No one alive could talk as well as he did

On points of medicine and of surgery,

For, being grounded in astronomy,

He watched his patient closely for the hours

When, by his horoscope, he knew the powers

Of favorable planets, then ascendent,

Worked on the images for his dependent.

The cause of every malady you'd got

430 He knew, and whether dry, cold, moist, or hot;[17]

16. **stone ... gold:** Alchemists at the time were searching for a stone that was supposed to turn ordinary metals into gold.

17. **dry ... hot:** the four humors, or fluids. People of the time believed that one's physical and mental conditions were influenced by the balance of four major fluids in the body—blood (hot and wet), yellow bile (hot and dry), phlegm (cold and wet), and black bile (cold and dry).

He knew their seat, their humor and condition.

He was a perfect practicing physician.

These causes being known for what they were,

He gave the man his medicine then and there.

All his apothecaries in a tribe

Were ready with the drugs he would prescribe

And each made money from the other's guile;

They had been friendly for a goodish while.

He was well-versed in Aesculapius[18] too

440   And what Hippocrates and Rufus knew

And Dioscorides, now dead and gone,

Galen and Rhazes, Hali, Serapion,

Averroes, Avicenna, Constantine,

Scotch Bernard, John of Gaddesden, Gilbertine.

In his own diet he observed some measure;

There were no superfluities for pleasure,

Only digestives, nutritives and such.

He did not read the Bible very much.

In blood-red garments, slashed with bluish gray

450   And lined with taffeta, he rode his way;

Yet he was rather close as to expenses

And kept the gold he won in pestilences.

Gold stimulates the heart, or so we're told.

He therefore had a special love of gold.

The Wife of Bath

You Need to Know The Wife of Bath is quite a character. Her great pride is the fine cloth she weaves, and she considers herself the most important woman in her church. She has been married five times and has already been on three pilgrimages. A big, red-faced woman who wears an enormous hat and bright red stockings, she enjoys laughing and talking with the other pilgrims.

18. **Aesculapius** (ehs kyuh LAYpee uhs): in Greek and Roman mythology, the god of medicine. The names that follow were early Greek, Roman, Middle Eastern, and medieval medical authorities.

Notes

A worthy *woman* from beside *Bath* city
Was with us, somewhat deaf, which was a pity.
In making cloth she showed so great a bent
She bettered those of Ypres and of Ghent.[19]
In all the parish not a dame dared stir
460 Towards the altar steps in front of her,
And if indeed they did, so wrath was she
As to be quite put out of charity.
Her kerchiefs were of finely woven ground;[20]
I dared have sworn they weighed a good ten pound,
The ones she wore on Sunday, on her head.
Her hose were of the finest scarlet red
And gartered tight; her shoes were soft and new.
Bold was her face, handsome, and red in hue.
A worthy woman all her life, what's more
470 She'd had five husbands, all at the church door,[21]
Apart from other company in youth;
No need just now to speak of that, forsooth.
And she had thrice been to Jerusalem,
Seen many strange rivers and passed over them;
She'd been to Rome and also to Boulogne,
St. James of Compostella and Cologne,
And she was skilled in wandering by the way.
She had gap-teeth, set widely, truth to say.
Easily on an ambling horse she sat
480 Well wimpled[22] up, and on her head a hat
As broad as is a buckler or a shield;
She had a flowing mantle that concealed
Large hips, her heels spurred sharply under that.
In company she liked to laugh and chat

19. **Ypres** (EE pruh) **and of Ghent:** Flemish centers of the wool trade.
20. **ground:** type of cloth.
21. **church door:** In Chaucer's day the marriage ceremony was performed at the church door.
22. **wimpled:** A wimple is a linen covering for the head and neck.

And knew the remedies for love's mischances,

An art in which she knew the oldest dances.

The Parson

You Need to Know The Parson is very different from the Monk and the Prioress. He takes his religion seriously, both in his studies and in the way he lives. Although poor himself, he gives generously to those in need. He goes on foot to visit the members of his parish even when he is ill or the weather is stormy. The Parson is kind and humble toward everyone. In short, he practices what he preaches, and he seeks to teach by his own example.

    A holy-minded man of good renown

There was, and poor, the *Parson* to a town,

Yet he was rich in holy thought and work.

490 He also was a learned man, a clerk,

Who truly knew Christ's gospel and would preach it

Devoutly to parishioners, and teach it.

Benign and wonderfully diligent,

And patient when adversity was sent

(For so he proved in much adversity)

He hated cursing to extort a fee,

Nay rather he preferred beyond a doubt

Giving to poor parishioners round about

Both from church offerings and his property;

500 He could in little find sufficiency.

Wide was his parish, with houses far asunder,

Yet he neglected not in rain or thunder,

In sickness or in grief, to pay a call

On the remotest, whether great or small,

Upon his feet, and in his hand a stave.[23]

This noble example to his sheep he gave

That first he wrought, and afterward he taught;

23. **stave:** staff.

Notes

And it was from the Gospel he had caught

Those words, and he would add this figure too,

510 That if gold rust, what then will iron do?

For if a priest be foul in whom we trust

No wonder that a common man should rust;

And shame it is to see—let priests take stock—

A shitten shepherd and a snowy flock.

The true example that a priest should give

Is one of cleanness, how the sheep should live.

He did not set his benefice to hire[24]

And leave his sheep encumbered in the mire

Or run to London to earn easy bread

520 By singing masses for the wealthy dead,

Or find some Brotherhood and get enrolled.[25]

He stayed at home and watched over his fold

So that no wolf should make the sheep miscarry.

He was a shepherd and no mercenary.

Holy and virtuous he was, but then

Never contemptuous of sinful men,

Never disdainful, never too proud or fine,

But was discreet in teaching and benign.

His business was to show a fair behavior

530 And draw men thus to Heaven and their Savior,

Unless indeed a man were obstinate;

And such, whether of high or low estate,

He put to sharp rebuke, to say the least.

I think there never was a better priest.

He sought no pomp or glory in his dealings,

No scrupulosity had spiced his feelings.

Christ and His Twelve Apostles and their lore

He taught, but followed it himself before.

24. **He . . . benefice to hire:** He did not hire someone else to perform his duties.

25. **find . . . enrolled:** He did not take a job as a paid chaplain to a guild.

The Pardoner

You Need to Know The Pardoner has long, yellowish hair like "rat-tails," bulging eyes, and a small voice that sounds like the bleating of a goat. If his appearance is unpleasant, so is his occupation. The Pardoner makes his living selling pardons for sins, as well as fake relics such as pig bones that he claims are the bones of saints. He travels from church to church, telling lies and pretending to be religious. In this way, Chaucer says, the Pardoner earns more in a day than the good Parson does in a month.

He [26] and a gentle *Pardoner* rode together,
690 A bird from Charing Cross of the same feather,
Just back from visiting the Court of Rome.
He loudly sang *"Come hither, love, come home!"*
The Summoner sang deep seconds[27] to this song,
No trumpet ever sounded half so strong.
This Pardoner had hair as yellow as wax,
Hanging down smoothly like a hank of flax.
In driblets fell his locks behind his head
Down to his shoulders which they overspread;
Thinly they fell, like rat-tails, one by one.
700 He wore no hood upon his head, for fun;
The hood inside his wallet had been stowed,
He aimed at riding in the latest mode;
But for a little cap his head was bare
And he had bulging eye-balls, like a hare.
He'd sewed a holy relic on his cap;
His wallet lay before him on his lap,
Brimful of pardons[28] come from Rome, all hot.
He had the same small voice a goat has got.

26. **He:** the Summoner.

27. **deep seconds:** harmonies.

28. **pardons:** small strips of parchment with papal seals attached. They were sold as indulgences (pardons for sins), with the proceeds supposedly going to a religious house. Many pardoners were dishonest, and even loyal church members often ridiculed them.

Notes

His chin no beard had harbored, nor would harbor,

710 Smoother than ever chin was left by barber.

I judge he was a gelding, or a mare.

As to his trade, from Berwick down to Ware

There was no pardoner of equal grace,

For in his trunk he had a pillow-case

Which he asserted was Our Lady's veil.

He said he had a gobbet[29] of the sail

Saint Peter had the time when he made bold

To walk the waves, till Jesu Christ took hold.

He had a cross of metal set with stones

720 And, in a glass, a rubble of pigs' bones.

And with these relics, any time he found

Some poor up-country parson to astound,

In one short day, in money down, he drew

More than the parson in a month or two,

And by his flatteries and prevarication

Made monkeys of the priest and congregation.

But still to do him justice first and last

In church he was a noble ecclesiast.[30]

How well he read a lesson or told a story!

730 But best of all he sang an Offertory,[31]

For well he knew that when that song was sung

He'd have to preach and tune his honey-tongue

And (well he could) win silver from the crowd.

That's why he sang so merrily and loud.

---

29. **gobbet:** fragment.

30. **ecclesiast** (ih KLEE zee ast): practitioner of church ritual.

31. **Offertory:** hymn sung while offerings are collected in church.

Federigo's Falcon, *from the* Decameron

Based on the Mark Musa and Peter Bondanella translation of Giovanni Boccaccio's masterpiece

Once a young man named Federigo Alberighi lived in the city of Florence, in what is now Italy. He was famous for his skill with weapons and also for his politeness and good manners. Federigo fell madly in love with a beautiful and charming lady named Monna Giovanna.

To win her love, he competed in jousts and tournaments—contests in which a knight on horseback carrying a long spear tries to knock an opponent off his horse. Federigo gave splendid feasts and spent his money extravagantly.

Monna Giovanna cared little for the things Federigo did to impress her, nor did she love him, but he loved her more than ever.

When he'd spent all his money, he was forced to leave Florence; he went to live on his small farm near Campi, where he passed his time hawking whenever he could. His falcon, one of the best in all the world, hunted birds and other small animals.

Now about this time Monna Giovanna's very rich husband became ill and died. In his will, as was the law at that time, the husband left his fortune to their young son. However, he loved his wife dearly, so he stated in his will that if their son died without having a son of his own, she would inherit everything.

The young widow and her son spent a year in the country, which was customary in those days. Her farm in Campi was very close to Federigo's farm, and her son and Federigo soon became friends. The boy began to enjoy working with hunting dogs and birds of prey—especially Federigo's falcon.

One day the boy became gravely ill, and Monna Giovanni was much grieved, for she loved her only child enormously. She begged him to tell her if there was anything he desired. "I will do everything possible to get it for you," she vowed.

"Fifth Day, Ninth Story" (retitled "Federigo's Falcon") adapted from *The Decameron* by Giovanni Boccaccio, translated by Mark Musa and Peter Bondanella. Retold by Holt, Rinehart and Winston. Translation copyright © 1982 by Mark Musa and Peter Bondanella. Reproduced by permission of **W. W. Norton and Company, Inc.**

Notes

Notes

"Mother, if you can arrange for me to have Federigo's falcon, I think I would be well very soon," he told her.

Monna Giovanna was taken aback and didn't know what to do. She knew that Federigo had loved her for many years although she'd never encouraged him. She thought, "How can I ask him for his famous falcon, which is his only means of support and his only pleasure?"

She considered all this for a long time and finally told her son, "Think only of getting well, and tomorrow I shall bring you Federigo's falcon."

The next morning she and a companion walked to Federigo's modest house. When he heard that Monna Giovanna was asking for him at the door, he was surprised and happy, and he welcomed her courteously.

"Greetings, Federigo!" she began. "I know that you have suffered on my account by loving me more than you needed to, so I have come to repay you for the harm I've caused. My companion and I intend to dine with you today—just a simple meal."

Federigo humbly replied, "Madame, I don't remember having suffered any harm because of you; on the contrary, I have received much good, and I am extremely happy to see you." He asked her to wait in his garden while he set the table.

Worried that he had nothing to serve her, he searched his house for money or for something to pawn to buy food, but he found nothing. Then, he spied his good falcon, perched in a small room. This, he thought, is worthy food for such a lady. He wrung the plump bird's neck and had a servant prepare and roast it on a spit.

He set the table with the whitest of tablecloths and called the two women to lunch. They never dreamed that they were eating the falcon.

After lunch, Monna Giovanni told Federigo, "You will be amazed when you hear why I came. I wish you had a child of your own that you loved because then I'm certain you would forgive me, at least partly. The common laws of motherhood force me—against my will and against good manners—to ask you for a gift—for your most precious possession—your falcon. I fear that my son, who lies very ill, may die if I don't bring it to him. I ask you not because of your love for me, but because of your own nobility."

Then, Federigo wept bitterly in her presence. He knew he couldn't grant her request, for she had just eaten the falcon. He wept and could not utter a word.

At first she thought he was crying because he was sad to lose his falcon. She almost withdrew her request, but she held back and waited for his reply.

"My lady," he said finally, "ever since first I loved you, Fortune has been cruel to me, but nothing compares to what she has just done to me; I will never be at peace with her again. I judged my falcon to be a food worthy of you, so I had it roasted and served to you."

As proof, he laid the falcon's feathers, feet, and beak before her. Monna Giovanna scolded him for killing so fine a falcon to serve as a meal to a woman, but she also realized that Federigo had a greatness of spirit that his poverty would never diminish.

She thanked Federigo for the honor he had paid her and for his good will. To her immense sorrow, her son died a few days later.

When her period of mourning ended, her brothers urged her to remarry, for she was very rich and still young. She did not want to remarry, but she began to think of Federigo's generosity, so she told her brothers, "I'd really prefer to remain a widow. But if you insist that I marry, the only man I'll consider marrying is Federigo."

"You foolish woman," her brothers laughed at her, "how can you want a man who hasn't a penny to his name?"

Notes

"I know that," she replied, "but I would rather have a man who needs money than money that needs a man."

Her brothers soon realized that she was determined, and although Federigo was poor, he was of noble birth. So Federigo and the very rich widow, Monna Giovanni, were married. He managed their financial affairs carefully, and they lived happily together the rest of his days.

The Renaissance: 1485–1660
Based on the Student Edition text by C. F. Main

(Notes)

We don't know what people of the future will think of our civilization. The same goes for Europeans of the Renaissance. Historical periods such as the Middle Ages, the Renaissance, and the Romantic period are useful labels invented by those who study the past. These historical periods do not have exact beginnings and endings, but we can recognize differences between one age and another.

Rediscovering Ancient Greece and Rome

The term *renaissance* is a French word meaning "rebirth." In history, it refers to the period of time following the Middle Ages. During the Middle Ages, the writings of ancient Greece and Rome had been forgotten. During the Renaissance, people rediscovered the marvels of the Greek and Latin classics.

The Spirit of Rebirth

People became more curious about themselves and the world. They began creating beautiful things and thinking new, daring thoughts. Today we still use the term *Renaissance person* to describe an energetic and productive person who has expertise in a variety of areas.

It All Began in Italy: A Flourish of Genius

The Renaissance began in Italy in the 1300s. There, much wealth had been gained through trade with the East and banking. This wealth led to an interest in art, the world, and the universe. Artists such as Michelangelo, explorers such as Columbus, and scientists such as Galileo all lived and worked during the Italian Renaissance.

Wealthy and powerful, the Roman Catholic Church supported many Renaissance artists and thinkers. Pope Julian II, for example, hired Michelangelo to paint scenes from the Bible on the ceiling of the Sistine Chapel. The figures in these scenes are bright, heroic, and noble. Many Renaissance artists shared Michelangelo's hopeful view of humanity.

Humanism: Questions About the Good Life

The Renaissance writers were part of a movement known as **humanism.** They read the old Latin and Greek classics to discover new answers to such questions as "What is a human being?" and "What is a good life?" Of course, Christianity already provided answers to these questions. The humanists accepted these answers but hoped to find support for them in the ancient texts.

The humanists had two tasks. First, they needed to find true copies of the ancient writings. Their searches through monasteries uncovered many long-forgotten texts. Next, they needed to share their findings. They set up universities and became teachers of the young men who, they hoped, would be the world's next leaders.

The New Technology: A Flood of Print

Around 1455, a German named Johannes Gutenberg (1400?–1468) printed the first complete book, a huge Bible in Latin. Before this, books had been written by hand. Now, books could be produced faster and more cheaply. Gutenberg's printing press made more information available to many more people.

Printing came to England in 1476, when a merchant named William Caxton (1422?–1491) set up a printing press near London. His press started the flood of print in English that continues today.

Two Friends—Two Humanists

A Dutch monk named Desiderius Erasmus (1466?–1491) is perhaps the best known of all the Renaissance humanists. Erasmus traveled widely, often visiting England to teach Greek at Cambridge University. While there, he became close friends with Thomas More (1477?–1535).

More was a lawyer and also a writer. Like Erasmus, he wrote in Latin. He produced poems, pamphlets, and biographies, as well as his most famous work, *Utopia* (1516). This work, which describes an imaginary society, became popular overnight. It has been translated into many languages and is often imitated. In addition, it has given us an adjective to describe idealized social systems: *utopian*.

The Reformation: Breaking with the Church

While the Renaissance was going on throughout Europe, another important event, the **Reformation,** was taking place in some countries. One feature of the Reformation was the same in all countries—the authority of the pope was rejected.

In England, conflicts with the Roman Catholic Church had been going on for centuries. By the 1530s, though, a break with Rome became unavoidable. Strong feelings of patriotism made the English resent the power of the far-off pope. Moreover, new ideas about religion were coming into England from other countries, especially Germany. There, a monk named Martin Luther (1483–1546) had started a new form of Christianity. It was based not on what the pope said, but on a person's own understanding of the Bible. In England, humanists like Thomas More began challenging the old ways of the Roman Catholic Church. Its superstitions, its immoral clergy, and its wealth, More said, all needed to be reformed.

King Versus Pope: All for an Heir

King Henry VIII had a problem: He wanted to get rid of his wife, Catherine of Aragon. Married for twenty-four years, Henry and Catherine of Aragon had not had a son who could inherit Henry's throne. In addition, a younger woman, Anne Boleyn, had become the king's "favorite." But the Church did not allow divorce.

Henry asked Pope Clement VII to declare that he and Catherine had never been properly married. When his request was denied in 1533, Henry declared himself the head of the English Church. He named a new archbishop of Canterbury, who declared Henry's marriage to Catherine legally over. Protestantism in England had begun.

The Protestant Reformation

Henry closed all of England's monasteries and sold their land to his subjects. Some of his subjects, though, remained loyal to the pope. Sir Thomas More—now a knight and Lord Chancellor of England—was one of them. For his disloyalty to Henry, the king had More beheaded.

Other people were dissatisfied with the new church for different reasons: They felt that it was not reformed *enough*. These people, known as Puritans, wanted to purify the church of all its outward "extras"—bishops, prayer books, even stained-glass windows. They saw religion as an inward, private matter between a person and God.

Henry VIII: Renaissance Man and Executioner

Henry VIII was the second of five Tudor kings. (His father, Henry VII, had seized the throne at the end of a long struggle called the War of the Roses.) During his reign, Henry VIII had six wives. These were Catherine of Aragon, Anne Boleyn, Jane Seymour,

Anne of Cleves, Catherine Howard, and Catherine Parr. The fates of these women can be summarized in this rhyme:

Divorced, beheaded, died,

Divorced, beheaded, survived.

Henry was unfaithful to his wives, but he couldn't bear being suspicious of them. Like Thomas More, Anne Boleyn and Catherine Howard paid the price of Henry's suspicions by being beheaded.

Despite his messy home life, Henry VIII was an important king. He created the Royal Navy, which increased England's power all over the globe. He supported humanistic learning. He wrote poetry, played musical instruments, and was a superb athlete. As an old man, he was bossy and self-centered. He died not knowing that his daughter would become the greatest ruler England ever had.

The Boy King and Bloody Mary

Henry VIII had three children: Mary, daughter of Catherine of Aragon; Elizabeth, daughter of Anne Boleyn; and Edward, son of Jane Seymour. Because he was the only male, Edward was first in line for the throne. Crowned Edward VI in 1547 at the age of nine, the sickly boy was a ruler in name only.

When Edward died in 1553, his half sister Mary took the throne. Mary, a devout Catholic, was angry with Henry VIII for divorcing her mother. In a fit of revenge, she restored the Catholic Church in England. She hunted down Protestants and burned many of them at the stake. She also married the king of Spain, a country England was beginning to fear. These actions, among others, earned her the hatred of many of her subjects. When "Bloody Mary" died childless in 1558, her sister Elizabeth became queen.

Notes

(Notes)

Elizabeth: The Virgin Queen

Elizabeth I (reigned 1558–1603) was one of the most brilliant rulers in history. Her first task was to bring back order in a country torn apart by religious feuds. She again declared the Church of England separate from Rome. To keep Spain happy, she hinted that she might marry Mary's husband, King Philip II.

Philip was the first of many noblemen who wanted to marry Elizabeth. But this "Virgin Queen" (after whom our state of Virginia was named) refused to marry anyone. She knew that her strength lay in her independence.

A True Daughter

A truly heroic person, Elizabeth survived many plots against her life. Many of these plots were the work of Elizabeth's cousin, Mary, Queen of Scots (in Scotland). This Mary was a descendant of Henry VII and next in line to the English throne. A Catholic, she was eventually removed from power in Protestant Scotland. She lived for many years under house arrest in England. Finally, Elizabeth had her executed.

The Spanish Armada Sinks: A Turning Point in History

Elizabeth rejected King Philip of Spain as a husband. She executed Mary, who, like Philip, was Catholic. In 1588, Philip was fed up and sent a huge fleet of warships—an armada—to attack England. With the help of some nasty weather, England's Royal Navy destroyed the Spanish Armada. This victory set England firmly apart from the Catholic nations of Europe. It was a great turning point in history and Elizabeth's finest moment.

A Flood of Literature

Now firmly sure of themselves, the English started writing as never before. Elizabeth became a much-loved symbol of peace and security. She inspired English authors, many of whom wrote about her in their poetry, drama, and fiction. Other writers honored this learned queen by dedicating their works to her.

A Dull Man Succeeds a Witty Woman

When Elizabeth died childless, James VI of Scotland came to the throne. (James was the son of Mary, Queen of Scots.) As James I of England (reigned 1603–1625), he lacked Elizabeth's skill and grace. James spent where Elizabeth had saved; he spoke poorly where she had been eloquent. He was a foreigner, while she had been a true Englishwoman.

James I tried hard. He wrote books, supported Shakespeare, and ordered a new translation of the Bible. He was a generous and peaceful ruler. But many of his subjects—especially the Puritans—greatly disliked his style.

The Decline of the Renaissance

James's son, Charles I (reigned 1625–1649), had an even worse time as king. His childish, stubborn ways earned him many enemies, and he was beheaded in 1649. For eleven years England was ruled by Parliament and the Puritan dictator Oliver Cromwell.

When Charles's son was returned to the throne in 1660, England had changed. The old Renaissance values were dying out. Educated people were becoming more worldly in their outlook. New scientific truths were beginning to challenge long-standing religious beliefs.

Meditation 17

Based on the meditation by John Donne

Notes

Nunc lento	Now, this bell tolling softly
sonitu dicunt,	for another, says to me,
Morieris.	Thou must die.

Perhaps the person for whom this death bell tolls is so ill that he does not know it rings for him. Maybe I think that I am all right; but those around me see my actual state, and toll the death bell for me.

The church is universal, and so is everything that happens in the church. When a child is baptized, we are linked together because both of us are now connected to the Head of the church—to Christ. In the same way I am affected by every death: We are all part of one book written by God. When one person dies, a chapter is not torn out of the book. He or she is translated, that is, moved into the afterlife by one of God's many translators—age, sickness and war, or justice. God both oversees the translation and rebinds the pages for the final opening in the Library, or Heaven. Just as the bell rings to call both the preacher and the congregation to the church service, so the death bell tolls for all of us—but especially for me, because I am very ill and near death. There was once an argument that went as far as a lawsuit as to which religious order should ring the bell that calls us to prayer in the morning. It was decided that the first one to awaken in the morning would ring the bell. And so it is with the death bell—we should be awake early to the fact that the bell tolls for us as well as the person who is dying. No one can ignore the tolling of this bell—it connects us all to one another and to death. No one person is an island, alone and unconnected. Every human is like a piece of a continent, a part of a mainland. If one small lump of dirt is washed away from this mainland, it is smaller—it is diminished. If one person dies, it is like that clump of earth being washed away from the mainland—all of us are affected, all of us are diminished. Therefore, you should never ask for whom the death bell is ringing; it tolls for you and for me. Every one of us must die, and another's death reminds us of our own death to come. We cannot call this a borrowing of misery and pain, as if we did not have enough misfortune of our own and had to get it from someone else. That would be like wanting someone else's treasure. Misfortune, pain and trouble are all a treasure—no one has enough of it. This treasure helps us get nearer to God. Like money, great trouble and misfortune have little worth when they are stored away out of sight. However, misery and misfortune are valuable when they are used to help others turn to God. We must welcome suffering because it helps us get to Heaven.

Notes

Tilbury Speech

Based on the speech by Queen Elizabeth I

(Notes)

You Need to Know Queen Elizabeth I wrote masterful speeches and political addresses. One of her best-known speeches is the "Tilbury Speech." Queen Elizabeth gave this speech in 1588. The news that the Spanish Armada had been destroyed had not yet reached England and Elizabeth believed the Spanish were on their way to invade England. She wanted to inspire her army to defend England against the Spaniards. In this speech, the English queen shows her deep feeling for—and pride in—her people and her nation.

My loving people: Some have tried to persuade us that it is dangerous to give you arms and ammunition. They warn that armed people might turn on us and attack us. But I assure you I do not want to live distrusting my faithful and loving people. Let tyrants—those who are cruel and absolute rulers—fear to arm their people. I have always behaved myself so that, under God, I can place my greatest strength and safeguard in the loyal hearts and goodwill of my subjects—my loving people. Therefore I am here with you, as you can see, not to amuse myself, but determined to be with you in the heat of the battle. I am here to live or die with you. I will die for my God, and for my kingdom, and for my people. I will let my honor and my blood be brought down in the dust. I know I have the body of a weak and feeble woman, but I have the heart and courage of a king—and of a king of England, too. I do not think that Parma, or Spain, or any prince of Europe should dare to invade the borders of my kingdom. So, not wanting to be a shameful coward, I myself will take up arms. I myself will be your general and your judge. I will be the person who rewards every one of you for your courage in the field of battle. I know that you already deserve rewards and crowns for your courage, and we do assure you, on the word of a prince, they shall be duly paid to you.

The Parable of the Prodigal Son *from* The King James Bible
Based on the Gospel of Luke 15:11–32

(Notes)

There was once a man who had two sons, and the younger said to his father, "Father, give me my share of the property." A few days later the younger son sold his share, took the cash, and left home for a far-off country, where he wasted it all.

A famine came into that country. Food became scarce, and the young man could not feed himself. So he went to work for a farmer, who sent him to tend the pigs. He would have been glad to eat the slops that the pigs ate, but no one gave him anything. Then he thought, "My father's servants have more food than they can eat, while I am starving! I will go to my father and say to him, 'Father, I am no longer good enough to be called your son. Treat me like one of your servants.'"

So he started out for his father's house. As soon as his father saw him, he was overjoyed. He had thought his younger son was dead.

The father sent his servants for his best clothes to dress his son in, and he told them to prepare a feast to celebrate his son's return.

The older son was on his way back from the farm fields. As he came close to the house, he heard music and dancing. He asked one of the servants what was going on. The servant told him they were celebrating the younger brother's safe return.

The older son was angry and refused to go in, even though his father came out and begged him. He said that his father had never even given him a goat for a feast with his friends, and now they had killed the fat calf for his good-for-nothing brother.

"My boy," said the father, "you are always with me, and everything I have is yours. How could we not celebrate this happy day? Your brother here was dead, and now he has come back to life. He was lost, and now he is found."

—Luke 15:11–32

NAME _____   DATE _____

The Restoration and the Eighteenth Century: 1660–1800

Based on the Student Edition text by C. F. Main

(Notes)

Between 1660 and 1800, English and European settlers in North America developed moneymaking ventures in the new Colonies. By the time the American Revolution succeeded, the United States was a new and energetic nation. In Europe, however, things were different.

From Tumult to Calm

During the 1600s, England had suffered many hardships: civil war, the plague, and a devastating fire in London. After such chaos, the nation wanted peace and order. By the mid-1700s, these goals had largely been achieved. New English settlements were being set up around the globe. The middle class was growing. The upper classes prospered. Thinkers and artists produced brilliant works and asked fascinating new questions.

Augustan and Neoclassical: Comparisons with Rome

England during this period is often compared to ancient Rome during the reign of the emperor Augustus (63 B.C.–A.D. 14). Augustus brought peace and order to Rome after the previous ruler, Julius Caesar, was killed. Similarly, after the civil wars and the beheading of Charles I, Charles II returned to the throne, the monarchy was restored, and peace returned to England. The people of both Rome and England were tired of war, suspicious of radicals, and ready to settle down to the good life.

In this age, the Latin classics were regarded as the best literary works. They were thought to present the final truths about humanity. Therefore, many English writers modeled their works on ancient Latin ones. Such writings were called **neoclassical**—"new classical."

Reason and Enlightenment: From *Why?* to *How?*

(Notes)

This period is often referred to as the **Age of Reason** or the **Enlightenment**. These labels tell how people were gradually changing their view of themselves and the world. In earlier ages, world events such as earthquakes and comets were seen as punishments or warnings. As the Enlightenment began, people started asking "How?"

For example, the astronomer Edmond Halley (1656–1742) took the terror out of comets appearing in the sky. He used math to calculate the length of one comet's orbit: seventy-six years. He was then able to predict that the comet would appear in 1786, 1834, 1919, and 1986—and it did. Such a reasonable explanation showed that there was no connection between the comet and human events. Seen in this way, natural events became much less frightening and superstitions began to fade.

Changes in Religion: More Questions

The new scientific explanations of nature began to affect some people's religious views. If comets weren't warnings from God, maybe God didn't meddle in human affairs at all. Perhaps the universe was like a giant clock, set in motion by a Creator who then sat back and watched it run on its own. This view was part of a larger movement known as deism. Some people worried that deism would make human beings lazy and self-satisfied. If the universe were a machine, wouldn't it run regardless of what human beings did or didn't do?

Although ideas about God were changing, few people dismissed religion altogether. Great thinkers like Sir Isaac Newton (1642–1727) and John Locke (1632–1704) remained religious. As it had in ages past, Christianity continued to play a central role in most people's lives.

Religion and Politics: Repression of Minority Sects

When Charles II came to the throne, he again declared the Anglican Church the official state church. (In the United States, the Anglican Church is called the Episcopal Church.) Furthermore, he tried to outlaw all church groups that were not Anglican, including Puritanism. These groups were persecuted throughout the 1700s.

The Bloodless Revolution

When Charles II died in 1685, his brother James II succeeded him. James was a Roman Catholic, and most people in England deeply distrusted him. After all, it was widely believed that Catholics were plotting to hand the country over to the pope! Opposition to the king, queen, and their Catholic son became very intense. Finally, in 1688, the family fled to France. After this Glorious (bloodless) Revolution, the throne went to James's Protestant daughter, Mary, and her Dutch husband, William of Orange. The rulers of England have been Anglicans ever since.

Addicted to Theater

From 1642 to 1660, all theaters in England had been closed. But Charles II, who lived in France at the time, had become addicted to theatergoing. Once on the English throne, he quickly repealed the ban on drama. A new excitement about theater rapidly spread. Now, female roles could be played by women—not by men and boys as before. Many great comedies were produced during this period, including William Congreve's *The Way of the World*. These plays reflected the life of the pleasure-loving upper classes. They also poked fun at this lifestyle, often showing the unromantic side of love and relationships.

The Age of Satire: Attacks on Immorality and Bad Taste

Alexander Pope (1688–1744) and Jonathan Swift (1667–1745) are now considered the best writers of the early 1700s. At the time, though, both were out of step with the values of the age—values that they criticized harshly. Many English people felt smug and satisfied with the world. Pope and Swift did not. They were horrified by the sloppiness they saw in art, manners, and morals. Pope, who loved order and discipline, attacked members of the upper classes for their bad behavior and bad taste. Swift, too, aimed to expose the worst of human nature—much like the artist William Hogarth (1697–1764), whose paintings showed the sordid underside of life.

Journalism: A New Profession

While Swift and Pope focused on the upper classes, a writer named Daniel Defoe (1660–1731) stood for middle-class values: thrift, hard work, and responsibility. Defoe and other writers were developing a new form of professional writing—journalism. These first journalists did not merely describe the events of the day. They also viewed themselves as reformers: What they wrote could change society. Some journalists today still see themselves in this role.

A Poetry of Mind, Not of Soul

Today great poetry is defined as a poetry of feeling. We admire such wide-ranging poets as Shakespeare, the Romantics, Emily Dickinson, and Robert Frost because their poetry comes from the heart. Poets such as Alexander Pope, however, had no desire to write from the heart. They wrote poetry of the mind, intending for it to have a public function.

A Public Poetry Conceived in Wit

Pope and his contemporaries would decide ahead of time to make a particular kind of poem, much as a carpenter decides to make a certain kind of chair. Many of these poetic forms came from the classics.

For example, if an important person died, the poets would celebrate that person by writing **elegies.** Such poems did not necessarily tell the truth about a person. Instead, they said the very best things that the poet could think of saying. On the other hand, if the poets felt that a person was behaving badly, they might write a **satire.** These poems did not tell the full truth about a person, either. They made fun of the person's weaknesses.

Another important kind of poem was the **ode.** Like the satire and the elegy, the ode used plenty of exaggeration. In lofty poetic language, odes expressed the feelings of society at large. An ode might be written, for instance, to celebrate the winning of a battle.

Like the fashions of the day, poems were carefully put together. To go out in public, a person was expected to put on fancy, formal clothes. Similarly, a poem was expected to be "dressed" in perfect rhythms and rhymes. In no way was the Age of Reason a casual one.

The First English Novels

By the mid-1700s, people were writing and reading long stories called **novels.** (The word *novel* means "something new.") Middle-class women particularly enjoyed these novels. They told of luckless individuals and their rambling, comical adventures.

The most important novelist of the 1700s was Henry Fielding (1707–1754). His novels are crammed with rowdy incidents and characters who are good, but not too soft. Others novelists such as Samuel Richardson (1689–1761) and Laurence Sterne (1713–1768) experimented with this new form. Richardson was the first to look closely at a character's emotions, while Sterne used the novel to challenge all the old "rules" of writing.

Searching for a Simpler Life

By the last decade of the century, the world was changing. Factories were turning cities into filthy slums. Across the English Channel, the French were about to murder a king and drastically change their society. The age of elegance seemed to be ending.

Writers, too, were turning in new directions. Disgusted with the cities, they looked elsewhere for inspiration—to nature, to the imagination, to the lives of simple country people, and to the past. A new literary age was quietly dawning.

Notes

A Modest Proposal

Based on the essay by Jonathan Swift

(Notes)

You Need to Know This essay, published in 1729, is Jonathan Swift's best and most famous pamphlet. He begins by describing the terrible conditions in Ireland and objecting to the way the English treat the Irish. For three years the Irish harvests had been so poor that farmers got very little money for their crops. The farmers could not pay the rent for their land demanded by their English landlords, who did not live in Ireland. That meant that little money remained to be spent on Irish goods in Ireland. Beggars and starving children were everywhere. Swift argued that England's policies kept the Irish poor. His aim in writing this pamphlet was to change these policies.

In "A Modest Proposal," Swift offers a solution to these problems—perhaps the most shocking solution ever offered. In this pamphlet, he takes on the role of a "practical" economic planner, pretending to use only facts. He seems to be full of common sense, even goodwill. It is this difference between its honest style and its shocking content that gives the pamphlet its force.

A Modest Proposal

FOR PREVENTING THE CHILDREN OF POOR PEOPLE IN IRELAND FROM BEING A BURDEN TO THEIR PARENTS OR COUNTRY, AND FOR MAKING THEM BENEFICIAL TO THE PUBLIC

Walking through the streets of Dublin, or the Irish countryside, it is very sad to see many women begging for food for their families. Each of these women has with her three, four, or even six children, all dressed in rags.

In these difficult times, I think everyone agrees that taking care of all these children is a great burden. For the first year of its life, of course, a baby may be fed cheaply on its mother's milk. But then what?

Notes

I have thought very deeply about this problem for a long time, and I have come up with a plan. Under my plan, these children will not suffer from the need of food and clothing for the rest of their lives. Instead, they will help feed and clothe thousands of others.

I calculate that every year in Ireland a hundred and twenty thousand children are born to parents too poor to take care of them. How can these children be made useful? These days, there is no work for them on farms or in manufacturing. Only the cleverest can make a decent living as a thief before the age of six, although of course most children learn the basics much sooner.

As for selling them as slaves, I have been told by merchants that no one will pay for a boy or girl under twelve years old, and even when they reach this age, they sell for three pounds at most. As the cost of their rags and scraps of food will have added up to at least four times that amount, this earns no profit for their parents or the kingdom.

Therefore, I now humbly suggest my own idea, which I hope will not raise the slightest objection.

I have learned that a one-year-old child, well nursed, makes a most delicious, nourishing, and wholesome food. It may be stewed, roasted, baked, or boiled—even fricasseed.

Here is my plan. Of the one hundred twenty thousand poor children born each year, twenty thousand should be kept for breeding, one male for every four females. (This is more than we allow for sheep, cows, or pigs.) The remaining hundred thousand, when they reach one year, shall be sold to wealthy people throughout the kingdom.

Their mothers must let them nurse as much as possible in the last month, to make them plump and fit for a gentleman's table. One twenty-eight-pound child should be enough for two dishes at a dinner party. If the family dines alone, the child will last several meals, and will still be very good on the fourth day, boiled and sprinkled with a little pepper and salt.

Notes

This food will be somewhat expensive, but very proper for landlords. After all, they have already devoured the parents with the rents they charge; why not the children, too? And, if they are thrifty, they may save the skin to make excellent gloves for ladies and summer boots for fine gentlemen.

A good friend of mine, and a true lover of his country, recently made another suggestion. He pointed out that many young people between the ages of twelve and fourteen are starving because they cannot find work. Why not use them in place of deer, or venison, for food?

But I believe the males would be too tough and lean; and to slaughter the females would be a waste, as they would soon become breeders. Besides, some overly tenderhearted people might consider such a practice almost cruel—and I could never support any project involving the smallest hint of cruelty.

What about the vast numbers of poor adults in Ireland who cannot take care of themselves because they are old, sick, or crippled? That problem does not concern me in the least. It is very well known that every day they are dying and rotting, from cold and hunger and filth, as fast as can reasonably be expected.

As for the younger people, their condition is almost as hopeful. They cannot find work, and so they cannot eat; then, even if they do get hired accidentally, they are too weak to work. In this way the country's problem will soon be solved.

But back to my subject. I think the advantages of my plan are clear. First, it will greatly cut down on the number of Roman Catholics in Ireland.

Second, the poor tenants will now have valuable property, which landlords can take to pay their rent, since the tenants have no money and their grain and cattle have already been taken away.

Third, it will help the economy, as the children will be raised and sold in Ireland, with no need for imports.

Fourth, the breeders will earn money from their children and no longer have to support them after the first year.

Fifth, this popular new dish will draw wealthy customers to taverns where skillful cooks invent the finest recipes.

Sixth, it would encourage mothers to take good care of their children. Men would value their pregnant wives as much as livestock, and would not beat or kick them for fear of causing a miscarriage.

I can think of no objection that could possibly be raised to my plan. Therefore let no one talk to me of other solutions: Taxing the profits made by absent English landlords, buying clothes and furniture made only in Ireland, rejecting foreign luxuries and practicing thrift, learning to love our country and forgetting our political differences, teaching landlords to show mercy toward their tenants, and shopkeepers becoming honest and hardworking, instead of cheating everyone.

No, let no one talk to me of such solutions, until there is the least glimpse of hope that they may be sincerely put into practice.

As for me, I had despaired of ever solving Ireland's problems, until I fortunately came up with my plan. If anyone has another plan that is equally innocent, cheap, easy, and effective, I would be glad to hear it. But before anyone rejects my idea, let them answer two questions.

First, as things now stand, how will Ireland find food and clothing for a hundred thousand useless mouths and backs? And second, I would like the absentee landlords to ask the poor of Ireland whether they would not have been happier to be sold for food at a year old, than to have suffered the endless hunger, the lack of clothing and shelter, the impossibility of paying rent without money or work, and the certainty of passing this miserable life down to their children.

My only motive in making this proposal is to help my country by improving our trade, providing for babies, helping the poor, and giving some pleasure to the rich. I cannot hope to earn a single penny, as my youngest child is nine years old, and my wife is too old to have more.

Notes

from Don Quixote

based on the John Ormsby translation of Miguel de Cervantes'
masterpiece

Notes

from Chapter 8

*About Don Quixote's good luck in the scary windmill adventure and
related events.*

Suddenly, Don Quixote and his assistant Sancho Panza
noticed thirty or forty windmills on the plain in front of them.
Instead of windmills, though, Don Quixote thought he saw evil
giants, so he decided to go into battle against them. Sancho Panza
tried to stop him. He explained to his master that they were
facing windmills with long blades that turned in the wind, but
Don Quixote insisted they were facing monsters with long arms.

"Clearly, you don't know much about this kind of adventure,"
he said to his assistant. "If you're afraid, stay behind and pray. I'll
do the fighting."

Then he spurred his horse Rocinante and charged toward the
windmills. Even when he got close, he still thought the windmills
were living giants and shouted insults at them. Next, the windmill
blades began to turn in the wind, but Don Quixote thought the
"giants" were threatening him with many arms. Then, thinking of
his lady Dulcinea to give him courage, Don Quixote rushed into
battle against the windmills. He charged at the first one so fast
that its whirling blades broke his lance and threw him and his
horse to the ground.

Quickly, Sancho Panza came to his master's rescue, insisting
again that Don Quixote had attacked windmills instead of
monsters. This time, Quixote agreed with his assistant, but he was
sure that his enemy, a magician named Friston, had turned the
giants into windmills as he charged at them.

Sancho Panza helped his master back onto his horse, and the
two rode off down the Puerto Lapice highway in search of further
adventures. Missing his broken lance, Don Quixote remembered
the story of a knight named Diego Perez de Vargas.

Notes

"When this knight broke his sword in battle," Quixote told his assistant, "he made a club from a heavy oak branch and pounded his enemies with it in battle. He was so successful with his club that everyone started calling him Machuca, the Pounder." Then Quixote announced that he, too, would find a club and use it so successfully against his enemies that Sancho Panza would feel lucky to be his companion in these adventures. Sancho Panza humored his master by acting as if he believed what Quixote told him.

As they rode along, Sancho Panza noticed that Quixote was slipping in his saddle and worried that his recent fall had left him shaken. Quixote agreed but said that a true knight would not complain about his injuries, no matter what. Being more realistic, Sancho Panza said that he himself would complain over the smallest injury. His master laughed and said that the rules of chivalry would allow a knight's assistant to complain as often as he wanted to.

It was time for the two men to eat. Don Quixote was not hungry, but he didn't mind Sancho Panza eating, so his assistant made himself comfortable on the donkey he was riding and began to eat and to take huge swigs from his flask. Sancho Panza kept his good sense of humor as he rode along, eating and drinking. He was willing to go along with his master, regardless of the hazards.

That night as they camped along the road, Don Quixote replaced his broken lance with a branch from one of the trees around them. He had read that adventuring knights always stayed awake at night remembering their sweethearts, so Don Quixote went without sleep, thinking of Dulcinea instead. Sancho Panza slept. He had a full stomach and had had nothing to keep him awake. He slept so deeply that when morning came, neither sunlight nor bird song awoke him.

When Don Quixote called out to him, Sancho Panza awoke and took a deep drink from his flask. It worried him to see how

Notes

little was left in the flask because he didn't think there would be a chance to refill it soon. Don Quixote didn't have breakfast; his memories of Dulcinea were enough for him. Then the two adventurers set out upon the road again.

That afternoon, they arrived at Puerto Lapice. When Don Quixote saw the city on the road before them, he got excited about the adventures they would have there. He warned Sancho Panza not to defend him if he got into a fight with high-ranking men. The rules of chivalry said that only another knight could assist him in a fight with someone of his rank. He told Sancho Panza, though, that the assistant could come to his aid in a fight with with men of lower rank.

Sancho Panza replied that he would obey his master's request, explaining that he was a peaceful sort anyway and didn't like to interfere in the quarrels of others. He added that if attacked himself, he would of course fight. "The universal rules of self-defense allow it," he said.

Don Quixote agreed but reminded Sancho Panza not to interfere if his master got into a fight with men of his own rank. Finally, Sancho Panza promised to go along with this request.

The Romantic Period: 1798–1832
Based on the Student Edition text by Harley Henry

Copyright © by Holt, Rinehart and Winston. All rights reserved.

In the spring of 1798, two young British poets sold some of their poems to raise money for a trip to Germany. Soon after they left England, their book, *Lyrical Ballads and a Few Other Poems,* was published. It included Coleridge's *The Rime of the Ancient Mariner* and Wordsworth's "Lines Composed a Few Miles Above Tintern Abbey." These works are now among the most important poems in British literature. At the time, though, no one knew that *Lyrical Ballads* would usher in a new literary age.

Turbulent Times, Bitter Realities

The Romantic period started with the French Revolution in 1789 and ended in 1832 with political reforms that led to modern Britain. When we think of this period, we think of two groups of poets. The first—Blake, Wordsworth, and Coleridge—were born before the period began. The second—Shelley, Keats, and Byron—were the second generation of Romantics.

The Romantic period was a stormy one, both in England and abroad. England was changing rapidly from a farming society into an industrial one. A new working class was growing restless in overcrowded factory towns. In addition, revolutions swept the Western world, causing historic change.

The French Revolution

For England the American Revolution was a huge economic loss and a loss of confidence. But the French Revolution of 1789 brought even more disturbing change. A ruling king was overthrown—a kind of revolution that could have spread to England.

Notes

Notes

The "New Regime"

Idealists such as Wordsworth were inspired by events in France. But in 1792, when hundreds of French aristocrats and clergy were beheaded by the new regime, even Wordsworth began to doubt the revolution.

In 1793, war broke out between England and France. Wordsworth, Coleridge, and other English liberals turned against France. During this shaky period, Napoleon Bonaparte became dictator and then emperor of France. In the end, he was as ruthless as the king who had ruled France before the revolution.

The Conservatives Clamp Down

All of these events made British conservatives nervous. As supporters of the king, they feared that a revolution would occur in Britain, too. To prevent such a thing, the government passed harsh new laws. It also fought a war against Napoleon, finally defeating him in 1815.

British conservatives believed this victory saved their country from a tyrant, but British liberals saw Waterloo as the defeat of one tyrant by another. Still, the Romantics continued to believe in a new and better era.

The Industrial Revolution Finds a Foothold

England was the first country hit by the Industrial Revolution. As factory-made products replaced handmade goods, people flocked to the cities for work. In addition, many small farmers were driven off the land when rich landowners took over. Many of these landless people looked for work in the cities, or took to begging or the poorhouse. The result was larger cities and terrible living conditions.

The Tyranny of Laissez Faire

The economic idea behind the Industrial Revolution was called **laissez faire** (LEHS ay FAYR). In economic terms this policy meant that buying and selling should be allowed to happen without government interference. The rich, of course, got richer. But this system was very hard on the helpless and the young. Poor children were often forced to work in factories or coal mines. In the mines, some children were harnessed to coal carts like animals.

The Rebellion of the Romantic Poets

The Romantic poets wanted a better world, and they believed in the power of literature. Frustrated by resistance to social change, they rejected the public, formal poetry that had come before them. Instead, they wrote lyric poetry that was private, free flowing, and emotional. These poets used the imagination rather than reason to respond to the rapid changes of the time.

What Does "Romantic" Mean?

Today, the word *romantic* often describes feelings of love. In literature, however, the word *romantic* comes from the term *romance.* The romance was a popular form of literature in the Middle Ages. It featured adventure, mystery, and fearless heroes. The Romantic writers sometimes used elements of the romance in their own works. It is for *this* reason—not because they wrote love poems—that they are known as the "Romantic" poets.

Today, the word *romantic* often describes the kind of cheap emotion found in best-selling novels about love. When we think of the Romantic poets, though, the word has three important meanings:

• **A Child's Sense of Wonder**
Romantics were inspired by the fresh and innocent way that children see the world.

Notes

- **Social Idealism**

Romantics believed that societies change in cycles and that it was the Romantics' role to change society by imagining a world with more happiness, justice, and well-being.

- **Adaptation to Change**

The term *romantic* implies an ability to accept change.

A New Kind of Poetry

In 1800, Wordsworth wrote a preface for a new edition of *Lyrical Ballads*. In it he declared that he was writing a new kind of poetry—poetry that was the "spontaneous overflow of powerful feelings." These **lyric poems** used ordinary language to describe common subjects—such as country life. In the country, Wordsworth saw nature's beauty and power. In addition, he saw an important link between nature and the power of the human mind.

The Mystery of Imagination

The Romantic poets were "mind poets" more than "nature poets." They wanted to find a connection between themselves and the world of the senses, and they found it in the imagination. They believed that both nature and the mind itself could stimulate the imagination. In addition, they saw both nature and the imagination as mysterious and inspiring. They believed that the imagination drives us to discover things we cannot learn simply by thinking. Finally, they believed that the imagination inspires the mind to imitate the power of creation. For the Romantics, poetry expressed this creative urge.

NAME _____ DATE _____

The Romantic Poet

According to Wordsworth, the poet is a special person, one who possesses "a greater knowledge of human nature" than most. In fact, all of the Romantic poets thought highly of the poet's role. William Blake saw the poet as an inspired teacher. Coleridge wrote that the poet "brings the whole soul of man into activity." Shelley called poets "the unacknowledged legislators of the world." Keats saw the poet as a "physician" to humanity. To sum up, the Romantics believed that poets were essential to society.

Lines Composed a Few Miles Above Tintern Abbey

by William Wordsworth

Notes

You Need to Know This lyric poem is a meditation on what nature, represented by the Wye River valley in Wales, has meant to the speaker. He first describes the valley's beauty. He then explains how his youthful, emotional response has become deeper and more thoughtful. He is glad that he no longer has to be physically in a natural setting to receive its healing powers. His memories alone can inspire him. Finally, the speaker addresses his sister, saying that having her with him makes the landscape even more precious to him.

Five years have past; five summers, with the length

Of five long winters! and again I hear

These waters, rolling from their mountain springs

With a soft inland murmur.—Once again

5   Do I behold these steep and lofty cliffs,

That on a wild secluded scene impress

Thoughts of more deep seclusion; and connect

The landscape with the quiet of the sky.

The day is come when I again repose

10   Here, under this dark sycamore, and view

These plots of cottage ground, these orchard tufts,

Which at this season, with their unripe fruits,

Are clad in one green hue, and lose themselves

'Mid groves and copses.[1] Once again I see

15   These hedgerows,[2] hardly hedgerows, little lines

Of sportive wood run wild: these pastoral farms,

Green to the very door; and wreaths of smoke

Sent up, in silence, from among the trees!

With some uncertain notice, as might seem

20   Of vagrant dwellers in the houseless woods,

1. **copses:** areas densely covered with shrubs and small trees.

2. **hedgerows:** rows of bushes, shrubs, and small trees that serve as fences.

Or of some Hermit's cave, where by his fire

The Hermit sits alone.

In Other Words It's been five years since I've been here. I again hear the sound of the river flowing down from the mountains. Once again I see these steep, high cliffs, which make me think of being completely alone. These cliffs connect the landscape to the quiet sky. I rest here, under a dark sycamore tree, and look out at the farmland and the orchards. It is not the season for ripe fruit—all the fruit trees are the same green color, blending into the woods. Once again I see the hedgerows, which are hardly even proper hedgerows—just lines of woods running wild. I see the farmhouses, with plants growing right up to their doors. I see smoke rising silently from among the trees. I imagine the smoke to come from the fire of a homeless person living in the woods, or from the cave of a hermit who sits alone.

These beauteous forms,

Through a long absence, have not been to me

As is a landscape to a blind man's eye:

25   But oft, in lonely rooms, and 'mid the din

Of towns and cities, I have owed to them

In hours of weariness, sensations sweet,

Felt in the blood, and felt along the heart;

And passing even into my purer mind,

30   With tranquil restoration:—feelings too

Of unremembered pleasure: such, perhaps,

As have no slight or trivial influence

On that best portion of a good man's life,

His little, nameless, unremembered acts

35   Of kindness and of love. Nor less, I trust,

To them I may have owed another gift,

Of aspect more sublime; that blessed mood,

In which the burden of the mystery,

In which the heavy and the weary weight

40   Of all this unintelligible world,

Is lightened:—that serene and blessed mood,

Notes

Notes

In which the affections[3] gently lead us on,—
Until, the breath of this corporeal[4] frame
And even the motion of our human blood
45   Almost suspended, we are laid asleep
In body, and become a living soul:
While with an eye made quiet by the power
Of harmony, and the deep power of joy,
We see into the life of things.

> **In Other Words** Even though I've been gone a long time, I have been able to see these beautiful sights in my mind's eye. When I've been tired, sitting alone in my room or surrounded by the noise of a city, the memory of this place has given me good feelings. These emotions run through my blood and my heart, into my mind, giving me peace and new energy. Perhaps these feelings will strongly influence a man to perform small acts of kindness and love. These memories have restored my balance and made me a kinder, more generous person. They have led me to a blessed mood in which I begin to see more clearly the meaning of life. In that peaceful mood we hardly breathe, our blood hardly moves, and our whole body seems almost asleep. We feel as if we were souls without bodies. The harmony and joy we have received from Nature lets us see into the quiet life of things.

If this
50   Be but a vain belief, yet, oh! how oft—
In darkness and amid the many shapes
Of joyless daylight; when the fretful stir
Unprofitable, and the fever of the world,
Have hung upon the beatings of my heart—
55   How oft, in spirit, have I turned to thee,
O sylvan[5] Wye! thou wanderer through the woods,
How often has my spirit turned to thee!

3. **affections:** feelings.
4. **corporeal:** bodily.
5. **sylvan:** associated with the forest or woodlands.

In Other Words Perhaps what I believe is not true. And yet, in the nights and days when the rushing, busy world has made me sick and unhappy, how many times have I returned to you. You, the River Wye, who wander through the woods—how often, in my mind, have I turned to you!

And now, with gleams of half-extinguished thought,
With many recognitions dim and faint,
60 And somewhat of a sad perplexity,
The picture of the mind[6] revives again:
While here I stand, not only with the sense
Of present pleasure, but with pleasing thoughts
That in this moment there is life and food
65 For future years. And so I dare to hope,
Though changed, no doubt, from what I was when first
I came among these hills; when like a roe[7]
I bounded o'er the mountains, by the sides
Of the deep rivers, and the lonely streams,
70 Wherever nature led: more like a man
Flying from something that he dreads, than one
Who sought the thing he loved. For nature then
(The coarser pleasures of my boyish days,
And their glad animal movements all gone by)
75 To me was all in all.—I cannot paint
What then I was. The sounding cataract[8]
Haunted me like a passion: the tall rock,
The mountain, and the deep and gloomy wood,
Their colors and their forms, were then to me
80 An appetite; a feeling and a love,
That had no need of a remoter charm,[9]
By thought supplied, nor any interest
Unborrowed from the eye— That time is past,

6. **picture of the mind:** primarily the picture in the mind, but also the picture the individual mind has of itself.

7. **roe:** deer.

8. **cataract:** waterfall.

9. **remoter charm:** appeal other than the scene itself.

Notes

In Other Words Now, this scene that I have pictured so often is here before me again in reality, although not exactly the way I remembered it. I stand here, enjoying not just the scene now, but also the thought of how the memory of this moment will give me pleasure in years to come. That is my hope. When I was young, I loved the natural world with a passion. I did lots of hiking. I accepted what I saw at face value. I did not look below the surface. I was more like a man running away from something I dreaded than like one seeking the things I love. I was no longer a boy, with the joy of a wild animal. Nature was everything to me then—I can't describe what I was like. The noise of a waterfall haunted me like a passion. The tall rock, the mountain, the deep wood, their colors and shapes, were something I hungered for. The feeling was immediate and direct. It didn't need any deep thought, anything other than what I saw in front of me.

And all its aching joys are now no more.
85 And all its dizzy raptures. Not for this
Faint[10] I, nor mourn nor murmur; other gifts
Have followed; for such loss, I would believe,
Abundant recompense.[11] For I have learned
To look on nature, not as in the hour
90 Of thoughtless youth; but hearing oftentimes
The still, sad music of humanity,
Nor harsh nor grating, though of ample power
To chasten and subdue. And I have felt
A presence that disturbs me with the joy
95 Of elevated thoughts; a sense sublime
Of something far more deeply interfused,
Whose dwelling is the light of setting suns,
And the round ocean and the living air,
And the blue sky, and in the mind of man:
100 A motion and a spirit, that impels
All thinking things, all objects of all thought,
And rolls through all things. Therefore am I still

10. **faint:** become weak; lose heart.
11. **recompense:** repayment

(Notes)

A lover of the meadows and the woods,

And mountains; and of all that we behold

105 From this green earth; of all the mighty world

Of eye, and ear—both what they half create,

And what perceive; well pleased to recognize

In nature and the language of the sense

The anchor of my purest thoughts, the nurse,

110 The guide, the guardian of my heart, and soul

Of all my moral being.

In Other Words That time is gone. Its painful joys and dizzy thrills are no more. I don't mourn it; time has brought me other gifts, which make up for that loss. I've learned to look at nature in a different way than I did as a thoughtless young man. Now, I hear the quiet, sad music of humanity. It isn't harsh, though it has the power to make me quiet and humble. And I have felt a presence that fills me with the joy of higher thoughts. I have felt a sense of something holy, which lives in the light of setting suns, in the ocean and the air, in the blue sky, and in the mind of man. It is a motion and a spirit, which draws to itself all thinking things and all things that are thought about, and is in everything.

So I still love the meadows, woods, and mountains, everything there is to see and hear on earth. I love both what is there and what I add to it with my thoughts and understandings. I am pleased to see that nature and my own senses are what make me my best self. They are like an anchor, a nurse, a guide, a guardian for my soul.

Nor perchance,

If I were not thus taught, should I the more

Suffer[12] my genial[13] spirits to decay:

For thou art with me here upon the banks

115 Of this fair river; thou my dearest Friend,[14]

My dear, dear Friend; and in thy voice I catch

The language of my former heart, and read

My former pleasures in the shooting lights

12. **suffer:** allow.

13. **genial:** creative.

14. **my dearest Friend:** Wordsworth's sister Dorothy.

Notes

Of thy wild eyes. Oh! yet a little while

120 May I behold in thee what I was once,

My dear, dear Sister! and this prayer I make,

Knowing that Nature never did betray

The heart that loved her; 'tis her privilege,

Through all the years of this our life, to lead

125 From joy to joy: for she can so inform

The mind that is within us, so impress

With quietness and beauty, and so feed

With lofty thoughts, that neither evil tongues,

Rash judgments, nor the sneers of selfish men,

130 Nor greetings where no kindness is, nor all

The dreary intercourse[15] of daily life,

Shall e'er prevail against us, or disturb

Our cheerful faith, that all which we behold

Is full of blessings. Therefore let the moon

> **In Other Words** Even without this teaching, I would not allow my creative spirit to go away. For you are here with me on the banks of this beautiful river, my dearest friend. In your voice I hear the language my heart once spoke. In the light of your eyes, I see the pleasure I used to feel. Oh, for just a little while, may I see in you, my dear sister, what I used to be. Nature does not betray those who love her. It is her privilege to lead us from joy to joy, through all the years of our life. Nature has the ability to affect our minds with quiet beauty and high thoughts, so that neither human unkindness nor the depressing events of daily life can bring us down or shake our faith that life is full of blessings.

135 Shine on thee in thy solitary walk;

And let the misty mountain winds be free

To blow against thee: and, in after years,

When these wild ecstasies shall be matured

Into a sober pleasure; when thy mind

140 Shall be a mansion for all lovely forms,

Thy memory be as a dwelling place

---

15. **intercourse:** dealings; social contacts.

For all sweet sounds and harmonies; oh! then,

If solitude, or fear, or pain, or grief,

Should be thy portion, with what healing thoughts

145 Of tender joy wilt thou remember me,

And these my exhortations![16] Nor, perchance—

If I should be where I no more can hear

Thy voice, nor catch from thy wild eyes these gleams

Of past existence—wilt thou then forget

150 That on the banks of this delightful stream

We stood together; and that I, so long

A worshipper of Nature, hither came

Unwearied in that service: rather say

With warmer love—oh! with far deeper zeal

155 Of holier love. Nor wilt thou then forget

That after many wanderings, many years

Of absence, these steep woods and lofty cliffs,

And this green pastoral[17] landscape, were to me

More dear, both for themselves and for thy sake!

In Other Words Let the moon shine on you as you walk alone, and let the misty mountain winds blow against you. In later years, when beautiful sights and sounds live only in your memory—then, if you should be lonely, or afraid, or suffering, remember me and my words with healing thoughts of joy. If I have gone where I can no longer hear your voice or see in your eyes glimmers from my past, do not forget that we stood together on the banks of this delightful river. Remember that I, who have worshiped Nature for so long, did not tire of my service. In fact, my love for Nature was even warmer, deeper, and holier. Do not forget, either, that after many years away from these deep woods and high cliffs and this green country landscape, they were even more dear to me—both for their own sake and for yours!

16. **exhortations:** strong advice.

17. **pastoral:** relating to herds or flocks, pastureland, and country life.

Kubla Khan
by Samuel Taylor Coleridge

(Notes)

In Xanadu did Kubla Khan
A stately pleasure-dome decree:
Where Alph,[1] the sacred river, ran
Through caverns measureless to man
5   Down to a sunless sea.

> **In Other Words** Long ago, in the mythical land of
> Xanadu, the emperor of China, Kubla Khan, put forth a royal
> order. A great domed monument dedicated to pleasure
> would be built above the holy river Alph. This river, it is said,
> ran underground through endless caverns to a sunless,
> underground sea.

So twice five miles of fertile ground
With walls and towers were girdled round:
And there were gardens bright with sinuous rills,[2]
Where blossomed many an incense-bearing tree;
10   And here were forests ancient as the hills,
Enfolding sunny spots of greenery.

> **In Other Words** So, the dome was built on ten miles of
> fertile ground, with walls and towers surrounding it. Within
> it were gardens that were made all the more lovely by
> winding streams. Trees with very fragrant flowers blossomed
> there, surrounded by an ancient forest.

But oh! that deep romantic chasm which slanted
Down the green hill athwart a cedarn cover![3]
A savage place! as holy and enchanted
15   As e'er beneath a waning moon was haunted
By woman wailing for her demon-lover!

1. **Alph:** probably a reference to the Greek river Alpheus, which flows into the Ionian Sea, and whose waters are fabled to rise up again in Sicily.
2. **sinuous** (SIHN yoo uhs) **rills:** winding streams.
3. **athwart a cedarn cover:** crossing diagonally under a covering growth of cedar trees.

In Other Words Yet crossing the tree-covered hills was a deep crack in the earth! This was a wild and dangerous place! It was a blessed and bewitched place, where one could easily imagine a woman crying for her demon-lover.

Notes

And from this chasm, with ceaseless turmoil seething,

As if this earth in fast thick pants were breathing,

A mighty fountain momently[4] was forced:

20   Amid whose swift half-intermitted burst

Huge fragments vaulted like rebounding hail,

Or chaffy grain beneath the thresher's flail:[5]

And 'mid these dancing rocks at once and ever

It flung up momently the sacred river.

25   Five miles meandering with a mazy[6] motion

Through wood and dale the sacred river ran,

Then reached the caverns measureless to man,

And sank in tumult to a lifeless ocean:

And 'mid this tumult Kubla heard from far

30   Ancestral voices prophesying war!

In Other Words Out of this deep crack came a gushing of water that tossed up huge rocks so that they seemed to fall from the sky like hailstones. From this fountain, the sacred river Alph flowed across the woods and valleys for five miles before returning to the endless caverns and the lifeless sea. Amid the sounds of this eruption, Kubla Khan heard ancient voices, warning him of war.

The shadow of the dome of pleasure

Floated midway on the waves;

Where was heard the mingled measure[7]

From the fountain and the caves.

35   It was a miracle of rare device,

A sunny pleasure-dome with caves of ice!

4. **momently** *adv.*: at each moment.

5. **thresher's flail:** heavy, whiplike tool used to thresh, or beat, grain in order to separate the kernels from their chaff, or husks.

6. **mazy** *adj.*: like a maze; having many turns.

7. **measure** *n.*: rhythmic sound.

Notes

In Other Words The pleasure-dome cast a shadow on the waves of the rushing river. From the river, one could hear the sounds from the fountain echoing chaotically within the caves. The overall impression was miraculous: as if the sunny pleasure-dome itself were built on icy caverns.

A damsel with a dulcimer[8]
In a vision once I saw:
It was an Abyssinian[9] maid,
40 And on her dulcimer she played,
Singing of Mount Abora.[10]
Could I revive within me
Her symphony and song,
To such a deep delight 'twould win me,
45 That with music loud and long,
I would build that dome in air,
That sunny dome! those caves of ice!

In Other Words I once dreamed of an exotic woman who sang of another paradise. If only I could remember the song she sang, then I would be inspired with such power that I could re-create the pleasure-dome of Xanadu in the sky.

And all who heard should see them there,
And all should cry, Beware! Beware!
50 His flashing eyes, his floating hair!
Weave a circle round him thrice,
And close your eyes with holy dread,
For he on honeydew hath fed,
And drunk the milk of Paradise.

In Other Words All who saw my creation would regard me with awe and fear. They would perform rituals to protect themselves from me, since I had touched the divine.

8. **dulcimer** *n.*: musical instrument that is often played by striking the strings with small hammers.

9. **Abyssinian:** Ethiopian. Ethiopia is in northeast Africa.

10. **Mount Abora:** probably a reference to John Milton's (1608–1674) *Paradise Lost,* in which Mount Amara, in Ethiopia, is a mythical, earthly paradise.

The Victorian Period: 1832–1901

Based on the Student Edition text by Donald Gray

Many changes took place in Britain during the reign of Queen Victoria (1837–1901). But unlike those of the early 1800s, these changes took place in a mostly peaceful, stable environment.

Peace and Growth: Britannia Rules

The British Empire was steadily expanding. By 1900, Victoria was queen-empress of more than two hundred million people living outside Great Britain. Meanwhile, back at home, the Industrial Revolution was creating new towns, new wealth, and thousands of new jobs. Government reforms slowly gave middle-class and working-class people more political power. Progress was being made.

The Idea of Progress

For one Victorian historian, progress meant improvements that could be seen, touched, counted, and measured. Historian Thomas Babington Macaulay wanted the London streets free of garbage. He wanted neighborhoods planned and houses numbered. He wanted people to be educated enough to read signs. Although some Victorians had lower standards than Macaulay's, most agreed that society was improving itself.

The Hungry Forties

The first ten years of Victoria's reign were troubled. Millions of people were out of work.

• **Poor Working Conditions**
There were terrible working conditions in factories and mines. Children worked such long hours that they were falling asleep on the job and getting caught in machines.

Notes

- **The Potato Famine**

In Ireland, a famine killed almost a million people and forced another two million to move. Some went to English cities, where overcrowding was already a serious problem. In the slums of industrial cities such as Manchester, twelve people might have lived in a single room; 250 people might have shared two toilets.

- **Pollution and Filth**

Because cities were growing very quickly, they were often filthy and disorderly. In 1840, 40 percent of Manchester streets were unpaved. London's Thames River was polluted with sewage, industrial waste, and runoff from graveyards.

The Movement for Reform: Food, Factories, and Optimism

During the 1840s, people held huge rallies to protest the government's failures. Food prices were high and many workers did not have the right to vote. Government officials became so worried that in 1848 they had the army ready to fight back against protesters.

- **Improvements in Diet**

Still, most middle-class Victorians thought that life was better than in the past and still improving. Living conditions did improve as the Victorian era progressed. After the 1850s, the price of food dropped. Diets improved as meat, fruit, and margarine became regular household items. Factories and railroads made clothing, furniture, and travel cheap.

- **The Reform Bills**

A series of reforms gave the vote to almost all adult males and limited the work day for children. State-sponsored schools appeared in 1870 and became compulsory by 1880. By 1900, more than 90 percent of the English population could read and write. Things were improving.

"Blushing Cheeks": Decorum and Prudery

The Victorians believed that they were improving morally, too. In fact, they were so concerned with proper behavior that the word *Victorian* now means almost the same thing as *prudish*. In books and newspapers, editors deleted words that might be embarrassing. In art and fiction, sex, birth, and death were softened into tender courtship, joyous motherhood, and saintly deathbed scenes.

Authoritarian Values

In the home, the husband was king. Middle-class women were expected to marry and make comfortable homes for their men. Unmarried women had few job opportunities. Working-class women might become servants, and middle-class women might become governesses or teachers. In literature, the middle-aged maiden was often a comic figure.

Many Victorians saw the hypocrisy behind all of this straight-laced behavior. But such behavior was slow to change because it, too, was seen as a kind of progress. Prudery and social order convinced the Victorians that they were in control—that they had evolved beyond the immoral, revolutionary behavior of the last century.

Intellectual Progress: The March of the Mind

Dramatic advances in science fueled the Victorian mind. Humans began to understand the earth, its creatures, and its natural laws. Charles Darwin and other biologists put forward new theories about evolution.

Notes

Thomas Huxley and the Game of Science

Some thinkers, such as Thomas Huxley, saw science as a high-stakes chess game with the universe. Like those Victorians who built railroads and pushed for reforms, these thinkers believed that the world offered a supreme challenge—one that could be met through human effort and intelligence. While warning that the game could be lost, they fiercely believed that it could and should be won.

Questions and Doubts

Many Victorian writers reassured their readers that the universe made sense, but others challenged this view. Some questioned whether people were bettering themselves materially without bettering themselves spiritually.

The Popular Mr. Dickens

Charles Dickens was one of these questioning people. This writer lived out a popular Victorian myth: Through his own effort and talent, he rose from poverty to wealth and fame. The happy endings of Dickens's novels are equally mythical, suggesting that things usually work out well for decent people. But an unsettling idea lurks at the core of many of these novels. Some of Dickens's most memorable scenes show decent people—often children—being abused and neglected. Could such a world really be a world of progress? Was society really advancing?

Dickens also raised questions about the costs of "progress." He often described the smoke and fire of industrial landscapes. In 1871, social critic John Ruskin noted a new phenomenon that we now call smog. This "storm-cloud of the nineteenth century," he wrote, "looks more to me as if it were made of dead men's souls."

Trust in the Transcendental—and Skepticism

Early Victorian writers trusted in a higher power. For them, the purpose of a poet or writer was to make readers aware of the connection between earth and heaven, body and soul. Midcentury writers changed their tune a bit, however. Some found it difficult to believe in an infinite power—especially given the miseries and injustices of society. Still others were saddened by what looked like the withdrawal of the divine from the world. In his poem "Dover Beach," Matthew Arnold strikes the major note of much mid-Victorian writing. "The Sea of Faith," he wrote, has ebbed. The old certainties are gone, and the only new certainty is disbelief itself.

By the end of the century, this kind of thinking was widespread. Earlier Victorian writers such as Dickens had created worlds in which happiness was possible. But in the works of Thomas Hardy and others, the world becomes hostile. Lovers and friends are hurt and betrayed by human troubles (such as unfaithfulness and war) and by natural troubles such as death.

Reflections on a Culture

No matter what its purpose, Victorian literature should be seen as a part of its society, not as a voice apart. Both its readers and its writers sought to move the world forward. But they also struggled against the world's grand contradictions and harsh realities.

Ulysses
by Alfred, Lord Tennyson

(Notes)

You Need to Know The aging Ulysses is recalling his past adventures. He longs for the exciting life he had when he was young. He rejects the security of a settled life and wants to keep testing his limits—experiencing new adventures. Ulysses speaks of passing his responsibilities as a ruler on to his mild, reliable son, Telemachus. Ulysses realizes, however, that the men he feels closest to are the sailors with whom he shared his adventures. It is with them that he wishes to set sail again in search of work that is of value—"of noble note."

It little profits that an idle king,

By this still hearth, among these barren crags,

Matched with an aged wife, I mete and dole[1]

Unequal laws unto a savage race,

5   That hoard, and sleep, and feed, and know not me.

In Other Words It's not much use for a king with no work to sit by this unlit fireplace, among these bare, steep rocks. My wife is old; I give out unequal laws to savage people who eat and sleep and do not know me.

I cannot rest from travel; I will drink

Life to the lees.[2] All times I have enjoyed

Greatly, have suffered greatly, both with those

That loved me, and alone; on shore, and when

10   Through scudding drifts the rainy Hyades[3]

Vexed the dim sea. I am become a name;

For always roaming with a hungry heart

Much have I seen and known,—cities of men

And manners, climates, councils, governments,

15   Myself not least, but honored of them all,—

---

1. **mete and dole:** measure and give out.
2. **lees:** dregs or sediment.
3. **Hyades** (HY uh deez): stars that were thought to indicate rainy weather.

And drunk delight of battle with my peers,

Far on the ringing plains of windy Troy.

> **In Other Words** I cannot give up traveling. I will live life to its last moment. I have enjoyed my life greatly. I have suffered greatly, both with those that loved me, and alone— on shore, and at sea during storms. I have become famous. I wandered with a hungry heart. I have seen much and known much—cities, the people who live in them, the way they act, their climate, their government. They all honored me. I took joy in going into battle with my fellow soldiers, far away in the flat, windy land of Troy.

I am a part of all that I have met;

Yet all experience is an arch wherethrough

20 Gleams that untraveled world whose margin fades

Forever and forever when I move.

How dull it is to pause, to make an end,

To rust unburnished, not to shine in use!

As though to breathe were life! Life piled on life

25 Were all too little, and of one to me

Little remains; but every hour is saved

From that eternal silence, something more,

A bringer of new things; and vile it were

For some three suns to store and hoard myself,

30 And this gray spirit yearning in desire

To follow knowledge like a sinking star,

Beyond the utmost bound of human thought.

> **In Other Words** I am a part of everything I've seen. Yet all experience is an arch through which shines the part of the world I haven't yet seen, its edge forever fading as I move. How boring it is to stop, to rust, not to shine in use! As if just breathing were really living! If I had more than one life, it still wouldn't be enough; and not much is left of the one life I have. But every hour I live brings new things to me. It would be horrible to shut myself up for years when my spirit longs to learn more, to go beyond the farthest edges of human thought.

Notes

Notes

    This is my son, mine own Telemachus,

    To whom I leave the scepter and the isle,[4]—

35 Well-loved of me, discerning to fulfill

    This labor, by slow prudence to make mild

    A rugged people, and through soft degrees

    Subdue them to the useful and the good.

    Most blameless is he, centered in the sphere

40 Of common duties, decent not to fail

    In offices of tenderness, and pay

    Meet[5] adoration to my household gods,

    When I am gone. He works his work, I mine.

> **In Other Words** This is my son, my own Telemachus, whom I leave to rule my island kingdom. I love him, and he is wise enough to do this work. He can slowly and carefully tame these rough people, making them useful and good. He can be trusted to do all the ordinary tasks at home when I am gone—take care of people, worship the household gods. He does his work, and I do mine.

    There lies the port; the vessel puffs her sail;

45 There gloom the dark, broad seas. My mariners,

    Souls that have toiled, and wrought, and thought with me,—

    That ever with a frolic welcome took

    The thunder and the sunshine, and opposed

    Free hearts, free foreheads,—you and I are old;

50 Old age hath yet his honor and his toil.

    Death closes all; but something ere the end,

    Some work of noble note, may yet be done,

    Not unbecoming men that strove with Gods.

> **In Other Words** There is the harbor, the ship with the wind puffing out its sail; there is the great, gloomy sea. We are old now. But old age still has its honor and its work. Death ends everything, but before it comes, we might still do some noble work, worthy of men like us who fought with gods.

4. **isle:** Ithaca, Ulysses' island kingdom off the west coast of Greece.

5. **meet:** proper.

The lights begin to twinkle from the rocks;

55   The long day wanes; the slow moon climbs; the deep

Moans round with many voices. Come, my friends,

'Tis not too late to seek a newer world.

Push off, and sitting well in order smite

The sounding furrows;[6] for my purpose holds

60   To sail beyond the sunset, and the baths

Of all the western stars, until I die.

It may be that the gulfs will wash us down;

It may be we shall touch the Happy Isles,[7]

And see the great Achilles,[8] whom we knew.

In Other Words The lights begin to twinkle from the rocks. The long day is ending; the moon slowly rises; the ocean moans with many voices. Come, my friends—it is not too late to look for a newer world. Push off with your oars; sit where you used to, and row together against the waves. My goal is still to sail beyond the sunset, beyond the stars, until I die. Maybe we will drown; maybe we will land on the Happy Isles and see our old friend the great Achilles.[8]

65   Though much is taken, much abides; and though

We are not now that strength which in old days

Moved earth and heaven, that which we are, we are,—

One equal temper of heroic hearts,

Made weak by time and fate, but strong in will

70   To strive, to seek, to find, and not to yield.

In Other Words Though we have lost much, much remains. And though we no longer have the strength that long ago moved heaven and earth, we are still what we are. Our heroic hearts, made weak by time and fate, still share one determination—to strive, to seek, to find, and not to give up.

6. **smite . . . furrows:** row against the waves.

7. **Happy Isles:** in Greek mythology, Elysium , where dead heroes lived for eternity.

8. **Achilles** (uh KIHL eez): Greek warrior and leader in the Trojan War.

The Bet

Based on Constance Garnett's translation of
Anton Chekhov's short story

Notes

It was a dark autumn night. The old banker walked back and forth, remembering a party he gave one evening fifteen years ago. Many clever men were there; at last, talk turned to the death penalty. Most of the guests thought it was wrong. They believed it was immoral and unsuitable for Christian countries. Some even thought it should be replaced by life imprisonment.

"I don't agree with you," said the banker. "I have not tried either one, but it seems the death penalty is fairer and more kindhearted. The death penalty kills a man at once, but going to prison for life kills him slowly."

"Both are equally wrong," said one guest, "for they both want to do the same thing—take away life. The state is not God. It has no right to take away what it cannot give back."

A lawyer was among the guests, a young man twenty-five years old. He said, "The death sentence and the life sentence are both wrong, but if I had to choose between them, I would choose imprisonment. Any life is better than none at all."

The banker suddenly hit the table with his fist and shouted, "It's not true! I'll bet you two million you wouldn't stay all alone in prison for five years."

"If you mean that," said the young man, "I'll take the bet, but I will stay fifteen years, not five."

"Done!" cried the banker. "Gentlemen, I bet two million!"

"Agreed! You bet your millions, and I bet my freedom!" said the young man.

And this foolish bet was carried out! The wealthy banker was delighted. He made fun of the young man, saying, "Give up this bet while you can. To me two million is nothing, but you are losing three or four of the best years of your life, because I know you won't stay longer. I am sorry for you."

Notes

And now the banker remembered all this and asked himself, "Why did I make that bet? What is the good of that man's losing fifteen years of his life and my throwing away two million? Can it prove that the death penalty is better or worse than imprisonment for life? No, no."

They had decided the young man should spend his captivity in a little house in the banker's yard. For fifteen years the young man could not go out the door, see human beings, hear the human voice, or receive letters and newspapers. He could have a musical instrument and books and could write letters, drink wine, and smoke. He could ask for these things in writing but could receive them only through a small window. Finally, the young man had to stay there exactly fifteen years. If he tried to break the agreement, he would lose, even if it was only two minutes before the end.

For the first year the prisoner was lonely and deeply unhappy. He played his piano day and night. He refused wine and tobacco. The books he sent for were novels with complicated plots, exciting stories, and so on.

In the second year the piano was silent. Three years later music was heard again, and the prisoner asked for wine. Those who watched him said all that year he did nothing but eat and drink and lie on his bed, yawning and talking angrily to himself. More than once they heard him crying.

In the sixth year the prisoner began studying languages, philosophy, and history. He studied so much that the banker had to work hard to get him the books he ordered. In the next four years, he went through six hundred books and learned six languages.

Then, after the tenth year, the prisoner sat at the table and read nothing but the Gospels. It seemed strange to the banker that a man should waste nearly a year over one thin book that was easy to understand.

Notes

In his last two years, the prisoner read books of all kinds. He demanded, all at the same time, books on chemistry and medicine, novels, and some works on philosophy. He was like a drowning man, desperate for something to hold onto.

The old banker remembered all this and thought, "Tomorrow at twelve o'clock he will be free. By our bet, I ought to pay him two million. But if I do pay him, I will have no money at all."

Fifteen years before, he had been rich, but gambling on the Stock Exchange and his own wild nature had lost his fortune. "Cursed bet!" muttered the old man, holding his head in despair. "He will take my last penny and enjoy life, while I will be a beggar and envy him. And then he will offer to help me! No, the only way I can keep from losing all my money is for him to die!"

The clock struck three o'clock. Everyone was asleep in the house. Quietly the banker took from his safe the key of the door to the young man's little house and went there. He called out to the watchman twice, with no answer, and decided that the man must be asleep somewhere.

The old man peeped through the little window. He could see the back and hands of the man sitting at the table. Open books lay everywhere.

The banker tapped at the window, but there was no answer. He turned the key in the keyhole. The rusty lock and the door creaked, but there was no other sound. He made up his mind to go in.

The man at the table sat very still. He looked as thin and bony as a skeleton, with long curly hair and a shaggy beard. His face was yellow; his hair was gray; you would not believe he was only forty years old.

He considered smothering the sleeping man then and there. No one would suspect foul play. But a paper on the desk caught his attention. He took up the page and read:

"Tomorrow at twelve o'clock I have my freedom, but before I leave this room and see the sunshine, I must say a few words to

Notes

you. I tell you that I despise all the things your books call the good things of the world.

"For fifteen years I have seen nothing of the world, but in your books I have drunk wine, I have sung songs, I have hunted in the forests, I have loved women. . . . In your books I have climbed mountains and watched the splendor of sunrise and sunset. I have performed miracles, killed, preached new religions, and conquered whole kingdoms. . . .

"Your books have given me wisdom. I know that I am wiser than all of you.

"And I hate your books. I despise wisdom and the blessings of this world. It is all worth nothing. You have taken lies for truth and ugliness for beauty. You would be amazed if frogs and lizards suddenly grew on apple and orange trees or if roses began to smell like a horse. I don't want to understand you.

"To prove to you how I hate all that you live for, I give up the two million that I once dreamed of. To make sure, I will escape from here five minutes before time and break the agreement. . . ."

When the banker had read this, he laid the paper on the table, kissed the man on the head, and went out of the little house. He was weeping. Never had he felt so great a hatred for himself. At home, his tears kept him from sleeping for hours.

Next morning, the watchmen ran in and told him they had seen the man who lived in the little house climb out of the window into the garden and leave. After checking to be sure that the lawyer was really gone, the banker took the paper and locked it up in his safe.

The Modern World: 1900 to the Present

Based on the Student Edition text by John Leggett and David Adams Leeming

Copyright © by Holt, Rinehart and Winston. All rights reserved.

Notes

Change on the Horizon

The Victorian age ended with the death of Queen Victoria in 1901. At that time it seemed as if Britain's power and majesty would sail on forever. But political and social events during the early 1900s would diminish Britain's strength. Several major colonies—Australia, South Africa, and New Zealand—would gain their independence. The rise in literacy, the growth of the Labour Party, and new ideas about government would transform British society and the world itself.

Darwin, Marx, and Freud: Undermining Victorian Ideas

Many of the social changes of the early 1900s had their roots in the work of three men: Charles Darwin (1809–1882), Karl Marx (1818–1883), and Sigmund Freud (1856–1939). These thinkers helped overturn many of the firm beliefs of British society.

Darwin's *Origin of Species* (1859) sets forth a new theory of evolution. According to this theory, species that adapt to their environments survive, and those that do not become extinct. Some people tried to apply Darwin's theory to human society. These social Darwinists held that only the fittest people should survive. They used this idea to justify many unfair practices, including racial prejudice.

German thinker Karl Marx spent his last twenty years in London. In *Das Kapital* (1867), he argues that economic injustice is rooted in private ownership. Therefore, all private property should be abolished. This revolutionary thinking led to sweeping changes in many governments, including that of Britain.

In Vienna, Austria, Sigmund Freud was changing the study of the mind. In *The Interpretation of Dreams* (1900) and other works, Freud argues that human behavior is controlled not by our conscious minds, but by our unconscious desires. Some people were outraged by Freud's claims, but artists and writers found his ideas fascinating.

The Great War: "A War to End All Wars"

In 1914, all of Europe was plunged into World War I, also known as the Great War. At first, British patriotism ran high. Thousands of young men enlisted. Six months later, thousands lay dead in the rain-soaked trenches of France. In four years, an entire generation of young Englishmen was killed. With the end of the war in 1918 came a new cynicism. The old values of honor and glory had led to war, a weakened empire, and a staggering loss of life. In place of the romantic values of the past, a bleak new realism settled in.

Experimentation in the Arts: Shocking in Form and Content

Before the war, new trends in art had appeared. Henri Matisse was making bold use of line and color. Pablo Picasso was creating his first cubist works. Igor Stravinsky was writing music that used strong rhythms and dissonant chords. Traditional ideas about beauty and order were being challenged.

A Revolution in Literature

After the war, these trends led writers to see the world in different ways. In her novels, Virginia Woolf rejected chronological order and experimented with shifting points of view. With a style called **stream of consciousness,** Woolf looked into the human mind. D. H. Lawrence rebelled against literary traditions and against British prudery, shocking British audiences with descriptions of relations between the sexes.

Most influential of all was the Irish writer James Joyce. His novel *Ulysses* (1922), based on Homer's *Odyssey,* tells the events of a single day in the life of a man named Leopold Bloom. In a wholly new way, Joyce drew from the deep wells of myth, symbol, and human consciousness.

The Rise of Dictatorships: Origins of World War II

By the 1930s, another war seemed bound to happen. A worldwide economic depression was helping dictators rise to power throughout Europe.

Italy and Germany fell into the hands of fascist rulers Benito Mussolini and Adolf Hitler. Mussolini held control through brutality and manipulation. Hitler and his Nazi party convinced many Germans that their problems were caused by Jews and other groups.

Russia's Communist government was based on the theories of Karl Marx. In the 1920s, Nikolai Lenin had sought to do away with private property. Lenin's successor, Joseph Stalin, sent as many as fifteen million people to forced-labor camps.

By 1939, Europe was again plunged into a bloody war. After the fall of France in 1940, Germany began bombing London and other English cities. The United States stepped in to help defeat Germany and its ally, Japan. On August 6, 1945, an atomic bomb was dropped on Hiroshima, Japan, by an American plane. The bomb ended the war, but it also wiped out the entire city. Small wonder, then, that much of the literature following World War II was dark and unhopeful.

Britain After World War II: The Sun Sets on the Empire

After the war, the Labour Party came to power in Britain and transformed the nation into a welfare state. The government became responsible for providing its citizens with medical care and other basic needs. Britain could not hold on to its colonies. Many of them, including India, became independent.

In 1998, an end to thirty years of violence in British-controlled Northern Ireland seemed near at hand. The leaders of Northern Ireland, Great Britain, and Ireland hammered out a promising formula for peace. It was approved by most of the war-weary Irish citizens.

British Writing Today

Before the war, politically radical poet W. H. Auden dominated the British literary scene. After the war, another group, known as the Angry Young Men, came into fashion. They disliked the intellectual snobbery of the Auden group. Many of their works made fun of the newly wealthy middle class.

Since 1960, diversity has marked British literature. At home, novelists such as Muriel Spark, Anthony Burgess, and Margaret Drabble have explored social issues and experimented with language.

The Growth of World Literature

Because of new technologies, writings in dozens of languages are now translated and distributed throughout the English-speaking world. Likewise, English works are similarly translated and distributed to non-English-speakers.

Seeking Cultural Identity: Postcolonial Literature

Much of current world literature focuses on political and social problems. Postcolonial writers (from former British colonies) write about finding their own identities and about the losses their native cultures have suffered.

African Expressions

In Africa, one response to colonialism was a literary movement called **negritude.** Writers, such as Léopold Sédar Senghor, looked to their past, before British colonialism, for inspiration. Some people have criticized this movement for idealizing the past. They call, instead, for a more realistic and critical examination.

White writers in Africa, such as Doris Lessing and Nadine Gordimer, write about the shame of racism and social inequality. Gordimer's novels have even been banned in her country because they so strongly protest the government's racist policies.

"Two Worlds or Ten": Literature in India

India is a country of many languages and many cultures. Writing in English, R. K. Narayan and Anita Desai capture the essence of their country. Narayan crafts characters with the pluck and stubbornness that is unique to India. Desai's characters face the country's competing social influences. She writes of the confused patchwork of India, which she sees as "two worlds or ten." New to the Indian literary scene is Arundhati Roy, a political activist. Her novel, *The God of Small Things* (1997), is a harsh criticism of India's extremely rigid class system.

Other Postcolonial Explorations

V. S. Naipaul, of Trinidad, writes strong, mocking criticisms of postcolonial nations. One of his characters sums up existence in a developing nation: "We lack order. Above all we lack power, and we do not understand that we lack power."

Another postcolonial writer is Naguib Mahfouz of Egypt. His novels show the struggles of Egyptians expelling foreign invaders. His writings also criticize Egypt's social conditions, suffering, and spiritual emptiness.

Latin America and Magical Realism

Latin American writers have responded to the changes to their society in many different ways. Poets Pablo Neruda (Chile) and Octavio Paz (Mexico) wrote about their cultural heritage and the effect history has on the present. Jorge Luis Borges of Argentina wrote stories that explore the nature of time and reality through fantastic twists of character, setting, and plot. His works foreshadowed the later literary movement of **magic realism.** This style of writing uses realistic details to describe incredible events as if they were parts of normal, everyday life. For example, in Columbian novelist Gabriel García Márquez's *One Hundred Years of Solitude* (1967), endless rains wash away the memory of mass murders.

Women's Voices: A "Second Sex" No More

Women writers have also become stronger since World War II. Feminist writers condemn the male-controlled world and seek to undo social inequalities. For example, French writer Simone de Beauvoir examines the middle-class views of women as second-class citizens and objects. Buchi Emecheta of Nigeria and her followers use motherhood (instead of marriage) for creative inspiration. Canadian novelist Margaret Atwood's *The Handmaid's Tale* (1985) is a dark warning to society. Her novel describes a future world where women are repressed and controlled by strict, religious rulers.

Never Forget: Responses to War and Government Repression

Widespread wars with periods of uneasy peace in between have defined world history since the early twentieth century. It is not surprising, then, that much of world literature has been in response to war. German author Erich Maria Remarque wrote about the physical and mental tortures of World War I. Italian

Notes

author Primo Levi and Romanian author Elie Wiesel have both written of the horrors of World War II's Holocaust. Japanese writers, such as Yasunari Kawabata, also have addressed World War II. Kawabata's works tell of the pain and suffering civilians suffered during the war. Writers from the former Soviet Union, such as Aleksandr Solzhenitsyn and Anna Akhmatova, and from China, such as Ha Jin, resisted strong governmental efforts to control their works.

A "Marvelous Capacity": The Promise of World Literature

The literature of the world tells many stories. One person couldn't possibly live all of life's experiences or participate in all the world's cultures. However, the variety of literature helps give us a wider, deeper understanding of the world and what it means to be human. As Aleksandr Solzhenitsyn has said, "The only substitute for what we ourselves have not experienced is art and literature." He believes that art and literature have a "marvelous capacity" for transmitting ideas across cultures.

In the Shadow of War

Based on the short story by Ben Okri

Notes

That afternoon three soldiers came to the village. They went to the bar and ordered palm wine and sat and drank amidst the heat and the flies.

Omovo watched them from the window as he waited for his father to go out. They both listened to the radio. The news talked about bombings and air raids in the country.

At that hour, for the past seven days, a strange woman with a black veil over her head had been going past the house. She went up the village paths, crossed the Express road, and disappeared into the forest. Omovo waited for her to appear.

His father gave Omovo his weekly allowance and said, "Turn off the radio. It's bad for a child to listen to news of war." Omovo turned it off. His father left quickly and walked to the bus stop to go to work.

Omovo sat on the windowsill and waited for the woman. The last time she came, the children said that she was a witch—that she had no shadow and her feet never touched the ground. As she went past, the children began to throw things at her.

Omovo noticed that whenever children went past the bar the soldiers called them, talked to them, and gave them some money. He ran downstairs. As he walked past the bar, one of the soldiers called him. He asked, "Have you seen that woman who covers her face with a black cloth?"

"No."

The man gave Omovo some money and said:

"She is a spy. She helps our enemies. If you see her, come and tell us at once, you hear?"

Omovo refused the money and went back upstairs. The heat got to him and soon he fell asleep.

"In the Shadow of War" adapted from *Stars of the New Curfew* by Ben Okri. Copyright © 1988 by Ben Okri. Retold by Holt, Rinehart and Winston. Reproduced by permission of **Viking Penguin, a division of Penguin Group (USA) Inc.** Electronic format by permission of **Ben Okri.**

When he woke, Omovo saw that the woman had already gone past. The soldiers had left the bar. He saw them following her, weaving between the houses. Omovo ran downstairs and followed the soldiers. When they got into the forest the soldiers stopped following the woman and took a different route.

Omovo followed the woman through the dense forest. She wore faded clothes, with the black veil covering her face. She had a red basket on her head. He completely forgot to look for signs that she was a witch—whether she had a shadow, or whether her feet touched the ground.

He followed the woman till they came to a crude camp near a cave. Shadowy figures moved about in the half-light of the cave. The woman went to them. He heard their tired voices thanking her. When the woman came back she did not have the basket.

Again he followed her till they came to a muddied river. Omovo saw the shapes of swollen dead animals lying on the dark water. A terrible smell was in the air. Then he heard the sound of heavy breathing from behind him. He recognized the voice of one soldier urging the others to move faster. Omovo hid in the shadow of a tree. The soldiers strode past. Not long afterward he heard a scream. The men had caught up with the woman. They crowded round her.

"Where are the others?" shouted one of them.

The woman was silent.

"You dis witch! You want to die, eh? Where are they?"

She stayed silent. Her head was bowed. One of the soldiers coughed and spat toward the river.

Another soldier tore off her veil and threw it to the ground. She bent down to pick it up and stopped, kneeling, her head still bowed. Her head was bald, and scarred with a deep groove. There was an ugly gash along the side of her face. The soldier pushed her, and she fell on her face and lay still. The lights changed over the forest and for the first time Omovo saw that the dead animals on the river were in fact the swollen corpses of grown men.

Before he could react, he heard another scream. The woman was getting up, with the veil in her hand. She turned to the second soldier, pulled herself up, and spat in his face. Waving the veil in the air, she began to howl dementedly. The two other soldiers backed away. The soldier wiped his face and pointed his gun at her stomach.

After he heard the shot, Omovo ran through the forest screaming. The soldiers tramped after him. As he ran he saw an owl staring at him from the leaves. He tripped over the roots of a tree and blacked out when his head hit the ground.

When he woke up it was very dark. Thinking he had gone blind, he screamed, thrashed around, and ran into a door. When he recovered from his shock he heard voices outside the room. He found his way out, and was surprised to find his father sitting on the sunken cane chair, drinking palm wine with the three soldiers. Omovo rushed to his father and pointed frantically at the three men.

"You must thank them," his father said. "They brought you back from the forest."

Omovo began to tell his father what he had seen. His father, smiling apologetically at the soldiers, picked up his son and carried him off to bed.

Shakespeare's Sister *from* A Room of One's Own

Based on the essay by Virginia Woolf

Notes

I find myself wondering why women did not write poetry in the Elizabethan age. I am not sure how they were educated or whether they even knew how to write or if they had a place where they could write. They had no money, apparently, and most probably had children before they were twenty-one. According to Professor Trevelyan, who wrote a history including the fifteenth and sixteenth centuries, they married at fifteen or sixteen.

Someone (I think it was a bishop who is now dead) declared it was impossible for any woman ever to have Shakespeare's genius. He was right in at least one respect. It would have been completely impossible for any woman to have written Shakespeare's plays in the age of Shakespeare.

Imagine, for instance, that Shakespeare had a wonderfully gifted sister named Judith. Will, her brother, went to grammar school, where he learned Latin, Greek, and logic. He married and had a child. Then off he went to London, where he quickly became a successful actor. He lived at the hub of the universe. He met everyone, practiced his art onstage, and even went to the queen's palace.

Meanwhile, his extremely talented sister remained at home. She had no opportunity to learn grammar and logic nor to read the Latin poets. She was just as adventurous and imaginative as her brother and wanted to see the world as much as he did. But whenever she tried to read, her parents told her to mend the stockings or mind the stew and to forget about books.

Maybe she wrote secretly but was careful to hide her writing. When Judith was sixteen, her parents arranged a marriage for her—even though she protested that she didn't want to marry.

Her father beat her severely and then begged her not to shame him. Although she felt she could not disobey him, one summer night she took a few belongings and ran away to London.

Judith was as gifted with words as her brother. Like him, she stood at the stage door of a theater and told the manager that she desired to act, but he laughed in her face. No woman, he said, could possibly be an actress—in those days none were. So she had no way to get any training in acting.

But she was young and pretty, so the actor-manager took pity on her. The result was that she found herself pregnant by him. One winter's night Judith killed herself and, as was common with suicides, was buried at some London crossroads.

That's how the story might go for a woman who, in Shakespeare's day, had the same genius that he had. But I think the bishop is right to say that no woman could possibly have had Shakespeare's genius then. For such a genius is not born among uneducated servants, and that is what most women, in essence, were. Women could not be geniuses because their work began almost before they left the nursery, and law and custom forced them to keep on working. Only rarely do writers like Emily Brontë or Robert Burns appear from among the working classes.

Whenever you read of a witch or a woman possessed by devils, or a wise woman selling herbs, or even a very remarkable man who had a mother, I think we are really on the track of a woman who wanted to be a novelist or poet but couldn't. It is women, I think, who wrote many of the poems attributed to Anon (Anonymous). Edward Fitzgerald, an English translator and poet, suggests women created the ballads and folk songs, crooning them to children.

No one can say whether he is right. But I am positive that any extraordinarily gifted woman in the sixteenth century would have gone crazy or shot herself or ended up in a lonely cottage as half witch and half wizard. She would have been so mocked and so frustrated that she surely would have lost both her health and her sanity.

Notes

Notes

No girl could have walked to London and forced her way before actors and managers without a great deal of anguish. For women were supposed to be chaste, or pure. A sixteenth-century woman living a free life in London and trying to write would have been under great stress that might have killed her. If she survived, whatever she wrote would have been twisted and deformed—the product of a guilt-ridden mind.

And if she managed to publish her work, it would have gone unsigned. She would have published anonymously or used a man's name, as did Charlotte Brontë, whose pen name was Currer Bell. Throughout history, women have been made to feel that they should remain anonymous.

A woman born with writing talent in the sixteenth century would have been terribly unhappy and would have had considerable inner conflict. Her life and her own instincts were hostile to the creative process.

But what mental state is most favorable for creativity?

Not until the eighteenth century did writers begin to record what went on in their minds as they wrote. From their autobiographies, we learn that writing a work of genius is almost always unbelievably difficult. Everything—barking dogs, interruptions, money problems, poor health—conspires against having a work transfer easily from the writer's mind onto paper.

In addition, the world is incredibly uncaring toward writers. No one asks them to create novels, poems, or histories, for the world doesn't need them. Nor will people pay for what they do not want. So young writers must cope with every kind of distraction and discouragement.

Women who wanted to write faced much greater obstacles than men did. To start with, no woman could have a room of her own unless her parents were very rich or noble. She had no money except what little she was given for clothes. So she couldn't go on a walking tour or a little journey to France, as Keats, Tennyson, and Carlyle, all poor men, managed to do.

Even worse, the world was not just indifferent to women's writing as they were to men's. The world laughed at women who tried to write, saying, Write? What's the good of your writing?

The Doll's House

Based on the short story by Katherine Mansfield

(Notes)

When old Mrs. Hay went back to town after staying with the
Burnells, she sent the children a marvelous doll's house. Because
it still smelled of fresh paint, it sat in the courtyard, propped up
on two wooden boxes.

The whole front of the house swung open, showing the living
room, dining room, kitchen, and two bedrooms. Isabel, Lottie,
and Kezia Burnell had never seen anything like it. There were
pictures painted on the wallpaper, complete with gold frames.
Red carpet covered all the floors except in the kitchen; red velvet
chairs sat in the living room; the beds had real bedclothes.

But what Kezia, the youngest of the Burnell sisters, liked more
than anything was the lamp that stood in the middle of the
dining-room table—a lovely little yellow lamp with a white
lampshade. The lamp seemed to smile at Kezia, to say, "I live
here."

The Burnell children hurried to school the next morning.
They could hardly wait to tell everybody about their doll's house.

"I'm going to tell first," said Isabel, "because I'm the oldest.
And I'm to choose who's going to come and see it first. Mother
said I could."

Playtime came, and a crowd of girls surrounded Isabel. The
only two who stood apart were the two who were always outside
any group, the little Kelveys.

The Burnells lived in a rural area of New Zealand, where there
was only the one school; therefore, the Burnell children had to
mix with children of all classes. However, the line on mixing had
to be drawn somewhere, and it was drawn at the Kelveys. Many of
the children, including the Burnells, were not allowed even to
speak to them.

"The Doll's House" adapted from *The Short Stories of Katherine Mansfield.* Copyright 1923 by Alfred
A. Knopf, Inc. and renewed 1951 by John Middleton Murry. Retold by Holt, Rinehart and Winston.
Reproduced by permission of **Alfred A. Knopf, a division of Random House, Inc.**

The Kelveys were the daughters of a washerwoman and a father who was said to be in prison. They looked strange. Lil came to school in a dress made from a green tablecloth of the Burnells'; her little sister, Else, wore a long white dress and a pair of little boy's shoes. But whatever Else wore, she would have looked strange. She was tiny, with enormous, serious eyes. Nobody had ever seen her smile; she scarcely ever spoke. She always held tightly onto Lil's skirt, so that wherever Lil went, Else followed.

Now they hung around at the edge of the circle of girls, listening as Isabel told about the doll's house—the carpet, the beds with real bedclothes, and the stove with an oven door.

When she finished, Kezia said, "You've forgotten the lamp, Isabel."

"Oh, yes," said Isabel, "and there's a teeny little lamp that stands on the dining-room table. You couldn't tell it from a real one."

"The lamp's best of all!" cried Kezia.

Isabel chose Emmie Cole and Lena Logan to come back with them that afternoon and see the doll's house. All the others, knowing they, too, might have a chance to see the house, were extra friendly to Isabel. The crowded around her and walked off with her.

The little Kelveys walked away; there was nothing more for them to hear.

Days passed, and as more children saw the doll's house, the fame of it spread. The one question was, "Have you seen Burnells' doll's house?"

"Mother," said Kezia, "can't I ask the Kelveys just once?"

"Certainly not, Kezia," said her mother.

"But why not?" asked Kezia.

"Run and play, Kezia; you know quite well why not," her mother responded.

Notes

Notes

At last, everybody had seen it except the Kelveys. At lunchtime, the children stood together under the pine trees. Suddenly, as they looked at the Kelveys eating their jam sandwiches wrapped in newspaper—always by themselves, always listening—the group of girls wanted to be mean to them.

Emmie Cole started it. "Lil Kelvey's going to be a servant when she grows up," she said.

"O-oh, how awful!" said Isabel Burnell.

Emmie nodded to Isabel in a meaningful way, just as she'd seen her mother do on similar occasions.

"Shall I ask her if it's true?" said Lena Logan.

"Bet you don't," said Jessie May.

"Watch! Watch me! Watch me now!" said Lena. She went over to the Kelveys.

Lil looked up from her sandwich, and Else stopped chewing.

"Is it true you're going to be a servant when you grow up, Lil Kelvey?" said Lena.

There was a dead silence. Lil only smiled her silly smile. This wasn't enough for Lena; she put her hands on her hips and shouted, "Yah, yer father's in prison!"

Then, Lena and the other little girls all rushed away, laughing and shrieking about the marvelous thing Lena had said.

That afternoon after school, Kezia was swinging on the big white gates of the courtyard. Looking along the road, she saw the Kelveys. Kezia stopped swinging as the Kelveys came nearer. Finally, Kezia made up her mind.

"Hello," she said.

They were so surprised that they stopped. Lil gave her silly smile, but Else only stared.

"You can come and see our doll's house if you want to," said Kezia.

Lil gasped; then she said, "Your ma told our ma you wasn't to speak to us."

"You can come and see our doll's house all the same. Nobody's looking," said Kezia.

But Lil shook her head still harder.

"Don't you want to?" asked Kezia.

Suddenly there was a tug at Lil's skirt and she turned round. Else was looking at her with big, imploring eyes; she wanted to see the house. So, like two little stray cats, they followed Kezia across the courtyard to where the doll's house stood.

"There it is," said Kezia.

Lil took a deep breath; Else was still as a stone.

"I'll open it for you," said Kezia kindly. She opened the front of the house, and they looked inside.

"Kezia!" shouted Aunt Beryl from the back door, staring as if she couldn't believe what she saw. "How dare you ask the Kelveys into the courtyard!" she shouted in a cold, furious voice. "You know you're not allowed to talk to them. Off you go immediately!"

The Kelveys did not need telling twice. Faces red with shame, huddling together, Lil and Else crossed the big courtyard and squeezed through the gate.

"Wicked, disobedient little girl!" said Aunt Beryl bitterly to Kezia and slammed shut the front of the doll's house.

When the Kelveys were out of sight of Burnells', they sat down by the side of the road. Lil's cheeks were still red with shame, but Else nudged her sister and smiled her rare smile.

"I seen the little lamp," she said, softly.

Then both were silent once more.